WEBMASTER SERIES

BUILDING AND MAINTAINING AN

NT WEB SERVER

WEBMASTER SERIES

BUILDING AND MAINTAINING AN

NT WEB SERVER

Jeff Bankston

CORIOLIS GROUP BOOKS

Publisher	Keith Weiskamp
Project Editor	Toni Zuccarini
Copy Editor	Jenni Aloi
Cover Artist	Gary Smith
Cover Design	Anthony Stock
Interior Design	Bradley Grannis
Layout Production	Rob Mauhar
Proofreader	Charlotte Zuccarini
Indexer	Lenity Mauhar

The Coriolis Group, Inc.
7339 E. Acoma Drive, Suite 7
Scottsdale, AZ 85260
Phone: (602) 483-0192
Fax: (602) 483-0193
Web address: http://www.coriolis.com

ISBN 1-883577-90-X : $39.99

Printed in the United States of America

10 9 8 7 6 5 4 3 2 1

Acknowledgments

No book is possible without the complete team of professionals that keep the author on track, on time, and on target. The original idea was perhaps the author's, or perhaps the agent's, or in this case a collaborative effort with the publisher. The Coriolis Group believes in one simple premise—keep it simple, and inform the reader with powerful information. That vision was shared with me by Keith Weiskamp, my publisher. Keith's vision for this book was key to its realization, and our combined efforts to turn the concept into reality was brought to fruition with the help of a good many people.

First on my list of those who were crucial to this book is my agent, Valda Hilley, who is president of Convergent Press Literary Group. She has been a guiding light to me, and an occasional swift boot in the rear when required; she's an absolute gem. Running a close second was Toni Zuccarini, the managing editor of the project. She did her best to keep the project on time, even when I was running on a hobbled Web server. I truly can appreciate her efforts, and I really did answer the phone when she called…well, most of the time.

Behind the scenes working the technical issues was Anthony Potts, Coriolis' technical guru. He ensured that those aspects of the project that needed an overview got it, and the server issues were examined. Dave Friedel worked on the CD-ROM that you'll use in the back of the book, and he did a fine job with it. Not to be left out, my copy editor Jenni Aloi whipped the manuscript that I thrust in front of Toni into shape. Jenni's comments and insights helped me to realize what I took for granted, and I thank her for them.

The book itself had several chapters of Web server software that will enable you to try-before-you-buy, in the form of evaluation versions of the products. These vendors helped immensely with the products themselves and ensured that the bases were covered for you, the reader. A special thank you also goes to my associate author, Marshall Copeland, who wrote Chapters 9 through 11 for the CGI and forms development systems.

Last, but not least, was the ever-loving and caring help of my beautiful wife, Anja Marie. No matter what the deadlines were, or how much pressure the book put on me, she always was there helping me with her thoughts and patience. This book would never have happened without her support and tender hand.

Contents

Chapter 4   Selecting and Setting Up Your NT Server Hardware   151

Chapter 7   Process Corp's Purveyor Web Server   283

Part 5   Appendices   447

Introduction

Every business that uses computers in conjunction with the Internet has a handful of users and administrators who really understand what the Web is all about; and there's another handful who really understand what a network server is all about. In between, there's the rest of the computing community that works with the devices that make up both the Web and the network, yet knows very little about either.

What happens when some of these blissfully unaware computer experts begin using the Web or find themselves building a Web server? Their knowledge of computers sometimes gets them "promoted" to computing guru and right into the Internet fire. *Building and Maintaining an NT Web Server* is a book for these users-turned-Web-administrators, or just for those folks who need to create or enhance their business' Web presence.

Building and Maintaining an NT Web Server is designed to show you how to get your business onto the Internet serving the public community, your private business' user base, or both. It will also show you how to run your applications on the Web server as a locally logged-in user, or from Hong Kong if you happen to be traveling. Various forms of server communications will be explored and exploited to increase your Web server's potency while keeping the costs under control. This book will also show you what tools you'll need to build a solid foundation for your Web.

Creating a network server isn't that difficult, but planning for its use on the Web requires some careful consideration and a lot of preparation. This book will provide the structured planning guide you need to help you breach the Web and make your business known to the world. In doing so, be prepared to spend time, money, and a few sleepless nights getting it right. However, you don't have to be completely at risk...read on and I'll show you what to do, when to do it, and a few things not to do as you put your business onto the Web.

This book is structured into four parts:

- Part 1 discusses the finer details of building a physical server to stand up to the rigors of the Web and the tons of users that you expect to see.

- Part 2 uses four Web servers to demonstrate different aspects and viewpoints of serving the Web. Those Web servers are Microsoft Internet Information Server, O'Reilly's WebSite, Process Software's Purveyor, and Quarterdeck's WebStar. I won't judge which one's the best, but rather show how I integrated each into my business' environment.

- Part 3 explores the Common Gateway Interface and Visual Basic to expand your Web server's power and flexibility. You'll learn how to use programmatical methods to conduct your business activities while accessing the Web server from the Internet.

- Part 4 discusses many aspects of Web server administration, including how to integrate a bulletin board service into the Web server for both augmentation of Web services and remote administration of the site.

The enclosed CD-ROM includes software for your Web site, including demo and evaluation software that you can use to build a test site and make sure that this is what you really want before dumping huge sums of money into the project.

This book is not a platform to learn NT Server itself. I used Windows NT Server as my platform, but if you simply use Windows, you'll find this book just as useful. In a few spots, I remind you of NT features and functions, but if you want to learn how to add a user to NT you'll have to find another publication to do this.

Instead, I concentrate upon the tasks you'll encounter when you create your very own Web server. These tasks are numerous, and vary in purpose and form, so be prepared to be flexible. Not every network server is capable of running a Web server, and not every Web server is up to the task of serving both the Internet and internal users.

When you finish, you'll have a firm understanding of how you want to approach the decision-makers with a plan to create the server, and some respectable figures to show them what it will cost the business to get online. You'll know what to expect in terms of server administration, emergency and normal maintenance, and system upgrades. One thing you'll truly learn is how to build a good Web server, and what happens when you don't.

Starting Out With Windows NT Server

PART

1

Windows NT Meets the World Wide Web

Microsoft's Windows NT Server has advanced over time to become one of the best network operating systems in existence today. As network systems go, there's been a vast array of guests at the networking party before Microsoft Windows NT Server came along. However, recent advances to this robust Network Operating System (NOS) has brought its functions and capabilities to the forefront of today's computing platforms. This book will demonstrate those advances in a manner that will convince you that this NOS is ready, willing, and able to support your every need in the Internet's World Wide Web, as well as your in-house networking infrastructure.

What You'll Learn

Throughout this book, you'll be introduced to many new aspects of Microsoft Windows NT Server that have evolved over time, and enhancements that position Microsoft Windows NT Server as a frontline NOS for your Web site. My goal is to show you how Microsoft Windows NT Server can be used to:

* Leverage the Web to provide a competitive business advantage

- Provide remote connectivity to field personnel requiring constant contact with the home office

- Provide a programmatical environment conducive to business productivity on the Web

- Integrate diverse environments into the Microsoft Windows NT Server NOS

I will be discussing four Web server software packages throughout this book: Microsoft's own Internet Information Server, Quarterdeck's WebServer, O'Reilly's WebSite, and Process Corporation's Purveyor Web server. Although I will not be conducting an intensive review of these products, I will provide instructions for the installation and configuration of each product and also an overview to give you a general idea of the most common of Web functions—browsing. I'll also get into the nuts and bolts of how each of these packages integrate into Microsoft Windows NT Server. You will learn how to maintain these servers, as well as discover the daily administration issues that will help you administer your Web site more successfully.

A Brief Look at Microsoft Windows NT Server

Microsoft Windows NT Server began its life years ago as a brand new NOS. Not something to be revamped, Microsoft Windows NT Server is a 32-bit powerhouse of a modular design. This means that subsections of the NOS are written as one group of functions and linked to others. If one subsection has to be enhanced or fixed, it doesn't directly affect other parts of the system or require other functions to be recoded. For instance, the security functions are in a group all their own, as are the OS/2-specific functions. Not all of the NT Server modules are depicted here, but Figure 1.1 illustrates the structure. Higher modules must go through the lower ones, such as the Kernal, in order to get to the hardware. No one application can misuse the hardware and crash the server.

Microsoft Windows NT Server has ample security to keep your business safe and sound from most intruders into your Web server. There are plenty of suitors willing to test your site's security merit, so I'll be discussing security in depth. Although not the preferred method, Microsoft Windows NT Server is capable of supporting both internal business requirements and

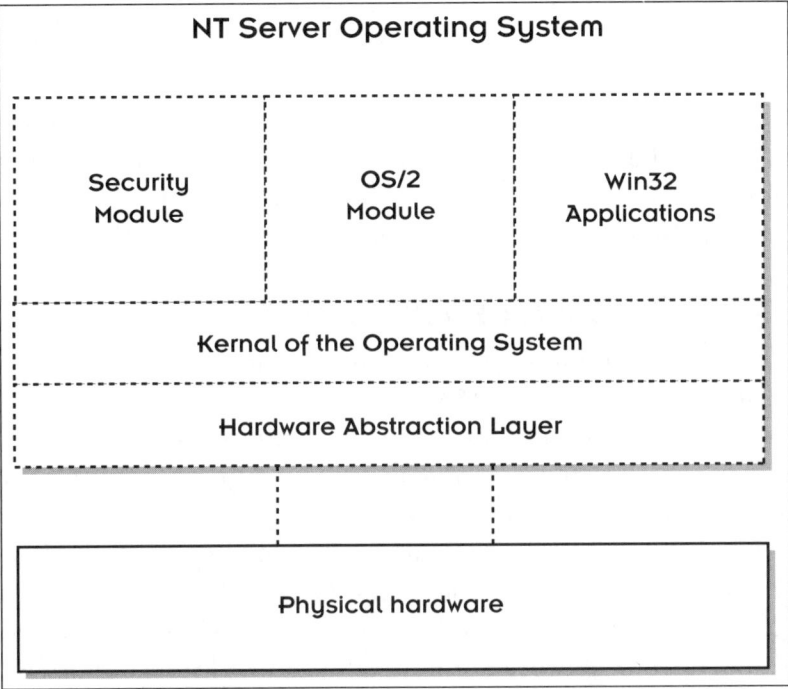

Figure 1.1   A model of Microsoft Windows NT Server's structure.

your Web site, as long as your system is at least a Pentium 120 MHz processor with 96 MB of memory! I'll show you how your business, if your CEO is unsure if a Web site is for you, can create, test, and wring out a prototype Web server using just a 486DX2-66 processor and 16 MB of memory. Yes, you heard correctly. With almost the same expense that a business might go through to equip a network user's desktop, the same business can build and test their Web site theory running Microsoft Windows NT Server.

Your Background

This book presumes that you already have a Microsoft Windows NT Server built for your business' network, and that you are familiar with server conventions. This server can be either a standard LAN server or a domain controller. What you'll be doing, though, is building a new server in which the normal NOS server is left alone while you create, test, and further develop the Web site. Once built, the Web server can then be placed online to the rest of the network so LAN users can get to the Internet, or run the Web server as a standalone site. However, if you want to use the same server for the Web site, I'll cover the necessary issues to let you know what you're in for. Lastly, for those of you who are new to Microsoft Windows NT Server, I have provided a section at the end of this book that previews the basic steps for installing Microsoft Windows NT Server; the hardware requirements are included in our discussions in the book.

Why NT Is Perfect for a Web Server

Approximately 75 million copies of the Windows 3.x desktop operating environment are in place and in use now. With this presence of Windows desktops, quite a few users and network administrators already have the experience and background to maintain Windows. Now, don't think that this is the only requirement to maintain Microsoft Windows NT Server, but if you know a good deal about the Windows desktop, you're well on your way to knowing Windows the server. The common areas are uncanny—the File Manager is still the File Manager and the Control Panel is still the Control Panel. For network administrators and advanced systems types of people, you already have the knowledge to administer the server. Rights are rights, such as read-only, system, hidden, sharable, etc. A few notable differences in the area of group rights include what Microsoft terms *tokens*, which regulate access to server resources.

The Advantages

If you put aside the visual differences, the underlying functions of Microsoft Windows NT Server lends itself to easy understanding. It supports NETBeui, TCP/IP, and IPX protocols effortlessly. If you have a Netware network and users that need access to the Web, yet the Web server is on Microsoft Windows NT Server, don't fret. You can run TCP/IP on both Netware and NT servers, and then route the services across to the Internet. You don't have to build a Web server for both Netware and NT LANs, just the Microsoft Windows NT Server running the Web software.

Another advantage to using NT as a Web server is that the Web software integrates tightly into the network functions of NT itself, and thus is faster and easier to administer. More and more applications and tools are becoming available for NT, and are increasing in stability as well. Experienced network administrators know what version 1.0 software is like, what it can do to you and your users, and the loss of hair that follows. Microsoft Windows NT Server is no exception, but the server itself is a stable platform tested and brought to bear in commercial settings. As a note of interest, the Microsoft Network, shown in Figure 1.2, runs Microsoft Windows NT Server and has been running Microsoft's own Internet Information Server (project-named Gibralter in beta) for quite a long time.

Lastly, we can't forget about the mighty Microsoft marketing machine. With such backing in marketing, logistics, and technical support, many Microsoft products succeed merely by the presence of Microsoft itself. This is not to imply that Microsoft turns out terrible software, because they don't, it's just that their market presence is formidable. When Microsoft Windows NT Server debuted, Microsoft told the corporate world that this is the NOS to beat all NOSs. Corporate America, on the other hand, knew that Microsoft Windows NT Server had yet to be proven in real-world, large-scale settings. If you were the administrator of a 5000 user network spanning 10 cities, would you drop your current NOS based upon someone's word? Even if it were Microsoft? Probably not, and the CEO would have you for lunch if you did.

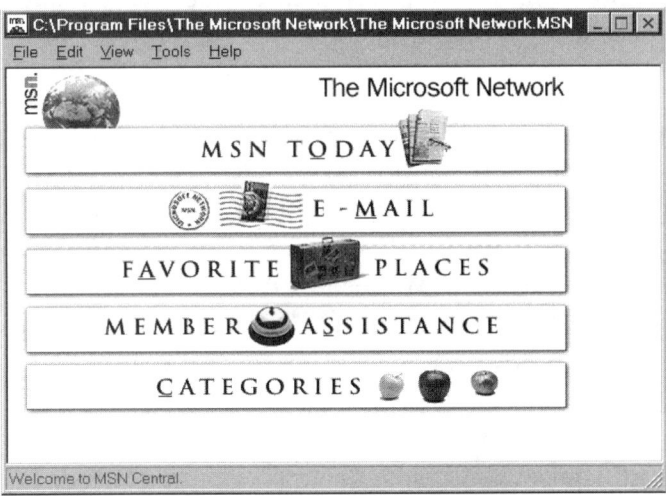

Figure 1.2   The Microsoft Network, which runs on the Windows NT Server.

The Competition

And that's exactly the stance that many corporations took—hide and watch. They wanted someone else to take the chances and experience the pains normally associated with the new NOS on the block. Novell Netware had made its mark as a departmental and corporate NOS with v3.12. Banyan VINES had long ago established themselves quietly as a TCP/IP wide-area-networking guru. Microsoft realized that if they were to succeed in the cutthroat networking world, they too would have to produce a viable enterprise solution. Microsoft Windows NT Server v3.1 was born in 1992. The problem was, in many people's eyes, that not only was it an untried NOS, but Microsoft tagged it Microsoft Windows NT Advanced Server v3.1 which used the same version number as the desktop operating system. To a few, this implied that Windows v3.1 desktop was expounded upon and the NOS was derived from it. Nothing could have been further from the truth. The only common bond was the user interface.

Even though Microsoft Windows NT Server was tagged as version 3.1, it really was a v1.0 product and carried the v1.0 stigma. As is normal with new systems, some corporations installed it anyway and tested the server. Over time, several more test sites went into place at sites ranging from five users to over 100. Still, Microsoft Windows NT Server wasn't widely accepted. Bugs were found, enhancements went into place, and version 3.5 came out; but still mainstream Corporate America wasn't convinced.

Then, something clicked in the Microsoft Marketing Machine—money. Novell Netware long held the common desktop captive to high costs of user licenses. It wasn't unusual to pay $20,000 for a 250 user network license pack even if you only had 120 users. Novell broke their licenses at 5, 10, 50, 100, 250, and 1000 users. You'd wind up wasting no small chunk of change for a few extra users. Microsoft heard the pleas of the estranged CFOs across the land, and money quickly became one of the primary junctures of Microsoft Windows NT Server becoming accepted on a much wider scale. Microsoft is now offering Microsoft Windows NT Server v3.51 at prices I recently saw as low as $700 in a wholesalers magazine, and then you buy whatever client licenses you need at whatever pace desired.

Suddenly, the face of networking changed overnight. Forget the features war, forget the marketing blitz, forget the rumors you may have heard from test sites of the olden days. Now, virtually anyone—including mom-and-pop shops across the world—could have Microsoft Windows NT Server at their fingertips, running on basic 486DX-based computers. With increased exposure and testing in more diverse environments, Microsoft was able to fix more bugs, refine the system, and respond to even more enhancement and feature requests. Microsoft Windows NT Server v3.51 is the current incarnation of this NOS with v4.0 due to release by the time this book is published. Version 4.0 brings new features, smaller memory requirements, faster performance, and a host of Internet functions built right into the NOS itself.

So, What Exactly Is the Web?

Such a hypothetical question, but an interesting one, to say the least. The Web as we know it, the World Wide Web, is a conglomeration of computer networks that form an infrastructure of data processing systems in a very wide-area setting. Virtually every major city in the world is represented by a Web server or two, as shown in Figure 1.3, and many corporate sites run a dozen Web servers to provide for the needs of private and public customers. Just like the spiderweb in your back yard, the Web (sometimes referred to as the WWW or W3) is connected by these computers with telecommunications such as frame relay, ISDN, and fiber optics.

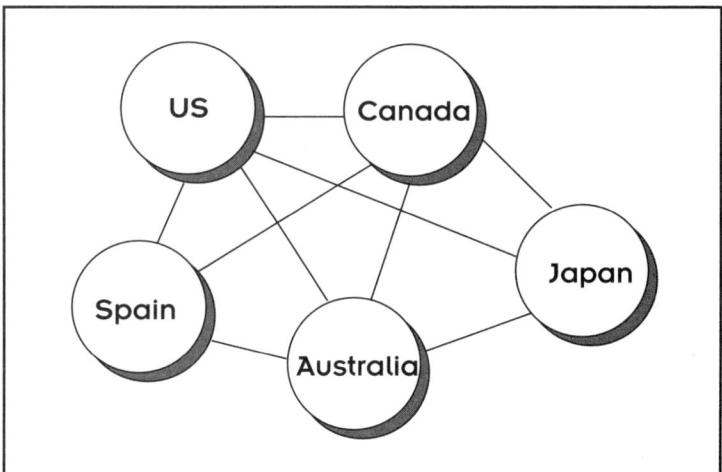

Figure 1.3   The World Wide Web (five sample countries connected).

Because each site is connected to many others, it's possible that even if one city's Web server goes down, then other portions of the Web itself continue to work by being routed back through operational sites. These interconnections form the core of the idea behind the same Web that the spider creates. The servers in this structure are of many types and designs, ranging from simple PCs to Sun workstations, all the way up to high-powered Unix servers, such as Silicon Graphics and DEC VAX systems. Many of these servers are multi-roled computers that are used at universities for research and development, or at corporations to analyze oil field data, and much more. While oil field blast and geological data require massive amounts of processing power, plenty of these computers have horsepower to spare. It's these machines that frequently do double duty as Web servers. To give you an idea of what a Web server has to do, let's consider three scenarios of Web servers and what they can do for you.

The Most Basic Web Server

Without getting into too many details about the hardware, even the most basic Web server can be used to host Web server software and the essentials for a Web site. While researching more material for this book, I built a Web site using a 486DX2-66 with 16 MB of memory and a 820 MB IDE hard drive with the usual compliment of I/O ports and accessories. Microsoft Windows NT Server itself installs in about 90 MB of disk space and uses around 12 MB of memory to get running. Sure, that leaves 4 MB of memory free, but NT will swap out to disk more than normal to accommodate the lack of physical RAM memory.

If you add more memory, it'll run a bit faster and smoother. Add more disk space, and you can install more applications. Add a larger processor, and you can host more simultaneous clients. It's all relevant to what you want to do, but this bare-bones Web server will at least give you a taste for Web life from the provider's perspective. Our bare-bones configuration is suitable for up to four concurrent users dialed in from a multi-I/O card such as the Equinox SST-4 processor card. If you used one of the Equinox SST-8 cards for eight ports, you could use up to six concurrent users on a 28.8 Kbps modem before the processor would start choking up. Even adding more memory didn't solve this problem, which leads me to believe that the processor was the limitation.

A Mid-Range Web Server

I polled several vendors and Web sites to see what some used for Web servers, and how they came to their decision. One common thread was that the average Web server consisted of a Pentium 90 MHz single-processor computer with 32 MB of memory, a single 1 GB hard drive for the NOS, and Microsoft Windows NT Server as the operating system itself. In this configuration, and running with a fractional T1 dedicated leased line, the average site can host 50 concurrent users accessing the site directly from the Internet without a single problem. This same server setup is also fully capable of hosting dialup clients for as many as a dozen concurrent users on 28.8 Kbps modems, along with those dozen Internet users beating on the server. That's a lot of processing going on under the hood, I assure you.

One aspect of the Web server business that eludes most sites is that when Microsoft Windows NT Server is working really hard, and a lot is happening, performance begins to level off at 32 to 48 users for single-processor computers. The one addition that helps the most is adding physical memory. One site I talked with said that upgrading their RAM from 64 to 96 MB caused the system to change from night to day in terms of how it performed. Wow! That much memory? Well, yes, and for a good reason. The operating system takes about 12 MB of RAM to run. Add to that another 8 MB for full TCP/IP operations and for the FTP server software. Add to that another 4 to 6 MB for the Web server software, and then perhaps 4 MB for the monitoring and email software. With 50 users online from the Internet, the server will use another 12 MB of memory. If we tally this up, we need 40 megabytes or so of free memory just to get the server off the ground with the desired operations to support the users. This really isn't a lot of free space given the server's purpose in life in a production world.

If you remember, I said you could prototype a new site on a 486DX2-66 and 16 MB of memory. That's still true, but now you see why putting one into production changes the picture considerably. Use the 486 to tell you the hows, whys, and wherefores of a Web site, but let the Pentium do the work for you properly in a production environment. But, I said they boosted the memory up to 96 MB. Yes, that's true, and here's why. In 32 MB of memory, the Web server is operating smoothly, providing FTP, Web browsing, and some email. This site then began using Microsoft SQL Server v6.0

and the Exchange Server for a more robust site and increased business opportunities. Whereas they once had 32 MB free memory, they now went to dirt poor conditions with the SQL Server and related software, even when they upped this number to 64 MB of memory. This isn't to say SQL Server is a memory hog, but in a production environment that puts heavy demands on the server, a lot of the physical server requirements went through the roof.

An Advanced Server

Whew! What an experience. The CFO of the company had things to say about the money dumped into that box, but the CEO now sees the light, as the saying goes. Increased business because their server is now in the Internet limelight; Increased referrals because satisfied customers now have effortless email contact with their vendor, and can refer new prospects; Increased productivity with employees because they can play network DOOM at lunchtime. Ooops! Going too far, eh? Well, you get the point. The business is booming because of a few little things they did, and it started with a little old 486 test bed Web server.

The shame of it all is that 18 months down the road, the Web server is noticeably slower than it once was. Our CEO is becoming less enthusiastic about the Web server than before, and you get called in on the carpet. You get read the Riot Act, told where to go and what to do, or else! There's a simple solution, you tell the CEO. Heck, all you need to do is add another processor, some more memory, perhaps another SCSI hard disk, and voila! Back in the Web server driver's seat once again. Your CFO, checking the cost of your requests, instantly gives you the thumbs down, but you convince the CEO that Microsoft Windows NT Server supports multiple processors for streamlined performance, and that the job can be done inside of 30 minutes, and you're back in the driver's seat.

Is this just some neat tale of computing? No, it demonstrates the flexibility of Microsoft Windows NT Server's multiple processor support so your machine can grow and mature over time without emptying your company's wallet in the beginning. Microsoft Windows NT Server supports up to 16 processors and 4 GB of physical memory in one box. That's a lot of horsepower and money sitting in the corner of the room, but be assured it does indeed work. As a real life working example, the Microsoft Network consists of specially built Compaq Pentium servers running 4 processors and 512 MB of RAM in each box, and there's tons of these servers running the network. True scalability in an Intel box? Pshaw, scoff the industry pundits, but it works. Microsoft Windows NT Server is truly ready to serve your Web needs right out of the box, given the proper hardware.

The Early Days of Networking

Now that you've been introduced to Microsoft Windows NT Server, let's talk for a minute about a historical perspective of networking that will help you understand how we can integrate Microsoft Windows NT Server into the Web. There are several functions of networking that I'll mention here to set the stage for the better part of this chapter. For you old hands of networking, just bear with me for a few minutes while the newbees are exposed to this technology.

Basic Network Design

To build you up to this thing called the Web, let's back all the way out to a local area network (LAN) design. With a LAN, PCs are connected with a physical cable to each other, and back to the server itself. No big surprises here. Figure 1.4 illustrates this concept.

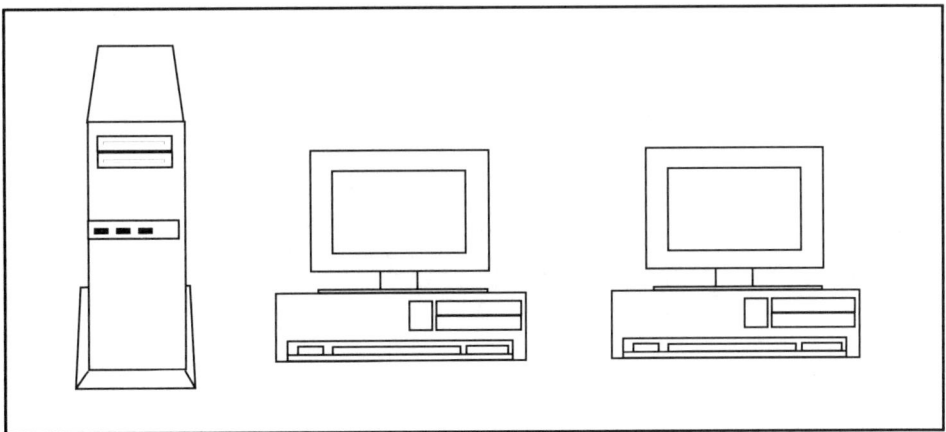

Figure 1.4   A basic local area network.

The next stage upward in network evolution is having two or more networks connected by any one of several means. The most common method is another copper cable connecting one server to another server, as illustrated in Figure 1.5.

This simple server link is sometimes referred to as *internal routing* because each server has two network interface cards (NICs) installed instead of one, and is then cabled between these cards. This situation forms a physical separation between networks, yet allows for a logical connection when the proper software is used. This is a common practice between Novell Netware IPX networks and Microsoft Windows NT Server NETBeui networks. The two are incompatible network protocols, and can't see one another. The same results can be effected by simply connecting both servers to a router. The router is a lot like a traffic cop on his box in the middle of the intersection where a red light doesn't work. You enter the intersection with your turn signal on (hopefully) to show your intentions. The policeman then says yes or no with hand signals. If this intersection has one road barricaded, then you can't go there no matter what. You know which way you want to go, but the policeman gives the final approval.

Routers, Routers Everywhere

The router is quite similar in its functions to the traffic cop mentioned above. It receives a packet of data, looks to see where it needs to go, and

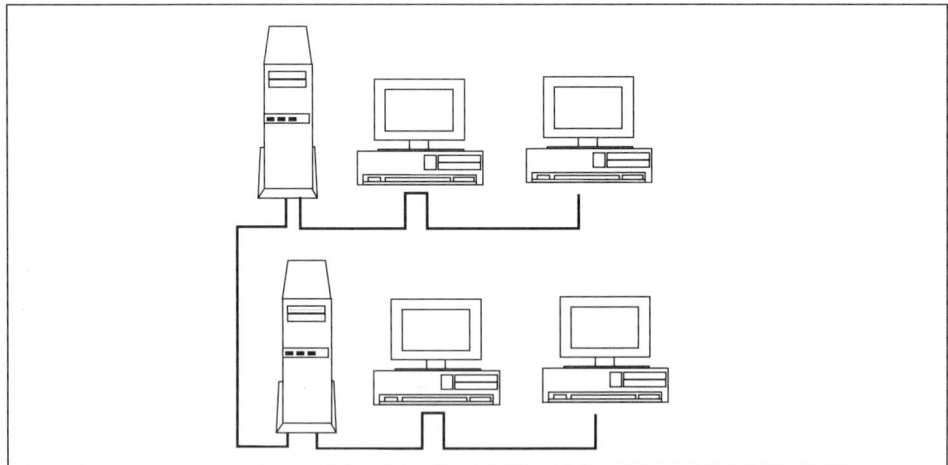

Figure 1.5   Server-to-server connections (two NICs in each server).

sends it onto that connection if it's possible. If not possible, it's returned to the sender much the way that you'd be denied access to a blocked off street. The router also acts much like the policeman—it doesn't modify the data packet that came into the router any more than the policeman modifies your desired route. Either it's yes or no. The downside to using a router is the cost of such a device. If you're routing the same protocol—TCP/IP to TCP/IP networks—then less versatile routers are required at a cost of perhaps $1000 or less. If you've got to route and filter packets of data for IPX, TCP/IP, and Macintosh systems, then a much more powerful and capable router is required. Such a device could easily top $10,000 from one of the best vendors.

So, what's the big deal with internal versus external routers? The external device is much faster because its only job in life is to receive a data packet and forward it on to the appropriate network, as shown in Figure 1.6. Keep in mind that the router has to be told which physical port on the router handles the data for which destination, and many routers have as many as eight ports to handle. If the data being moved stays on the same physical network, then it never has to be routed and performance is never an issue.

The server performing internal routing has plenty of other jobs to handle, and this internal routing function simply adds to the workload. If you've built a server from basic components for a basic job, then you'll get basic performance. This is one reason why Web servers are separate machines performing only Web functions.

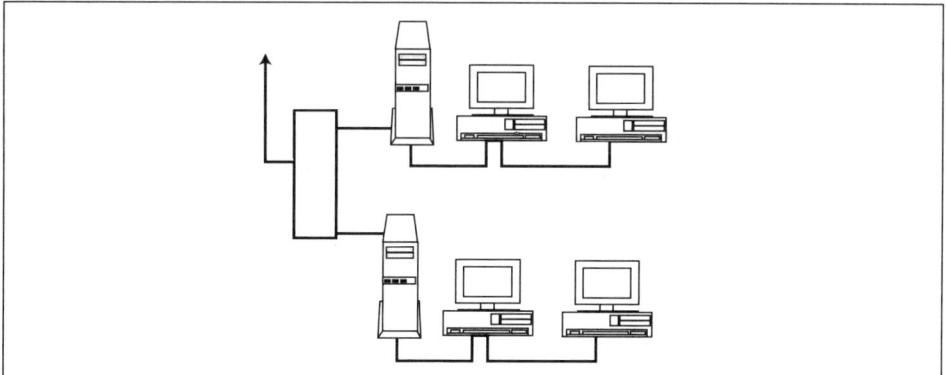

Figure 1.6   Basic router processing.

The Internet Routing Scheme

Now that you've seen how networks are put together, let's see how this pertains to Microsoft Windows NT Server and the Web. Actually, the Internet is made up of literally thousands of networks interconnected to one another by massive numbers of routers of all types and designs. Because these systems are so diverse, the common thread between them is the protocol—the means of moving data between servers. English is the predominant language of the United States. In France, it's French. All across the world, each country, and even divisions within the country, have their own dialect. If you had to connect computers together and bridge the language barrier between the possible languages, that'd be a highly formidable task indeed. It'd be really nice if there was a way everyone could easily understand one another, but that got fouled up a few thousand years ago.

In the computer world, a very similar situation exists. Novell servers speak IPX as their native tongue. Microsoft's dialect is NETBeui and NetBIOS. Banyan VINES has it's own version of TCP/IP called VINES-IP. None of these know anything about the other, so to connect each of these systems together calls for a common language. TCP/IP is it. Transmission Control Protocol/Internet Protocol is the name, seamless connectivity is the game. If you install TCP/IP in each of these servers, then all of them can talk to each other without caring what is running underneath it. What this does is form a common bond from Hong Kong to Vienna to Los Angeles. Remember the lost common language a few thousand years ago? Well, we can't get that back, but TCP/IP does that for computers. Even as I write this manuscript, I'm connected to my Internet provider and checking mail, grabbing a file from an Internet site in Germany, and browsing the Web at Microsoft's campus. Figure 1.7 clearly shows how the Internet is put together.

Mail, file transfers, and Web browsing are going on at the same time. TCP/IP allows for this simultaneity by using *sockets*, which are connections from the application software and the operating system. Having the ability to create and manage multiple sockets is one feature that TCP/IP uses and that makes your world on the Web so much fun. As we get into later chapters, we're going to build a Web server that is capable of supporting multiple users and functions at the same time. When you see these things happening, you'll understand why. This understanding is important for those days when things just don't seem to be working correctly.

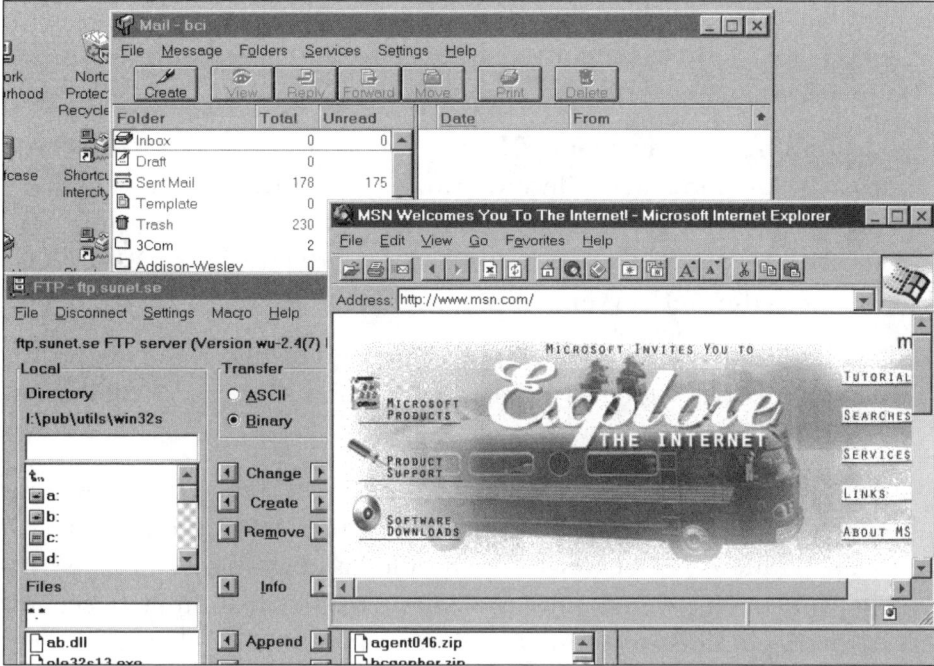

Figure 1.7   A walk on the Internet.

Some Basics of Windows NT Networking

Before firing up your Web server software, you need to have a little understanding of Microsoft Windows NT Server networking. It's not very hard to set up the server, and we've assumed that you already know about networking under NT Server. However, most new and even some experienced network administrators do not fully understand the Microsoft Windows NT Server domain model and how it reflects upon new servers. Let's take a minute to discuss this model, what it signifies, and how it affects your usage of Microsoft Windows NT Server as a Web server.

The Microsoft Windows NT Server domain model is an abstract logical structure used to define the network server's principle area of responsibility. In this model, there are several types of servers:

- **Primary Domain Controller (PDC)**—One server designated as the focal point for all security, user accounts, system administration, and related critical controls for the network as a whole. It typically contains the user database, security rights database, and critical system controls. This server typically does the duty of a PDC only, and no other functions, in a heavily used network.

- **Backup Domain Controller (BDC)**—A separate network server whose primary duties include a file and print server for the general populace, and which provides a backup replication of the databases stored on the PDC. In a light duty setting of less than 100 users, the BDC could be used as the Web server.

- **Standard Network Server**—A regular file and print services server for the users. This is what most Microsoft Windows NT Server installations are doing these days.

The last option is one that I found a client in several weeks before writing this manuscript. In that situation, the customer had asked for a new Microsoft Windows NT Server to be installed and configured for five users. No problem, it seemed, until the completed installation saw a second server coming online for testing and development work. When user security and system issues came up, they couldn't get some devices shared or permissions set properly. During the evaluation of the network, I discovered that no domain controller had been created! There was no way to centrally or categorically control user access to the network. Luckily, because the first server was installed as a simple file and print services server, the second server could then be installed as a domain controller and solve several issues.

What does all of this mean to you? Well, first, I hope you installed the first server as a PDC. That's the best way to go. If you need other functions split off of the PDC, then create a second server as a plain old network server, or even as a BDC. The backup process for domain databases isn't strenuous on the BDC at all, and can function as the Web server in most cases.

 If you create the Web server as a BDC, then be aware that you could be vulnerable to intrusion into your network. For this reason, many businesses build their Web servers as completely standalone machines, unless they can secure the Web server from intrusions by using firewalls or proxy servers.

One alternative to creating a standalone machine is to use a router and attach the Web server to the internal company network so that all incoming traffic is routed to the Web server only. With the use of a proxy server, any incoming traffic from the company's own people can be allowed access to the main network. The combination of network passwords, user account security, firewalls, and proxy servers should suffice for all but the most stringent security requirements of a Microsoft Windows NT Server network.

Applications and Servers

As previously mentioned, your mix of applications and the company's internal data processing vision will define how the network uses the Web server, and how the users use the network by way of the Web. It's a two-way street that causes much concern two years down the road, when the most ambitious plans for a Web site go awry the first time the Web server itself comes crashing down due to an overload. How is this possible, you ask? When the Web server first went online, it ran like a banshee and was faster than the network server itself. Naw, just not possible.

Well, it *is* possible, despite even the best laid plans of mice and MIS. Perhaps the company has had a changeover in personnel, with a new WebMaster who uses every possible resource within the company to maximize the return on investment. Noble gesture, to be certain, but faulty thinking when it comes to a Web server. What was once a screaming little machine has become something my 8 year old can outtype on the old 386. There's a place for applications that function with the Web server, and there's a place for applications that don't. Ah, I thought I said that quite a few paragraphs back, so what do I mean? When your Web server gets online, you're bound to find new uses on the Web for the site. One of these will be used in Part 3 of this book to demonstrate the use of Visual Basic, the Common Gateway Interface (CGI), and scripting to provide professional business services on the Web.

While creating and maintaining these services, I found one customer that had all of the programmatical tools installed on the Web server itself and was performing the actual programming, compiling, and debugging on the same machine that was the Web server! Twenty users were on the Web site, and all were barely able to perform functions at the time. It was the company's policy to perform the work on the same server as the Web software for these reasons:

- The possibility of viral attack was reduced by making the Web server stand alone.

- The results of the new programming could be seen immediately.

- The company did not have to purchase additional routers and a desktop PC for the developer.

That was really not the best thing to do, as the customer found out, especially because one of the miffed users was the CFO! Needless to say, the CFO loosened the purse strings to get a developmental PC for the programmer. This is just one example of what not to do with your Web server. In later troubleshooting, more less-than-optimum circumstances will be reviewed. It does, however, point out that having the Web server connected to the main business network isn't all that bad; the developer can now access the Web server internally to test changes and post updates. Any tasks that need to be done can be done from the server console.

Styles and Architectures of the Network

While not directly related to the Web, let's take a minute and talk about internal network infrastructure and how it relates to the Web server. There are four common types of network infrastructures defined and in use today—bus, star, token ring, and FDDI ring. I want you to know what to expect in the way of performance when your Web server comes online and you have employees accessing your internal network from the Internet connecting inwards.

Star-Coupled Systems

If you've ever gazed into the night sky (and know something of astronomy), you can pick out clusters of stars that are commonly called constellations. In the midst of these clusters, you can pinpoint a star that forms the nucleus of the group. A similar analogy is the wagon wheel of the Old West. Spokes

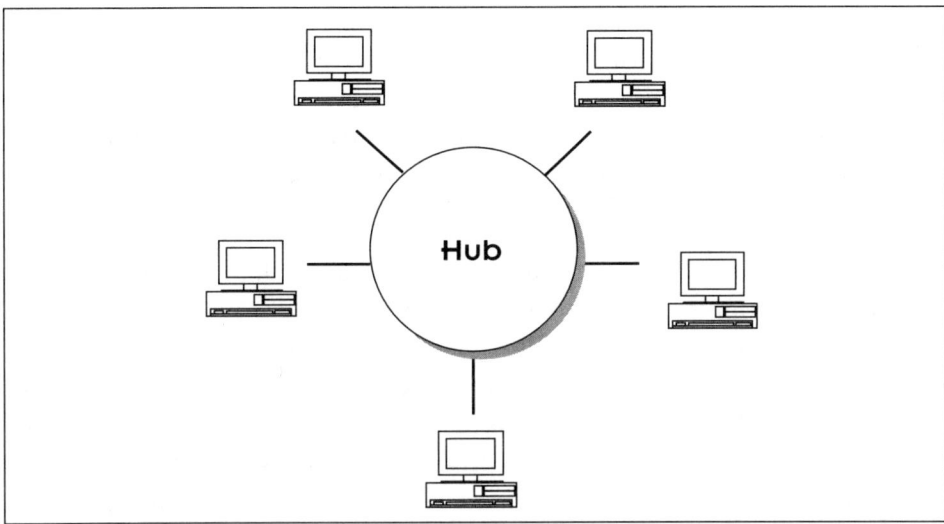

Figure 1.8　A star-coupled LAN.

connect to the hub to form the wheel and provide strength to carry the load. If one of the spokes breaks, the wheel will continue to function. Star-coupled LANs work in much the same way, as shown in Figure 1.8.

Star-coupled systems use the broadcast methodology to get data to each workstation on a signaling rate of 10 megabits per second. That is, the server or workstation sends out the data packet to each connected device on the network, and only the one with the proper address accepts the data. All other devices ignore the data packet. If any one workstation should go bonkers, it usually doesn't affect any other part of the network. *Usually*. The exception to the rule is if the NIC goes bad. In this case, the server can broadcast packets of data all across the network, causing a flood in the cables. In 99.9 percent of all cases, only the one workstation is ever affected. This is very good for this kind of design, and for the business in general. The only single point of failure is the hub. Naturally, if it goes out, the show is over.

The Common Bus Structure

The bus structure was perhaps the first style of network cabling systems. It has its good points, but it has a few weaknesses as well. Unlike the star-coupled system, the bus structure can be thought of as the city street. It starts at one point (terminated), and proceeds to its other end (also terminated). All along this street, houses (workstations) are built and occupied. There can be a corner convenience food store (printer), but the street must have a large grocery store (network server) to serve the masses. When all is said and done, the entire assembly of the city street (network cable) forms the community (LAN). Figure 1.9 illustrates the common bus structure network.

The bus-coupled system sends data out to the network devices in the same way as the star-coupled system. Now, let's consider one very important aspect of the bus structure. What if a sewer pipe directly in front of the grocery store (network server) breaks? What a mess. Guess you'll have to live off of the cookies and milk in your house (workstation) for a time while the problem is resolved. The problem with this network system is that the single point of failure is now possible on any span of the entire cable system, at any workstation, the network server itself, or even power. This potential problem can be very unsettling to some network administrators, but should not dissuade you from considering the bus option. A little later on in this chapter, I'll discuss the pros and cons of a cabling scheme that show how this bus structure can be a rather appealing option for small LANs of 50 or fewer users.

Token Ring

Token rings are similar to the star-coupled scheme, but differ in the signaling speed and the connections. Like star-coupled LANs, token rings are less susceptible to outages because one workstation usually doesn't down the network. Unlike the star-coupled system, token ring systems pass the *token,* or data packet, from workstation to workstation in sequential order until one workstation qualifies to receive the packet. If no device is to receive

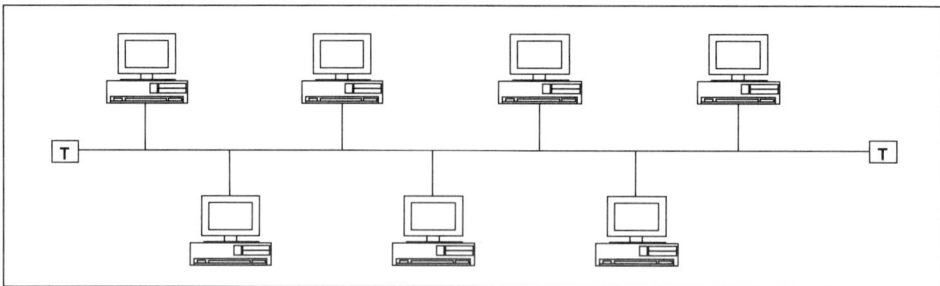

Figure 1.9   A bus-coupled network.

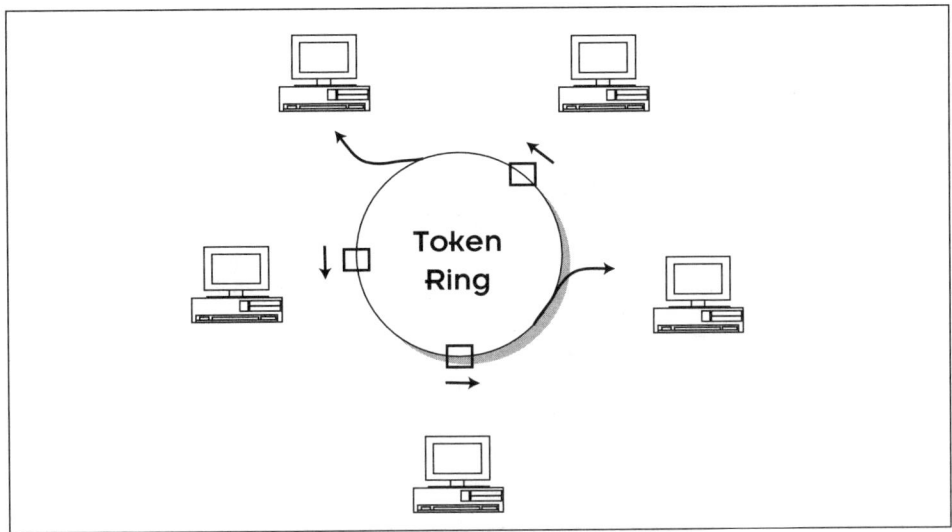

Figure 1.10　A token ring system.

the packet, or the packet got corrupted en route, it is discarded. Figure 1.10 illustrates a token ring system.

This standard is in use almost exclusively by IBM systems or others using IBM networks. The signaling rate is either 4 or 16 megabits per second, depending on the type of cable used and the NIC. One disadvantage to token ring systems is the cost of the NICs, the wall plates to make the connections, and the size of the connections. This is a very reliable standard, and the cabling scheme requires a knowledgeable technician to install and build the cables.

FDDI and Double Fiber Rings

Fiber Distributed Data Interface, or FDDI, is a standard in which fiber-optic cables are used to form the same style of network cable as the bus structure, but the major difference is in the use of glass as the medium instead of copper. Yes, that's right! Fiber cabling is composed of a glass center core that varies in diameter from 50 microns to as large as 165 microns. A *micron* is one millionth of an inch. To give you a decent perspective, the average size of the human hair is 300 microns. Or, if you prefer, a particle of dust that floats in the sunbeams in the window averages 100 microns in thickness. Figure 1.11 illustrates the size of a fiber cable core.

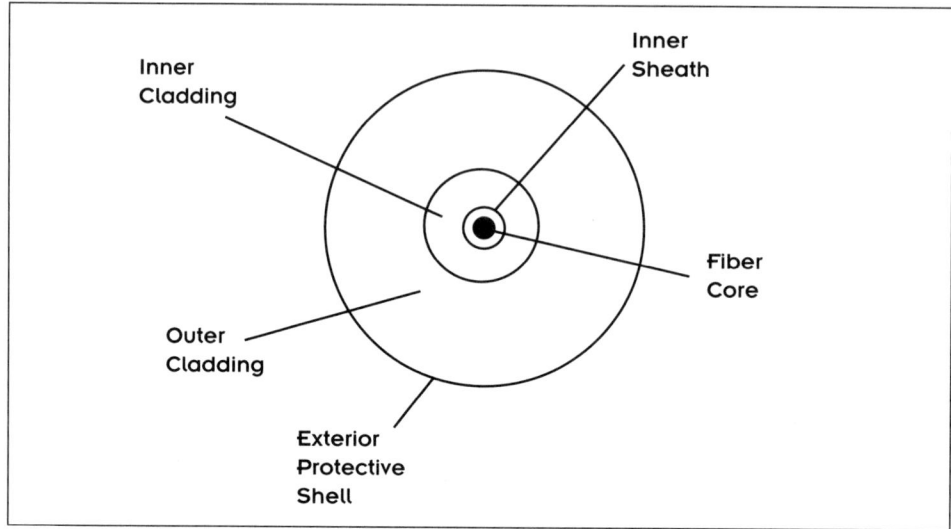

Figure 1.11 Fiber cable core, in perspective.

There are several types of fiber cable in use, but the two most common are called *single mode* and *multi-mode*. The most common fiber cable in use is the multi-mode version. Multi-mode is 62.5 or 125 microns in diameter, depending on a few circumstances which we'll discuss later in the chapter. Why the multi-mode? What does it do, play AM and FM at the same time? Add a CD? Well, not really, but it's close to that versatility. Basically, multi-mode fiber uses a standard type of light system in which the light is transmitted down the fiber to form the carrier for the data. Think of the carrier as a bus going down the street. The bus is used to get you from here to there safely; likewise, the light in the fiber is used to carry the data safely from one point to another. The glass fiber is the medium, the light is the carrier in the glass. As such, using standard light sources to carry the data allows for inexpensive fiber (yes, you heard right) cable, but restricts the distances used to no more than 5.2 miles on a single segment without the use of a fiber repeater.

Single-mode cable is 50 microns in size. This type of cable employs a bona fide laser as the carrier of the data. Laser in the truest sense of the word! This laser allows for use in considerably longer distances, but the light source is expensive, the cable is expensive, and the maintenance is expensive. Did I mention that this networking system is expensive? Average distance with single-mode fiber on a single segment without a repeater is 35 miles.

Let's take fiber optics one step further. One way to provide redundancy in your LAN is to make sure the cabling scheme not only stands up to the pressures of the users, but also holds up under the physical environment. If you live in California, you surely know the story there. Here in my home state of Florida, we have salt water corrosion, huge field rats, and hurricanes to contend with, as well as users that move the equipment around whenever they feel like it. That's not so bad, but if they only knew what they were moving! This is the problem with bus structures. You never know when something is going to be moved in the attic, the cellar, or within the walls that may affect the LAN as a whole. An FDDI double ring is two sets of fiber cables that run converse to one another in opposite directions. At strategic locations, the fiber rings are connected by routers that provide a replicated path to remove the possibility of failure—no matter what goes wrong at most points on the circuit. Figure 1.12 shows the double ring system.

While this cabling scheme is among the most reliable, and the most capable, it is also the most expensive solution of all the choices. If you're building a document imaging network, then FDDI is your choice. If you're building a city-wide network, sometimes referred to as a MAN (Metropolitan Area Network), then FDDI is your choice. If you're building a network

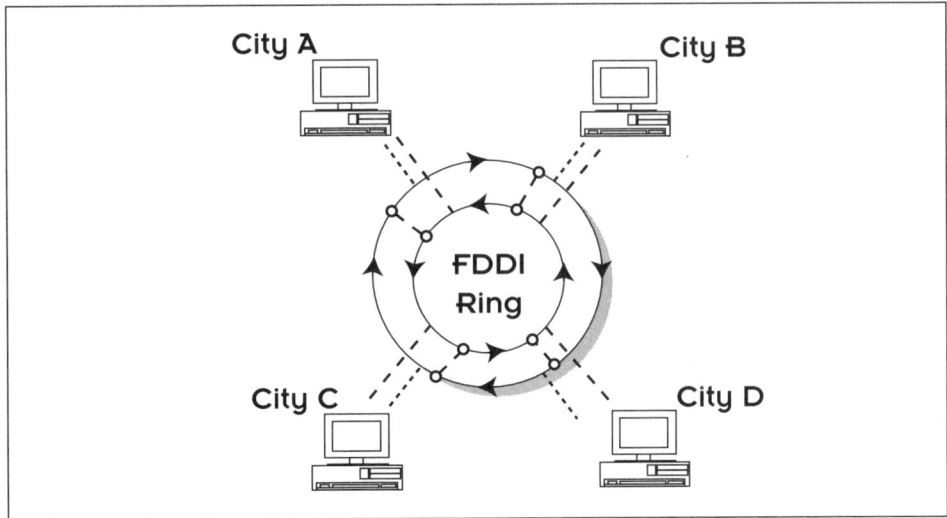

Figure 1.12 An FDDI double ring networking system.

that has hundreds of users with few having seriously intensive applications but that are spread out in separate buildings, then FDDI is probably for you. In nearly all other applications, fiber optics is simply out of reach in terms of cost to the company and technical ability of the cable installers.

Fiber Optics Principles

Among the choices, fiber has been stated as the most expensive. No truer words have been spoken. If you decide to use fiber, be prepared. The connectors for fiber can cost as much as $20 each, with the need for two connectors at each end, one to transmit and one to receive. If you foul up any part of the cable, you have to start from scratch, usually replacing the other connector as well. This gets expensive in a hurry. You will also have to contend with an unusual safety issue. Remember that center core of the fiber? Glass? That glass core is only 62.5 microns in diameter, and if it breaks off and gets into your fingers, off to the surgery room you go! There's no picking the glass shard out; I can assure you from personal experience.

The previous cabling systems were made of copper, and could withstand various forces of nature and humans. Fiber, on the other hand, is less resilient. Fiber can tolerate only a ninety degree bend in six inches without compromising the integrity of the fiber core, whereas copper can be twisted nearly into a pretzel before this problem occurs. If you want to assure extra longevity of fiber, install it into conduit pipe. More expense you say? Well, at an average of $2 per foot for fiber, it's definitely worth it. Here's a summary of the steps to build a fiber-terminated connection:

1. Clean a two foot length of the cable, starting from the end, with 9 percent alcohol.

2. Plug in and turn on the fiber kit's heating and curing tool. This warms up to about 350 degrees.

3. Using the special knife provided in your fiber optics cable kit, cut off the end of the cable two inches back from the very end of the cable. Make sure there aren't any fragments hanging from the cable.

4. Using the special sheath knife, remove the outer cladding to the cable two inches from the end of the cable.

5. Using the same knife as in step 3, remove the inner cladding to the fiber.

The raw glass core is now exposed! Failure to exercise proper safety techniques can result in damage to the fiber or harm to personnel. Always wear proper safety gear and observe safety precautions.

6. Carefully insert the exposed glass core into the fiber connector shell. Measure the amount of glass core protruding out of the end of the connector and observe the amount of protected cladding on the backside of the connector. There must be at least one-half inch of protruding glass out of the end of the connector with the protected end snugly in place.

7. Pour the epoxy material into the connector shell to fill the gaps all around it.

8. Once the epoxy settles, insert the connector into the curing tool and bake the epoxy for 15 minutes.

9. Remove the connector, allow it to cool, and then cut off the excess glass core.

10. Once the cooked connector has cooled, use five levels of resistive paper to polish the glass end of the connector so that the connector is perfectly perpendicular to the end of the glass core. Use a "figure 8" pattern, starting with the 200 grit paper and finishing with the emery cloth which is equivalent to 1000 grit.

These are the basic steps to building one fiber connector. There are two connectors on each end of the cable, and four connectors total. So, conservatively, you've invested two hours for one cable set. And that's not to mention the $150 for materials. But who cares, right? You're done. Not yet, bucko! Get your handy-dandy fiber test set out and check the integrity of the cable. Not quite up to spec, eh? Guess what? You get to do it all over again from the start! All that time and money wasted. The moral of this story, and this story happens all the time, is if you decide on fiber for your site, you might consider sending one of your best technicians to fiber maintenance school, or hire a competent cable installation company.

What's all of this architectural stuff got to do with the Web, especially fiber optics? Well, when your wildly successful Web site is due for renovation and moving up the ladder to better equipment because your CEO is completely convinced that it's worth the money the CFO doesn't want to spend, one way to provide better and more reliable service is to use better and more reliable equipment. If your telecommunications provider has the solutions for it, then fiber optics from primary points of service will get you cleaner and more stable lines than what some of us have to tolerate. My Web server now is suffering from RBOC-ous non-ous fix-ous syndrome. Meaning, if they (the vendor) can pick up the phone and get a dial tone, they're convinced the line must be fine. If you live in an area where 9600 baud modems are a luxury, you know how far behind the times a communications vendor is that doesn't care too much about quality lines, much less digital circuits.

This is a rather bold statement about the state of our telephonic circuits, but it really means that the Information SuperHighway is all too often rerouted up and over Small City, USA to avoid these unpleasantries or expensive investments. Even if they bring advanced computing resources to town, most telephone companies won't see a return on their investment for the next two years or so, so kiss your modern link goodbye!

The Corporate Windows NT Network

This topic is interesting to consider. You've been introduced to the Microsoft Windows NT Server domain model, what it is, and how it affects certain operations. There are as many thoughts on how to create your domain plan as there are changes in the wind on any given day. The domain plan you apply to the Web server placement can affect several security and operational issues. Take a look at the domain implementation shown in Figure 1.13. Using this figure, we can see how the plan affects the location and serviceability of the Web server. One thing to point out here is that this corporation deemed it necessary to create four separate domains so that Engineering could be autonomous from Accounting and MIS, but still reported to The HeadShed. (*Everyone* reports to the HeadShed.)

This view of the corporation makes one wonder where the Web server is to be placed, and why. Does the central accounting office host it? Not really, no good reason for the number crunchers to maintain it. So, shouldn't MIS have it located in their Glass House computer room? Sounds logical

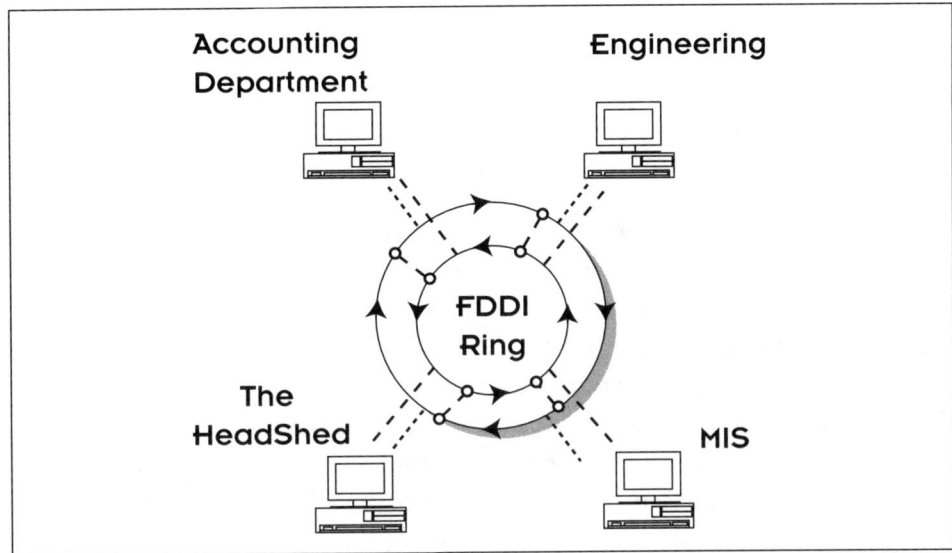

Figure 1.13   A sample corporate domain plan.

since they maintain the hardware and software. But MIS has it geographically located in a most remote spot—away from the employees that use it, and away from the developers that need direct access to it the most. Not such an easy solution, eh? In this case, MIS, the CEO, and the people who are most closely involved with the Web server should sit down with the customers that could also use the Web server and see just exactly what the needs are, could be, and are projected to be in the future.

In dispersed settings such as this one, it would not be unreasonable to have multiple Web servers hosting specialized core parts of the business' services, yet have connectivity to the other Web servers. This setup provides only what the customers want, yet gives access to the seldom used information as needed. Additionally, it reduces network traffic to only those segments of the network for each Web server. In Chapter 12, *Web Server Administration*, we'll preview analysis software for just this purpose; to chart and monitor your Web server's progress and usage.

The Internet, by Comparison

Okay, so the internal business perspective of a Web server has become a bit clearer than before, so now let's turn our attention to the Internet aspect of the Web server. Basically, take the business' network and replicate its basic form and functions about 10,000 times across the globe, and you've got the Internet. Sure, it varies with Sun servers and IBM servers and DEC VAX systems, but the core principles are the same. Connect all of these servers together, and you've formed the Internet.

To get from one Web server to another, as we've said before, the data gets routed all over. The transition from one router to another is called *making a hop* in networking lingo. The trip from server to server can be traced with utilities that measure the time to get from point A to point B, the number of routers that the data traversed, and any lost packets. In the test, the number of routers traversed is referred to as the *hop count*. I did a test of a hop count from my place to a customer's site just seven miles down the road, and found that it took 23 hops to get there! When I did a test called a *trace route* between the same two sites, I found that my request went from my site in Northwest Florida to Atlanta to Dallas to seven sites on the West Coast, across seven northern tier states, and then back to the customer's site. My data is more well traveled than I am!

This is a real-world situation that points out that no matter how close you physically may be to your customer, the route that your information takes can be thousands of miles long. The Web servers that form the connection could be down for maintenance, down for upgrades, or down for the count, you have no way of knowing. It reflects the true nature of the Internet, that it uses a best-delivery method of distributing data. Return receipts requested of email guarantees little except that the email made it to the first point of contact capable of sending the receipt. One customer I see often has four servers in which the first point is a Banyan VINES server that hosts the email software. This is where the return receipt is generated, yet the mail itself has about three more servers to go through before actually getting to the user.

Protocols of the Internet

As you build the server, keep in mind that there are several transport methods to get data moved around the Internet. These form the nucleus of all data movement, and you should be aware of them. TCP/IP is the protocol used to talk to each computer, but the protocols I will be discussing are different because they apply to the data itself. When you build your Web server, keep in mind the tools that you'll need to use for the average site's support. Not necessarily in the order of importance, these tools are:

- **HTTP Web browser server software**—Allows you to view Web documents

- **FTP server**—Transfers files to/from clients

- **Email server**—Sends and receives email

- **Gopher server**—Handles database search and retrieval software

- **Server analysis**—Measures the usefulness of the Web site

Let's talk a little bit about each of these tools, keeping in mind that the soon-to-be-released newest version of Microsoft Windows NT Server has several of these tools built right into the server. Those items are the HTTP Web server, an enhanced FTP server, a Gopher server, and the new Microsoft Internet Explorer v2.0 client.

HTTP stands for *Hyper Text Transport Protocol* and is the predominant function used in daily Internet activities. This protocol moves data from Web servers, such as O'Reilly's WebSite, to the requesting client. FTP, or *File Transport Protocol*, is used to move files, either binary or textual, from one location to another. When files are transported, two possible modes are used—ASCII and binary. ASCII preserves the formatting of simple text documents while binary moves the file byte for byte regardless of the content of the file. If you use ASCII format to move a binary file, chances are that the file will be useless. You can, however, move a text file using binary mode without harming the document. Email uses a couple of protocols, one called POP, which stands for *Post Office Protocol*, and one called SMTP, which stands for *Simple Mail Transport Protocol*. POP is used for the clients connecting to the Web server to retrieve email, while SMTP is used for outgoing mail from the server. And while you're getting mail, you might have a file attachment to an email. These files use several methods of transport. A couple of them are *UUEncode, MIME*, and *Base 64*.

This underscores part of the problem of setting up that new Web site—there are a lot of things at stake here. How much experience should the new WebMaster have? A little? A lot? Know where the on/off switch is located? Hard to say sometimes, but a safe bet is someone that is fluent in computer terminology, the basics of network designs, industrious and adventuresome, thick skinned, and has a brass jaw. Well, the last two are of my own device, but it means that if you build the server, be ready to field some pointed questions about how it operates.

Transmission Speeds of Your Web Server Links

Why would this be important to Microsoft Windows NT Server as a Web server? Okay, how about this scenario. You're in the field working at a customer's site when you realize you need to connect back and get a special file of updates to fix a key problem. You've sent email back to your boss explaining the problem, the message comes back telling you where on the site the file has been put, and off you go to get it. After making the initial connection, a great big error dialog box pops up saying there was a network error in the connection. No biggie, you've seen this before and it always goes away. Not this time...it persists. And it persists again. Finally, a bit flustered, you email the boss about the problem and ask if he could email the file as an attachment. After all, email isn't nearly as strenuous as FTP, right?

As it turns out, the problem stems from a timeout factor in which the FTP server can't possibly respond to the FTP client's request fast enough because the connection's link speed is insufficient to support the volume of users. This problem is typical of sites that underestimate the needs of the Microsoft Windows NT Server network along with the new Web site. In Chapter 2, you'll develop a Web server game plan and then implement it in Chapter 3. Part of this plan takes into account traffic volumes, now and in the future.

The New Kid—Windows 95

In every sandbox, it seems as if there's a new entry into the playing field every week. The desktop operating systems are no stranger to this, and Windows 95 is no exception. While billed as an evolutionary process of Windows 3.1, the old tried-and-true operating environment, Windows 95 is different. Several years ago, Microsoft started changing and improving Windows 3.1 with two primary goals—make it easier to use and a more productive computing environment. It maintains vestiges of its 16-bit world to ensure compatibility to the hordes of 16-bit applications, yet it advances the cause of 32-bit applications significantly. Communications and printing, specifically, got a much needed boost in performance. During one series of tests I did on the product, I had a desktop machine running a 486DX2-66 and 16 MB of memory, that had two 28.8 Kbps modems connected to online services downloading files. Both connections were getting about 3 Kbps, which is slightly above the average for those modems.

In addition to those two downloads, I was compiling a large C++ project and writing manuscript all at the same time. The system performed admirably, better than I expected, but was surely a solid indication of how well Microsoft had improved upon Windows. This isn't to say Windows 95 is a perfect product, because it has its limitations and problems just like the rest of them. What it does say is that the average user and novices alike will enjoy the changes made to the user interface that substantially improve productivity. For some, the new user interface is just too drastic a change to be useful to them until they've had time to adjust to it. For others, they'll take to it like a duck to water.

Whatever the case, one of the principle efforts behind Windows 95 was an increase in productivity by making the desktop more friendly and easier to use. Windows 95 succeeded at this to a degree, depending on who you talk to, and in what context. If someone is using an old 16-bit DOS application that was errant in its days in Windows 3.0, then there'll certainly be problems running it in Windows 95. Printing was the single most disgusting part of Windows 3.1 that I can remember. Let a print job get hung up, or out of control, and it was useless to fight it. Print Manager was often totally useless in that regard. Windows 95 lends a bit of relief by way of the new property sheets for each printer and the amount of control each print queue has for management.

Networking in Windows 3.1? A lesson in hair loss at your own hands. Just terrible. Windows 95 got a tremendous boost in ease of networking and the user got plentiful relief in configuring the average desktop for networking. I can have a new Windows 95 PC configured and online to Microsoft Windows NT Server in fewer than five minutes! It's that easy, but don't think it's error free. Some NICs are problematic at best, and impossible to work with at worst. These are the ones that'll challenge you and Windows 95 to get configured properly for the network. Oh, and if you thought this was something new or singular to Windows 95, OS/2 has similar problems, as does VINES, as does Microsoft Windows NT Server. If the

NIC is a pain, then brace yourself for the installation process. Aside from that, the overall networking abilities of Windows 95 are a token of the improvements made to the desktop. These network drivers are all 32 bit and run with the speed and efficiency you'd expect of them. All of these options, drivers, changes, and settings are available in one centrally located dialog box, as shown in Figure 1.14.

With that said and done, one of the forthcoming enhancements to Microsoft Windows NT Server v4 is a new shell that very closely resembles the one Windows 95 sports now. The power of NT is soon to be merged with the ease of use of Windows 95, a really neat advance in networking that will be reviewed later in the book. This also says that Windows 95 workstations on the Microsoft Windows NT Server network with the Web server will have an easier time managing and administering the Web server as a whole. There is one drawback to using Windows 95 with Microsoft Windows NT Server, and that's that you can't use NTFS partitions on a Windows 95 workstation. This omission is necessary for proper security and rights.

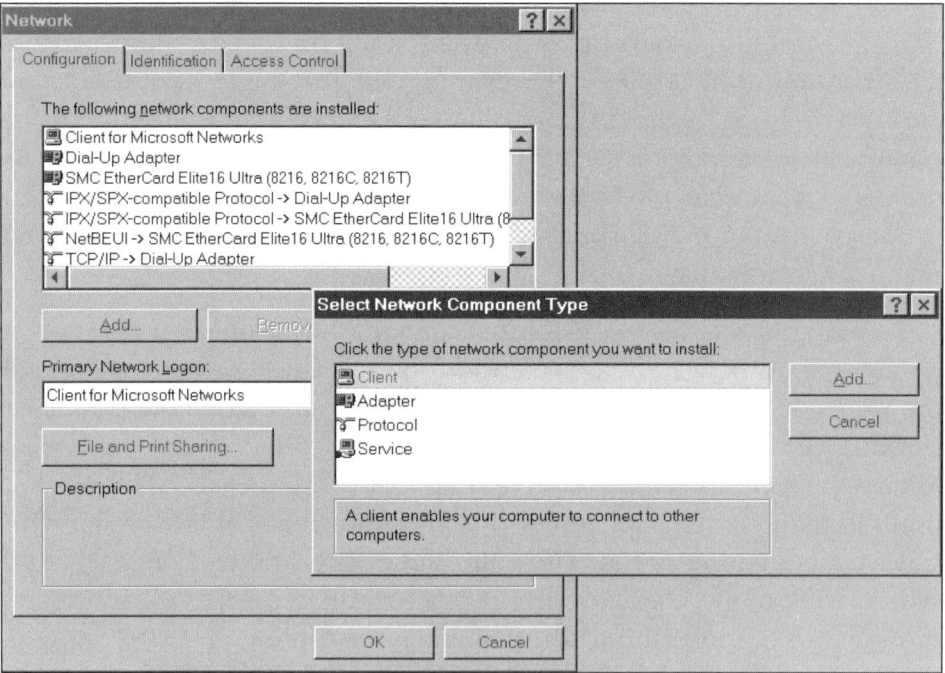

Figure 1.14   The Windows 95 networking options.

Windows NT Workstation

If you now think that Windows 95 is the cat's meow at running on a Microsoft Windows NT Server network, you're right, but try NT Workstation the next time you get a chance. This client is really a scaled down mini-NT server without all of the server side software and controls for security. It has nearly the same look and feel as Microsoft Windows NT Server, but without the overhead. It's fast, clean, and integrates directly into the Microsoft Windows NT Server network. It also has FTP services where outside users can FTP to the workstation anywhere on the network and move files. You don't have to do it to/from the Web server all the time, but rather you can have an NTFS partition on your networked PC that runs TCP/IP and access the PC remotely.

The Overall Picture, and What It Means for Windows NT

Okay, we've gone through a lot in this first chapter, most of it is introductory in nature and geared to get you in the frame of mind to create and maintain a Microsoft Windows NT Web Server. It's fun, interesting, expands your horizons, and makes for really good résumé material. With the explosive growth of the Web, anyone that has Internet and Web server experience will surely have a better chance finding and keeping a job in these turbulent times we live in. If you've followed NT along it's trail, you'll remember that it was positioned originally as a direct competitor to Netware and VINES as a LAN server.

However, even Microsoft couldn't immediately turn the tide away from Netware at first, so they took what appeared to be an alternative direction—the Internet. Microsoft has a long-term strategy for Microsoft Windows NT Server, and it's flatly geared to the Internet and online services. The entire computing community got a sense of this new direction when Microsoft released their Internet Information Server and made it available to anyone absolutely free! Yes, free. Talk about market penetration, this is one sure way to do it. This will get them the presence on the Web they wanted, but there's more to it. For a business environment to really get the most out of the SQL Server, you can use it as a back-end database engine, and then add front-end tools such as Visual Basic, along with some CGI tools, to build a searchable database to get at the company data while

Figure 1.15   Yahoo search results.

accessing your Web site across the Internet. Did you ever see a search result from something like Yahoo? Check out Figure 1.15.

Guess where that came from? A database query. Not necessarily Microsoft
SQL Server, but other search engines that gather data at all times of the
day and night. The point is that a very active and productive business Web
site will make use of all available resources to promote the business and
enrich the bottom line.

What's Next

While you've gotten a good start into the Web server business with Microsoft
Windows NT Server, here's a summary of how we're going to get you going
strong, with a preview of some of the things we'll look at and do in the
coming chapters:

• **Chapter 2**—Develop a game plan to build your Web server.

• **Chapter 3**—Review some of the business points of interest in a Web server.

- **Chapter 4**—Define and build your Web server.

- **Chapters 5 to 8**—Evaluate four Web servers, including Microsoft's Internet Information Server, O'Reilly and Associates' WebSite, Quarterdeck's WebServer, and Process Corp's Purveyor.

- **Chapters 9 to 11**—Extend your Web site by using Visual Basic programming with the Common Gateway Interface and scripting.

- **Chapter 12**—Review how your Web server is performing, how to maintain it, and a few ways to access your Web server remotely. I'll feature the WebTrends analysis software along with Raptor's firewall software. An extra benefit will be the installation and review of the Wildcat for Windows NT Server bulletin board service, customized with the use of Equinox Super Serial intelligent processor boards, to access your Web server and the network as a whole.

- **Chapter 13**—Ensuring Web server security and general user issues.

- **Chapter 14**—Disaster recovery and troubleshooting procedures to remember when it all goes wrong!

Developing Your Web Server Game Plan

This chapter will play a significant role in your Web site. You'll be better able to determine why you or your business wants a Web site, what to expect in the way of things to do and obstacles to overcome on the way there, and more. You'll get a secondhand look at a real-life Web site that was built from the ground up—mine! I'll make a few comparisons, at various points, to other Web sites I've been involved in, ranging from other NT Servers to Sun Microsystems-based Unix servers. Each offers a unique perspective of what you'll do, or need, for your site.

Specifically, this chapter addresses:

- Designing your site from scratch from a desired need or goal

- Planning the hardware construction of your site

- Acquiring your domain name and address

- Acquiring the physical communications link

- Designing and planning the actual software installations

Systems Integration—The Process of Planning

Systems and network integration is one of two primary functions of my business, and one that I've enjoyed tremendously over the years. I've been pleased with the success I've had, the customers I've helped, and the business relationships I've forged. Perhaps the one thing that has brought me the most pleasure has been the reward of having a customer thank me for keeping them from jumping off into an abyss of wasted money and development time in their projects. I want to keep you from jumping into the abyss, too, so together we'll be developing the Web Server Master Plan. This plan will keep you on the straight and narrow as you embark on your Web adventure. The plan is included on the accompanying CD-ROM as plan.doc. The document starts off as plan01.doc and increments upward to the final document, plan05.doc. By breaking the plan into segments, you will be able to see what tasks you need to tackle and in what order.

Most of my customers are small businesses that have goals and aspirations exceeding those of their big cousins in Corporate America, but don't have the cash to handle the project. Even those that do have the cash—or investment partners—to handle Web site projects, don't have a firm grip on what they're getting into until it's too late. It's not until the server is built, the software is installed, and a few customers are online that they realize what they *should have* done.

Sure, you can make improvements during off-peak hours or by scheduling downtime and notifying the customers. (In fact, scheduled maintenance is very worthwhile and should be performed once a week at a minimum. We'll get to this concern later on.) But why recover from continual problems when you can get it right the first time? The solution is really quite simple, and I already mentioned it—planning. Developing a workable plan is the primary purpose of this chapter. When you set out to tackle the Web, you'll need to consider many different things, starting with why you want this site.

Why Set Up a Web Site?

Somewhere along the line, someone mentioned that Joe Blow from Company ABC found a really neat piece of software that has helped his business in some way. So, being the savvy businessperson that you are, you inquire about the source of this information. "The Web," he replies. "Can't be," you scoff. "That large conglomeration of computers and gobbledy-gook?" You eventually find out that not only did Joe find the software on the Web, but it was even *easy*! "Wow!" you think to yourself. "I wish we could do that for our customers."

Well, you can, and it is one of the most frequently chosen reasons for having a Web site. Customer support of your product is chewing your right financial arm off at the elbow, and the CFO knows it. What if you could give your customers complete access to your tech support databases and reference materials? And automate it for remote access? Now that's a superb reason for a Web site. And these same customers have computer-literate technical folks on staff to wade through all you offer.

Now imagine that your business has 500 PC users split up into several groups. There's an Engineering department, an Accounting department, a Logistics department, and, of course the HeadShed. Each department has unique needs and support issues, so why burden them all with the same server? Or the same server topics? Again, here comes Microsoft Windows NT Server to the rescue. NT's disk sharing and resource utilization makes for a fine separation of unwanted groups of topics or users.

In the planning stages of this book, I considered several different ways I could write it. My publisher and I had many discussions determining the goals we wanted to meet. You, too, will have to determine your goals—whether they be technical support for your customers or meeting the needs of your company internally—if you want your Web site to be a success, not to mention pain free (well, almost). So let's get right to it.

Determining Goals for the Site

We're going to use my own Web site as a target environment for this chapter. We've discussed some pretty ambitious goals. Before we can set any plans into motion with any degree of success, it's important to know what we want to accomplish. These four goals represent the core of our support issues:

- Private Web access for our Internet-based customers

- NT Server Remote Access Service for our WFWG, Win95, and WinNT Workstation customers

- Private bulletin board access for customers with none of the programs listed above

- Direct server-to-server connections for our major customers to our NT Web and LAN servers

Sure, these seem like a not-too-demanding list of things to accomplish, but you'd be amazed at the hoops we'll jump through, prerequisite tasks we need to complete, and the little issues that can easily derail or compromise installation. For instance, will the customers be accessing data using the CGI scripts on the server? Will any of the users be doing programming for you? If so, they'll need special access, including rights and permissions. Did you get the proper licensing for network access? Like I said, the little things. Now that we have these four primary objectives defined, we can begin to plan for the future. Using this approach, we might even be able to purchase the equipment now that we'll need to successfully meet these goals.

Of course, these four goals are our primary concern, but the bigger picture holds more for us. Next, I'll let you know what our other goals are, and how we want to implement them.

Alternative Goals for the Site

Even the best leaders have to work out kinks in their great plans for conquering the world. But the rewards are well worth the effort. Our situation is no different and also holds the prospect of financial and personal rewards if implemented correctly. Unfortunately, we have a limited time scale—two to four years. However, considering the turnover rate of today's technology, even one year can be construed as excessive. For instance, I purchased a 2 gigabyte SCSI-2 drive last year in July for $990 and today the price is down to $600. Motherboards and other component parts of my server have similarly come down in price at the rate of 40 percent or more. Overall, a server that cost $3500 in July of 1995 now can be purchased for $2000. That's a mighty big drop, and you can consider it all lost money if your server isn't earning you a solid return. The moral: Make sure you are earning a solid return!

You should have alternatives ready to put into play or even as a supplement to your existing strategy. In my business, we're planning to offer a few more services to preferred customers. Here's a list of the ones we'll be implementing:

- Public Internet Service Provider (ISP) connections to the Web server over a dialup modem.

- Public bulletin board access for local business customers using a 1-800 access. In the rural areas of my county, all phone calls are either local long distance or toll calls at the rate of 25 to 50 cents per call. The 1-800 number offers a value-added incentive to do business with us. The BBS also provides a gateway to our Web server, giving these remote customers Internet access across a modem.

- Public bulletin board access for home-based businesses and personal users needing technical support for their computers. These customers represent a huge growing market across the nation, as more people begin working at home.

As you can see, there's plenty to do in a short span of planning. Obviously, you'll have to evaluate the merit of any project you do with the return on the investment. And remember, in the business world, time also equals money; if the task will be one of low cost in terms of up-front funding, but high cost in terms of time to get it going, it may not be as viable as it appears. One more factor, and a very important one at that, is to check out the market presence around you to see if any other companies have implemented similar services. You'd be foolish to set up a Web site where a major ISP with a healthy customer base has already set down roots—unless you've found a top-secret way to entice their customer base to your site.

 Most ISPs do not offer private Web access to transfer files and other related confidential information. This is one way in which your Web site could garner membership—by offering secured access customer-to-customer, or customer-to-your-business.

Customer Interaction

Now that you have defined the goals and aspirations for your Web site, it's time to begin drafting the initial planning document that you'll use during this process. Wait a minute, this is only a Web site, you say. Just build or buy a new machine and start loading the software, right? Well, I wouldn't. The people that'll be using your site may or may not have special needs. They may have Macintosh computers and need to access your Microsoft Windows NT Server. Not exactly what I'd call a compatible set of kids playing in the sandbox. Also, they may not even have modems! Are you going to leave them in the dark to decide how to get connected? I'd surely hope not if you want to keep these people as paying customers.

You should definitely involve your customer base in this very critical stage of planning. While you're developing your master document, talk to them. Perhaps a telephone conference with them and several of your people will get the creative juices flowing, and uncover idiosyncrasies such as a customer having insufficient phone lines to handle the needs. Alternatively, you could create a small survey and mail it to each customer asking what they'd like to see, how they intend to connect to the Web server or the BBS, if they have special needs, etc. These are the small behind-the-scenes issues that can (and usually do) cripple the best of plans. Here are some key issues for you to consider:

- How is this site being offered to the customer? Extra charge to existing contracts? Gratis for preferred customers?

- How many of the customer's employees are you going to grant this access to?

- Are there hourly usage limits?

- Will there be restrictions to accessing the Web site—time of day or day of week?

- How will you assist the customer in getting connected? When it breaks?

- What existing hardware and software does the customer have now to access your site? Any upgrades required?

This is but a sampling of the issues that you'll have to consider when you speak with each customer. Oh, with each one? Doesn't this apply to most of them? Not really. It could, but it's only a starting point for the work you've now got in front of you. I hope you didn't think this was going to be a walk in the park. It'll take some significant planning, but the rewards are worth it in a well-designed Web site.

Your First Rough Draft

Our first set of plans is the rough draft, which is located on the CD-ROM in a file called plan01.doc. As you can see, it's nothing more that a condensed version of the last few pages. We'll be adding more detail to the plan as we consider all of the alternatives to this site. As with any good plan, our document will undergo a lot of revisions before the site is firmly established. One Autocad drawing I saw during a recent design stage went through 140 changes. We won't go quite that far, but it's important that you understand that your plan is a living document.

This rough draft should give you some idea of what you're likely to want in your Web site, even if it's nothing more than a skeletal picture of the site. Don't let this bother you. If your site goes through a dozen changes or drafts, then I'd say that's about normal. As I've stated before, it's far better to make mistakes now and correct them now than to wait until the site is operational. There's nothing worse than a handful of irate customers to ruin your Web site dreams, not to mention the business.

Initial Design Review

When you've created a baseline game plan, and have reviewed and/or edited it for the tenth time, it's time to get the entire gang together and conduct an internal formal business review of how you intend to implement the initial goals of the Web site. At this stage, you (hopefully) have not yet purchased anything, nor have you issued a request for quotes to any computer resellers. This is the best time to make changes or clear up any misgivings that may exist about the Web site. It's terribly important that everything is laid out on the design table at this time. Make no bones about it—mistakes from here on out can be costly and delay the implementation of the site. Additionally, mistakes can be quite costly down the road when the site needs to be updated because the plan was too shortsighted.

So just how does this initial design review help us? It states the obvious needs for the site—you plan the purchases, set the tempo for the site, involve the customers so they know what to expect, and show your CFO what to expect in next month's accounts payable bin. Aside from that, the review also uncovers some of life's little unexpected matters, such as how much training is needed and for whom. The review shows you how much you knew about building sites, how much you didn't know, and an idea of what to expect for the future. All of these educational things you've learned before spending a penny and committing to the site. This is the ideal time to delay creation or modify the intent of the site.

Whether you knew it or not, the initial design review, if you took notes and did an outline, has provided you with a baseline document usable for writing the site's guidance and manuals; remember, someone has to operate the site. This task entails daily administration, security issues, customer contacts, and related matters. You'll probably want to devote a single person to the site's overall needs, and this person is usually called a *WebMaster*. You may have someone that can do double duty in two or more positions, but many businesses create a new position dedicated to that job. For the first six months of the site, I'd highly advise the business to devote a knowledgeable networking person to this task.

Okay, so you've had your series of meetings and decided upon a core set of needs the business would like to support for the customer base. The site is still to be a private venture for the first year. In order of importance, here are the most strategic goals to be addressed in this first version of the site:

- Provide required server access for customers

- Provide employee services, such as traveling sales representatives checking on leads and orders

- Give the WebMaster and MIS full access for remote control and administration

To provide the solutions for this target environment, your customers need to be polled to determine their requirements and special needs. Once this review has been completed, you will have identified the following system-level issues that have to be addressed with the site (the list below contains sample figures from my own site-building work). These concerns are common to all of your customers:

- A need exists to have at least 50 MB of disk storage for your 15 most preferred customers.

- Your site will need 700 MB of temporary storage for file transfers, program operations, and such.

- Disk space growth is estimated at 20 percent per year per customer for the next five years.

- The business has five customers whose data is critical to the point that a loss of one hour of downtime can cost as much $5000. Data protection and recovery are of the utmost importance.

- Only 10 people will have no possible need for Internet access, but rather need simple file transfer from the Web site's server locations. This group represents those people who have no earthly idea what the Internet is, how to operate it, and have no time to learn it.

In-Progress Design Review

Now that we've made some concrete decisions regarding system-level issues, it's time to get down to the final decisions. We know the goals of the site, the minimum requirements of the site, and the customers' requirements. The designers of the site have a firm grasp of the requirements, and these people may indeed be the same team that builds the server. In fact, that's the most desirable position possible, but not always doable. At this stage, if your designers and builders are not the same team, it's time to hand off the project to the builders. Your game plan should now look something like plan02.doc. And it is this stage of the plan—the part that has all those final decisions in writing—that needs to go to the builders of the site. Let's take a look at the nuts and bolts of the plan at this point.

Choice of Servers

I'll make a couple of blanket opinions about the Web server hardware as suggestions because you already know that Microsoft Windows NT Server can handle the task with great aplomb. Get the best affordable server hardware possible, and buy brand name equipment from the start. There's Dell, AST Research, DEC, IBM, Compaq, and a host of other vendors that will meet your every need in server hardware. All will suffice, and provide years of reliable service. However, the age old adage is still true—you pay extra for a good name, but you also get what you pay for. I've built quite a few computers from scratch, ranging from simple desktop machines all the way up to multi-processor network behemoths. In time, I learned how to pick and choose the parts needed, by vendors, to have a very reliable system. By the same token, if you build the machine this way you can expect to be totally responsible for all hardware and warranty support for the server.

On the other hand, if you buy a prebuilt server, most will come with some level of on-site support or provide warranty support by phone with the vendor. Be cautious about on-site support! On-site to the majority of vendors means that they've contracted with a computer shop near you to take care of your needs if the server requires it. I'm not knocking these local providers of support, but most of them have no clue about your situation and specific needs. You'll have to spend time on the phone with the vendor to diagnose the problem, and then the vendor will tell the local support shop what they need to bring to you to fix the problem. If it doesn't work, then they'll have to try again. Usually, the vendor sends the parts to the local shop who then brings them to you. If more parts are needed, then your site sits down a bit longer until the vendor gets the additional parts to the local shop.

In situations where Web servers are in critical positions, this situation is totally unacceptable. Sites with servers that are this important must be staffed by networking technicians that can handle any job that comes around. For this reason, you may opt to purchase the server without site support and handle that issue on your own. Even if your package does come with on-site support, just ignore it unless doing so would void the warranty. Yet another option is to purchase additional hardware as spare units ready for use should the main equipment go out.

All about Spare Hardware

If you purchase spare hardware, the most important thing you can do is to proof test it just as soon as you can to validate its readiness for the job. If this is to be a critical hard drive that contains the operating system, then you should prepare the drive and reload the operating system to the point that it's configured as close to normal site operations as possible. This includes creating the core user accounts, permissions, security, etc. Once you've tested and prepared the unit, then store it in a safe location *that several people know about.* Yes, that's right! I went to a customer's site once where the server hard drive was having measurable difficulty processing data. The customer had a spare drive handy because the inventory said they did. The person holding the inventory knew that the network administrator kept the drive in the logistics room, which looked like my 8-year-old son's room. After two hours of searching, the decision was made to call the on-vacation administrator who could not be reached. Unfortunately, this person wouldn't be back for two more days—just about the amount of time required for me to order a new drive and have it installed.

As it turned out, all of the network spare hardware was placed in an unlocked cabinet behind the kitchen in the office. Readily accessible, but no one knew where it was, so the site spent the next two days down. I'm glad I wasn't there when the administrator came back!

Core Server Requirements

Okay, enough war stories about misguided intentions and down to the nitty gritty of Web server design. As I mentioned before, Web servers have different requirements than normal network servers. This is true of our server, as well. We'll tailor the Web server to our customers' needs with an emphasis on future business plans. Later in this chapter, we'll go over the actual hardware and software requirements of the site, and issues surrounding their use. If you're in a smaller organization, you will be able to build your server from scratch using clone parts and hardware. If you're in a large organization, you probably have a logistics department that has buying power with numerous vendors. In that case, you'll probably buy brand name servers already built to a large degree. In a later section, we'll talk about the actual server requirements. Also, the data links will be explained and you'll see how I went through the data communications jungle with my providers.

Final Process Review

When you've made it this far, you can pat yourself on the back because you've survived the most important parts of making your Web site a reality. But you're not done yet. After building the physical server, installing the software and proof testing the basics, you need to consult with your customers (and employees) again to see if their requirements have changed. This is still the best time to make changes to the server and site configuration without altering the bottom line too much and risking the wrath of the CFO.

This stage is called a *final process review* of the site, and you conduct the review as you would conduct the initial design review. The difference, however, is that you've purchased all of the required hardware and software. The pieces of the puzzle have been put together, you're finishing most of the construction process, and you can consider the site 95 percent completed. It's not yet online and ready for business, but you're close to it.

What, then, are the relative merits of this review? Well, for one thing, you've had the chance to use the server and see how the hardware performs. You can, in fact, build the Web site and make it operational as a test bed for the MIS group to pound upon and see how it reacts. If you don't have an MIS group, let some of your computer hacker buddies beat on it. You'd be surprised at what you'll uncover in the way of anomalies when you first proof test it. You'll also learn what amount of disk space is consumed when the core software is installed and brought to life. Just remember that this is perhaps the last time you'll be able to make the changes necessary to give your customers a bandaid-free site that flows and works smoothly. Band-Aid free because once the server is brought online, you want your only down time to be for performing basic tasks and installing patches to bugs.

Unfortunately, mistakes happen. Every time you make adjustments or quick fixes, you're opening your site up for potential trouble. I once saw the most simple and fundamental of site inspections go bad and cause a minicomputer to be down for 48 hours when all they wanted to do was oil the bearings of a cooling fan. True story! To get to the fan, a shelf had to be removed. To remove the shelf, a 10-pin connector had to be moved out of the way to get to a screw on the shelf. When that connector was moved, its safety hooks broke from old age and removed primary signal connections to eight disk drives on the critical run of disk drives for the processor— and down came the system. All for the love of oiling a bearing on a two dollar fan. The repair of the connector cost $650 in labor and time lost ordering a new connector.

The moral to this story is to get it as close to perfect as possible before taking the site public, or private as it is in this case. It's really never too late to fix what needs to be fixed, but it's always too late when you fix what isn't broke.

What's left to do? Something called *site acceptance*, which is sometimes tied into site testing and qualifications. It's a lot like Boeing Aircraft Corporation building a new jet and selling it to Delta Airlines. You can bet that Boeing has a solid reputation as a premier builder of planes, but Delta is still going to test the plane before giving Boeing a single penny. So, Delta test pilots will fly it, land it, and wring it out for all it's worth. If they give the thumbs up, then the plane is accepted for commercial service.

Site Acceptance

But, we're not flying airplanes here! Web sites aren't nearly as critical as airplanes, where lives are at stake, you say. I'd agree with that from the humanistic standpoint, but could you accept your company's data being stolen and destroyed by intruders? Or could you accept one of your best customers getting faulty data from the Web site and making a bad decision because of it?

I didn't think so, and I definitely would not want to be in the board room while the customer was yelling at the CEO who then flares up at the CFO because she approved the purchases for the site. I think I'd rather have a site tested to the highest level possible. Don't go to extremes, but make sure the site is protected from intruders with a good firewall. Make sure the allowed users have the proper permissions to get them into the server areas necessary to do their jobs. Make sure the essentials and important stuff is covered. You'll have to sit down with your customers and tell them what they'll see, what's expected of them, and what you'll work with them to achieve. When all else fails, have a good set of server backups handy.

So, the equivalent to having your site signed off and accepted as a formal site would be to have every customer begin a 30-day testing period. This test period should be as in-depth and intense as possible. Transfer as much data as possible, use as many of those forms and CGI scripts as possible, and beat the server as hard as possible. While your customers are doing this, check the NT Server error and monitor logs to see what's going on and how the physical server is performing. You'll also want to pay special attention to the communications link and observe the statistics of the link. How's that critical portion of the site performing?

When this acceptance testing period is over, you should gather all of the data together for analysis. Look for weak spots in the performance of the server, and review the performance log files of Microsoft Windows NT

Server's diagnostics. This information is critical in deciding if you're ready to put the Web site online officially, or if you need to make final changes. At this point, your planning document should resemble plan03.doc.

 This is a great time to show the CFO that her money was well spent because you've built a primo server.

Planning for Internal and External Web Sites

A Web server is a Web server, true or false? It is, unless you're using the same server for both private (internal) and public (external) usage. What's the difference between these two server types, you ask? An internal Web server, shown in Figure 2.1, is one that is attached to the business network as a whole; an external server, shown in Figure 2.2, is a completely standalone server that is not attached to the network and is accessible to the general public. This perspective of using a Web server can be confusing and is worth a few words. Internal Web servers are those in which the server itself

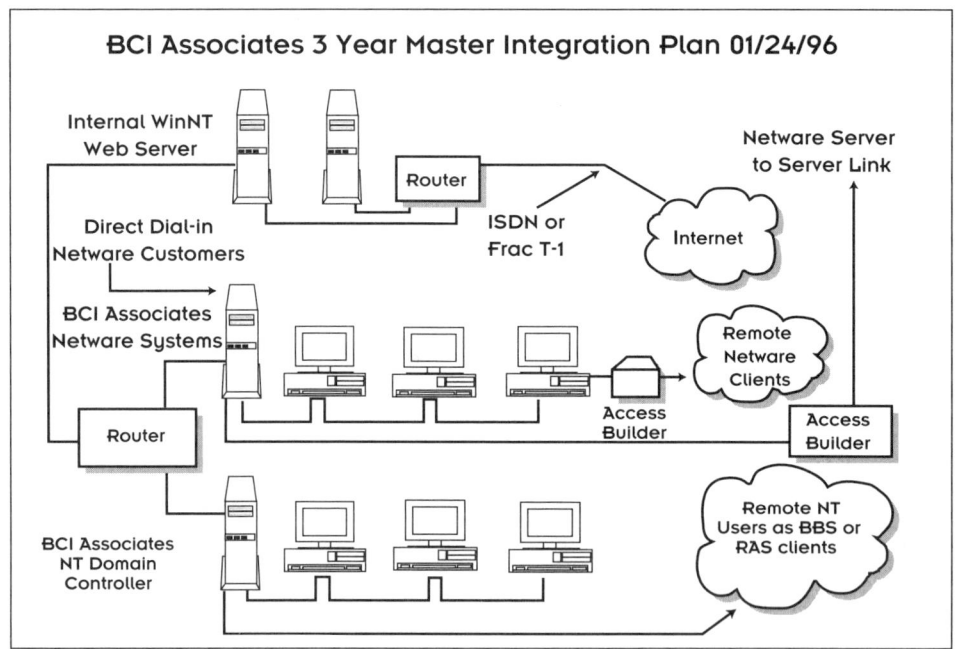

Figure 2.1 An internal Web server.

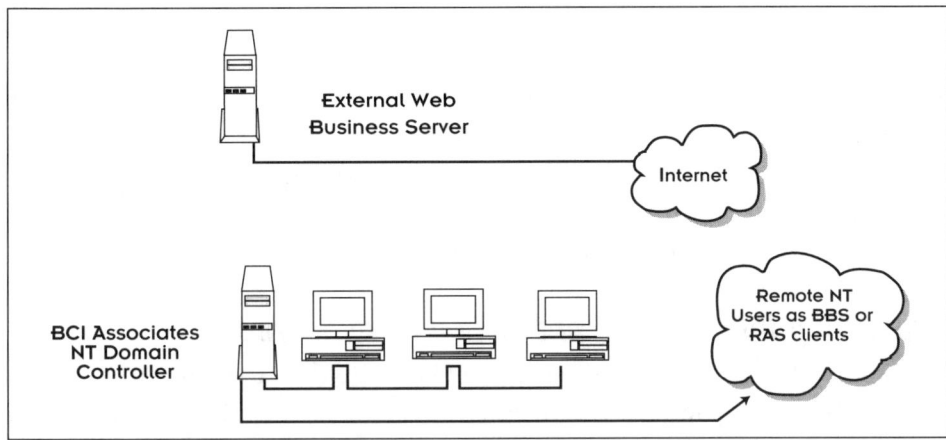

Figure 2.2   External Web server.

allows network users to access the Internet by routing TCP/IP traffic from the network across the wire. External Web servers are those in which the users accessing the Web site do so from across the Internet itself. This server typically is a Microsoft Windows NT Server sitting all by itself and not connected to anything else but the Internet. You are probably scratching your head wondering, "Do I have separate physical servers for each? Is it worth that kind of an investment? Why would I want separate servers?" These are some great questions and deserve detailed answers.

The Differences between Internal and External Servers

You can see from Figures 2.1 and 2.2 that the physical differences are apparent, but what about the logical ones? The users allowed to log on are the most prevalent issue. When they log onto the external server, this server is the only place they can go. Users do their work, get the files they want, and leave. Not much else to do, not much else they could do anyhow. They still have full access all across the server just like any other Web site for which they have rights. The external Web server can only be administered from the console instead of through remote links by the WebMaster. The external server also requires more local hardware to accomplish some tasks, such as backing up the server.

As I mentioned previously, internal Web servers provide the ability for network users to access the Internet from their network workstations. If necessary, users can access Internet sites or their own Web server. They need special routing hardware, which is usually installed at the server, to get their network request out to the Internet. These workstations have to run TCP/IP software, in addition to any other Internet client software, for their network I/O cards to be able to connect out to the Internet. The system administrator of the network has global access to the Web server and any other resources on the network. This makes updates not only easier, but accessible from any place where the WebMaster can log in.

Examining the Dangers of the Two Server Types

What possible dangers does the external Web site have to deal with? There's no possible intrusion into the business network. If the server crashes, no other part of the business is affected. So what is affected? The term *danger* isn't exactly correct. The potential problems are generally operational, such as when the administrator who has to access the core functions of the server when something goes wrong is on vacation, and no one else is trained to handle server problems. There's also a chance that the WebMaster needs to use resources of the Web server that are accessible only from the network. Other than situations like this, there's not much that can be hurt with an external Web server. One other possible drawback of an external server is that the machine must have the horsepower to handle any request, whether it be a simple FTP transfer or a CGI SQL Server request.

The internal Web server, by contrast, has a lot to worry about. If there's a physical connection to the business network from the Web server connecting to the Internet, then the internal network is just as vulnerable as the Web site. A virus that gets into the Web site can get into the internal business network. A user that can get into the Web site can get into the internal network with a goodly amount of hacking. It doesn't seem like a pretty picture, and it might not be at times, so let's get into the reasons why each has good points.

The Benefits of the Two Server Types

External Web servers are, all other things being equal, faster than their internal site brothers. No other kind of traffic has to be routed or processed from users or other sources, as shown in Figure 2.3. Other resources include backend SQL Servers that process CGI requests for data and related

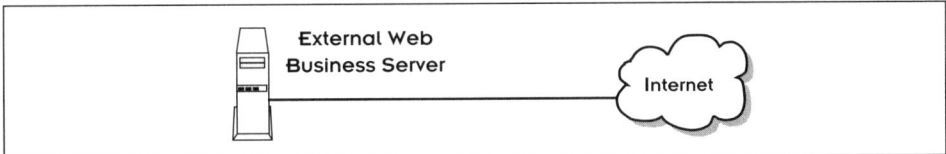

Figure 2.3 External Web site processing.

queries. If the Web site has to be taken down for maintenance, no other part of the business infrastructure is affected.

The internal Web site has a lot going for it in the plus column. Included here is the WebMaster's ability to access and administer any other part of the network from the Web server to which he has rights. The internal Web server, having connectivity to the other business resources, offers redundancy for Web server resources such as the file repositories. This redundancy comes in many forms and offers several advantages. For example, if your network runs Windows NT Workstation and uses NTFS partitions, you can use TCP/IP in the workstations and perform nearly any Web task to the network work-station that can be performed to the Web server itself. Figure 2.4 illus-trates internal Web site processing.

An internal server provides a key aspect to critical processing of Web sites because it gives you instant redundancy and protection. Microsoft Windows

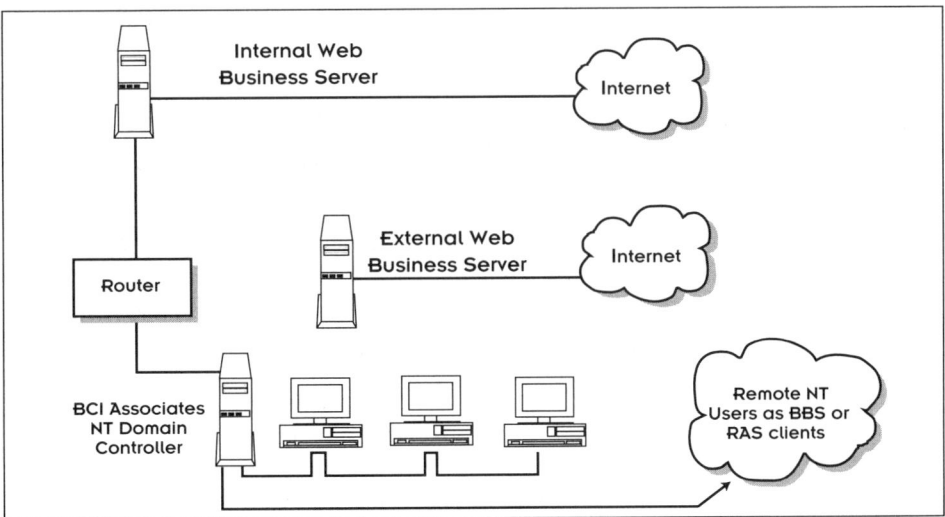

Figure 2.4 Internal Web site processing.

NT Server offers directory replication for security of data, true enough, but having accessible alternatives is nice. Consider this: Your site comes to life and flourishes for two years. Your plans are largely successful, and the site brings much joy to the CFO. The Web site only needs a few changes to configurations and a new software package to make everyone content with the Web site.

This changes dramatically when word gets out that your Web site offers wonderful services and you suddenly have three new prospective clients. Each company has their own requirements, and all three appear to be really hot tickets. You don't want to lose them at any cost. How do you leverage the internal Web site to your advantage? The solution is simple. Use one of the Windows NT workstations on the network as a temporary Web site running any one of the Web server software packages I'll discuss in Part 2 of this book. By the way, Windows 95 can operate as a Web site given the appropriate hardware.

Estimating Volume of Users

Figuring out how many users will visit your site has to be one of the most frustrating aspects of creating a Web site. You can guess all you want as to how popular your site will be, and market the site until you're blue in the face, but what it all boils down to is how you present the site with interesting and compelling information. You've got to make the site worth someone's online dollar and make it sparkle so they'll come back. If the site performs poorly, you can count on a decline in visitors.

You need to recoup the cost of the site—unless, of course, money is of no concern. Money is a huge concern to me, and I have to have some form of repayment to recoup the cost of the site. The CFO isn't likely to continue investing money into a dead horse, I assure you. If this is a private business site, you've got an edge in the user count. You should already know to within 5 percent the amount of users that will access the Web server. With this information, you can figure out the communications link requirements pretty closely. The volume of users, and the bandwidth requirements for the same, are critical to building the proper Web server.

> *For the remainder of this chapter, all discussions will focus on an internal private Web server. While there are distinct issues that differentiate a private from a public Web server, most of the discussion applies to both.*

So, let's state the figures that will drive us to the decisions that lie ahead. Let's assume that we've got five customers employing five people that will access the Web server by way of the Internet. Because direct Internet users do not have specific bandwidth requirements like modem users do, direct Internet users can retrieve and manipulate data on the Web server as fast as the Web server can process it. For our purposes, let's say that each direct Internet user equals a modem user at 28.8 Kbps speed.

Our clients also employ four direct modem users that will dial into the Web server for Web server access using modems of 28.8 Kbps speed rating. These users will be the traveling folks that can never tell where they'll be in relation to a local Internet point of presence. You'll have 800 numbers for these users because you value their business. Table 2.1 summarizes the connection speeds and type of access that we know will occur.

I've thrown in the third connection of a server-to-server link because there's a chance that one of these customers may need to have their Microsoft Windows NT Server directly integrated into your environment. Later on, when we discuss links, I'll introduce you to something called *ISDN*, which is rapidly becoming the next communications wave to overtake computing. ISDN has been around for quite some time, but it has only recently become viable in terms of its widespread presence and lowered cost. ISDN, which is illustrated in Figure 2.5, is a fantastic solution for linking servers together over dialup routers for local solutions. From this perspective, the important point to note is the Internet connection speeds. ISDN's maximum rate is 128 Kbps, and our link requires up to 144 Kbps if all four users connect to the Web server at the same time. This implies that ISDN isn't right for us capacity-wise, but you'll soon see this is not necessarily true.

Look at Figure 2.5 carefully because there are hidden costs with this circuit. Although ISDN has the capacity to run at 128 Kbps link speed, it's a digital

Table 2.1   Summation of Web Server Connection Requirements

Volume of Users	Type of Access	Speed of Connection	Cumulative Bandwidth
4	Modem	28.8 Kbps	115.2 KB
5	Internet	28.8 Kbps	144.0 KB
1	Server to Server	10 mbps	10 mbps

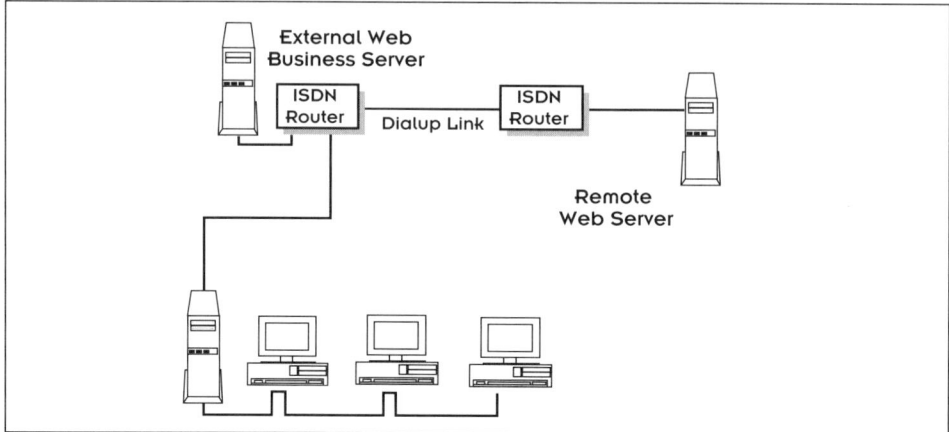

Figure 2.5   Using ISDN to connect servers.

service that requires numerous checks to be performed before it can be brought into play. ISDN also must be available within your local area, to some extent. Don't let a measly 128 Kbps connection between servers give you the impression this is insufficient. Nothing could be further from the truth unless you've got servers that are passing tons of data constantly. For the vast majority of sites, ISDN is a decent alternative. If this concepts sounds confusing, don't worry. We'll discuss ISDN in depth shortly.

Types of Connections for Corporate Users

Let's take a few minutes to discuss the types of connections we may need. There are as many ways to get connected as there are directions for the wind to blow, but the four most prevalent are:

• Microsoft Windows NT Server's Remote Access Server

• Internet Access to your Web server

• Bulletin board dialup service using a modem

• Server-to-server connections

NT Server's Remote Access Server (RAS)

If you've ever logged into a network, then you know you have to supply a user name and a password to gain access to the resources of the network, such as a printer or files on the network server. These are the most basic and fundamental workings of a network infrastructure. You're a member of the network users group who have specific access rights, belong to membership groups for centralized control, and a host of other things. These things you do at the office from your desk or other suitable accommodations.

However, when you're away on vacation or traveling for the company, you're no longer a user on the network, right? Sure, but that is only applicable as far as a modem will take you. When you need to get back to the office, and you're running software compatible with Microsoft Windows NT Server's RAS functions, you can use a modem to connect back to the main network server, as shown in Figure 2.6. This compatible software comes in the form of Windows 95, Windows for Workgroups, and Windows NT Workstation. When you use this type of connection, you'll log into the network just like you do from your desktop. The only difference is that the speed of the modem controls the performance of your work.

This is a very easy way to continue working while you're away and check up on things at the office. (Perhaps your spouse would rather you *couldn't* connect to the office when you're supposed to be enjoying a relaxing trip to Mexico!) When you connect to the server, you appear to the server just like you do when connected locally. You can check mail, run applications, move files, and anything else you might want to do, including print. Once again, the only difference is the speed at which things happen. This is where a fast modem or even an ISDN dialup adapter is nice to have.

Direct Internet Access from the Web

The next form of connectivity that we'll need to employ is direct Internet connections. We've stated that we'll have up to five concurrent users on our site at any given time. If we make a blanket statement that we consider

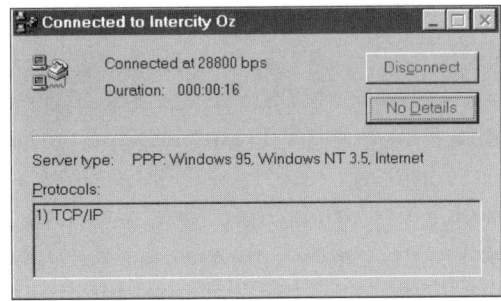

Figure 2.6　RAS connection to NT Server using Windows 95's dialup networking.

each connection will be at 28.8 Kbps, then we'll need 144 Kbps of through-put. This seems inappropriate for ISDN's maximum of 128 Kbps, but is it? Let's dissect this situation and see why it should work just fine.

When users connect to your Web server directly across the Internet, they may be doing so from a workstation on a network, from a PC using a modem from their Internet Service Provider, or from a Sun workstation that doubles as a server at some university. You just don't know which one, and any of those could, in fact, be powered to download files at 56 Kbps transfer rates. Just two of those users maxes out the ISDN connection alone! Unless you've got continued service requirements like this, what actually happens is that as much as 75 percent free bandwidth is available as data flows across the line.

When a user connects to your Web server, the initial log-on procedure is but a momentary blip in the performance of the link. When files are transferred or a Web page is accessed, the data is moved relatively quickly and the link is again idle. These bursts of traffic are what most sites experience during the course of normal operations. As such, an ISDN-equipped site could support as many as 18 users with compression turned on and resulting in an equivalent transfer rate of about 9.6 Kbps. So let's keep this in mind as we progress forward. A 9.6 Kbps link may not seem like much when it comes to Internet access, but remember that the most we're anticipating during this startup period is five concurrent users. In a section to come shortly, you'll see why I'm suggesting ISDN as a startup and we'll consider dedicated links at that time.

Bulletin Board Access for Modem Users

In a worst case scenario, you may have some users that have no reason, purpose, experience, or wherewithall to use the Internet. All they need to do is read/send mail and move files. If these people had one of the prerequisites mentioned earlier for NT Server Remote Access, then they could simply use dialup RAS connections. However, quite a few of them (in fact, most) have standard laptops running standard DOS and Windows software. None of these laptops are equipped to run Windows NT Workstation or Windows 95. They could, however, be running Windows for Workgroups with the Remote Access Server add-in programs.

This would solve the problem of access, and would enable them to have direct access to the Web server. These users would appear as normal users on the network, as far as the NT server is concerned. However, as a practical matter, we can't count on that. What we can count on is that if these people have DOS or Windows communications software, then they can get connected to our bulletin board. From the BBS, they could perform an operation called a *door*. This operation works like a door in your house. Open the door, and you leave the BBS and go into another room such as another BBS. In this case, the door leads to the Web server and full Internet access. Figure 2.7 illustrates the use of doors. While the process requires an additional piece of software, this little bit of leverage is really a neat aspect of alternative connectivity.

Server-to-Server Connections

Another interesting aspect of this process is the technique of connecting a customer's network server to our server and then routing TCP/IP traffic from them to us and out to the Internet. This is normal life for many sites

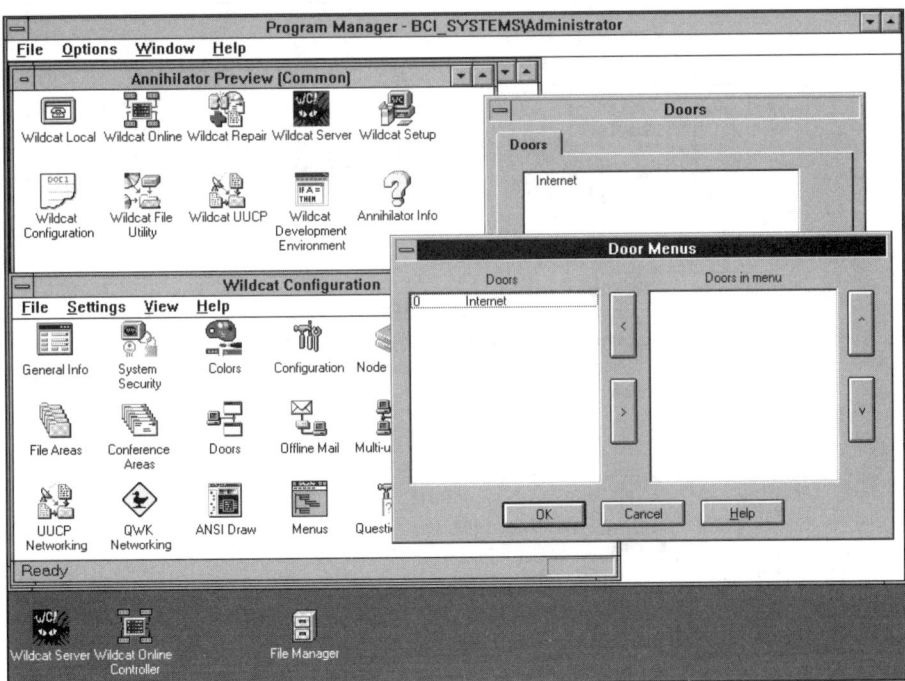

Figure 2.7 Doors to the Internet.

and isn't anything special in the world of networking. It is new for customers that have never experienced life on the Internet nor considered alternative ways of connectivity. All that happens here is that, in a Microsoft Windows NT Server domain model, the customer's network server is a member of the NT domain. When the customer's server connects to our regular NT network, which our Web server is part of, we route the customer's TCP/IP traffic across our Web server out to the Internet, as illustrated in Figure 2.8.

Server-to-server connections are just another form of indirect Internet access. This type of situation lends itself to ISDN connectivity and remote access server products to form the core link.

 If it looks like the traffic is getting to be too much, you can always increase the link capacity. The point is to provide whatever services our customers need. Keep them happy, and it'll all come together.

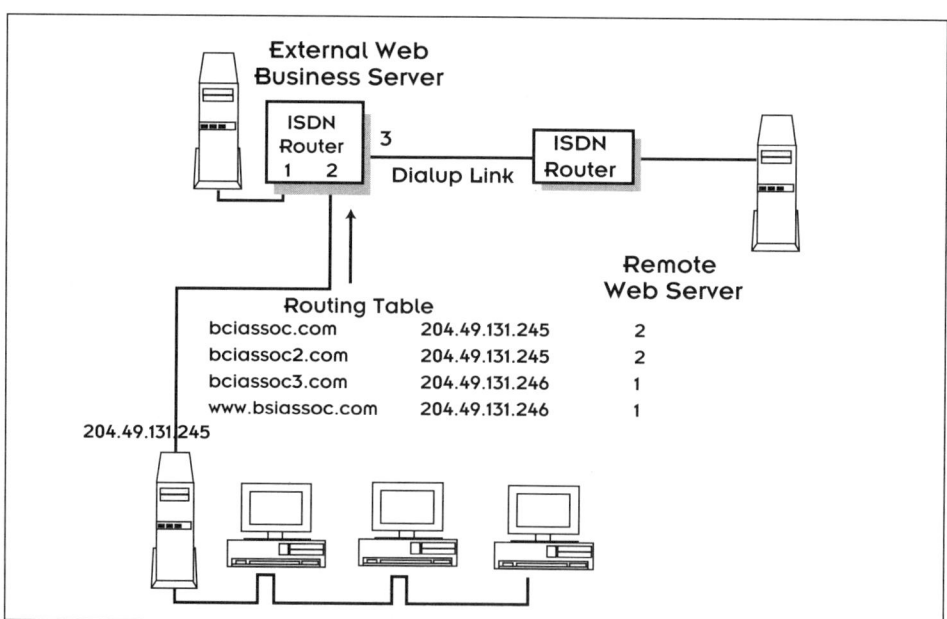

Figure 2.8   Routing TCP/IP traffic from our customer.

Monitoring Connected Users for Future Estimates

When you get the site operational, use the tools provided with the Web server software for monitoring the activity of the server. The tools will show us how much of the site is in use and by whom. Microsoft Windows NT Server itself has server diagnostic tools and monitoring tools, shown operating in Figure 2.9, that show us how many users are connected, to where, and for how long. We can see how much of the server's resources are being used, how much of these resources are free for the system, and an average loading factor on the physical server. Over time, all of these statistics will be necessary to determine future upgrades and to find problem areas of the Web server's capabilities.

You can define monitoring parameters, which allow you to review average CPU time, interrupts per second, and other related information. Simply save all of the information for later analysis. As a matter of policy, you should gather these log statistics once a week and review them as well. In the case of my own servers, my Web server doubles as a Microsoft Windows

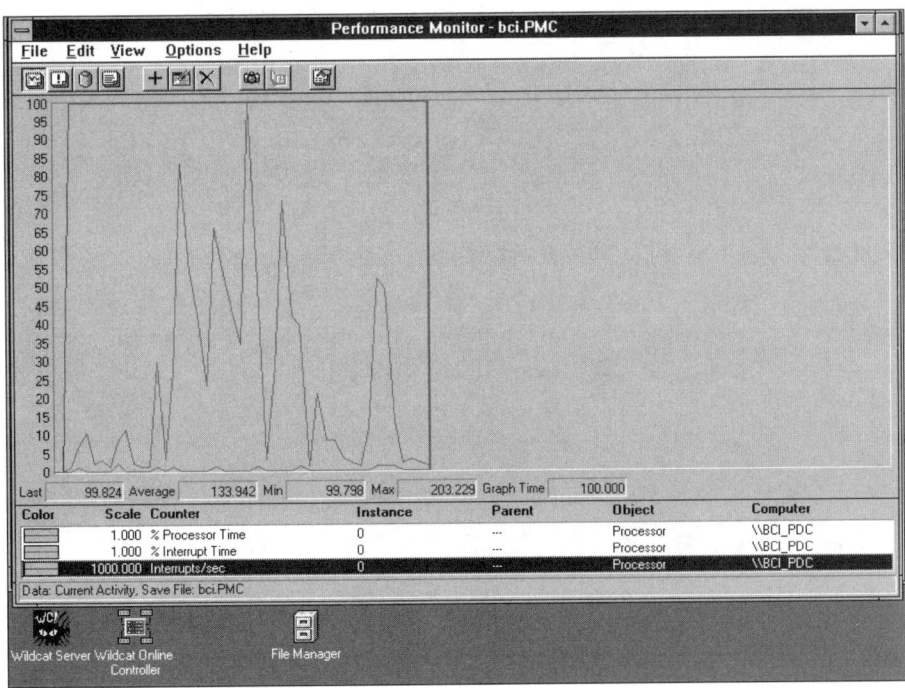

Figure 2.9 Microsoft Windows NT Server performance monitoring.

NT Server Backup Domain Control (BDC). Periodically, this BDC resynchronizes with the network's Primary Domain Controller (PDC). When this occurs, the BDC's user databases are updated with any changes to the PDC, including new users, changed rights and permissions, etc.

Internet Link Capacity

We've already discussed ISDN as a solution for connecting 20 or fewer users. That's fine, but what are the alternatives? There are numerous alternatives to ISDN for more demanding needs, so let's examine these. Table 2.2 illustrates some of the connectivity options available in today's market. Understand that even though these options exist now, they may not be available in your immediate area.

This table was built from data that I gathered from calling several vendors, including AT&T, SprintLink, and others involved in the communications business while I was building my site. As you can see, it can get quite pricey very quickly. The CFO would have a canary if you put the bill on her desk for a T-3 link. So, what I did was use a 28.8 Kbps modem link to proof test the basics of the Web server until I was sure that all was well and that the site was going into full scale operation. This is a real money-saving trick. All you're really doing at this stage is building the Web pages, getting the basics built, making sure it works, and showing the CFO you have an idea of what you're doing.

Table 2.2   Relative Merits of Different Communications Links

Available	Type of Connection	Speed of Link	Startup Cost	Monthly Cost
Immediate	Modem access	Up to 28.8 Kbps	None	Up to $30
30—60 days	Dialup ISDN	Up to 128 Kbps	Up to three months fee	Varies, but can be as little as $400
30—90 days	Dedicated *FT1	56 Kbps to 768 Kbps	$3500 (56 Kbps) $12,000 (768 Kbps)	$1650 for 56 Kbps $4800 for 768 Kbps (graduated)
30—90 days	Dedicated T1	1.544 mbps	$15,000	$6000
90—120 days	Dedicated T3	45.1 mbps	$135,000	$75,000
90—120 days	Frame Relay	56 Kbps on demand	$1200	$3000

*FT1 means fractional T1 speeds which range from 56 Kbps up through 768 Kbps.

So, what do these speeds have in common with your needs? Most of them are flexible enough to suit your needs, except for the modem link. But even modems have witnessed a boost in technology that upped their throughput to 33.6 Kbps and over 57.6 Kbps with compression turned on for a single link. This advance puts the pressure on single line ISDN, which is 57.6 Kbps normal and over 80 Kbps with compression turned on. Using the plain ISDN connect last week, I got 8.4 Kbps effective transfer rates on files, which equates to roughly 84 Kbps link speed. Not bad at all! But, when the data really gets moving, these modem and ISDN links begin to suffer from a decided lack of horsepower. It's now time to explore the real world of dedicated connectivity.

Upgrading the Link to Meet the Need

As you probably know, modem lines are capable of what modems do, and nothing more. Frequently, we see even less productivity with noisy lines and moisture in the lines, and ISDN tops out at 128 Kbps with multiplexed channels. When this happens, you'll need more room to grow. This is where the downside to ISDN hits squarely in the pocketbook. Whatever investment in ISDN you've made to date is usually down the tubes. It's been fun, but that's about the extent of it.

The new and faster links require different hardware on both ends. Because ISDN is a digitally mastered modem, it's sometimes considered to be a "smart" modem. As such, the local telephone company or source is also running similar ISDN equipment, so they're not likely to be able to support your upgrades on the same equipment. All the way around, new equipment and costs are jumping right out at you. Table 2.3 shows the costs that I incurred with my local Bell South office when setting up my 128 Kbps multiplexed dialup ISDN in comparison to a similar 128 Kbps FT1 dedicated link with SprintLink.

You can see that my monthly ISDN cost is $488 for 128 Kbps, no matter how much or how little I use it. I have to purchase an ISDN router for this link, and my provider configures it for me. All I have to do is connect it up, and away I go. If the link drops out, the ISDN router will automatically try to reconnect all the time. The only issue here is that if the link goes down, and the router can't connect (usually a physical problem on the wire),

Table 2.3   Actual Connectivity Costs

Function	Startup Cost	Monthly Fee	Lease Required
128 Kbps ISDN basic	$210	$93 flat rate	None (Bell South)
ISDN Internet Acct	None	$395 flat rate	None (UUNet Tech)
ISDN Router	$1100	N/A	One-time cost
128 Kbps FT1 dedicated	$2800	$1200	1 year (Sprint, all functions)
FT1 Router	N/A	$275	1 year

then the site is down until this can be repaired. Bell South treats this as a standard phone line outage, which is exactly what it is. The *D* in *ISDN* stands for digital, which means that the data traveling across the line is digitized data moving along a standard telephone link.

This repair process can take up to a week at times but they try to get to it within 48 hours during the normal work week. If the link goes down on Friday morning, then I can pretty much count on my site being down over the weekend. By contrast, if the SprintLink goes down on a dedicated circuit, Sprint reroutes the link to another spare circuit. If the outage is between my site and the closest point of presence, then Sprint gets to work on it right away without delay. They realize that the reason you've got the dedicated link is for business purposes, and wastes no time at all in circuit restoration.

This is the reason why dedicated links exist. If you want to compare raw costs per link, you'd see that the dedicated link is more expensive at a 3:1 ratio. So why all the fuss over these links? My suggestion is to use a 28.8 Kbps modem to get the Web server talking to your provider. This is quick and painless. So far no obligations. Next, if your immediate user count is 20 or fewer, try using dialup ISDN to proof the rest of the site. If that proves less than optimal, you can always jump to the dedicated FT1, which should solve all but your most demanding needs.

If you intend to build your site as an Internet Service Provider, don't waste your time and money on a 56 Kbps link of any type! I've had to bail out three customers that thought 56 Kbps was sufficient, but could not possibly serve the public with more than five users connected. The lowest speed you should consider using is a 384 K FT1. You can always bump up the speed to full T1 if necessary.

What Happens When You're Way Off?

Ah, yes. Someone didn't heed the warning block above, and has gotten into a jam and a half. In the situation described previously, I found that I was able to upgrade the link, with SprintLink and AT&T, from 56 Kbps all the way up to full T1 using most if not all of the existing equipment that these customers had in service for 56 Kbps. Not too much of a hassle, but that's not even the half of it. The major factor was that the Web server itself was built on a 486DX4-100 processor and 32 MB of memory for 10 users on the 56 Kbps link. Even though the link was upgraded to T1, the Web server wasn't up to the task of handling 30 concurrent users!

Faulty planning all the way around and misguided intentions left this wanna-be Internet Service Provider hanging in the breeze and counting change to foot the bill. I watched the server's console and noticed that the time clock wasn't updating at all. Yes, a locked up server and on a T1 connection. If you calculate the average cost to the provider per second, the dialup ISDN at 128 Kbps is 67 cents per hour while the full T1 is around $2 per hour. You do the math and tell me if the CFO would be ticked off if the server was down over the weekend and no one noticed.

In the next section, we'll go over the actual Web server hardware and software requirements for building a respectable Web server that won't embarrass you, your CFO, or the customers. By now, your plan should look something like plan04.doc. Keep in mind that your server requirements may change, but this should help you consider the many aspects of creating a Web site.

Web Server System Requirements

We've talked a lot about the planning stages and some requirements to building a good site. Planning is always key to a successful site, so it's time to start naming names and taking notes about hardware. As a matter of standard practice, I generally don't back one hardware vendor over another unless my years of systems design clearly point out a winner that's head and shoulders above others. There are just certain things in life that mean more to me, and one's a reliable vendor of hardware and software.

System Hardware

In considering our goals for the customers, we've concluded that we may have as many as 25 concurrent users online at any one time. In the future, it's feasible that our Web server will have as many as 100 users at one time. In light of this consideration, I feel justified in saying that for proper performance you should start the server at a Pentium-120 or higher with at least 64 MB of memory. By the time NT itself gets running and the Web server software starts going, the server will have used 26 MB RAM. Once the ancillary software starts, and a few users get logged on, you'll easily be using 32 MB of memory.

Because you're running a Web server with business data, RAID 5 disk subsystem components are essential to a successful site. The two most common forms of RAID are type 1 and type 5. Type 1 is nothing more than a mirroring of a drive; type 5 is used in database operations where security of the data is paramount. Figure 2.10 illustrates the RAID disk subsystems. The idea here is that a set of SCSI disk drives are teamed with a SCSI controller to form one logical drive out of several physical drives. The end result is data safety, because in RAID systems no one physical drive holds all of the data. It's spread out among the cluster of drives in such a way that if one physical drive quits running, you can replace the bad drive and let the operating system rebuild the data.

Many Web servers are afterthoughts for company marketing and are not deemed essential to the bottom line, so these do not run RAID. However, if you intend to process a lot of requests, you should consider RAID because these systems are generally faster in response than singular disk drives. The expense can't be ignored, either; RAID subsystems require a special

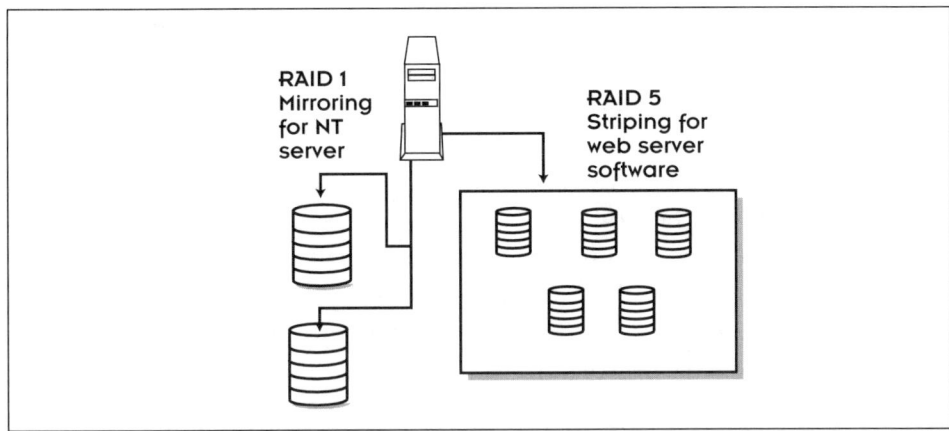

Figure 2.10 RAID disk subsystem types 1 and 5.

controller card. There's plenty on the market now that are up to the task, including Mylex, Adaptec, BusLogic, Seagate, and more. I've personally used the Mylex DAC-960 RAID controller and have had very good success with it. One glaring problem exists with RAID—if a drive quits, the controller or operating system *has to notify you!*

Yes, I had a drive die once and found that my Banyan VINES operating system continued to operate—although sluggishly due to the dead drive. The only way I knew the drive had quit was by the amount of user problems with their data. The RAID was restoring the data on the fly as users needed the data, and this imposed a significant overhead on the server in addition to normal operations for 200 users. Using the system logs, I identified the failed drive and replaced it and let RAID rebuild the data.

 If you choose RAID, make sure that the controller works with NT, but also make sure it has provisions to notify NT of a failure and/or otherwise handle the event.

With the advent of SCSI-3 disk drives and the increased performance they can bring, I recommend you use them. Because you'll need three drives as a minimum for the RAID 5 factor, choose drives of sufficient capacity to last you. For example, if you choose 2 GB units, then three drives result in an effective storage of 4 GB, because 33 percent of the cumulative drives is used for RAID overhead. The same three drive set of 4 GB units gives you an effective storage of around 9 GB, which should suffice for most starting Web sites. One last comment on RAID: Although not really documented anywhere, I've found that instead of using three drives of 2 GB, five drives of 2 GB are your best bet for a faster performing system. If one drive in the three-drive set dies, the data is stored on only two drives. A system rebuild or continuing operations will be very sluggish. In a five-drive setup, a downed drive leaves four units still operational. I have found this to be a more reliable situation. The proverbial "more is merrier" rings true in this case.

Okay, that's it for the core of the server—processor, memory, and disk drives—so let's hit the ancillary equipment. Because the server doesn't have much interaction at the console, the video subsystem is negligible. I use plain 16-bit SVGA cards to keep the cost down. No use putting a Ferrari engine in a VW, because the frame would fall apart at Mach 2. Same thing with the keyboard; I use a standard 84-key keyboard. For the mouse, I'm partial to the Microsoft Serial mouse for the touch and feel, since most operations under Microsoft Windows NT Server are mouse driven. Certainly, you are free to pick your favorite rodent. For serial ports, two are fine, but make sure they're using the 16550 UART-designed models.

My Web server is aided by the use of a four-port serial card from Equinox Corp. in Sunrise, Florida. I know. I said I seldom bespeak a single vendor's name. Well, I renege here because this SST-4 four serial port card from Equinox works like a dream with NT and my BBS software, Wildcat for NT Server. When I find something that works this well, I've just gotta say it! One of the best attributes about this card is if you have two serial ports on the Web server to start, this card starts its ports off as serial port 3. If the Web server had four ports on it, the SST-4 starts off as port 5. Effortless operations, to be sure. Equinox can be reached at 800-275-3500 ext. 247 or across the Internet at *info@equinox.com*. Equinox has many other cards supplying up to 256 ports on a Microsoft Windows NT Server. I will provide more information about this card in Chapter 12, when we get into generalized Web site administration.

Next, you certainly want to protect your data with good backups. Don't waste your time fiddling around with tape drives of less than 500 MB. Get one of the speedy Digital Audio Tapes (DAT) version 3, which can give you up to 8 GB on a single tape. As the site grows, you'll surely need the capacity. One more thing is that if you implement the idea of having another workstation on the network serve as an FTP site, then that'll need to be backed up, as well. With a good DAT drive, you can backup across the network with ease. New software is flooding the market. Third-party vendors have really come through to solve your most demanding backup needs with Microsoft Windows NT Server.

Let's see, what's left? Oh yes, case and power supply. Make very sure that the case is large enough to support your projected expansion, and make sure there are cooling fans installed in it! Heat is the number one killer of computer systems, followed closely by power disturbances. You can be most assured that power protection is paramount to the server's extended lifespan. To calculate the required capacity needs, add up all of the amperage draw of the components that you want to protect. Multiply the amperage by 120 to give you the wattage. The surge load of the protected equipment can be as high as three times the maximum operating amperage draw—an important technicality to keep you from blowing up the Uninterrupted Power Supply (UPS) and frying everything in sight. Now that you know the power consumption of the devices, pick a UPS from your favorite vendor. Take their rating, which is in volt-amperes, and multiply that by .707 to get the true wattage rating that the UPS can handle.

Never, never, never, put a laser printer on a UPS unless that UPS is rated at over 3000 watts of protection! The average desktop laser printer runs at a nominal 8 amperes of continuous power with an initial surge load that can exceed 30 amperes for less than a second. Even though the wall power breaker may handle this load, a UPS is much more sensitive to these power transitions and will attempt to supply the correct power to the printer, mistaking the initial surge as a loss of power. This error has often resulted in fried laser printers, fried UPSs, or both. And that's not to mention the possibility of an electrical fire.

Let's do an example and then discuss the types of power protection. Before getting into the example, I'd like to emphasize the difference between the terms *volt-amperes* and *wattage*. The two are drastically different in their meaning and application, but the industry has seen fit to use the ratings in what I've seen to be contradictory places. When you go to the computer store and see a UPS on the shelf, it'll have a numerical rating on the outside of the box. This is the *volt-ampere* rating which indicates a relative value of the UPS' input voltage and power. The true effective capacity of the device is the *wattage* rating. Take the volt-ampere rating on the box and multiply it by .707 to get the wattage rating. My server has a 300 watt power supply for all of the internal components of the server. While none of them are drawing full power, the most that is being drawn is 300 watts, which is the maximum rating of the power supply. My monitor pulls 6 amperes on startup and 2 amperes continuous running. So, the monitor uses 2 amperes multiplied by 120 volts equals 240 watts of power. The combined needs of the monitor and computer total 540 watts of power. So to get the best UPS for my system, I'll need a UPS of 771 volt-amperes or higher to properly sustain the system during normal runtime.

Two other power protection devices—*online UPS* and *sine wave UPS*—differ from the standard UPS in that not only do they provide backup power to the computer, but they also provide a higher degree of filtering and protection from power transients such as brown-outs and line sags. Think about when the refrigerator or furnace comes on in the house. Many homes experience a brief dimming of lights. This is called a *sag*, and occurs when the line voltage momentarily drops below 100 volts. While the power is low, your wonderful power company senses the decrease of power and the transformer outside your house dutifully boosts up power to compensate. By the time that occurs, the furnace has caught up and now the excess voltage reaches as high as 150 volts. This is called a *surge*. Sags and surges, pictured in Figure 2.11, of less than 20 volts are not normally noticed in computers, but larger swings can cause computers to reboot. A more devastating form of power problem is called a *spike*. Spikes, which are illustrated in Figure 2.12, do some real damage when they hit the electronic world, because standard power supplies aren't built to handle the momentary power spike of up to 10,000 volts that can sometimes occur in less than one tenth of a second.

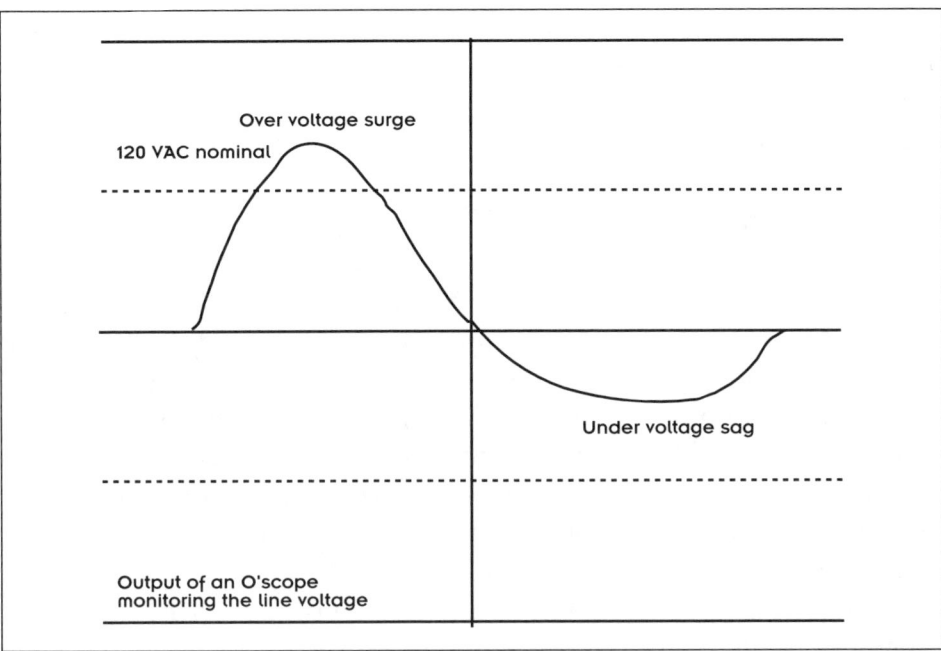

Figure 2.11   Sags and surges are relatively minor electrical anomalies.

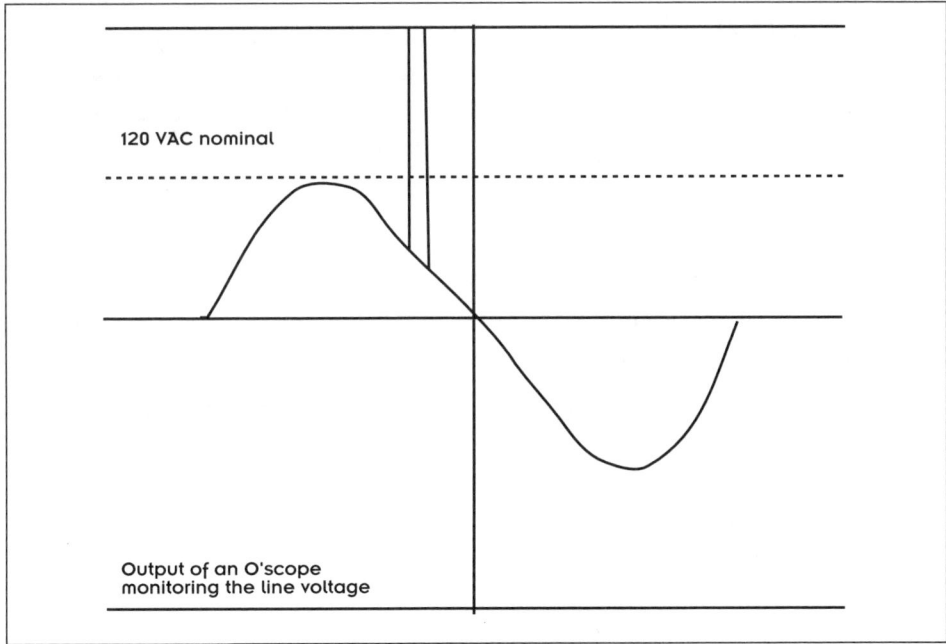

Figure 2.12   Spikes raise up to 10,000 volts in less than one tenth of a second.

To counter these types of power anomalies, protection devices, such as the online filter, exist to stabilize the line at 120 volts nominal. When these unruly power waves hit the beaches of your Web server, nothing will occur except normal operations.

System Software

Next, let's peruse some of the software that is required to get your Web server operational. Of course, there's Microsoft Windows NT Server itself. This takes about an hour to install, and about two hours to configure and get the network protocols working, add a few users, set basic security and permissions, and otherwise get the server running. Plan on a day to do this, just to be safe. Then, there's the Web server software. This isn't too terribly difficult to do for any of the packages that we'll look at, but just the same it takes time to accomplish. Next, there's the FTP configuration. FTP takes only a few minutes to install and set up, but it is a disaster to fix if you don't define your directories properly. Try to choose a proper layout based upon your needs and the types of software to be stored. Figure 2.13 shows a simplified tree structure of my FTP site.

Finally, you'll need to install all of the ancillary tools, such as Visual Basic v4 for the CGI work. If you're using Microsoft SQL Server as the backend engine, this is a tremendous load on the server. Count on using over 150 MB of disk space and a full day to configure it, at least. Table 2.4 summarizes the configuration requirements for the server software. The table only summarizes the major tools you'll be needing. You're bound to run across some smaller tools that you're sure to want to install.

Basically, you can have the server installed and operational with the minimum taskings in a day and a half, or two full work days if you're taking your time. The FTP Space requirement of 500 MB is a starting point for your needs, and as I mentioned earlier you should set aside as much disk space as you can imagine is required. Starting out with 1 GB is not unreasonable.

The WebMaster

The WebMaster is the single most important position in the company after the Web server comes online, as far as the server is concerned. This person is the server's primary caregiver. When it acts up, the WebMaster will fix it.

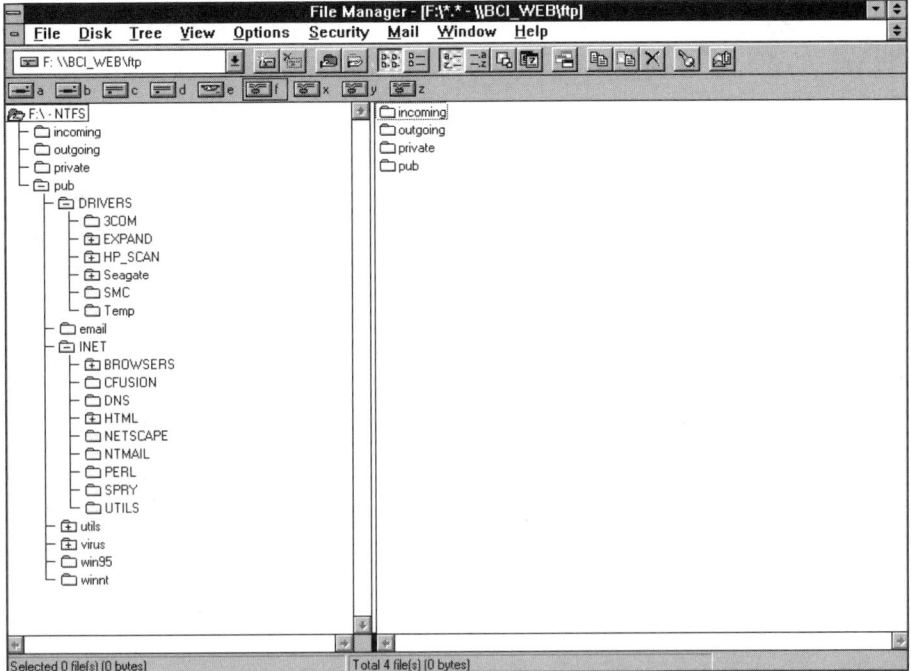

Figure 2.13   My FTP directory layout.

When it needs help for a user, the WebMaster will take care of the account issues. When the disk fills up and crashes the server, the WebMaster is the one that the CFO chews on when someone says that all it takes is money to

Table 2.4   Relative Configuration Requirements of Server Software

Software	Space Size	Time to Install/Configure	Required to Use
NT Server	100 MB	8 hours	Yes
Web Server	~50 MB	4 hours	Yes
FTP Service	10 MB	1 hour	Yes
FTP Space	>500 MB	1 hour	Yes
Email	25 MB	3 hours	No
Gopher Server	10 MB	1 hour	No
Remote Access	5 MB	½ hour	No
Bulletin Board	10 MB	3 hours	No

fix it. Any way you look at it, the WebMaster is the focal point of the daily operations for the Web server.

As such, the WebMaster is worthy of some training on Microsoft Windows NT Server and how to accomplish the many daily tasks required to maintain accounts and user needs. Once NT is set up, it's very reliable and easy to deal with. However, in the changing world of the Internet and the World Wide Web, the WebMaster may find it a busy day at the office every day. The WebMaster should have a solid TCP/IP background and know the terms and troubleshooting techniques of the average network infrastructure. The WebMaster should be well versed in data recovery and server restorations in the unlikely event of a crash of the worst magnitude.

All in all, the WebMaster is the Top Dog of the Web for your company. Ideally, the WebMaster will have at least one assistant that knows the hows, whys, and wherefores of the Web server and the WebMaster's procedures for maintaining the same. A little written policy goes a long way towards solving the needs of the users.

Future Plans for the Site

All the while that the site is being built or otherwise being planned, always strive to be looking forward to the needs of the site. In this day and age, even if the site doesn't pan out in a year's time, the components of the server can be used elsewhere. For instance, a 2 GB drive can be used to expand the storage on a workstation that is highly graphic in nature. Or you may have a programmer on staff that has lots of experience and is branching off into Windows programming. This person could use a powerful PC, and the Microsoft Windows NT Server operating system could be removed and reloaded with something else. The server has lots of memory, disk space, and other goodies that would make it a fine programming platform.

These are the things that could be useful later on, or make future Web server upgrades easier to do. One of the worst possible things that a new Web site can do is focus on one technology and one vendor to solve all of the site's needs. This just isn't practical, and is downright wasteful of company resources. True, SCSI can take care of storage needs quite easily, but I saw a test site that used IDE drives go into production using one IDE drive as the sole storage medium. IDE works great, and is inexpensive, but leaves very little room for expansion when it occurs. To add more storage, you'll have to down the site and add a drive or a new SCSI controller and drive. All of this takes time, which keeps your customers offline.

Where You're Located—The IP Address

How do people know where to find you on the Internet? Why through your address, of course. Just as your friends locate your home by its street address, users locate your Web site through your *Internet Protocol* (IP) address. An IP address is a 32-bit (or 8 byte) numerical designation of the placement of a computer within the global network that we call the Internet. If you don't have an address, no one can find you.

You need to make your presence known publicly by officially registering yourself. The *Domain Name Service (DNS)* locates everyone that is officially registered on the Internet. More on this topic later.

The IP Address of Where You Live

IP addresses are composed of 32 bits of format in an octet base. This means that IP addresses will never exceed the number 9. My server's temporary address is 204.49.131.245 and has an *alias* of www.bci.com for the time being. By the time this book goes to print, I'll have a more permanent situation in which the IP address will change and the Web site will be www.bciassoc.com. An alias? What's that? Well, the human-readable form of a name is easier to remember than the numerical one, so the DNS registers my name of www.bci.com and equates it to 204.49.131.245. This means that when you type in *http://www.bci.com* in your Web browser, DNS looks that alphabetical name up in the directory listing and translates it into the numerical one. Why does it do this?

To get from one location on the Internet to another, a device called a *router* is used to move the data in the appropriate ways to get from point A to point B. Routers know nothing of alpha names, only numerical addresses. What's more, routers have the numerical designations in a listing called a *router table,* which tells the router how to send the data from place to place.

From Figure 2.14, you can see that the steps to get from place to place are as follows:

1. Server examines the destination address typed in.

2. If numerical, bypass DNS (step 3) and go to step 4.

3. If alpha, use DNS to obtain numerical address.

4. Send desired IP address to your closest router. Router then finds closest connection point to hand off the same request and get to the next router. Process continues until destination IP address is reached or fails.

5. Destination IP address device either responds with an authoritative return, or errors out.

6. Destination IP address device then processes request to provide data.

While these steps present a simplified version of the process, you can still see why your request can sometimes take forever. The request has to make the route from location to location. If one path fails, the request, in a sense, backs up and tries another path. This process is called *finding the path* and can be followed by a really neat Microsoft Windows NT Server utility called *TraceRoute*. Examine Listing 2.1 and you'll see how TraceRoute

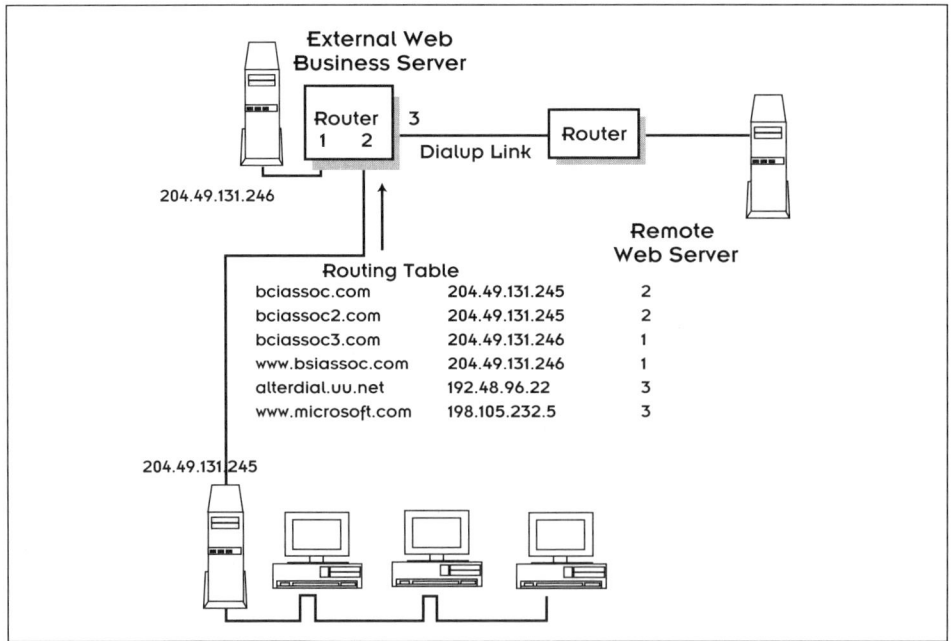

Figure 2.14   Moving data by routing.

can be used to see where the data has to go, and what it has to go through to get around. As a sample, I did a trace from my modem connection to my Internet Service Provider to Microsoft Corporation's Web server, *http://www.microsoft.com*.

Listing 2.1   Actual TraceRoute to Microsoft's Web Server

```
Tracing route to www.microsoft.com [198.105.232.4]

over a maximum of 30 hops:
  1   161 ms    150 ms    146 ms   gulf98.interoz.com [204.49.131.98]

  2   158 ms    146 ms    148 ms   router.interoz.com [204.49.131.1]

  3   171 ms    145 ms    167 ms   cisco1-gulfnetpc.mariana.cntfl.com
      [204.49.129.5]

  4     *         *         *      Request timed out.

  5     *         *         *      Request timed out.

  6   197 ms    174 ms    171 ms   204.49.62.2

  7   180 ms    172 ms    195 ms   cisco_5.cntfl.com [204.49.7.2]

  8   187 ms    200 ms    188 ms   cisco-sl.cntfl.com [199.44.9.65]

  9   216 ms    211 ms    212 ms   border1-serial3-5.Atlanta.mci.net
      [204.70.16.65]

 10   214 ms    201 ms    356 ms   core-fddi-0.Atlanta.mci.net [204.70.2.49]

 11   219 ms    190 ms    206 ms   core2-aip-4.Atlanta.mci.net [204.70.1.70]

 12   327 ms    219 ms    228 ms   core1-hssi-2.Dallas.mci.net
      [204.70.1.114]

 13   237 ms    259 ms    276 ms   core-hssi-3.KansasCity.mci.net
      [204.70.1.118]

 14   295 ms    232 ms    262 ms   core2-hssi-2.Denver.mci.net
      [204.70.1.157]

 15   325 ms    283 ms    296 ms   core-hssi-4.Seattle.mci.net [204.70.1.90]
```

```
16    295 ms    311 ms    273 ms    border1-fddi-0.Seattle.mci.net
      [204.70.2.146]

17    321 ms    302 ms    324 ms    nwnet.Seattle.mci.net [204.70.52.6]

18    333 ms    309 ms    333 ms    seabr1-gw.nwnet.net [192.147.179.5]

19    367 ms    267 ms    288 ms    microsoft-t3-gw.nwnet.net [198.104.192.9]

20    313 ms    280 ms    297 ms    131.107.249.3

21    339 ms    274 ms    311 ms    www.microsoft.com [198.105.232.4]

Trace complete.
```

The first thing you should notice is that the *Trace* function did a DNS resolution as the very first item. Why press onward if the alpha address is not a valid site? When the alpha address resolves, as it's called, it means that the Microsoft site was properly registered with the people that handle the DNS services, AT&T. Also notice that two of the sites timed out, and had to be retraced along an alternate route. The principle services that the Internet operates by are:

- *Directory and Database Services*—Provided by AT&T Corp., these services provide all of the information for finding people, places, and sites on the Internet. Think of them as the "White Pages" of the Internet.

- *Network Registration Services*—Provided by Network Solutions, Inc., this service creates and registers the domain and IP addresses of customers. To obtain new domain registrations, Network Solutions normally deals directly with Internet Service Providers or with users such as myself that have a domain but connect to an Internet Service Provider.

Now, look back at the trace and notice how the many of the first IP addresses use the figure 204 during the trace. This number represents the class of addresses. There are three distinct classes of IP addresses governed by the size of the networks involved. Class A addresses are for the largest networks while class C represents the smallest networks. Table 2.5 illustrates this concept. The term *hosts*, represents the number of PCs that are connected to the particular network. For instance, my current provider uses a class C address of 204.49.131.xxx which allows for addresses of

Table 2.5   IP Class Addresses

Class	Number of Networks	Number of Hosts
A 1-126	126	16,777,214
B 128-191	16,384	65,534
C 192-223	1,097,151	254

204.49.131.0 through 204.49.131.254. If this provider ever exceeded 255 concurrent users, then they'd have to get another block of IP addresses for another network.

Significance of Class Membership

Each computer and each network has a significance on the Internet and is classified by its hierarchical position, or pecking order, on the Internet as a whole. When the number of host computers supported by the ISP is large (as with an enterprise-wide network with 50,000 computers), then the ISP takes on a class A address. The number of servers are few but the number of supported users is quite large. By contrast, most of the ISPs that are being sold to us little users by modem are class C addresses. During testing, the address for my Web server is 204.49.131.245. The leading 204 indicates a class C designation. Class C is by far the most common network you'll see from a provider. Class A is generally reserved for development and internal use by the InterNIC.

When you apply for and obtain a class address—we'll use the class C block that I obtained for my server—you receive the address from the available pool of your provider. The provider gets them assigned to them from the InterNIC's master pool of IP addresses. Along with the address, I had to select a domain name for my server. Selecting a domain name is not mandatory, but it's advisable, so you can have an alpha name for your site. If you go to *http://www.internic.net* and choose the registration services, there's a query that you can use to see if a particular domain name already exists, as shown in Figure 2.15. I applied for my name, bciassoc.com, but I checked with InterNIC first to see if it was available. When the process is complete, the InterNIC sends confirmation for the domain name. As of February 1996, the registration cost was $100 for a two-year period.

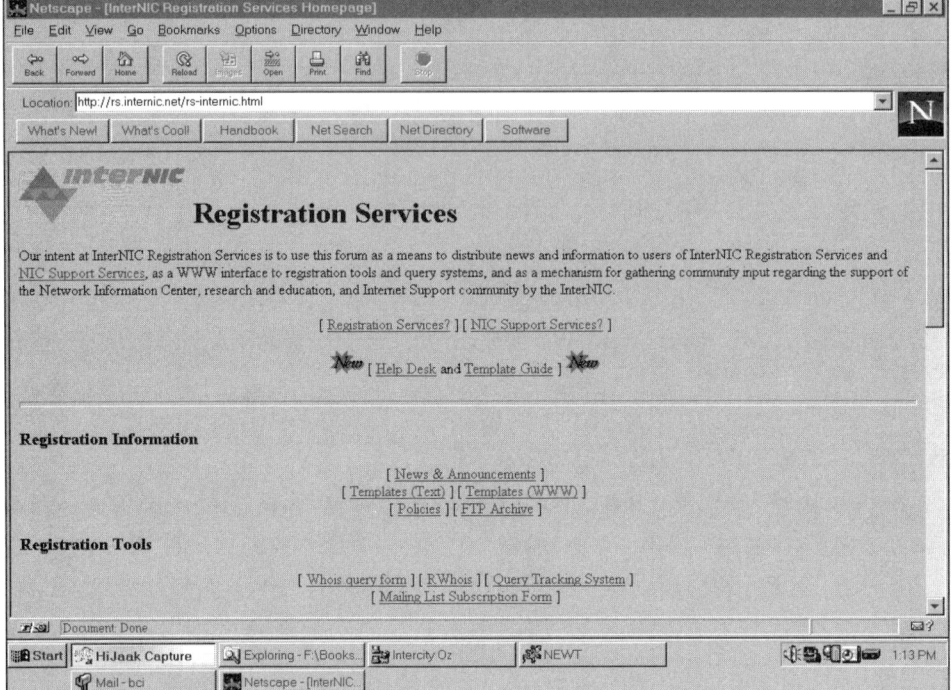

Figure 2.15   Registration test for domain name.

The next step is to associate the two addresses (the numerical and alphabetical) in the DNS listing from your provider. You can maintain your own DNS if you like, or pay a nominal fee to have your provider do it. The DNS basically tells other computers that www.bciassoc.com refers to 204.49.131.245. Table 2.6 shows a sample DNS resolution file.

The DNS is nothing more than a simple text file that allows any computer to determine the IP address for any server. Once the data makes it to the server, the internal router on the network takes over and sends the requests to the

Table 2.6   Sample DNS Resolution File

Name	IP Address
BCIASSOC.COM	204.49.131.245
BCIASSOC2.COM	204.49.131.245
TEST.SERV.COM	204.49.131.245

appropriate location. This DNS process is also the source of many headaches. Have you ever gotten the ill-fated message that an alias cannot be resolved? This error occurs because the destination can't be found, the destination isn't properly (or at all) registered with the NIC, or the server is truly offline.

Your Relationship with Your Vendor

So, now you've obtained a domain and block of IP addresses for your Web server, and you're officially online. One thing you should remember is that you don't own the block of IP addresses. You're paying for them by virtue of the monthly service fees you pay to the ISP for the account. The domain is yours to keep as long as you keep it active. If for some reason you leave the ISP, then the registered block of IP addresses returns to the free IP pool of the ISP. Getting the connection back with someone else requires you to go through the same process all over again, including the DNS for the domain. By the time you've made it here, your Web Plan should look similar to plan05.doc.

The Connection—Getting Online with a Domain

Way back in the beginning of the chapter, I mentioned that we'll need to form a *domain* for our Web server to get online. This is still true, and now's the time to do that. I also mentioned that you should get to the Network Solutions site. Let's go through this process in detail now and make the final process bear fruit.

What Is a Domain?

If you've got Microsoft Windows NT Server experience, then you may have knowledge of the domain model. If you do, just bear with me as I explain the difference between a Microsoft Windows NT Server domain and an Internet domain model. One of the most useful things you can do is get a copy of the Microsoft Windows NT Server Resource Kit. The kit contains a program called the Domain Model Planning Guide that you can use to create your most basic game plan for Microsoft Windows NT Server. This guide will also prove to be helpful for planning your Web server.

Basically, a domain is a territory. Consider this analogy: The lion of Africa has an invisible area of land that he patrols and claims ownership to by virtue of his own way of knowing the perimeter of land. You can't define the territory concretely as a lion does, but you can observe him over time and get a rough idea of the area that he commands. A business has a territory that's within its control, as well. For the most part, a business can define a range in terms of buildings or specific desktops. This is not always practical to do, so creating a domain from an abstract thought makes planning and control easier to manage.

Your Place in the World—Creating Your Domain

Let's go through the domain model creation process, first for Microsoft Windows NT Server and then for the Internet model. If you have the Microsoft Windows NT Server Resource Kit, then you have the software handy. If not, then follow along and get a glimpse of what the Domain Planner can do for you. Start the planner from the installed Resource Kit group. The opening screen looks like the one shown in Figure 2.16.

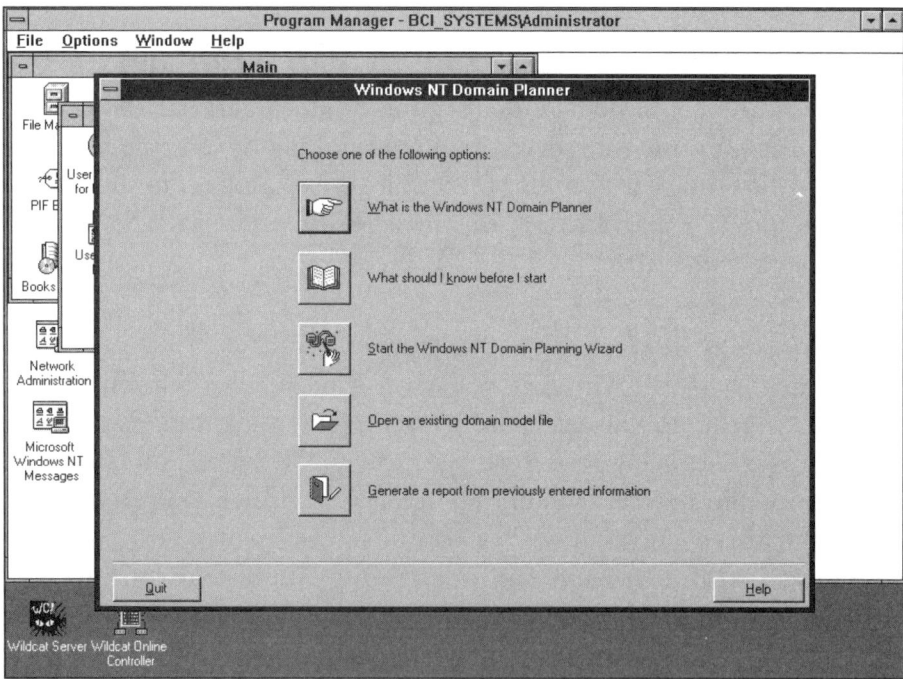

Figure 2.16 Opening screen of the Domain Planner.

Selecting the first button starts a very good tutorial of the Microsoft Windows NT Server domain model. It points out a few interesting aspects of the model, and what you can expect from it. Once you're done with that, press onward and select the third button from the top and start the Domain Planner. When you start it, you'll be asked a number of questions regarding the setup of your network, how many workstations and of what types, if you want centralized management, and a host of other issues to be considered. When you're finished with the process, you'll be presented with a preview of the document that details your domain and how you can best set it up and use it. The file dom_plan.doc, which is located on the accompanying CD-ROM, is a copy of the report that I did on my business and related interests, with two sites titled NCS and CPLG. Both are geographically separated from my business, and both are separate businesses on their own. As such, they have their own domain, but are also trusted domains into my business domain which is the master. Sounds a bit confusing, but you'll be able to see the structure without a problem.

Now that you have an idea of the Microsoft-centric domain model, let's take a look at the Internet domain. Seeing these two models side by side will give you a good understanding of the differences between the two domains. Because you'll be hearing the same term used concurrently within two contexts, this understanding is important. You can choose an Internet domain name based on a number of factors, including the name of the business, a favorite product of the business, or some closely relevant idea of the business. Because the Internet places few restrictions on domain names, you could choose a name that has no relevance to your business, but I wouldn't hold your breath waiting for visits if you go this route.

The Domain Registration Process

My business' name is BCI Associates, so I chose bciassoc.com as an abbreviation of the business name. With a name picked out, and several backup names in case yours is already taken, head off to the InterNIC and do a check for the domain name. Figure 2.17 shows the NIC registration documents. If you're getting your server connection from an existing ISP, then chances are they'll submit the papers for you and report back with the domain name and a block of registered IP addresses. If not, then you can

```
>          INVOICE FOR DOMAIN REGISTRATION & RENEWAL
>
>****************** Please DO NOT REMOVE Version Number ********************
>
>Invoice Version Number: 1.0
>
>***************** Please see attached detailed instructions *****************
>
>Invoice Information
>1a. Invoice Number......................: 960110.932
>1b. Invoice Date.........................: 10-jan-1996
>1c. Invoice Due Date....................: 09-feb-1996
>
>Domain Information
>2a. Registered Domain Name............: BCIASSOC.COM
>2b. Associated Tracking Number.........: 951220.3129
>2c. Period Covered......................: 03-jan-1996 - 03-jan-1998
>2d. Initial Registration Fee............: $100.00 USD
>2e. (A)ccept (R)eject Charge...........:
>
>Summary Information
>3a. Total Charges......................: $100.00 USD
>3b. Total Amount Accepted..............:
>
>Payment Method
>4. (CH)eck (CR)edit card, or (AC)count:
>
>Credit Card
>5a. (V)isa, (M)astercard, or (A)MEX....:
>5b. Credit Card Number.................:
>5c. Name on Credit Card...............:
>5d. Expiration Date....................:
>5e. Authorized Signature and Date......:
```

Figure 2.17   NIC registration form.

submit the domain name electronically to the InterNIC, as I did. You'll receive confirmation by email, or by fax if you choose, of the name selection or a message indicating that you need to try again. You'll also receive an electronic bill for the registration with instructions on how to pay it. That's all there is to it.

Types of Domain Connections

Types of domain connections? What kind of a section is this, you ask? Well, I just wanted to point out a few differences in how the server is being connected to the Internet and why it affects the connection. If you use a modem to make the link, the server still uses an IP address to get connected, but is obviously limited to the speed of the modem. You should keep this in mind when it comes time to work with time-sensitive connections and test your Web server. Even though I said you can use a modem to proof test the Web server, and that still stands true, keep in mind that if the phone line gets ratty, then data is easily corrupted and some operational parts of the server can get lost in the shuffle. If you used RAS to make the connection, run the RAS monitor and watch for the little red light to come on the monitor indicating corrupted data transmissions. If this happens once every minute, then there's the real possibility that the modem line is completely unreliable. Also, in a modem connection, no users on the internal network can get out to the Internet.

Making the connection with the dialup ISDN terminal adapter is the next best solution. This solves, for all practical purposes, the dirty line problems. However, like the modem, no internal network routing can be performed.

As a third option, using a dialup ISDN device such as the Ascend series of routers provides both reliable digital circuits and internal network routing functions. This little gem gets your users onto the Internet from your internal business networks. The drawback? More than 15 or 20 users will choke up this link.

 The best way to get your domain online is the dedicated link, which keeps you online all the time and at faster rates. You pay for this extra speed, but you can get higher processing rates on the same port with a few minor changes at the ISP.

Getting an Online Connection

Getting the actual connection can be a real trial in patience, but one way to get started is to use a known list of sites, such as the one found at *http://www.yahoo.com/Business/Corporations/Internet_Access_Providers/Indices*, which I found by using the Yahoo search engine. This is a very good list of the major and some not-so-major ISPs around the nation. Keep in mind that there are perhaps ten times this number of sites. Don't discount the spare room in an large closet, either. Servers and modems can fit almost anywhere!

Other than modems, the local exchange carrier controls the ISDN to your server if you choose that route. Such major vendors as AT&T long distance services aren't yet allowed to compete in that market, but that appears to be changing thanks to Congress. The dedicated and switched Internet links can be had from SprintLink, MCI, and AT&T.

All about Email

As common as the modem is these days, the email process is used so often that I've heard that whole businesses would collapse if email was to end. That's a bit of an exaggeration, but you get the idea. Electronic mail has quickly replaced the telephone and the post office as the most often used form of communications in a business environment.

What Is Electronic Mail?

Email is the electronic form of the paper letter, nothing more. Email is also the single largest component of a Web server that promises to kill a new server. Why is that, you ask? I was recently a victim of an email flurry on a system where some nitwit sent the email to "*@*@*", which is a global address on our email system. What actually transpired was that over 20,000 users got the email message and over half of them didn't have the sense to realize what the message was, and replied to it. Now, in addition to that return email, the original is attached to the reply so now 10,000 new messages are floating around that are twice the size of the first message. In a very short time, about 200 servers started croaking under the load of the email running loose in the wide area network.

So, what is email? An ever-convenient method to converse with someone, a group of people, or the world. If you're not careful about this, you'll bring the world to it's electronic knees. Yes, it can be done (and is on occasion). And that's the not the only dastardly deed of which email is guilty. Let's find out what other evils lurk in email.

Attachments and the Dark Side

Email with an attached file is a neat way to move files from one place to another. So you've been introduced to the evil email product, but did you think to consider what would occur if an errantly attached file was sent to the same global users? It'd crash that system in a hurry. Furthermore, in some email systems, if an email is sent to a group of 25 users, and all have the same attachment, and one of those 25 users can't receive the email, guess what happens? Yes, *all 25* get the same email sent to them all over again! Even if those first 24 got the message, the last one caused the retransmission to the failed delivery point. However, the email system has no way of knowing that the list of recipients is more than just one user. If one fails, all of the recipients get the message again. When you pick a mail system, make sure it doesn't do this to you!

Multiple Recipients

If you've got a list of users that you need to send the same letter, you can compose each individual message offline—to save connection fees—then go online and transmit them all at once, but that means creating a bunch of individual messages. A better solution is to use a mailing list. Mailing lists save on time and money by creating one message and sending it to everyone on the list. This is the essence of what is known on the Internet as *list servers,* or *listserv* for short. You can subscribe to a listserv to get on a common mailing list for messages, updates from a vendor, and such. Your Web server may or may not provide a listserv for your customers for you to update them on coming events, upgrades, special product notifications, and so on.

However, list servers are for disseminating fixed information (usually) and discussion groups. The information isn't normally for dynamic usage like a Web page would be using Perl or VB4.

Return Receipts, and What They Don't Mean

When you send out an email message, you can do much like the post office does and request a return receipt for both delivery and for when it gets read. That's a nice idea, and has the best of intentions, but it's worthless in many situations. Here's why. Think back to the router example of the internal network. When an email leaves the source, weaving its way through the Internet, it passes through many gateways on its way to its final destination. A return receipt is generated by the first point capable of responding. This may or may not be the final destination. So you can see how the return receipt misleads the source into thinking that the mail made it when in fact it may not have.

The second most useless part of email receipts is that is doesn't indicate whether or not the recipient has actually *read* the email.. If the recipient stores the email in a folder but never actually reads the message, the "message read" receipt never gets sent back to the sender.. We know that the email made it past the first server because the return receipt was generated. Perhaps it is stuck in the processing software on the user's server, and the user is totally unaware that mail has been lost. Unfortunately, this happens all too often. Be careful when you select your email package.

Utilities at Your Disposal

As you administer your new site, you'll find some indispensable resources that are crucial in keeping the server operational and working smoothly. Down time or poor operation could cost you potential customers, so you'd better be ready.

Basic System Tools

Some of the most basic tools are free, and you've got a pile of them. A couple of them I'll talk about shortly, but first, here are the tools that are included with the Microsoft Windows NT Server installation:

- Server Diagnostics allow you to track the progress of each part of the server, ranging from memory utilization to CPU time slices to ancillary devices in use

- System, security, and applications log files generated by NT server itself provide an ongoing analysis of recorded events such as failed logons, successful directory accesses, time on the system, and more

- Server Performance Monitoring

- User Statistics

- General Disk Administration

Recovery Tools

The recovery tools provided with NT amount to a precious diskette that maintains a copy of the boot record, system files, user and system critical files, and a means to boot the server when it dies. It can restore the core part of the system that would otherwise prevent it from booting up. You can make a new emergency diskette by running the RDISK program in the SYSTEM32 directory. Follow the instructions, and it updates your emergency disk easily. In addition to that, you might want to make a backup of the disk registries and critical areas by running the Disk Administrator

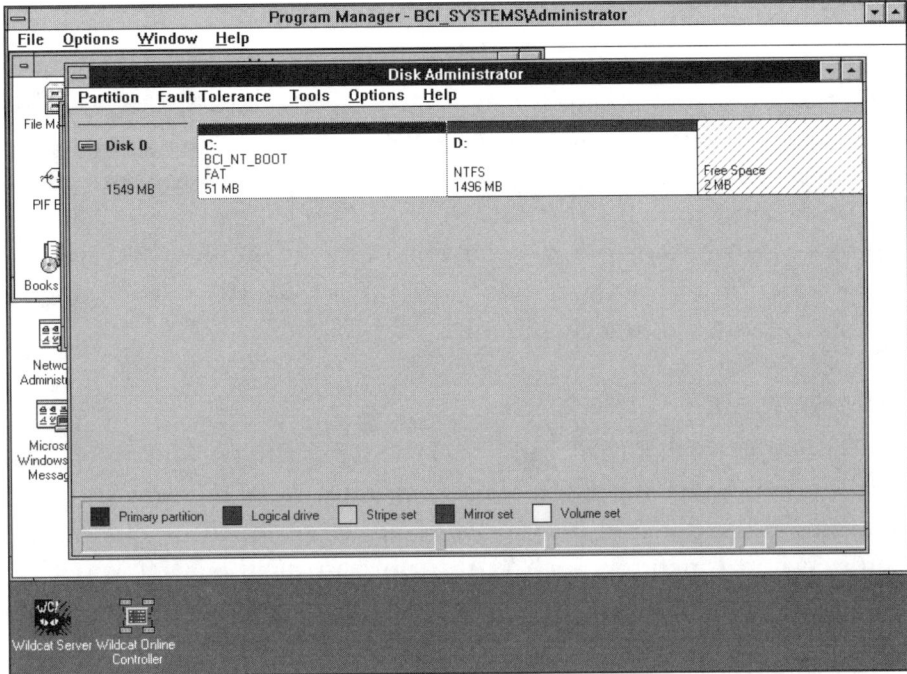

Figure 2.18   Disk Administrator configuration.

and saving the configuration, as shown in Figure 2.18. A worthwhile gesture, I assure you. Wait until you've been caught in a failure, and you'll *never* forget to do it again!

Basic Supported Backup Tools

The NT-supported backup program is a no frills, few thrills program designed to work with the most common backup tape drive in the industry. Any common QIC-40 or QIC-80 drive should work fine. The program performs routine backups in an orderly manner, and professes to use compression when it's running. While it may, I saw little compression being used on my Iomega Tape-250 drive, which is QIC-80 format. I normally get 170 MB on a 307-foot-long tape, and my test run of the backup system pretty much equaled that. Depending on how much data you've got that changes, these QIC tapes are next to useless in a full-scale server implementation. Your best bet is to use one of the commercial-strength solutions from any one of the available products supporting up to 8 GB on one tape.

Watching the Attached Users (Admin Tools)

One of the neat administrative tools that comes with Microsoft Windows NT Server allows you to monitor the users connected to the server, where they are in the system, what they're doing, and many other things. If you open the Administrative Tools group, then run the Server Manager program, shown in Figure 2.19, you'll see a concise listing of users connected to the Web server and to any other computer in the network. This is a normal function of the Microsoft Windows NT Server, but I thought it interesting enough to tell you about it.

NT Resource Kit

As I mentioned earlier, this double CD-ROM set with accompanied documentation is perhaps the single most important set of documents next to the Microsoft Windows NT Server docs themselves. The RK includes a host of utilities and functions, such as the Domain Planner, Net Watcher, a UUEncoder and Decoder, support for multiple desktops, an image editor,

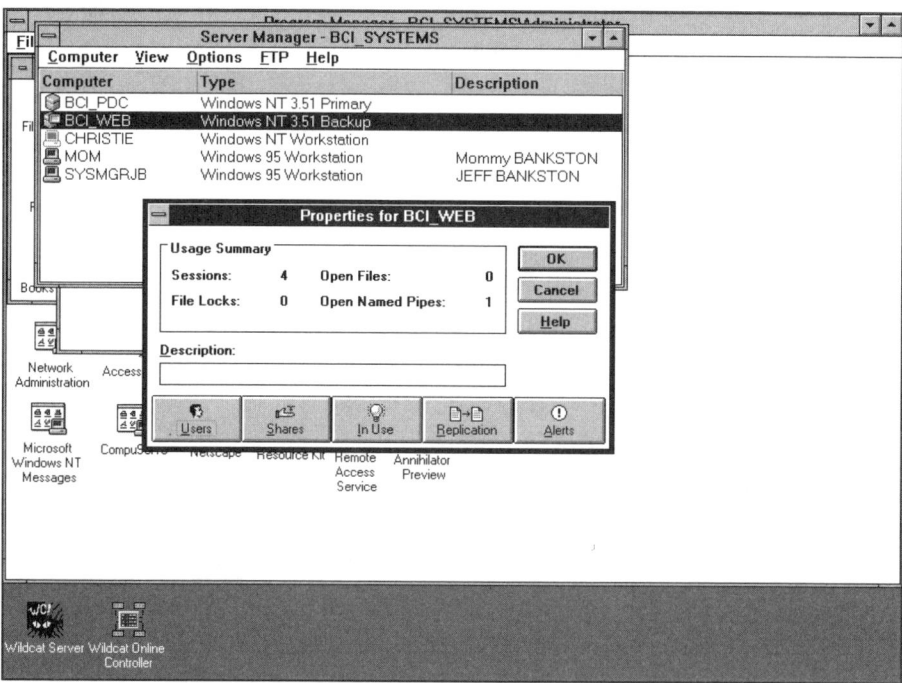

Figure 2.19 The Server Manager keeps its eyes on you.

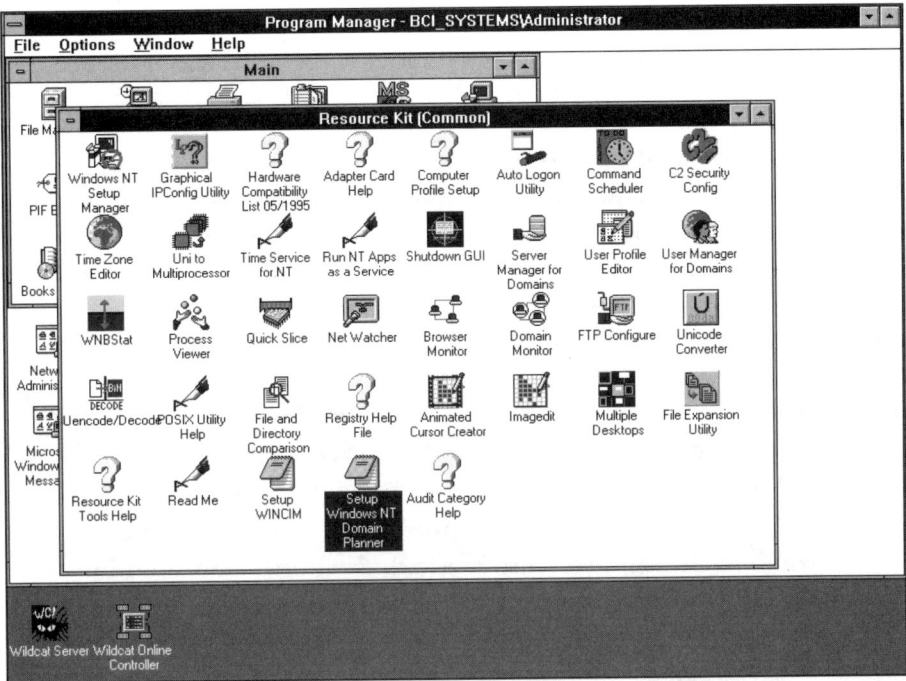

Figure 2.20 The NT Resource Kit group.

and more. The RK is shown in Figure 2.20. I paid $395 for the full set in January 1996, and it is probably still close to that now. If you're serious about maintaining your Web site in top working order, this is definitely required reading.

Microsoft TechNet Subscription

The last item I want to go over with you is called the TechNet subscription. TechNet is a whopping double CD-ROM set issued monthly and every month's arrival offers to install and update your existing installation of the TechNet database indices. This guide is chock full of technical tips, new driver updates, the Microsoft Knowledge base, and tools and tips to maintain nearly any Microsoft product. While it's true that we're installing and maintaining mostly third-party software onto Microsoft Windows NT Server, the plain and simple fact is that TechNet contains installation notes and fixes for many other applications as they relate to NT or other Microsoft products. Are you trying to configure Microsoft SQL Server for your Web server's databases? Check TechNet to see if there's a technical note or tip on how to do what you want. TechNet's main screen is shown in Figure 2.21.

While these are the predominant tools that make the Web server easy to administer, we'll be talking about other tools in *Chapter 12, Web Server Administration. Appendix B* also provides an in-depth look into the resources mentioned in this chapter, with specific emphasis on working with the server when problems arise.

Summary

This has been a complex, but fun-filled chapter! We covered many topics, including defining the Web site as a whole, why we're doing it, what we'll use to build the site, our basic working parameters, and a host of related matters. We've defined the nominal and best-case hardware for the server and why some of the choices were made. I also addressed such important issues as communications links, including the ups and downs of the choices

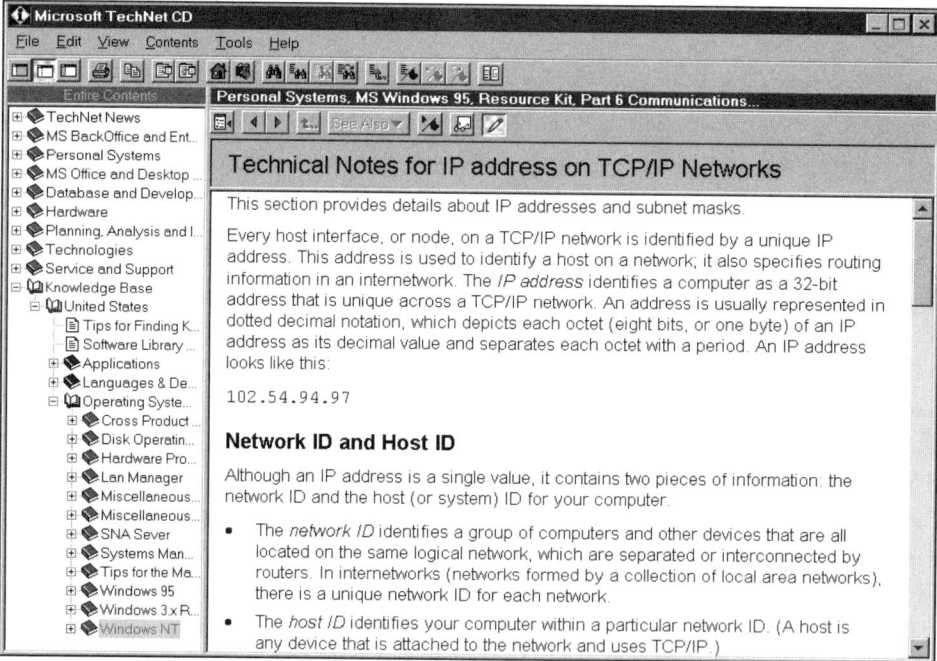

Figure 2.21 The TechNet main screen showing the topics available.

available. I hope this discussion has prepared you to accept or reject some of the theories you've had about your own site and some of the things to be watching out for during construction. You definitely need to keep the CFO hard hat on during all phases of server building, but let the CEO and customers know what fun and newfound productivity they'll receive as a result of all their hard work and patience!

CHAPTER

Web Services from a Business Perspective

Now that you have a solid understanding of Windows NT Server and how to create a strategy for implementing a successful Web server, I would like to show you how, in addition to your other business needs, your Web server can function as a money-making machine. I know, you've already decided that the Web site would be private—to keep it to your customers—but once you've seen the unparalleled opportunities that the Web offers, you're likely to change your mind.

Specifically, in this chapter I will explore:

- Selling Web pages on the server

- Discussing the types of, and transformations of, the HTML language

- Selling or leasing disk space on your server

- Some of the many Web server consultant roles you can perform, for a fee

- Operating your site as a beta test site center

- Advertising on the Web

- Running a news service

- Operating an Internet list server for your customers

- Implementing front end tools for your business data

There's plenty more, and I'd love to share them with you, but the book would then be large enough to boost a small child at the dinner table.

Selling Web Pages

Perhaps one of the most pervasive topics on the World Wide Web is the subject of selling Web pages stored on a Web server. You've got the server, why not use it to its fullest extent. We'll get into the details in a moment, but before I get in too deep, I want to define a few terms. A *Web page* is an HTML document that displays on a Web browser. A *home page* is simply the top-most Web page of a particular Web site. *HTML*, or *Hyper Text Markup Language*, is the language that's used to create the Web page—the graphics and links you see are part of the HTML code. HTML has seen several incarnations and enhancements, of which v3.0 is the latest. It supports an improved set of commands and enhancements, including better audio, video, and representative markups to help make the most of your Web sites. Finally, a *link* is a portion of the HTML code that is used to launch users through cyberspace to another location containing related information.

To further clarify these concepts, let's hop up to the Microsoft home page, shown in Figure 3.1, at *http://www.microsoft.com*, and make note of some key ideas there. I'll assume you're using Netscape's Navigator for this little expedition. However, if you're using Microsoft's Internet Explorer, you will find it to be quite similar in operation to Netscape.

This is the very first Web page that is accessible when you want to access the Microsoft Corporation via the Internet. This is their home on the Internet, hence the term home page. All of the links are underlined and are displayed in blue. This display is Netscape's default and you can change that anytime you want. Continuing our tour, move your mouse to the Microsoft Internet Explorer link. Notice that the arrow turns into a hand with a finger pointing to the link; this symbol shows you that the text is in fact a link to another site or another place on this site. In this case, the link is to another Microsoft location—perhaps even on this same server. At the bottom of Microsoft's home page, the link *http://www.cdt.org/speech.html* takes you to another site altogether.

Figure 3.1 The Microsoft Corporation home page.

Now, let's hop over to the Coriolis Group's site, *http://www.coriolis.com*, click on the Frames option and enter the Coriolis web site, as shown in Figure 3.2.

Notice that the bottom portion of the figure is subdivided into *frames* of information. Frames, which are simply a way to organize a Web site, are one of the latest rages of the Web to hit the streets. A frame is nothing more than HTML code that focuses Web page content so that common items are contained within a frame, much like glass windows are sectioned off in frames. Each frame is independent from the others, yet sometimes related in content.

As your site prospers, you should consider adding frames to your home page, as a way to advertise your customers. If your Web server is as capable as the one we created in Chapter 2, then it will weather the additional hits without any problem. You'll make extra money for little or no work, and your customers will have just one more reason to praise your existence!

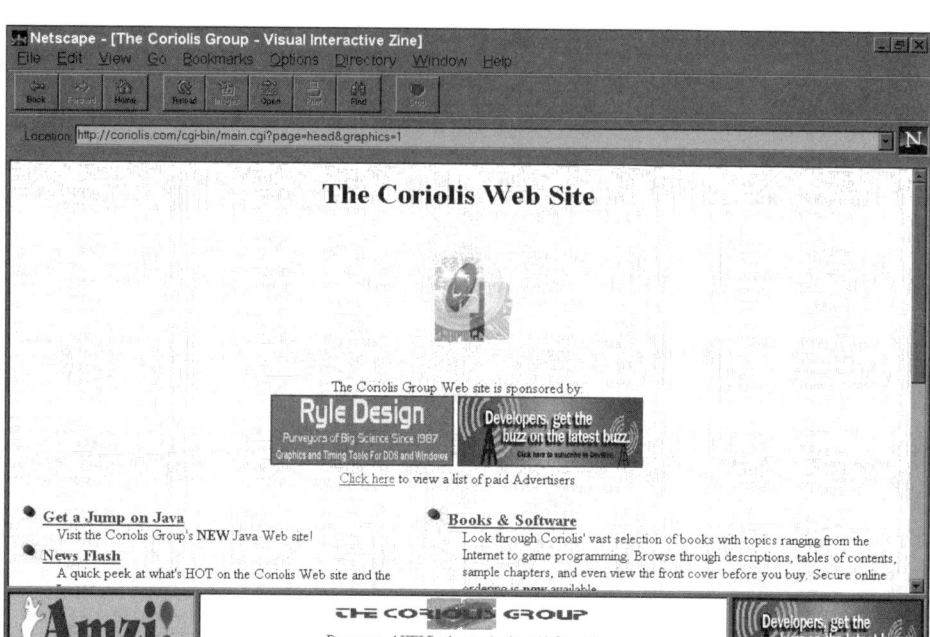

Figure 3.2   The Coriolis Group has a really neat Web site.

There's one small drawback: maintenance. What's all of this got to do with maintenance, you ask? Consider this: You change and control your site as you deem necessary for the customers, and for good business as well. Those other sites? Well, they're doing the same, which means that if you have links that cross to other sites, then at one time or another, you'll wind up with useless links that don't go anywhere. When links break down, someone has to fix them…and pay for it! So, without further ado, let's proceed onward to the topics of maintenance and money.

Maintenance

The maintenance of a Web page involves several aspects of programmatical venturing. HTML is a fairly easy language to learn and master. As I mentioned earlier, there are lots of interesting things that you can do with HTML—display neat graphics, link to other sites, link to your own information, and much more. If your company won an award for excellence in its field, you might want to add a graphic of the award and list your accomplishment on your site. Or, maybe a client who keeps a page on your server tells you about a really cool site on widget technology that he wants added to his page. So off you go to add a link to this site. Sounds like a piece of cake, right? Well, it is, as long as you're careful.

You make your first changes on the test files, save them, and test them. Looks fine until you put them in place. The first person that accesses the page gets sent off to Siberia! Not exactly what you wanted. Puzzled, you start debugging the problem. Are you responsible? Sure, you maintain these pages! The customer pays you for this, so dutifully you go off and find out, two days later, that the site you're referencing has moved and not bothered to let anyone know. You programmed everything perfectly, but it wasn't your fault. And it certainly wasn't the customer's fault. Now what do you do?

This is but one of the many problems of Web page maintenance that will confront and confound you. What is your level of responsibility towards the customer and Web page maintenance? Generally the amount of responsibility is determined in your negotiations with the customer at the onset of your service. You have several options: You can post the Web page into the server when the customer creates or modifies the page; you can give the customer access to the page storage location and let him create, modify, and process the page; or you can handle the modifications yourself. These factors affect all of the ways that you can make money on the site processing Web pages.

Rates

Ah, yes. It all boils down to money. Doesn't everything? If you decide to sell Web page space, then be prepared for several new issues to arise, such as a crashing end to the privatization of your Web server. Once you go public, you'll have to contend with a whole new set of administrative issues. See Chapter 2 for information regarding those issues. Aside from these concerns, you need to decide how much you want to charge for your Web pages. What criteria do you use to determine the cost and rates for ongoing Web page support?

This can be a bothersome issue for customers who don't understand what a Web page can do on the Internet, so on goes your PR hat. First, you must explain what a Web page can do for them, such as:

- Offer standard advertising of products and services on an ongoing basis, unlike a newspaper that charges for a finite period of time

- Offer prompt and timely updates to Web pages in response to changing market conditions or new customer products offered on the market

- Offer other Web connections to relevant products, technical support, and product updates via the Web page links

- Empower the customer with the ability to provide customer support to their own end users

After you've shown them how beneficial a Web page can be, you need to discuss maintenance issues:

- Frequent changes require time-consuming effort on your part, and effort does not come cheaply.

- Maintenance costs can be large if the pages are maintained on a per-change basis.

- Complex Web page modifications can cause echoed problems if one change causes another page's links to be broken. For instance, if a customer's home page has links to 15 other pages on his site, and those 15 pages each have 10 distinct links, one change to a link in a strategic location can cause half of those links to break.

- Subservient actions on a Web page can cause the need for lots of disk storage on the Web server, costing more for disk space than was needed for the Web pages themselves.

As with other business ventures, to build up a reputable and profitable Web business, you need to invest capital. In other words, you need to spend money to make money. Consider this analogy: You own a small business making and selling widgets from your home. The first year, your office consisted of a work bench in the garage. You had one employee—yourself—and you used existing tools and space. As widgets became more popular, you sold more and needed help to build and ship them. Your garage became increasingly crowded with no room to grow. So, to make more money and sell more widgets, you had to hire more people and build an attachment to the garage. A Web-based business is no different. If you profit from the Web pages, and your buyers demand more, then you should create more pages or enhance existing pages to further reflect your mission.

Now that you know what's involved—and there is a lot of stuff to digest here—I bet you're wondering what kind of figures you can expect to see. Most sites charge $25.00 per page per month to store their customers' pages. Pages are generally limited to 3,000 bytes. This price includes only posting and storage fees. If the customer wants changes, many sites charge around $35.00 per month per page, and they average about four changes per month. If this is a really hot site that requires many changes each month to keep up with the changing market conditions, then charging up to $100.00 per page per month is not unreasonable. However, when the customer's changes get this numerous and frequent, they generally hire their own Internet expert or negotiate special rates with you to maintain their pages.

You have to be very careful when you agree to do page maintenance because the volume of changes can soon find you making changes on a full time basis. When you get to that point, it's time to assess your position on the issue. Do you hire a Web page maintainer, or train the customer to do more on their own, losing their monthly payments? I hope not. After all, you're doing this for the money. My advice is to have your eye on an HTML expert, preferably waiting in the wings if possible. You also need to consider if the maintenance agreement with the customer includes keeping the last few revisions around for historical reasons. If this is the case, then your disk storage requirements rise sharply. Suppose 10 customers had five Web pages, each page averaging 3 KB in size. If the last three revisions had to be held for historical reasons, then you're storing four sets of pages for each customer. That's 600 KB of disk storage per customer. While that's not a huge number, consider these same 10 customers creating two more pages for each of the existing pages. This addition jumps the storage to around 1 MB for basic Web services. I've seen sites that have 200 customers in this situation, which means 120 MB of disk space is used just for Web page contents—and that's only counting text content. Most pages use graphics of some kind to enhance the display, so add 30 MB for each of these 10 customers. Add another 30 MB for sound files or other enhancements. We're talking a whole lot of storage here. These issues should play a role in your decision of whether or not to pursue the business of selling Web pages. Either way, you'll, at the very least, be dealing with your own Web pages, so let's talk a little bit about the languages—HTML and VRML—that you'll be using for your own needs.

An Introduction to HTML

Web pages are written in HTML—a text formatting language that tells a browser how to interpret and display pages like the ones you saw in Figures 3.1 and 3.2. HTML is simple to learn and use, but there are several programs and utilities available that allow you to create HTML pages with ease. Check out the Word for Windows utility add-in, which is free, or the shareware program HTML Assistant. Both are neat and simple to use, and produce code like that shown in Listing 3.1. The resulting Web page is shown in Figure 3.3.

Listing 3.1   Sample Web Page HTML Code

```
<TITLE>Panama City, Fla.'s Premier Web Site</TITLE>
<H1>Welcome to BCI Associates</H1>
<H2>A Systems Integration Firm</H2>
<P><P>
<H3>We're pleased you've chosen to visit our site, and welcome your
comments.</H3>
```

I'm not going to get into an HTML discussion because there are already dozens of books out there to tell you how to write and debug HTML pages. What I'm going to do is emphasize a few items of interest that can help you make your Web pages more exciting. The code in Listing 3.1 is in plain old HTML from the earliest days. Since then, numerous changes and enhancements have been made to the language. HTML 3.0 is the current version. To understand some of these concepts, let's look at the HTML source from the Netscape site, which uses the frames feature we discussed earlier. Listing 3.2 shows the HTML used by Netscape to create frames.

Listing 3.2   Netscape's Frame Source Listing

```
<FRAMESET ROWS="*,93">
        <FRAME
            NAME="content"
            SRC="/ndx.html"
```

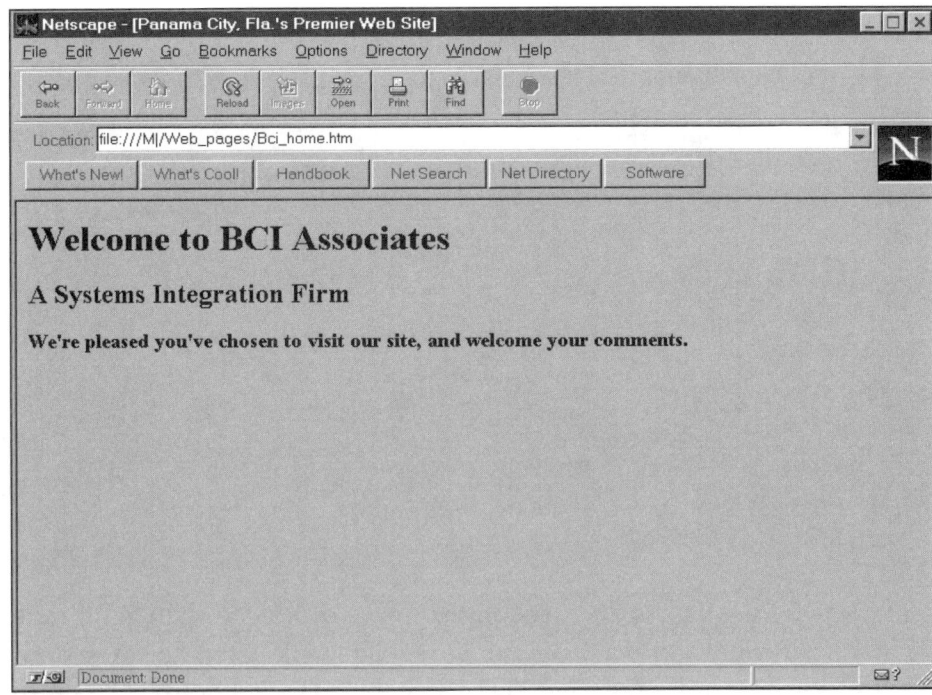

Figure 3.3 The HTML code from Listing 3.1 creates this Web page.

```
                MARGINHEIGHT=5
                MARGINWIDTH=10
                SCROLLING = "auto"
                NORESIZE>
<FRAMESET COLS="150,160,160,*">

     <FRAME
                NAME="frame1"
                SRC="/navigate/f1.html"
                MARGINHEIGHT=3
                MARGINWIDTH=0
                SCROLLING = "no"
                NORESIZE>


     <FRAME
                NAME="frame2"
                SRC="/navigate/f2.html"
                MARGINHEIGHT=4
                MARGINWIDTH=0
                SCROLLING = "no"
                NORESIZE>
```

```
<FRAME
        NAME="frame3"
        SRC="/navigate/f3.html"
        MARGINHEIGHT=4
        MARGINWIDTH=0
        SCROLLING = "no"
        NORESIZE>

<FRAME
        NAME="frame4"
        SRC="/navigate/f4.html"
        MARGINHEIGHT=4
        MARGINWIDTH=0
        SCROLLING = "no"
        NORESIZE>

</FRAMESET>
</FRAMESET>
```

Netscape's home page is an excellent example of how to spruce up a site to provide customers with a site that's worth their online charges. You don't have to have the latest version of HTML to do this, but it helps. The downside to creating such a site lies in the HTML learning curve—using the latest versions of HTML can and usually does take up more of the WebMaster's valuable time. When you decide to go fancy, a dedicated Web page creator almost becomes mandatory.

Another neat thing that you can do with Web pages is to create a search engine for databases. This is done using a form to enter in data as a request to find something, and then submitting the form to a backend processor, such as SQ Server or Oracle database engines. Let's look at the ever-famous Yahoo! search Web page, where hundreds of thousands of people visit each month to find information on the Web. Listing 3.3 shows a portion of the HTML code for the page, while Figure 3.4 shows the actual page.

Listing 3.3   The Yahoo Search Engine

```
<FORM METHOD=GET action="http://search.yahoo.com/bin/search">
<INPUT size=30 name=p>   <INPUT type=submit value=Search>
     <A HREF="/search.html">Options</A>
```

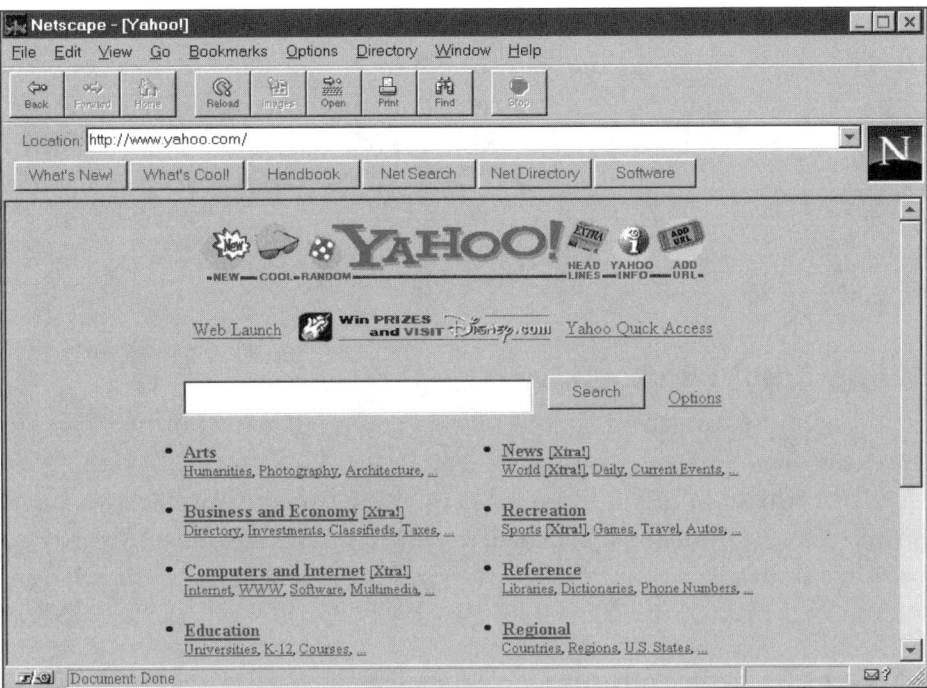

Figure 3.4   The Yahoo search engine.

The extracted source, which is partway down the listing, shows the search function. The user types in the requested search parameters or data to find, or selects the Options link to specify the conditions of the search. This step is useful to help narrow the search to the pertinent information so that you don't get 10,000 sites returned in the results.

And that's the brief rundown on HTML. If you'd like further information, I suggest you pick up a copy of *The New Netscape & HTML EXplorer* by Urban A. LeJeune (Coriolis Group Books, 1996, ISBN 1-883577-91-8). This superb reference goes into many aspects of HTML, CGI, forms, and scripting, to provide you with a detailed background of using the language. Next, we'll talk about a newcomer to the Web, VRML.

An Introduction to VRML

Virtual Reality Modeling Language, or VRML, sprang onto the Web about a year ago and provides an interesting extension to the Web page by using a 3D technique. This newcomer is astounding and demanding at the same time. To use VRML, add the VRML add-in component to your HTML-capable browser, and head off to the Netscape home site for a preview. When I was last there, they had a VRML graphic on screen as part of their home page. You might also want to check out the VRML Forum, shown in Figure 3.5, at *http://vrml.wired.com:80*. If you don't have a VRML add-in for Netscape Navigator, go to *http://home.netscape.com:80* and check out the new add-in products.

Adding Sound and Video to Web Pages

Two of the most appealing aspects of Web pages are the addition of sound and video files. Sound comes in several forms: WAV sound files and AVI video files, which include full sound capabilities in addition to video capabilities. WAV sound files are usually small in size and are used for such sounds as the alarms and radio files found in your Windows installation. Less than 50 KB in size, these files transfer from the Web to your system

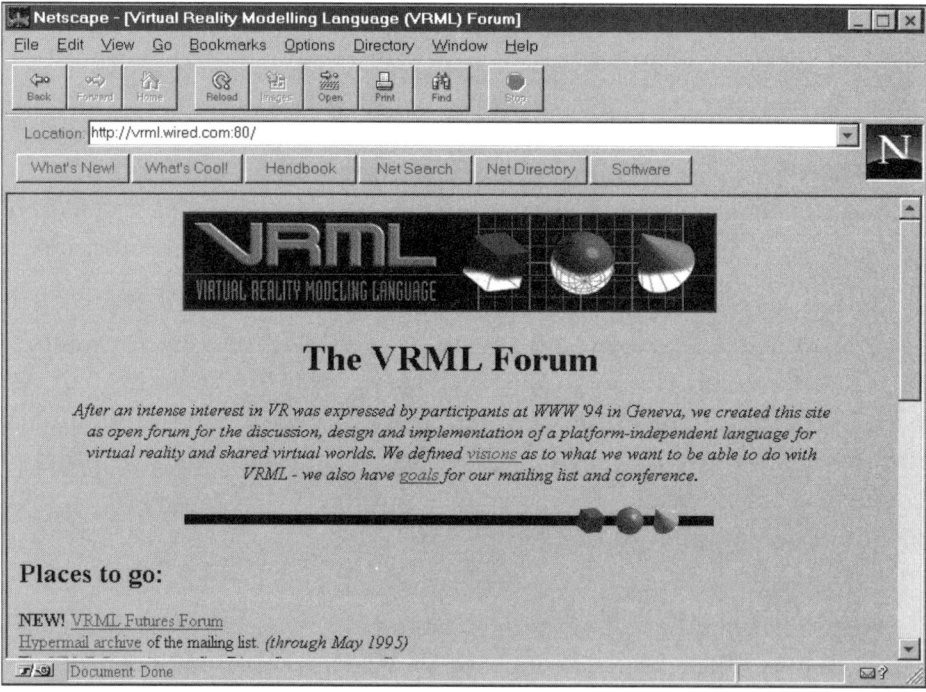

Figure 3.5   The VRML Forum.

relatively quickly and easily. The catch is that either your operating system has to support these files, or you'll have to get an add-in product that plays the files for you.

Netscape allows you to add this support by using *helper applications.* Simply download the product you need and install it on your system. Then add the helper application to Netscape's list of supported applications. Windows 95 supports audio WAVs and video MPEGs with built-in viewers. When either of these two types of files are downloaded as a result of surfing a Web page, Windows 95 starts the correct helper application automatically.

Both WAV and AVI files can be a great advantage to your Web page, but don't get overzealous. Video files are often very large, sometimes exceeding 5 MB in size. Just wait until a user hits one of these links and spends the next 30 minutes downloading the video file only to find out she went to the wrong link. She can cancel the file transfer, right? Yes, she can, but she may not know she is at the wrong place until it's too late!

The moral of the story is that sound and video can enhance your site and presentations, but you should caution the Web surfer that these files exist and you should post their relative sizes right next to the link. For an example of this technique, stop in at *http://sdsc.edu/SDSC/Partners/vrml/ examples.html,* which is shown in Figure 3.6. This is a VRML site, but the lesson still applies.

Selling FTP Space

Ah, yes. Now we get down to more money issues. Your business has spent thousands of dollars building this Web site, and your CFO would like to see some of this come back into the company. Can't blame the CFO, for sure, because this is what the Web site is supposed to be doing. To accommodate your customers' storage needs (based on your discussions with them and the 10 MB that's generally offered gratis) you decide to purchase a 4 GB drive at the onset of the project. However, after your site becomes operational, some of the customers have decided that there is no need for disk space at all, regardless of the cost (or lack of cost). You're stuck with lots of extra real estate. What to do, what to do. My suggestion: Sell the space as rented "office space" to compliment the Web pages that

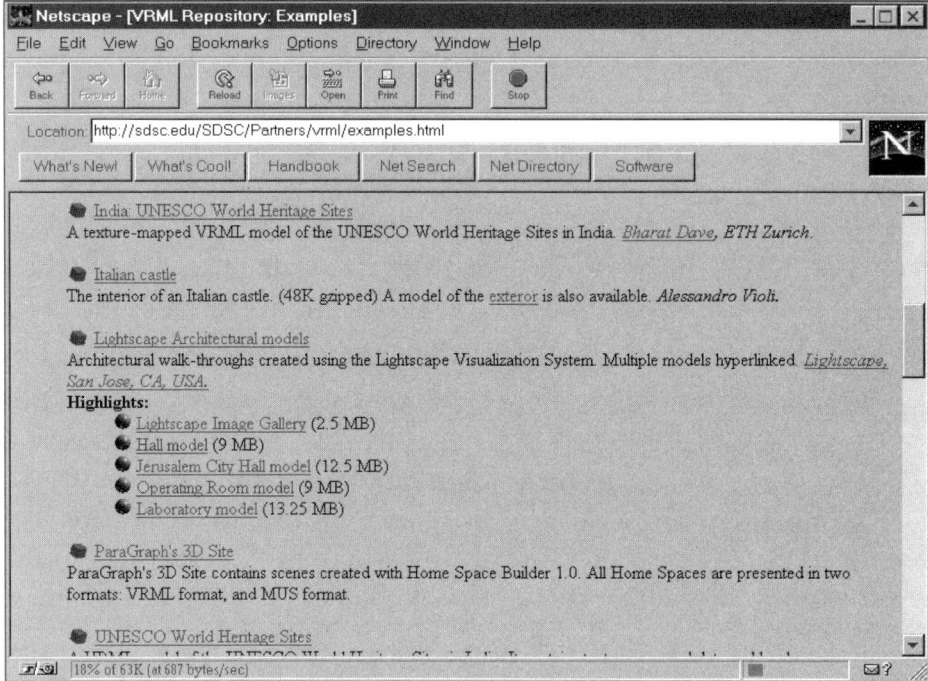

Figure 3.6 It's important to note huge files!

you've sold earlier. Now, your customers that have Web pages can store the files that compliment the Web pages right on the same server!

As an example, let's examine the HTML code from McAfee's Web page offer to download their anti-virus software from their Web site (Listing 3.4). Pay special attention to their usage of HTML to get to an FTP site.

Listing 3.4   References to Site Links

```
Download McAfee </TITLE></HEAD>
<BODY bgcolor="ffffff">

<P>
<P><CENTER> <IMG src="/gif/downban.gif" align="Middle" alt=""></P>

<P>
Fully functional, 30 day evaluation copies of all McAfee software
packages are available from these McAfee Associates FTP servers.
```

```
<UL><UL>
        <em>Note:</em>  You can select the <u><i>00-index.txt</i></u>
        files in any directory for some clues as to which directories
        contain which packages. For example, for anti-virus products
        you'd look in the <b>/pub/anti-virus/</b> directory. </UL></UL>
</P>

<P><HR><H2>
<A href="ftp://mcafee.com/pub">
Download Evaluation Copies of McAfee Products</A><BR><BR>

<A href="ftp://mcafee.com/pub/3rdparty">
Download Third Party Products</A> </H2></P>
```

Figure 3.7 shows the actual site. Notice the arrow that I captured pointing to the FTP link at *http://www.mcafee.com/down/download.html.* Nothing more than HTML code, no trickery.

Pretty neat stuff! So, keeping with the tone of providing the customer with a viable business solution, the use of Web links can achieve all sorts of

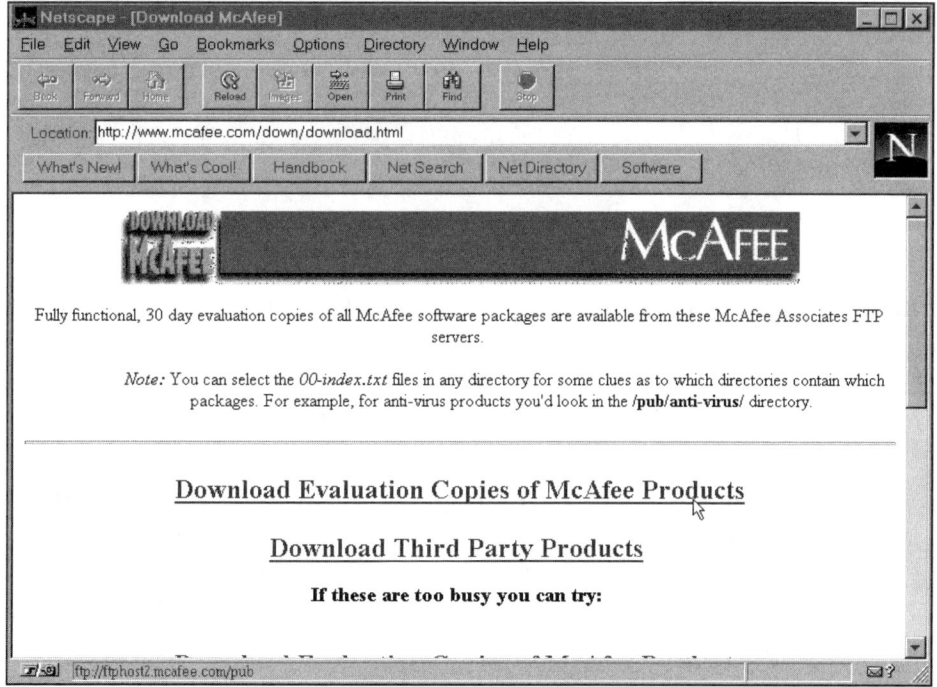

Figure 3.7   The McAfee Web site pointing to an FTP site.

productive tasks. If your customer so desires, you can maintain complete libraries of files for their users by simply posting the file to the FTP site and changing the Web link. This technique is especially helpful for novice users—they can simply enter the URL to go right to a file location.

Enough said about the necessities; what about money? This depends on a number of factors, but essentially you'll have to negotiate rates with each customer. One site I know of provides 10 MB free with each account, whether they use it or not. Exceeding that allocated amount results in fees ranging from block increases of 1 MB at a time to a per kilobyte charge. Generally, fees are $1 per megabyte per month per account, above the initial supplied amount. For a user of 125 MB with a 10 MB initial allocation, the fee would be $115 per month. Because it would take two years for this user to spend the amount of storage fees that would equal the cost of a decent-size drive to support this locally on the user's own PC, this provides both a needed and economical service. Of course, if you have 20 users with the same disk requirements, then you'll soon wind up with a disk farm to satisfy their needs, as shown in Figure 3.8.

How's that for supporting the user's storage needs? Using a monster disk array along with optical storage is a unique method of giving users dynamic storage without breaking your CFO's wallet right away. In the next few sections, we'll go over some of the related needs of an FTP storehouse, aside from the obvious fees to pay for it.

File Formats

In the computer world, there are as many file formats as there are wrong turns to take on the Web. However, you'll generally run across the more common types of files. It's nice to be aware of these file types when you start servicing your customers, because not all of them will know how to handle these files. Hey, there's another use for Web pages! Informational specifications called *FAQs*, or Frequently Asked Questions. These are short info sheets that provide pertinent information about common topics. For example, you could have an entire FAQ series on how to process files. Table 3.1 lists a few of the more common files, something about them, and how to process them.

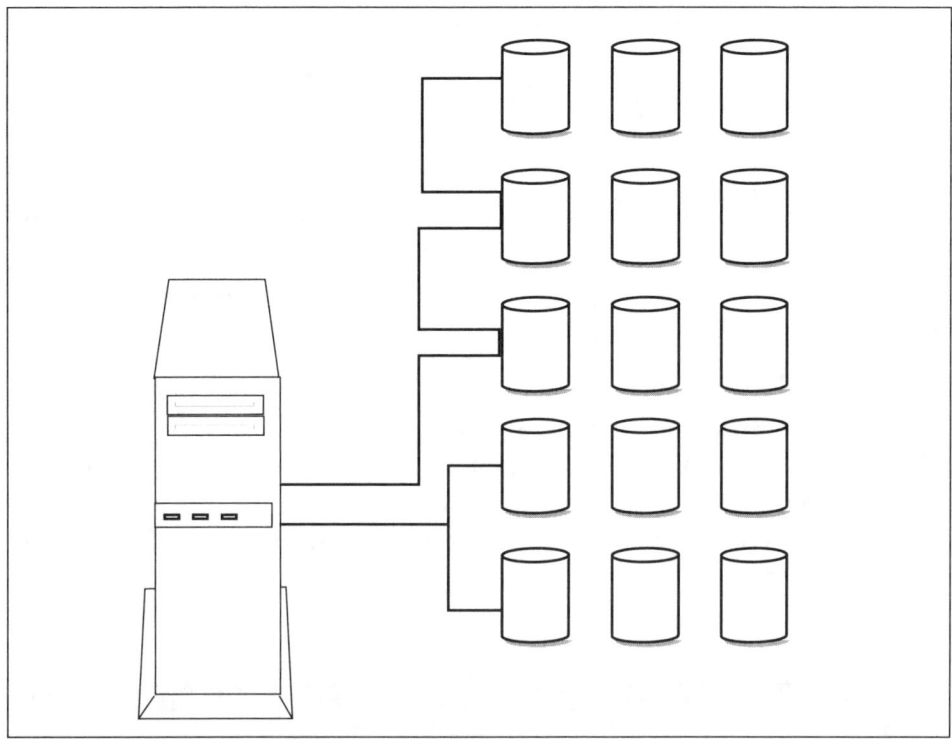

Figure 3.8   Representative view of a disk farm.

These are but a few of the files you'll find scattered across the Internet, but they're the ones you're most likely to run across and have to process. To help your clients out, you might consider purchasing the required files

Table 3.1   Several File Formats Found on the Web

File Type	Extension	Native Environment	Processor
DOS archive	ZIP	PKWare's PKZIP	PKUNZIP.EXE v2.04g
DOS Archive	EXE	PKWare's Self Extractor	ZIP2EXE.EXE
DOS Archive	LZH	Lharc, by Yoshi	LHA.COM
DOS Archive	ARC	DOS archives	ARCE.COM
Unix Workstation	Z	native Unix	Unix System
Unix Workstation	TAR	native Unix	TAR archiver on Unix

and posting them on your server so your clients can use these archives. These programs don't take up much space, and are relatively inexpensive. One more thing you might want to consider placing on your site is a program to process long file names. Figure 3.9 shows the 3Com FTP site root directory. Although several of the file names listed in the directory are standard DOS-style file names—up to eight characters plus a three-character extension—you can see a few that have longer names. If you look deeper into 3Com's directory tree, you'll see that some of the directory names are also longer than eight characters.

All of these longer names get truncated in displays and files of regular DOS formats, such as DOS and Windows 3.x. Windows 95, Windows NT Workstation, Windows NT Server, and OS/2 all support long file names, but if you *download* one of these long file name files, DOS users will see the name truncated. For example, the file name TEST_SYSTEM_FILE.EXE would be shortened to TEST_S~1.EXE. The 1 stands for the first iteration of the named file. Figure 3.10 shows an example of truncated files.

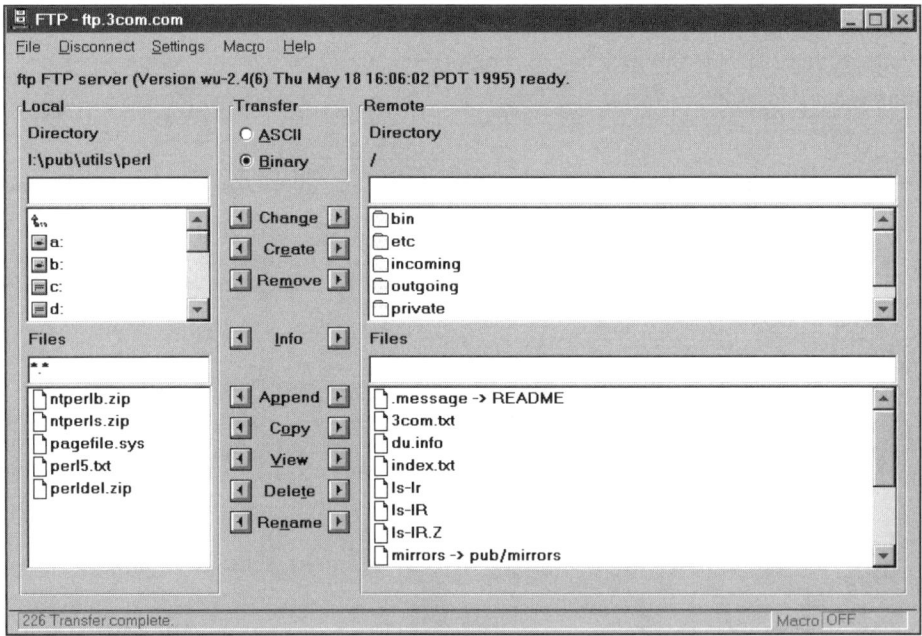

Figure 3.9   3Com's FTP site root directory.

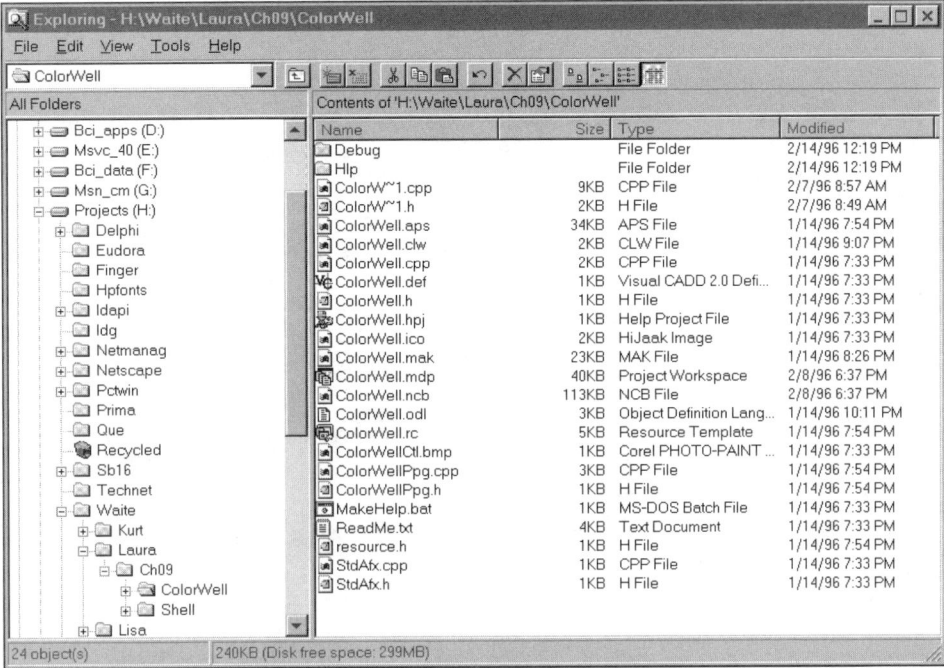

Figure 3.10 My truncated files.

The situation becomes sticky when you download files with a long file name, extract the short file name version, and then run the program. You may get an error message indicating that the program cannot find some of the files required to run the program. Sure it can't find them, the names have been truncated! Files with the "~" symbol (called the "tilde") are unusable as far as the programs that use these files are concerned, although DOS, Windows, and Unix can work with them just fine. You'll have to rename them to the correct names to use them. But how do you do that?

Using a program like WinZIP v6, open the archive to see the long file names preserved. From there, simply re-enter the correct file name. Figure 3.11 shows an archiver that preserves long file names.

Self-extracting files are the most commonly used because they require nothing on the part of the user except the ability to type in the name of the file. This also has the benefit of sharing files with unknown systems or destinations because if they can run a DOS program, then the self-extractor can be used to get to the files. I prefer to use self-extracting files wherever possible.

Name	Date	Time	Size	Ratio	Packed	Path
AppBarWnd.cpp	02/02/96	08:23	7,983	64%	2,858	Shell\AppBar\
AppBar.aps	02/02/96	08:21	33,936	74%	8,881	Shell\AppBar\
AppBar.clw	02/02/96	08:21	1,340	59%	543	Shell\AppBar\
AppBar.rc	02/02/96	08:21	5,344	73%	1,463	Shell\AppBar\
resource.h	02/02/96	08:21	1,012	63%	372	Shell\AppBar\
appbar menu.tif	02/02/96	08:16	201,548	99%	2,432	Shell\images\
AppBar.cpp	02/02/96	08:10	1,318	58%	560	Shell\AppBar\
AppBarWnd.h	02/02/96	00:43	1,453	55%	654	Shell\AppBar\
Subfolder.mdp	02/02/96	00:31	37,888	94%	2,285	Shell\Subfolder\
Subfolder.ncb	02/02/96	00:31	107,520	90%	10,713	Shell\Subfolder\
AppBarData.h	02/02/96	00:19	1,207	54%	558	Shell\AppBar\
AboutDlg.cpp	02/02/96	00:12	1,009	59%	411	Shell\AppBar\
AboutDlg.h	02/02/96	00:12	809	52%	388	Shell\AppBar\
AppBar.h	02/02/96	00:10	755	53%	354	Shell\AppBar\
AppBar.ico	02/02/96	00:10	1,078	68%	341	Shell\AppBar\res\
AppBar.rc2	02/02/96	00:10	398	57%	170	Shell\AppBar\res\
StdAfx.cpp	02/02/96	00:10	204	34%	134	Shell\AppBar\
StdAfx.h	02/02/96	00:10	502	44%	283	Shell\AppBar\
subfolder - change to the DLL version of MFC.tif	02/01/96	21:57	601,443	99%	7,463	Shell\images\
Subfolder.dll	02/01/96	19:11	57,856	77%	13,350	Shell\Subfolder\Debug\
early version of Subfolders.tif	02/01/96	17:43	15,197	66%	5,115	Shell\images\
create new class CProperties.tif	02/01/96	17:42	19,621	29%	13,880	Shell\images\
Subfolder.mak	02/01/96	17:34	11,674	83%	1,946	Shell\Subfolder\
Subfolder.aps	02/01/96	17:33	42,180	77%	9,658	Shell\Subfolder\
Subfolder.clw	02/01/96	17:33	1,213	60%	485	Shell\Subfolder\
Subfolder.rc	02/01/96	17:33	4,642	71%	1,362	Shell\Subfolder\
SubfolderPage.cpp	02/01/96	17:21	6,643	64%	2,424	Shell\Subfolder\

Selected 0 files, 0 bytes   Total 136 files, 2,161KB

Figure 3.11   An archiver that preserves long file names.

Storage Requirements

Alas, one of the main functions of a Web site now comes into focus. Every Web server has to have sufficient disk space to run normally, and you should give yourself enough for emergencies as well. Counting the operating system and basic Web server software along with the basic utilities, you'll use in excess of 400 MB of disk space just to get started. For a new site, I suggest that you have 500 percent of disk space free above the disk space used. For instance, if you've occupied 400 MB after the installation of NT Server and all of your Web server software, then you should have an additional 2000 MB free for the inevitable expansion that will occur in the coming months as the other issues of Web servers come to light. This may seem excessive at first, but trust me. Been there, done that, felt that. And it hurts when you get caught by the ears!

I've seen this aspect of Web server development bite many planners squarely in the wahoo. But it doesn't have to be this way. One way to ease this sting it to use SCSI controllers and devices. By using SCSI controllers you can operate as normal and then add storage like you usually do to SCSI controllers—one device at a time! It's nothing to shutdown the Web server and pull the cover to add a new drive. Fire it back up, format the drive, and boom—you're back online! You repeat the process each time you near capacity with the current drives. This approach presumes you're using standard drive architectures and not RAID. If you're using RAID, this is another story entirely. To increase RAID storage, you'll have to do a complete backup of all of the data on the RAID, add the new drive, reformat the entire RAID system, and then restore the data. This is true of nearly all RAID systems because RAID treats all of the physical drives as a logical unit of one drive. So, misplan your RAID storage, and you could be in for an exciting night at the office.

Perhaps one of the most underused storage mediums in the industry is optical solutions. You see plenty of CD-ROM drives and juke boxes for CDs, but how many rewritable drives are in the business office? One estimate recently placed the corporate environment as the next big push for computer resellers with rewritable optical solutions. These solutions include everything from small "zip drives," such as the Bernoulli 100 MB floptical unit, all the way up to the big 8-inch, 12-gigabyte platters. At one time, I contemplated the purchase of a 5½-inch 1.2 GB rewritable drive for my storage needs. The drive and controller cost $1700 and the media cost $49 per blank disk. Not exactly what you'd consider economical, so these kind of drives languished in the market. The next optical drive to make its debut was a little 3½-inch magneto optical drive like the Fujitsu DynaMo unit. This little gem holds about 217 MB of data after being formatted. It's the same size as a standard 3½-inch floppy, but twice as thick. The price of the drive, which is SCSI-1 compliant, was $700 when I bought mine, and the media is now $19 apiece. Now, the drive is priced at barely $500, but the media price hasn't dropped much.

When you are determining your storage requirements, the primary piece of information you'll need to know is: How much storage are you using on a weekly basis, and what percentage of that number is actual Web server storage? Obviously, if you've had to add a physical disk you know the impact on the Web server. Now, if you use a very large rewritable optical drive, you can amass up to 2.4 GB of storage using two of the 5½-inch SCSI rewritable drives. When the media fills up, just replace it with a fresh disk. An instant 1.2 GB per drive ready to go!

However, a time may come when you need access to the data on an existing disk but the disk will have to be changed out. If you're traveling 2000 miles away, that's kind of hard to do, since the physical disc will have to be switched. One solution to this problem is to go with jukebox optical disks the size of CD-ROMs that are used in a device that closely resembles the jukebox full of 45 records in the old ice cream shop. It's an expensive device, but with it you can store up to a terabyte of data that is immediately accessible to the users. Jukeboxes are especially useful because a 50-platter device can use up to 50 CD discs that will switch automatically under software control, so you won't have to physically switch the discs.

So, you can see that optical storage is a very viable alternative to many storage solutions. This type of storage provides you not only with adequate storage requirements for the present, but for the near and far future of your Web site. Figure 3.12 illustrates the architecture that I built for my Web server initially for testing, and then for the final Web server. I used the former to test the "proof of concept" model of the site, and the latter for security of data.

Employing a Hierarchical Tree Structure for Your Web Server

A hierarchical tree structure? What does this have to do with anything, you ask? Well, in a nutshell, your users will find it easier to navigate a responsible tree structure than to wander around your site trying to figure out what's what. Let's begin by examining the directory structure of my Web server, as viewed from the File Manager. This view is shown in Figure 3.13. Figure 3.14 shows the same directory tree as seen from an FTP logon from the Internet.

See the difference? While you can see the full tree from File Manager, the FTP view is considerably different. Why in the world would you use a subdirectory of "games" under the "drivers" directory? You wouldn't, so creating such would cause much distress for one of your regular visitors trying to get the latest update to a game you wrote. This is a quiet and seldom seriously thought out process that deserves some attention. In planning out your FTP usage, keep in mind the Web server as a whole. How are

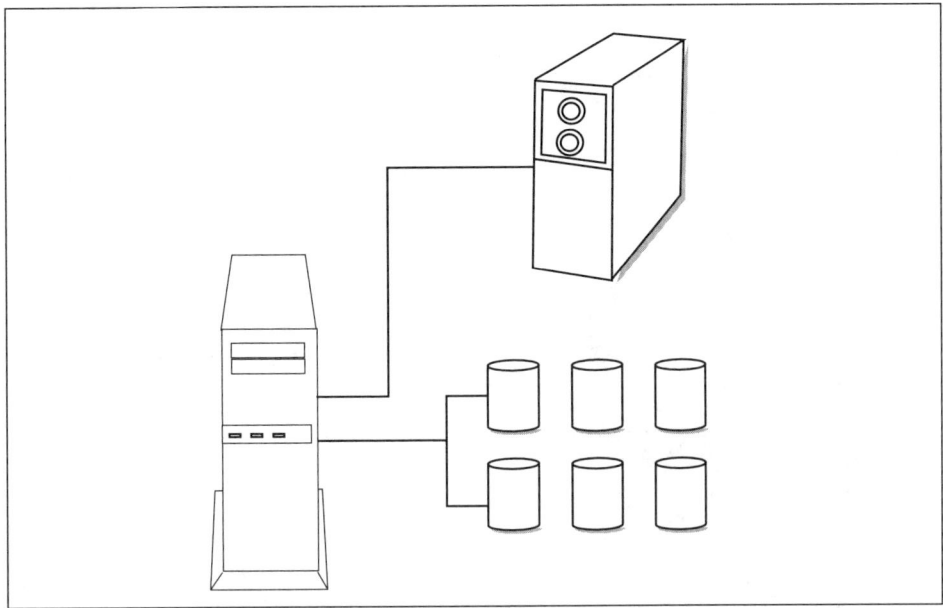

Figure 3.12 My Web server's disk subsystem.

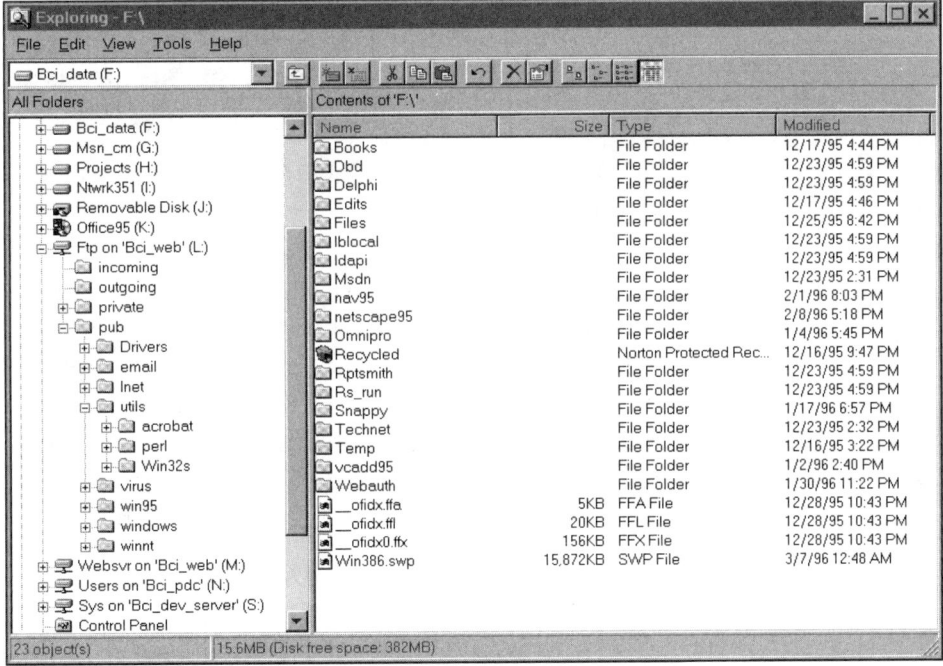

Figure 3.13 File Manager's view of my Web site.

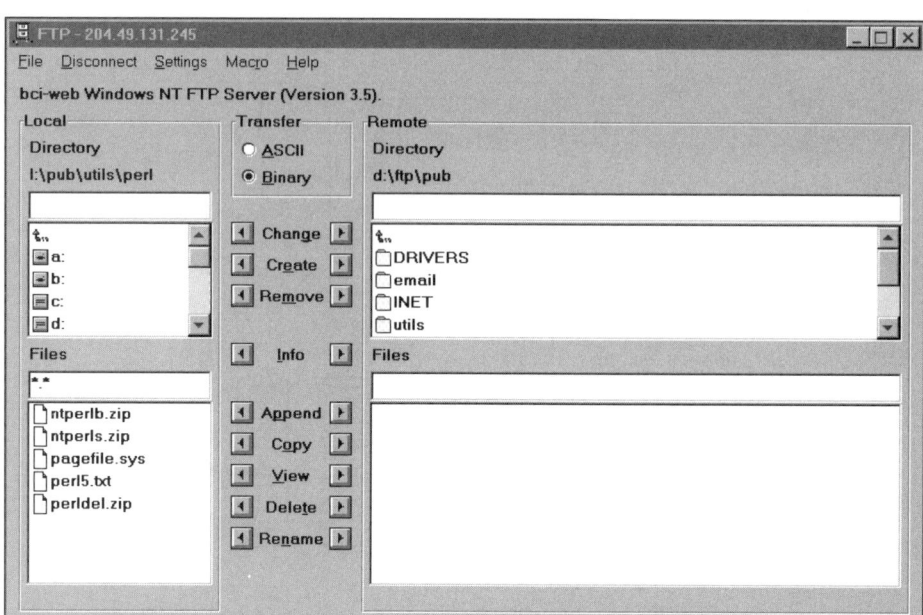

Figure 3.14   An FTP Internet view of the same site.

you serving your customers, and the business in general? Are there program or data files that the business' most important customer needs access to on an ongoing basis? Are these files top secret?

If they are, I guess you'd better protect them. (We'll talk about security in a moment.) How about those games updates? Give them away to any customer as a freebie, and you'll need to grant public access. Microsoft Windows NT Server makes this kind of sharing of data as easy as pie, but there's a little trick to remember. When you grant the proper permissions to the users, don't forget to share the directory! Set the same permissions to the same groups you do in the Security settings of File Manager. Once this is done, sit back and enjoy the secured environment of file access. Figure 3.15 shows the groups I've added to the FTP access. These are the basics of my site, and new users need only be added to a group when they're created on the Web server.

Client Access

Perhaps the single most important part of the Web server is security. Security is crucial to the proper growth and livelihood of your new toy. Give the wrong

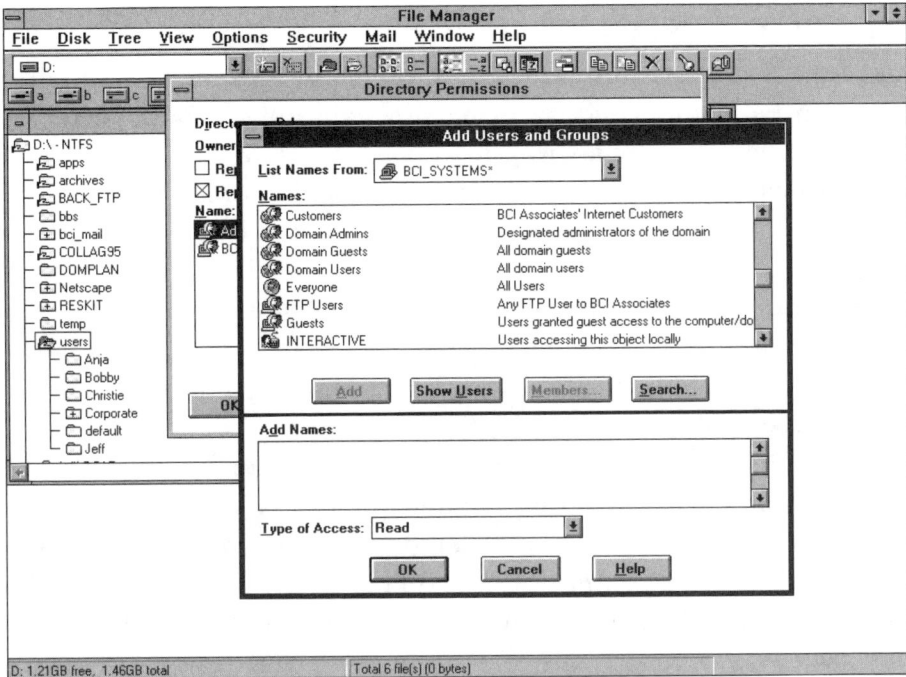

Figure 3.15   Changing the security permissions from the File Manager.

access, and one of your best customer's most vital business plans goes into the wrong hands. It's a lot like jumping off into a pit of pungie sticks. You know it's going to hurt, and you shouldn't do it, so be careful and *don't* do it!

Because your customers connect to the Web server in different ways, you have to institute proper security and procedures for all connection avenues. Mustang Software's Wildcat for NT Server, the Bulletin Board System (BBS) software that we'll use later in the book, has a function that allows you to connect to the BBS, then gateway out to the Web server just as if you're a network user. This form of access requires multi-level security and controls within the BBS itself and then in the Web server.

Network clients have a different set of concerns than do BBS users, as do Remore Access Server (RAS) users, and you'll have to address them at the proper time. If you have super-sensitive issues, then you may consider using a firewall for limited Internet access. In Chapter 12 I will discuss using Raptor Systems' firewall software to seal up any possible security breaches before they occur.

Web Server Consultant Services

One of the ways that you'll keep your CFO happy is to show how the Web server can be manipulated to further the cause of the bottom line. All across the Internet, there are ways to find information, but organization of that information is in a sorry state. This section will introduce you to a few ideas on how to use that information to leverage your business' Web server for a more profitable venture. In a manner of speaking, you'll bring together several aspects of the Web to your server, and entice customers to use you as a sole point of contact.

Marketing Surveys

Have you ever been sent one of those goofy marketing surveys that just chill your bones? They generally include questions requesting all sorts of information that you would never ever give out to anyone, let alone a stupid form. They ask you to verify all sorts of personal information including your income, number of kids, and social security number. I never send mine back.

Well, there's one way to set up a marketing survey, ensuring 100 percent response, and store the information away in a database for use at a later time. If you want what is offered at a site, even just a software demo package, then you must complete a survey form in its entirety. No gaps and no substitutions, it must be completed. Both Netscape and Microsoft use this technique for users wanting to download their Web server software. Their surveys take the form of an application, although I've never known anyone to be turned down. Figure 3.16 shows the survey you get when you download the Microsoft Internet Information server.

After you fill in the form, the data is sent to the Microsoft server backend tools that process the request, and they send you a return mail message that let's you know the status of your request. Although I do not know what these companies use their information for, I assure you it's used for something, or else they'd not have gone to the trouble to create and maintain the form.

Your Web server can be of great help on your (or your customer's) data gathering venture. Here are some suggestions for information you can

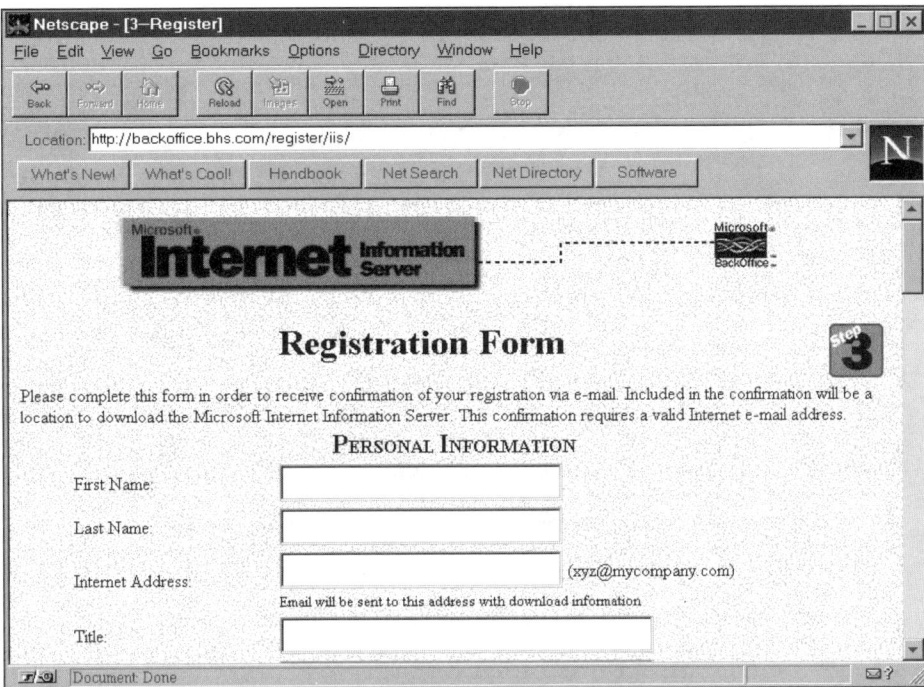

Figure 3.16 Downloading the Microsoft Internet Information server.

request and ways to use your server to gather data:

- Find the type of operating system your software users have

- Gather data on problem calls to your computer repair shop

- Register any of your software that the user has bought

- Send in a suggestion or complaint on the service of the Web server

- Perform an information-only request for proposals from vendors

- Send in product FAQ updates remotely

- Ask users what they want in a new or enhanced product

So you see, not every marketing survey is a real pain in the behind. Take your individual wants, needs, and company desires forward to the following sections and imagine how and where you could use such a form to solve a particular need or fill the gap in something the server software can't do. Remember that these surveys generate files and use disk space, so if a customer of yours is requesting surveys, the disk space they use goes up. Also, if a set of surveys reach a set demand or the results hit a specific volume, then you can generate email to someone to pay special attention to this fact. You can also be billing for the volume of email generated. You don't always have to bill for this data, but it's a potential you'll have to evaluate.

Creating New Servers

If you can build a new Web server, or rebuild an existing one, you have a very lucrative potential to become a consultant. In Chapter 2, we discussed Web server requirements from both a hardware and software standpoint. Let's quickly review these points:

- Perform a site survey to determine the actual needs of the server

- Talk to the customer, and many of the customer's users, to determine the overall purpose of the site

- Propose a Web server platform and finalize it

- Install and configure the prototype server

- Final configuration review

- Perform acceptance testing

Most of these tasks could turn into billable services if you were an Internet consultant.

Logistics Issues

Where there are servers and connectivity, there's the potential for disaster and mayhem. These two brothers seem to run hand in hand with Murphy and his law, so modern computing infrastructures are bound to fail at some point. This is the basic and most important premise of support issues. Here's a list of the most important issues that will cause great consternation to the CEO.

- If the Web server goes down, the business starts losing money immediately.

- If the Web server goes down, critical customers lose connectivity to other sites. Not a direct loss of money to you, but your customers are now without *their* money-making functions.

- If natural disaster strikes, the Web server would be unable to be recovered.

- If man-made disaster strikes, the Web server would be unable to be recovered.

Each of these items is catastrophic to the business, either in the basic premise that the data has been destroyed, or the access to the data has been removed. I added the last two to differentiate between unavoidable disasters, such as flash fires at the office over the weekend, and avoidable disasters like hurricanes, that generally come with a warning. In all of those circumstances, the opportunity to avoid disaster and continue supplying services to the customer is very possible.

 Critical data on the server should be backed up consistently over the weeks that the server is being built and then put online. This means purchasing a good tape drive, software, and a whole slew of tapes if these items weren't purchased in the initial server build. Power protection devices, utility software, and other issues such as this encumber the customer with a host of logistics questions that you can answer.

Billing Issues

Of course, all of this has to be paid for somehow. Not the server, but the services that the customer uses and allows their own customers to use. If you use the Web server to do double duty as a partial Internet Service Provider, then the customer may need someone to track the online time used by those connected to the Web server. You can also have billing set in place for selling FTP disk space, Web pages, and the like. All of these things allow you to use your Web server to help your customers, or if the need exists, for your customer to support and sell excess server space to their customers. It's a lot like leasing a building and then subleasing each of the suites.

Server Maintenance

All servers at one time or another need some kind of support, whether it's minor maintenance, training the new user, training the WebMaster on how to use the server, installing new hardware, or even providing routine support. There are plenty of businesses out there that would love to have the Web server earning its keep, but haven't the time, inclination, or the personnel to perform normal maintenance.

A perfect example of this is a past client of mine. I supported this client's 200-user network. The customer had plenty of their own computer people available to do the job, but they believed that they could save money by having their employees work a different and hopefully more productive job. The change was to hire outside technical support to do the same job that their own employees used to do. It's becoming more common these days to *outsource* service and support of networking systems.

Along the same vein, you can always find companies that need someone to create, test, maintain, and support their Web server or Web businesses while they simply use the results of the Web server's performance. Most server actions can be and are performed by outside maintenance sources, and many of these tasks are done remotely across the Internet. All you have to do is prepare the server for remote access by you or your assistant.

Sales Projects

By now, you've gotten the idea that Web servers are a massive advertising machine, if nothing else. This is how and why most sites realize significant gains in their products, or are accepted by the public. Well, not completely, but with the explosive growth of the Internet, the Web holds the best promise for small companies to look just like large ones. This is perhaps one of the best benefits of the Web. On the Web, a two-employee company seems just as large as IBM or Compaq. If you can create and maintain an enticing Web page, then you're likely to have a lot of visitors on that fact alone. Web surfers like to see what all of the hubbub is about, even if they're not buying. And window shopping has led to a substantial amount of sales.

Your most important sales event or product can be advertised on your home page as a current event. In fact, most Web sites actively involved in these kinds of sales have a "Coming Events" section. You'll also find lot of "New and Improved" or "News Flash" sections. If you head off to the Microsoft Corporation home site at *http://www.microsoft.com,* you'll see a "What's New" light bulb in the top center of their home page, as shown in Figure 3.17.

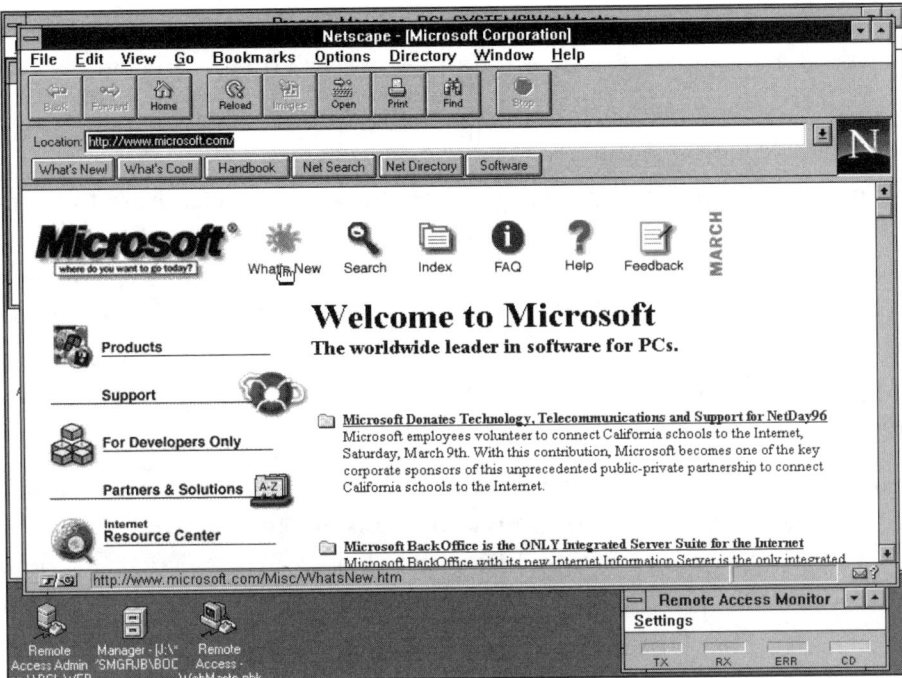

Figure 3.17 The "What's New" section of the Microsoft home page.

Look for these kinds of updates to clue you into the latest and greatest. Software vendors like Netscape often change their home page daily to keep up with the changing times. Be prepared to do the same for your customers if you expect them to get the most out of the Web server.

Beta Test Projects

This is one part of the Web that is so underused that it's not even funny. If you've ever been involved with the beta testing of new or improved products, you undoubtedly know that CompuServe has many forums for these vendors to host private testing forums for their products. Although this technique is still popular, many vendors have moved to private BBSs to do some of their testing. Few, if any, that I know of use the Web for such activities, although Microsoft Windows NT Server is fully capable of supporting private ownership and private operations.

So, how would one set up a Web server as a beta test site? Well, for one thing, design it to support as many users as you see posting bug reports, downloading file updates, and generally accessing the Web server at the same time. I was once refused admittance to a beta forum on CompuServe in which the maximum users were 250, so I was at least number 251 trying to get online.

To support that many users on a Web server, you'd at least have to have a T1 link, a Pentium 150 MHz server, and about 256 MB of RAM. This would be a massive server with a price tag to match. Who would such a server benefit? Actually, the business producing product ABC that manipulates the widgets discussed earlier needs to have some software debugged and prepared for the masses. A beta test Web server is perfect for this situation, and should be explored.

Here's how it would work: you use Web pages to let the users know of updates, the FTP server to download updates or post bug reports, the list server to carry on conversations about the beta project, the email server to send comments in or generally talk to others in private, and private home directories to store miscellaneous software. So you can see how a Web server can easily double as a beta test site, just like CompuServe forums do. Next, let's review the possibilities of using this very same configured server not as a beta test site, but as an Internet Service Provider.

Internet Service Providers

The Internet Service Provider (ISP) business is booming all across the country, and is expanding in Europe as well. Let me give you a brief tour of what it takes to be an ISP. I've been actively working with providers in my local area, and have done vast amounts of research into what it takes to provide Internet services. Do you remember the Web server we built in Chapter 2? Well, take that Web server and make sure it has at least 8 GB of disk space, and is configured as a RAID 5 system. Also, start the server off with 64 MB of memory, and be prepared to boost it up to 128 MB if necessary.

To provide decent access to the Internet, you'll need to use a T1 line, which costs $7000 to install and about $3200 a month in access fees for a full time dedicated connection. So to become an ISP, you're already looking at an initial investment of about $15,000 for hardware, software, and communications, with recurring costs of $3200 a month for the link. Let's not forget modems for the T1 link. Decent 28.8 Kbps modems can be had for about $200 (less for external modems), and you'll need a pile of them. How many is a pile? Well, to recoup just the monthly line charges of $3200, and this doesn't count the administration costs of the site, you'll have to have 128 paying customers at $25 a month. In these days of Internet providers on every corner, most ISPs are charging between $20 and $35 a month for unlimited access. Another popular pricing scheme charges $19.95 for 20 hours a month, and $1.25 for each additional hour.

ISPs often make money back by selling Web page services, as we discussed earlier, but that takes disk space and possibly the addition of another worker at the site. You can also sponsor special events in your hometown using your Web server, so there's use for an ISP. Even if you have people that don't use Windows 95 or Windows NT Workstation, some of them surely use Windows 3.1 and can get the Windows for Workgroups add-in. Native Windows operating systems connect to NT Server very easily and reduce connectivity problems significantly. If these users don't have any of the Windows-based software, then using a TCP/IP protocol software such as Trumpet WINSOCK is a superb solution. Because Microsoft Windows NT Server uses a Point to Point Protocol (PPP) schema to make remote connections, then Trumpet and other packages such as Netmanage's Chameleon TCP/IP software works well. As you can see, there are alternatives out there to solve the connectivity needs of the most finicky user.

The one issue that escapes some ISPs is that new Internet users have no software at all to start out! If they join up, how are you going to get then connected to your server? When you sign on new users, mail them an installation kit, and then assist them over the phone to get connected. One 3½-inch floppy, one package of shareware, and you've got another happy Internet user. Once connected to the Internet, then they can get as much software as they want, or that you can store on your own Web server.

Training and the Web Server

For this final portion, let's talk about your WebMaster. What are the qualifications of this person? How will he respond to a crisis? How well will he handle the pressure of dozens of users calling to find out why they're not able to connect? If you think this is a joke, or could never happen to you, then you're in for quite a shock! Quite a shock indeed, and a heck of a rude awakening.

I suggest that you have someone with a significant level of expertise with the Internet and Microsoft Windows NT Server perform a peer evaluation of the proposed WebMaster. You should also consider sending your WebMaster to a Microsoft Certified Training Center to provide advanced training with the Microsoft Windows NT Server and networking in general. Add to this a generous sprinkling of systems administration, and you've got one competent WebMaster.

Advertising on the Web

As your Web site expands, you may want to take it public and earn more, as I mentioned earlier in this chapter. Advertising is the most obvious and most lucrative approach, but how do you get up to speed? In this section, we'll explore advertising and identify how your business can leverage various functions of a Web server to make money and provide a competitive advantage.

Running a List Server

List servers perform automated mailing and messaging functions, and are nothing more than an automated BBS in which a message you post gets automatically sent back to a defined number of users. Let's take a look at a listserv we'll call ABC. This listserv has members 1 to 5. If user 1 posts a new message to the listserv, then member 2 can reply to it. However, the reply not only goes to member 1, who created the message, but also to members 3 through 5. In the meantime, member 4 also replies to member 1. Member 4's reply gets sent to all list users, as well. As you can see, this is a great way to disseminate information, but can result in massive amounts of data being transmitted across the server. Remember the suggestion I had for a rather large hard drive for the server? Thought I was joking, eh?

In Chapter 12, *Web Server Administration*, we'll be examining the list server in depth. We'll be using NTList from SoftDisk Corporation as our Microsoft Windows NT Server list server. NTList is included on the accompanying CD-ROM. It's fully functional, but you have to apply for a key to use the product at *http://www.ntsoftdisk.com*. Having said that, I'd like to let you preview the steps that will be necessary to form a list server:

- Install the list server software
- Define new lists

- Add users to the list

- Specify distribution

- Monitor disk space and performance

Not much to it, but there are a few things to watch for, and disk space is one. If you're planning on running many lists, then running them on a separate physical or logical disk from the FTP, Web, and operating systems is a good idea. Periodic purging of old list members and message traffic is also a good idea.

Another excellent use for a listserv, and this is one that is used all the time, is for users to subscribe to a list and receive messages for updated products, materials, services, and notices of problems. I subscribe to several in which I receive the Microsoft Windows NT Server BackOffice mail for happenings and updates to BackOffice. I also receive updates from several book publishers so I know when new books hit the marketplace. The NTList product I used for this book sends me update notices, bug fixes, and enhancement notices.

Business Resources

Every business—including your Web site—needs to have backing of one type or another. When I was looking for support for my business in some expansion projects, AT&T Capital Services (*http://www.att.com*) was one that I turned to for help. There's similar support available all across the Web in the form of research shops, search engines like Lycos and Yahoo, but also the Microsoft Knowledge Base articles. The next section will talk about Gopher and how that can help you, but for now let's keep the discussion to what you can do for your customers.

An exciting prospect of customer support is self-help in which the customer uses your resources to help themselves. If the problem is something the customer can't resolve, then you come to the rescue—and that means money in your pocket. One way to help your customers help themselves is to use a networked CD-ROM tower. This device allows seven drives to function as a single entity by using software that maps all the drives to one drive letter. You could then purchase a network license for products such as

Microsoft's TechNet technical solutions resource and put it on the network for your customers.

While you may think that paying $2,000 for a networked CD and another $5,000 for the CD-ROM tower is a bit pricey, consider the alternatives. Last summer one of my clients' servers crashed and died a horrible death. Upon finding that the problem was a bad hard drive controller, they were fully capable of replacing it and bringing the server back online knowing that they'd have to update the NOS drivers for the new controller. However, restarting the server yielded numerous system crashes that were unresolvable and seemingly pointed to another, more serious problem.

In reality, the problem was that the new controller's native operating mode was to support drives faster than those that existed in the server at that time. So, they were hung out to dry, right? Wrong. Using one of these CDs for technical support, they found the solution was to jumper the new controller to operate at a mode of data transfer that was compatible with the existing drives. But isn't that what the manuals are for, you ask? Well, the manuals for the controller cover installing the controller and installing the NOS drivers, and that's about it. A few minor troubleshooting tips and hints, but nothing of the magnitude they saw. But what about tech support? Tech support can be wonderful, but consider this: Your drive crashes at 2 AM on a Saturday morning of a three day weekend. A critical business decision has to be made bright and early Tuesday morning, and you can't get through. Somebody's toes are in the wringer over this one if it doesn't get fixed.

This situation really happened to a very good customer, and now they're an even better customer! Why? We had a CD-ROM of technical support handy on our server; they dialed into our 1-800 link and found the solution. It was a single-user version of the network edition, but it did the job nicely, thank you. Oh, and Murphy truly rules the roost in the computer room after midnight. 'Nuff said.

Another approach you might take is to include custom-written applications on your server using CGI and Visual Basic to access your business files where applicable. I'll go into detail on this subject in Chapters 9, 10, and 11, but remember that business opportunities exist wherever you make them happen. Serve your customers a full plate of options and services and they'll be eating out of your hands.

Using Gopher

If you've ever used the Web as a single user rambling through the Internet, then you've probably used a Gopher server to help you find information. Gopher got it's name as the mascot of the University of Minnesota, where the gopher is a native animal of the area and the Gopher server started. Gophers make their way around by burrowing through the small areas to find virtually anything! The Internet Web server packages we'll use in future chapters will exploit Gopher servers in much the same way. Unless you're using the Microsoft Internet Information Server, which has a gopher server built right into the software package, you'll have to purchase a gopher server. One excellent place to find NT products is at the Beverly Hills Web site, shown in Figure 3.18 and located at *http://www.bhs.com*.

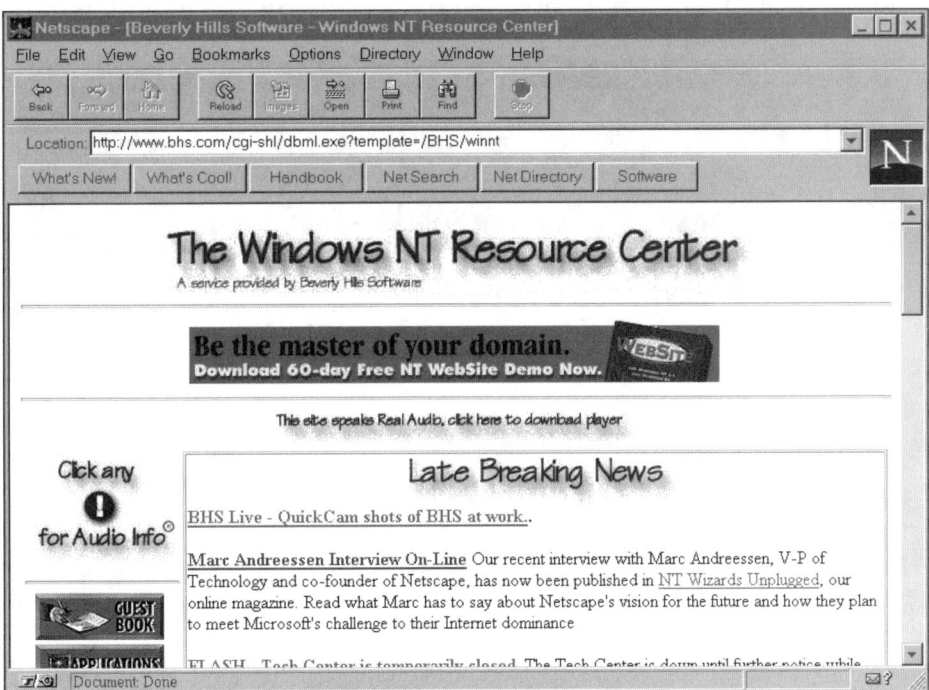

Figure 3.18   Beverly Hills software's Windows NT Resource Center.

This site is dedicated to serving the needs of the Microsoft Windows NT Server community, and is one of my top picks for products and general information about Microsoft Windows NT Server. They perform some really serious checks across the Web for new and exciting products, and they also sponsor many topics such as finding NT support, services, and NT user groups.

Internet Shopping Malls for Advertising

Shopping on the Web for the general public has grown significantly over the last two years. It has become such a lucrative business that many Web sites have included links to stores offering related items or just fun stuff, as a courtesy to their clientele. Sometimes, you can find good deals on a vacation plan or cruise, and other times you'll run across a Web site like the one shown in Figure 3.19.

The PC Cyber Shop (*http://Web2.pc-today.com/browse.html*) is chock full of computer deals. When you've browsed the Web as long as most of us have,

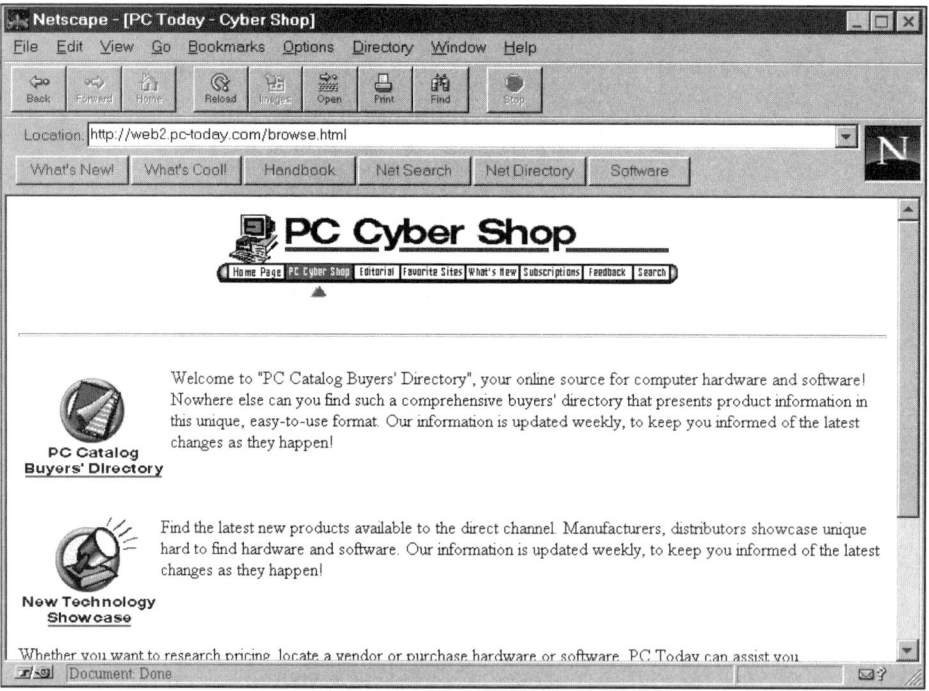

Figure 3.19 PC Cyber Shop.

you eventually compile a Web link base of dozens of juicy places to go and find things, do things, or just keep you informed. There's so much out there that many larger companies, and some small ones too, devote one person a day to cruising the Web locating sites with similar content to their site (a real dream job). Adding these links to your Web server for your customer base is a good business move and excellent advertising on the Web.

Think about the prospect of having a link on your Web page that has a button icon right next to it telling the reader about a new tool your business now has ready, or a really sweet deal for new clients. All they have to do is click on the button one inch from the links, and voila! Instant advertising for you on their way to other sites on the Web.

Etiquette on the Web

One of the last things I want to discuss about advertising is when and where to do it, and when and where not to do it. You see, there's an unspoken set of rules by which you must abide if you wish to prosper on the Web. If you send email or advertising to an unwanted party or parties, then count on getting some unruly responses, called *flames*, about your requests and/or your heritage. People pay for email accounts and other useful items on the Web, and to receive someone's unwanted literature about products and paraphernalia is a sure bet to get you smacked.

If you receive a large volume of flames regarding an unsolicited message, your server may slow down tremendously. This happened recently at an East Coast company that violated the unwritten rule of the Web, and these folks got slammed with enough mail that their ISP crashed their twin Web servers. Needless to say, this company got kicked off of the ISP as soon as they found out what happened.

The moral to the story of advertising is that if you want to pitch your goods and services, do it on your own server, so people come to you. Don't send unsolicited email to anyone if you don't want to have their unhappy responses swamping your server. If you want to advertise outside of your server's realm, go to one of the many shopping malls that exist all across the Web and buy office space on their servers. If you don't know where to look, go to *http://guide-p.infoseek.com/Titles?qt=shopping+mall* and look at the list that comes up. Figure 3.20 shows the search results.

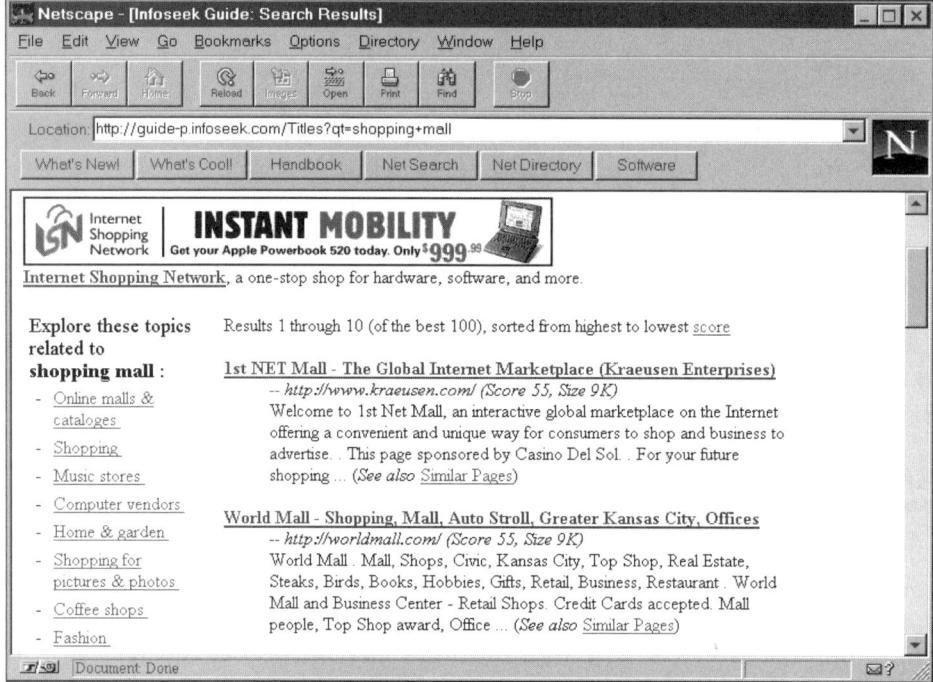

Figure 3.20   Shopping malls on the Web.

News Services

Running a news service is much like operating a business. You've got customers with different needs, different expectations of what news is, and how to use it to their benefit. When you consider adding a news service to your offerings, you need to determine the volume of news so that you can decided whether or not to use a completely different physical server, or just install the software on the same server as the Web server itself. If you don't have a news service from your ISP, you might be interested in trying one of these free services:

- news.sisna.com

- mediasoft.net

- ulke.himolde.no

- news.cis.nctu.edu.tw

- ccnews.ke.sanet.sk

- news.ak.net

If one of these won't work, you may have to resort to using a paid service to feed you a full news system. Try one of the following services:

a2i communications
1211 Park Avenue #202
San Jose, CA 95126
Data: (408) 293-9010 (v.32bis, v.32), (408) 293-9020 (PEP)
 (log in as "guest")
Telnet: a2i.rahul.net [192.160.13.1] (log in as "guest")
FTP: ftp.rahul.net [192.160.13.1], get /pub/BLURB
info@rahul.net (a daemon will auto-reply)
(UUCP, news feeds, mail feeds, MX forwarding, name service)

Anterior Technology
P.O. Box 1206
Menlo Park, CA 94026-1206
Voice: (415) 328-5615
Fax: (415) 322-1753
info@fernwood.mpk.ca.us
(UUCP, connectivity, name service, MX forwarding, news feeds)

CERFnet
P.O. Box 85608
San Diego, CA 92186-9784
Voice: (800) 876-CERF
help@cerf.net
(connectivity, name service, MX forwarding, news feeds)

Colorado SuperNet, Inc.
Attn: David C. Menges
Colorado School of Mines
1500 Illinois
Golden, CO 80401
Voice: (303) 273-3471
dcm@csn.org
(UUCP, news feeds)

connect.com.au (Australia)
Attn: Hugh Irvine (hugh@connect.com.au)
 Ben Golding (bgg@connect.com.au)
Voice: 61 3 528 2239
(UUCP, connectivity, name service, MX forwarding, news feed, PPP, SLIP)

Demon Internet Systems
internet@demon.co.uk
(Internet access, SLIP, PPP, name service)

DPC Systems
537 Cloverleaf Drive
Monrovia, CA 91016 (Los Angeles County)
Voice: (818) 305-5733
Fax: (818) 305-5735
Data: (818) 305-8444
Email: connect@dpcsys.com
(UUCP, name service, MX forwarding, news feeds)

ExNet Systems Ltd
37 Honley Road
Catford
London, SE6 2HY, UK
Voice: 44 81 244 0077
Fax: 44 81 244 0078
exnet@exnet.com or exnet@exnet.co.uk
(UUCP, mail and news feeds)

Gordian
20361 Irvine Avenue
Santa Ana Heights, CA 92707 (Orange County)
Voice: (714) 850-0205
Fax: (714) 850-0533
Email: uucp-request@gordian.com
(UUCP, name service, MX forwarding, news feeds (for SoCal sites only))

Hatch Communications
8635 Falmouth Avenue, Suite 105
Playa del Rey, CA 90293
Voice: (310) 305-8758

Email: info@hatch.socal.com
(UUCP Usenet news and email, SLIP connections for ftp and telnet)

HoloNet
Information Access Technologies, Inc.
46 Shattuck Square, Suite 11
Berkeley, CA 94704-1152
Voice: (510) 704-0160
Fax: (510) 704-8019
Modem: (510) 704-1058
Telnet: holonet.net
Email: info@holonet.net (automated reply)
Support: support@holonet.net
(UUCP/Usenet feeds, local to 850+ cities nationwide)

infocom Public Access Unix,
White Bridge House,
Old Bath Road,
CHARVIL, Berkshire,
United Kingdom,
RG10 9QJ
Voice: 44 [0] 734 344000
Fax: 44 [0] 734 320988
Data: 44 [0] 734 340055 (you can register online interactively)
Email: info@infocom.co.uk (send a message with ALL in the subject)
(UUCP, Usenet Feeds and Internet Email to UNIX, DOS, ATARI, AMIGA, MAC)

Internet Initiative Japan, Inc.
Hoshigaoka Bldg.,
2-11-2, Nagata-Cho,
Chiyoda-ku, Tokyo 100 Japan
Voice: 81 3 3580 3781
Fax: 81 3 3580 3782
Email: info@iij.ad.jp
(UUCP, news feeds, mail feeds, MX forwarding, name service, anonymous FTP and UUCP services, domain registration)

Iowa Network Services
312 8th Street, Suite 730
Des Moines, IA 50309
Voice: (800) 546-6587
FAX: (515) 830-0345
Ftp: ftp.netins.net
WWW: http://www.netins.net/
Gopher: gopher.netins.net
Email: info@netins.net
(UUCP, news feeds, mail feeds, MX forwarding, name service, domain
registration, SLIP)

JvNCnet
B6 von Neumann Hall
Princeton University
Princeton, NJ 08543
Voice: (800) 35-TIGER
market@jvnc.net
(connectivity, name service, MX forwarding, news feeds)

MSEN, Inc.
628 Brooks Street
Ann Arbor, MI 48103
Voice: (313) 998-4562
FTP: ftp.msen.com [148.59.1.2], see /pub/vendor/msen/*
info@msen.com
(UUCP, connectivity, name service, MX forwarding, news feeds)

MV Communications, Inc.
P.O. Box 4963
Manchester, NH 03108-4963
Voice: (603) 429-2223
Data: (603) 429-1735 (log in as "info" or "rates")
info@mv.mv.com
(UUCP, name service, MX forwarding, news feeds)

NEARnet (New England Academic and Research Network)
10 Moulton Street
Cambridge, MA 02138

Voice: (617) 873-8730
Fax: (617) 873-5620
nearnet-join@nic.near.net
(connectivity, name service, MX forwarding, news feeds (for
NEARnet sites))

Netcom—Online Communication Services
4000 Moorpark Avenue, Suite 209
San Jose, CA 95117
Voice: (408) 554-UNIX
Data: (408) 241-9760 (login "guest," no password)
Telnet: netcom.netcom.com [192.100.81.100] (login "guest")
Email: info@netcom.com
(UUCP, connectivity, name service, MX forwarding, news feeds,
other services)

NET GmbH—Network Expert Team
Figarostr. 3
70597 Stuttgart, GERMANY
Voice: 49 711 97689-21
Data: 49 711 97689-22 (login "guest," no password)
Fax: 49 711 97689-33
Email: info@N-E-T.de
(Internet access, SLIP/PPP, ISDN, UUCP, connectivity, name service,
MX forwarding, news feeds, mail feeds, domain registration,
other services)

Northwest Nexus Inc.
P.O. Box 40597
Bellevue, WA 98015-4597
Voice: (206) 455-3505
Data: (206) 382-6245 (log in as "new")
Fax: (206) 455-4672
info@nwnexus.wa.com
(Internet access, SLIP/PPP (dial-up, dedicated, 56k, FT-1), UUCP,
news feeds, mail feeds, MX forwarding, name service, NIC
registration, Nutshell books)

The PC User Group
P.O. Box 360
Harrow
London
Voice: 44 81 863 1191
Fax: 44 81 963 6095
hostmaster@ibmpcug.co.uk or hostmaster@ibmpcug.uucp
(UUCP, mail and news feeds)

Performance Systems International, Inc.
11800 Sunrise Valley Drive, Suite 1100
Reston, VA 22091
Voice: (703) 620-6651 or (800) 827-7482
Computerized info: all-info@psi.com
Human-based info: info@psi.com
(UUCP, connectivity, name service, MX forwarding, news feeds)

Portal Communications Company
20863 Stevens Creek Boulevard, Suite 200
Cupertino, CA 95014
Voice: (408) 973-9111
Fax: (408) 725-1580
Data: (408) 973-8091 (V.32/PEP) Call for local node near you. Nodes
provided by Sprintnet or Tymnet have additional charges.
Telnet: portal.com
Email: CS@portal.com
(UUCP, news feeds, mail feeds, MX forwarding, mailing lists, file
archives, domain registration, FTP, SLIP/PPP, commercial
menu-based online service, shell, telnet, irc, gopher, interface
software available for Amiga, PC, and Sun)

SURAnet
8400 Baltimore Boulevard
College Park, MD 20742
Voice: (301) 982-3214
Fax: (301) 982-4605
Email: news-admin@sura.net
(connectivity, name service (for SURAnet sites), news feeds (for
SURAnet sites))

TDK Consulting Services
119 University Ave. East
Waterloo, Ontario
Canada N2J 2W9
Voice: (519) 888-0766
Fax: (519) 747-0881
Email: info@tdkcs.waterloo.on.ca
(UUCP, news/mail feeds)

Telerama
Luce McQuillin Corporation
P.O. Box 60024
Pittsburgh, PA 15211
Voice: (412) 481-3505
Fax: (412) 481-8568
28.8 K: (412) 481-2392
Email: info@telerama.lm.com
(UUCP and ?)

UUNET Canada, Inc.
1 Yonge St., Suite 1400
Toronto, Ontario
Canada M5E 1J9
Voice: (416) 368-6621
Fax: (416) 369-0515
info@uunet.ca or uunet-ca@uunet.uu.net
(UUCP, connectivity, name service, MX forwarding, news feeds)

UUNET Technologies Inc.
3110 Fairview Park Drive, Suite 570
Falls Church, VA 22042
Voice: (703) 204-8000
Fax: (703) 204-8001
info@uunet.uu.net
AlterNet (network connectivity) info: alternet-info@uunet.uu.net
(UUCP, connectivity, name service, MX forwarding, news feeds)

UUNORTH, Inc.
Box 445, Station E

Toronto, Ontario
Canada M6H 4E3
Voice: (416) 537-4930 or (416) 225-UNIX
Fax: (416) 537-4890

Xenon Systems
Attn: Julian Macassey
742 1/2 North Hayworth Avenue
Hollywood, CA 90046-7142
Voice: (213) 654-4495
postmaster@bongo.tele.com
(UUCP, news feeds, mail feeds)

XMission
P.O. Box 510063
Salt Lake City, UT 84151-0063
Data: (801) 539-0900 (log in as "guest")
Telnet: xmission.com [198.60.22.2] (log in as "guest")
FTP: xmission.com [198.60.22.2], get/pricing
support@xmission.com
(UUCP, news feeds, mail feeds, MX forwarding, name service, SLIP/PPP)

XS4ALL
Postbus 22864
1100 DJ Amsterdam, HOLLAND
Voice: 31 20 6200294
Data: 31 20 6222174 (V.34 28k8)
31 20 6265060 (ZyXEL 19k2)
Fax: 31 20 6222753
Email: account@xs4all.nl
(Internet access, SLIP/PPP, ISDN, UUCP, name service, MX forwarding, news feeds, WWW home pages)

News Servers

News servers operate on many different protocols, but the most commonly used is called *NNTP*, or *Network News Transport Protocol*. The predominant news server, however, is ruled by Unix machines using the *UUCP*, or *Unix to Unix Copy Protocol*. These servers run under one of two operating modes:

SUCK feed, which means that your news server receives only the news that you ask for; and forced feed systems, which means you get the entire newsgroup system. This latter method means that, at any one time you could be receiving as much as 4 GB of news articles and updates daily.

And, at that kind of volume, a lowly ISDN or FT1 link is next to useless. For that reason, most ISPs generally use an established news server or tag onto another server for the feed. This approach usually incurs some charges for your site, but is worth it in the long run if you're short handed in the maintenance and support department. The following information was extracted from the Usenet news FAQ, which is stored in its entirety on the CD-ROM included with this book as file newsfaq.txt:

If you just want to read Usenet yourself, then putting your machine onto Usenet is probably not what you want to do. The process of doing so can be time-consuming, and regular maintenance is also required. Furthermore, the resources consumed by a full Usenet setup on a machine are significant. You need to consider:

- Disk space for the programs—a few MB for the binaries, another couple of MB for any sources you keep online

- Disk space for the articles—currently (as of August, 1995) around 450 MB a day, although it is possible to minimize the amount of disk space consumed by articles by carefully selecting which newsgroups and/or hierarchies you wish to receive

- Communications bandwidth—for practicality, you should have either a 14.4 Kbps/28.8 Kbps modem link or 56 Kbps or faster NNTP link; it is no longer possible to run a full feed over 28.8 Kbps modems or 56 Kbps TCP/IP NNTP links

- Fees—if you're paying someone to provide you with a news feed

A serious Usenet server system, carrying all of the standard eight Usenet hierarchies, a large hunk of alt.*, and various regionals, is typically going to need a Sparc 2 or better, with 32 MB or more RAM, and at least 3 GB of disk space. One particularly good high end, but inexpensive, configuration is INN 1.4unoff2 on an HP 9000/712 system, with 96 MB of RAM, and 5 GB of disk space.

A home system can usually fit into a much smaller machine, such as a Sun 3 or 386-class PC compatible, plus 25-50 MB of disk for news. Until recently, one supporter's home machine was an AT&T 3b1 (about the performance of an IBM PC/AT) with 60 MB of disk. The setup worked just fine for a small news feed and a fair amount of mail.

If you plan on running a Microsoft Windows NT Server as a news feed, plan on running equivalent news servers.

If you decide to create your own news server, pay close attention to Chapters 5 through 8, where we'll install, configure, and test run four Web servers. At the same time, we'll integrate a news server in those environments so you can see how it's done.

Newsgroups

The news services are structured according to the intended topics. There were nearly 20,000 newsgroups the last time I checked, and more are being created weekly. However, fewer than a dozen core newsgroups form the classifications of the rest of the entire news service. Here's a rundown on the major groups:

- alt—Alternative news, which involves everything from cooking to submarine screen door maintenance

- comp—Anything related to computers

- biz—Business matters

- rec—Recreational issues

- news—Learn about newsgroups

The CD-ROM included with this book contains a file called newsgrps.txt, which lists all the current newsgroups. From this reference, you can search—offline—for any prospective newsgroups you may want to join.

Naughty News

Ah, yes. The wild and wooly Internet offers many things to many people, including some of the not-so-charming aspects of the Web. Your business should tag the marketplace you intend to use to please your customers, and steer clear of the less-than-desirable remaining groups. You can subscribe your server to the most applicable groups and filter out the undesirables in much the same way a client does, as in Figure 3.21.

After you've used enough newsgroups to last you a lifetime, you'll realize that the existing newsgroups are about as complicated and useless to some people as screen doors on a submarine. At this point, the WebMasters often decide to create a newsgroup to solve a particular need instead of finding groups that only partially meet the needs of your customers.

Front End Tools to Access Your Business' Data

I want to give you a preview of how your business can leverage the Web with many different methods. This last section goes over some of the ways

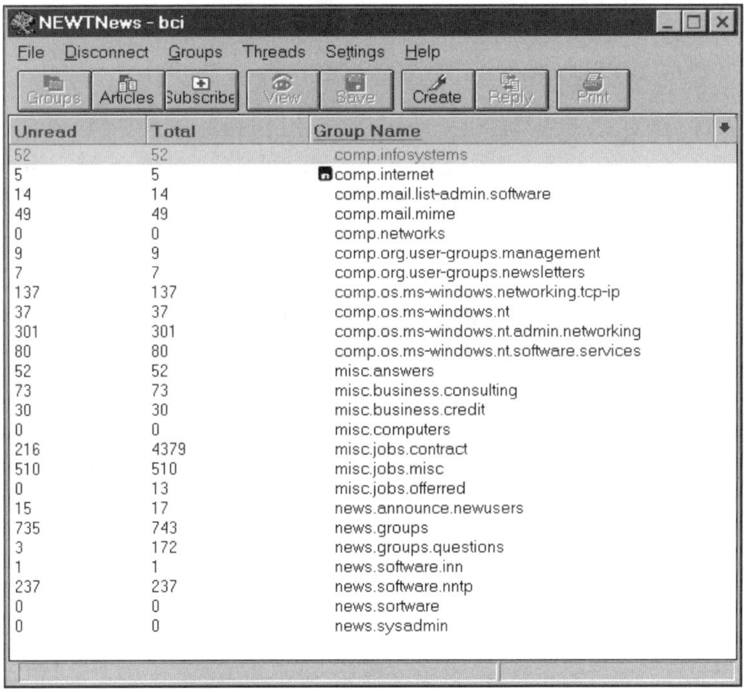

Figure 3.21   Subscribed newsgroups.

that each of the functions below will manipulate data and return favorable and useful results to your users. This section serves as a preview of Chapters 9, 10, and 11.

HTML

Hypertext is a neat way to create and build Web pages along with handling the usual support issues. I pointed out earlier that HTML is nothing more than a textual markup language that is interpreted by the Web server software and executes certain commands. It has a defined set of commands, just like what is considered to be regular programming languages such as C or C++. Unlike those compiled languages, though, HTML has to be parsed into distinct commands. If these commands are not readable, then it fails. There are dozens of HTML authoring tools available to you, many of them are free, but many of them are quite expensive.

When we install the Web servers and create basic Web server home pages, we'll be using HTML Assistant Professional v2. We'll create dual HTML versions of Web pages because not everyone uses a Web browser client that works with HTML v3.

CGI and Visual Basic

Users interface with HTML to enter data that is presented in a form made easy for the user to understand. Once the data is entered, it is ushered back to software running on the Microsoft Windows NT Server. The software packages that process the data are called *backend servers*, and include packages such as Microsoft SQL Server, Oracle, and Sybase. These backend servers cannot interpret HTML, so a middle processing system is required. Enter the Common Gateway Interface, or CGI. CGI comes to the rescue along with some programming language to tie these two—CGI and the backend—together. Because these CGI functions are likely to change weekly, it's nice to use an easy and effective programming language. We'll be using Microsoft's Visual Basic v4.0 for this task, and the source code is supplied on the CD-ROM for your altering pleasure.

Scripting

Scripts are another form of utilizing the data entered into the HTML form. In this case, the data is used to automate sets of actions to get a desired result.

For example, you can use scripts to register a user onto a list or a product listing database. Scripts are basically a kind of batch file for the Web.

Summary

In this chapter, we've learned about many things dealing with business on the Web. There's so much to cover that you could easily write an entire book about business on the Web from a purely business perspective. The topics we covered included:

- Selling Web pages

- Offering FTP space on the server

- Giving Internet Service Provider-style services

- Learning about Web server requirements

- Learning how to entice your customer with new business arrangements on the Web

- Learning about advertising on the Web

I hope you found this information enlightening. There are a lot of business opportunities on the Web just waiting to be discovered. After completing this chapter, you're up for the challenge!

Selecting and Setting Up Your NT Server Hardware

Chapter 4 is our first big step into actually building our Web server. The previous three chapters have provided an excellent introduction into the hows, whys, and wherefores of business Web servers. Now, it's time to explore the inner workings of your Web server. We'll begin our exploration by examining the hardware designs of different servers. I'll present three options for server configurations, providing information on specific vendors' types of systems and designs that will help you keep that pestering CFO happy for a time. More specifically, we'll cover:

- The different styles of Web servers you can build

- Memory requirements for the server as a whole

- Different RAID subsystems

- Internet connectivity options

- Web server applications and disk usage

- Server backup operations

- Ways to avoid the temperature demon

- Power protection devices

When you finish with this chapter, you'll be armed to the teeth with genuine practical data to make the installation of the Web server software a cinch. All of this information comes from years of experience, research, hours of lost sleep, and months of reading in my technical library. It thrills me to no end to be able to bring this to you, so let's proceed! If you want to shake up your current distributor, take a look at the Web page at *http://Web2.pc-today.com/browse.html* and check out the vast array of computer components advertised there.

Practical Hardware Solutions

In this section, I will specifically address the core issues behind, or rather within, a Web server—that is, the hardware ideally geared to the Web server. As I mentioned before, I won't be covering the installation of a Microsoft Windows NT Server; I assume that you already fully understand that process. My goal is to illuminate the reasons why a normal network server may or may not serve your purposes as a Web server, depending on the volume of traffic you'll have, and what you can expect to invest to ensure your building a productive Web server. These next three sections profile the minimum, average, and optimum physical server hardware needed to perform as a prototype, low volume usage, and a very serious Web server, respectively. Each section is broken down further for consideration of the processor, memory, disk systems, and other I/O devices, such as serial ports.

Minimum Server Hardware

I consider this server setup to be a testbed environment to get your server baselined. If nothing else, you can use this model to get your thoughts together and decide upon a course of action without getting into too many money, time, and configuration issues. For this discussion, I'm using a standard desktop PC (by 1996 standards). This server model is likewise suitable for low volume user groups of fewer than 25 users.

Processor

As processors go, the 66 MHz processor is largely considered to be the minimum to use. As for vendor, I use Intel, but I've also used AMD successfully; other specialists have reported using Cyrix and others with no problems. The 66 MHz processor is capable of performing at the rate of 2.1

MIPs, or millions of instructions per second. At one time, this was considered to be a real barnburner of a CPU, but has since been overshadowed by stronger performers.

The other aspect of 486DX processors is the use of the internal 4 KB cache located inside the processor. A *cache* is a temporary holding area for data while the CPU processes the data. You can think of a cache as a small handheld shopping bag—like one of those little hand-carried plastic baskets you use when you only need to pick up a few items. This is where you keep your goodies before you get to the checkout stand. If you think you've forgotten something, you simply refer to the carrier to see if it's there. If not, you go back to the aisle and get one of whatever you need.

A cache is used in much the same way, as shown in Figure 4.1. The CPU retrieves data from the disk drive for its usage, but it also keeps a copy of the most recently ordered 4 KB worth of information in the cache. If the CPU needs more information to work on, it refers to the cache. If the cache has it, then the CPU gets it from there. If not, the CPU retrieves it from the disk in a second disk access. Because the cache is closer to the CPU electronically, and the cache is faster than the disk system, this process has a net effect of speeding up overall system operation to a degree. To further clarify, I'm talking about the *internal* cache (within the physical processor itself), not the level 2 cache installed on the motherboard.

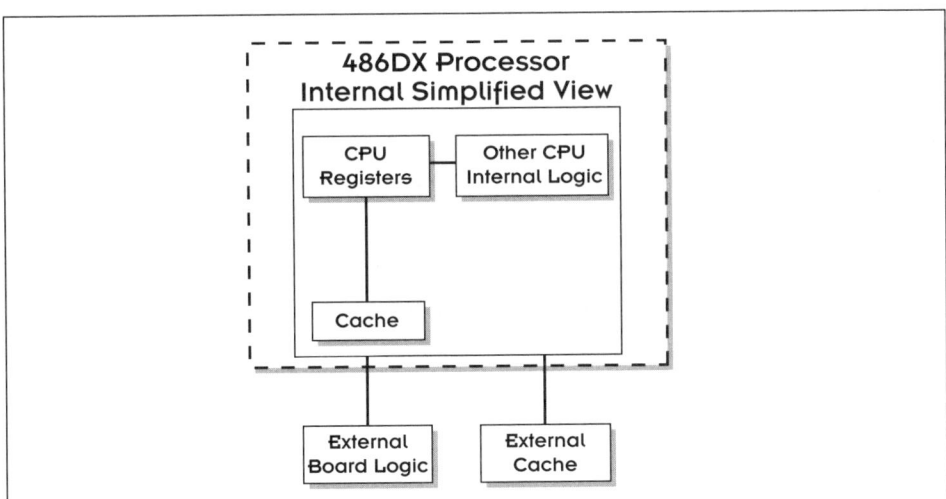

Figure 4.1   A cache subsystem.

However, not all caching operations are good! As in much of life, too much of a good thing isn't always good for you…or your CPU. Just like parking lots, the larger a cache is the more time it takes to find the desired information—or a car, in the case of the parking lot. The CPU will then spend much of its time waddling around looking for information that may or may not be present. To put this into perspective, the cache system in these slower 66 MHz CPUs runs at an average of 35 nanoseconds access time. This means that to get to the data inside the cache, it takes an average of 35 nanoseconds to set up the physical cache chips to be accessed plus 250 nanoseconds to set the rise time and circuit access time. Additional overhead for the cache can amount to as much as 25 more nanoseconds. These figures are general times meant to keep the intricate details out of this discussion, but you get the idea. Now, we're up to 310 nanoseconds of processing time, or roughly one third of a microsecond.

So what's a nanosecond? It's one thousandth of a millionth of a second, or one billionth of a second. That's humming right along as far as you and I are concerned, but it's relatively slow as far as the processor is concerned. The CPU itself can handle 2.1 million instructions per second. If you do a little quick math, then you'll see that if one cache operation were to support one CPU instruction, then only six cache access cycles would be available per CPU instruction cycle. This isn't a very hospitable working relationship between the two, so something's got to give. Normally, such a CPU/cache system would support in excess of a 20:1 ratio. When we get into our discussion on faster systems, I'll show how this problematic situation is cured, resulting in much improved system throughput.

Memory

Our minimum server must start out with at least 16 MB of memory no matter how you configure it. Because of their initial configuration and the popularity of the 30-pin memory modules, these 486 systems have a widespread installation base. Unfortunately, this popularity presents a unique problem for the industry. Most, if not all, of these 486DX2-66 processors are installed in motherboards that exclusively use these 30 pin memory modules, and only use eight memory slots. This means that the Microsoft Windows NT Server installation had better work on 32 MB of memory, or you've got a problem. Memory is not upgradable in most of these systems unless you use one of the add-in 16-bit memory cards, such as the AST RAMPage. These are fine devices, but on the ISA bus they're murder on performance.

The problem? On a normal installation of Microsoft Windows NT Server, up to 24 MB of this main memory is in use to get the server off the ground. Use the RAS component, and another 4 MB of RAM is in use. So you can see from this that these minimum servers are good for prototyping and a few users, perhaps up to 10 concurrent users either from your network or dialing in remotely. One solution to this is to use some of the new memory conversion modules on the market. These conversion modules take four of the 30-pin modules and effectively make them a single 16 MB module. Another approach is to purchase an adapter that uses the newer 72-pin memory and mates it to the 30-pin memory slot of this motherboard. The kicker is that the motherboard's memory controller has to have a *legal memory configuration* available to support this new memory capacity. A legal memory configuration is one where the memory module you install must match the motherboard's allowable usage.

On 486 and above systems, you must install four of these 30-pin modules at a time to have a proper installation. Because these are 32-bit computers, the memory must also match. The 30-pin modules are 8 data bits wide, so four of them must be used at a time. These four modules together are called a *bank* of memory. Table 4.1 illustrates part of the legal configuration of my 486 testbed's system. All amounts are in megabytes.

It's important to notice the placement of the memory modules to accommodate these values. There's no place for 24 MB of memory, nor can 4Mx9 modules be placed in Bank 1 by themselves, as they can be in Bank 0. You

Table 4.1   An Example of a Legal Memory Configuration

Amount	Type	Bank 0	Bank 1
4	1Mx9	1Mx9	
8	1Mx9	1Mx9	1Mx9
16	4Mx9	4Mx9	
20	mixed	4Mx9	1Mx9
32	4Mx9	4Mx9	4Mx9

must carefully consider these restrictions if you want to have a successful server. What do you do when it's time to increase memory? Blame the CFO for not funding a better server? Not likely. This table is one reason that these systems are best relegated to test servers, or desktop PCs for a user.

Disk Systems

Disk drives have evolved over the years into something that none of us ever thought was possible. Certainly, this is one of the most important parts of the server that exists, and it is also the most neglected. While it's nothing to swap out a disk drive or add in new storage, this is not the case with Microsoft Windows NT Server when it comes to Web servers. Although this process was a cinch in Windows 3.1—all you had to do was complete a full backup across the drive, install the new drive, and restore the old software—NT's intricacies change the situation radically.

Many of the existing computers today still have 300 to 500 MB hard drives installed, which is fine for desktop or prototype Web servers installing the bare minimum software. When you get into production servers, however, do yourself a favor and stay away from drives with less than 1 GB of space. Even if it means using the 486DX we've talked about here with its 500 MB drive and adding a second drive of 1 GB, as shown in Figure 4.2. Such a scenario may exist for a 486DX2-66 that used to reside on a desktop running a 340 MB IDE drive. As common as these are, very inexpensive drives of nearly 2 GB capacity exist now for EIDE and SCSI. It's simply a matter of adding a second drive or perhaps a second controller, if you choose to go the SCSI route.

 Give yourself the capacity required of even a bare Web server. As soon as you figure out what you'll be using the Web site for, you can then migrate the extra drive out of this minimumly configured server into a more powerful one by removing the drive and controller as a pair, if the controller is usable in the new system.

I/O Devices

Always the topic of conversation, but never remembered until after the fact, the I/O devices may or may not be important to your server. With this

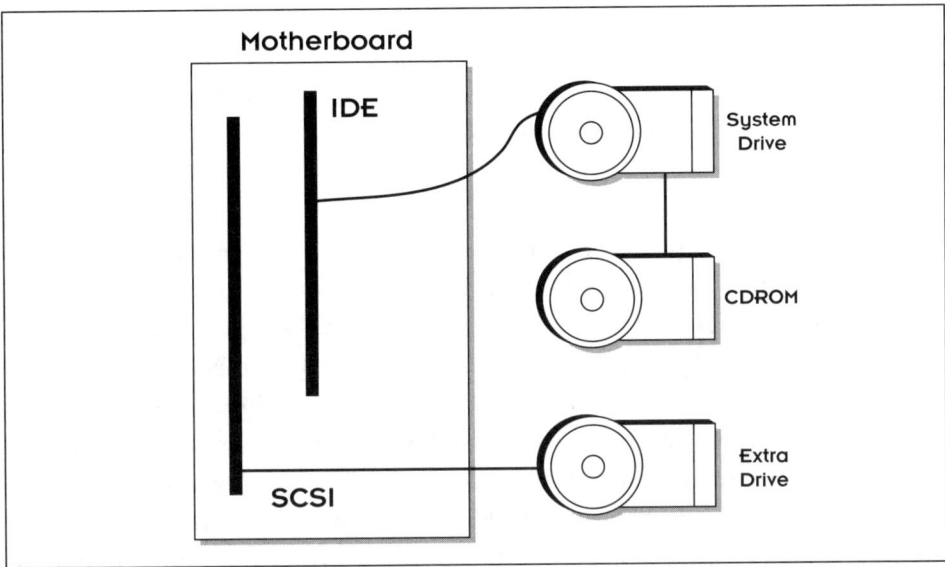

Figure 4.2 Adding a second hard drive.

minimum server, you'll surely have the basics of I/O installed: two serial ports and one parallel port. A game port may or may not be installed, but is obviously not required and it won't hurt anything by being there. This basic I/O card is necessary for the mouse to run on the serial port, since most of these older systems used a serial mouse. The second serial port is useful as a modem port for an external modem so you can remotely log in and take care of your assigned duties.

I'll get into specifics in the next section, but these older I/O cards do not have the capacity to sustain high-speed modem data transmissions. As such, they're relegated to the role of maintenance connections and general data usage. I wouldn't count on them at all for serious communications. One of the minimum devices used is a 14.4 Kbps modem to proof test the server links to other sites. While 14.4 Kbps seems aggravatingly slow for data, consider that this barebones Web server is being used to propagate ideas into reality, and as such needs no serious money thrown at it.

Average Server Hardware

This is where we begin to bring our server into the modern day of computing. Not all the way, mind you, but close enough that you'll begin to see how Web server performance is affected by the use of better hardware to support the software. We'll also begin exploring some hardware not considered to be the normal usage in the Microsoft Windows NT Server world, but that will benefit us for the Web server.

Processor

The processor now graduates into something a bit more powerful. As I mentioned before, the absolute minimum processor from the previous section was a 66 MHz 486DX model, but today the 486 goes all the way up to 120 MHz speed demons. Sure, the Pentiums rule the roost around the PC these days, but does this mean the high-end 486s should be forgotten? Intel has killed off the 60, 66, and 75 MHz Pentiums so far with rumors that the 90 and 100 MHz processors aren't far behind, given the advances in processor design. As of March 1996, the 166 MHz Pentium Pro is out on the streets and tearing up the competition with the high-end processors. The prices match, I assure you. But so does the performance!

A Pentium 166 handles the system at about eight times the horsepower of a 486DX4-100 because of its sheer speed and enhanced design. One of my customers uses a Pentium 90 single processor network server to handle 150+ users on a daily basis, running Unix on the server, and the system is averaging 60 percent utilization. This leaves 40 percent of the processor's abilities available for those extra-demanding times.

To put it into another perspective, my testbed 486DX2-66 running 32 MB of memory recently averaged 85 percent utilization when I was downloading files from one network station directly to the server, had a second machine downloading files via a modem and then moving the files across the network, and a third user was logged into the Web server doing his thing. Memory utilization was at 95 percent to match the processor's load factor. This means that a fourth user was likely to cause all sorts of problems if a demanding task was requested of the Web server. It all points to considering the Pentium 90 as the average Web server's processor of choice. Because Intel is killing off the 486 line and the earlier releases of Pentiums up to 100 MHz, the Pentium 120 is likely to become the minimum processor available for your average Web server. This isn't necessarily a bad thing. The next section about memory ties into the processor to show how they complement one another.

Memory

This is where building a Web server gets interesting. To start things off on a good foot, you'll want to put at least 32 MB of memory in this system. It doesn't matter what the makeup of the memory is at this time, but 32 is a good figure to start with and get you going. An average Web site means including FTP and Telnet capabilities and perhaps one Web server software package to support users browsing the Web. Don't include Microsoft Windows NT Server's remote access into this equation, as 32 MB will just about be used up for this server. You can have as much FTP storage as you want, just watch the extra applications you may want to run.

Memory Types

I said that memory type and design does influence the performance of the system, and now I'll explain how and why. The form itself—30-pin or 72-pin memory modules—doesn't matter. What does matter is the speed of the module now that you're getting into a more serious Web server. I'll explain briefly. The speed rating of the module represents the average time required for the processor to retrieve the data in the module itself, and is rated in nanoseconds. If the processor has to do too much waiting to get data out of memory, then the processor waits for one clock cycle while the memory bus controller catches up.

It's a lot like sitting at a red light with three cars in front of you, and the first car in line is a very timid driver. This person won't press onward when the light turns green for fear of a last minute driver buzzing the intersection, and the light is one of those 45 second wonders. You'll eventually get through, but it takes time. If the processor (you) has to wait for someone else to get going (the timid driver), the only recourse is to wait until this situation is resolved.

One way to resolve this is by using something called *page mode interleaving* of the memory system. This means that while one part of memory is waiting to have data placed into it, the other part of memory is being used by the processor. When the first part of memory gets its data, the other part will be done servicing the processor. Now, the processor switches to the second part of memory that was being filled while the first part was being used, and the processor doesn't miss a beat...usually. Figure 4.3 illustrates page mode interleaving. While this is a really simplistic view of memory

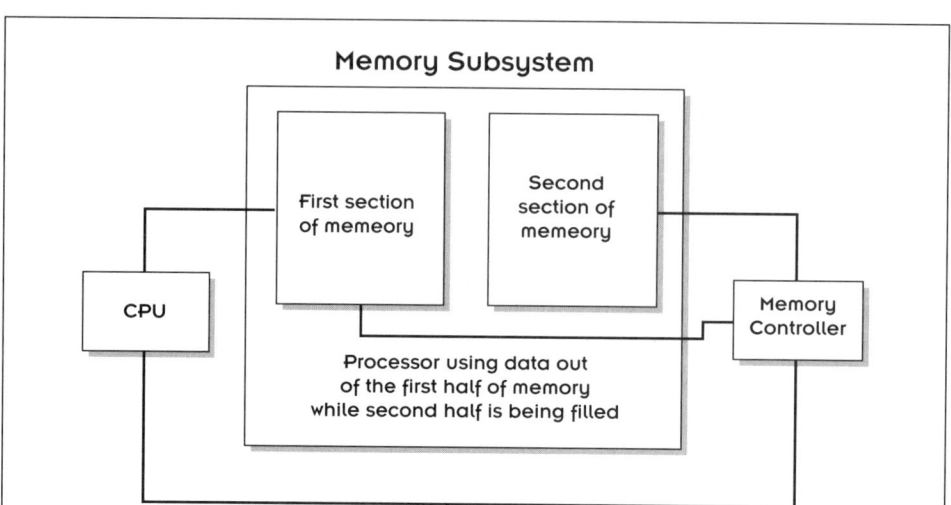

Figure 4.3   Page mode memory demonstrated.

management, this is the basics of how the processor uses memory for different tasks. The processor is perhaps six to ten times faster than the memory subsystem, and page mode is one way to speed things up.

So, how do you know if your memory uses page mode? You don't. Check the motherboard's manual, or the computer's manual if you were shipped a whole box complete, and see what kind and type of memory it takes. I say this because on some systems, in order to use page mode you have to install two of whatever type of memory you choose to install. If it's 16 MB modules, then two are required. Guess what? Back to the CFO for more money! That should go over like a lead brick in a balloon shop, but rest assured that most motherboards shipped today use this kind of memory architecture built into the motherboard itself. It's just something to be aware of.

 The use of faster memory in a page mode interleaved motherboard can improve system performance by as much as 40 percent. If you can find them, use the 40 nanosecond variety for best performance. While more expensive, they're worth it in the long run.

Memory Architectures and Capacity

I already said that 32 MB is the minimum acceptable for a midrange Web server. This gets you running and operational. As you plot and plan this system, you'll find an increasing number of motherboards that accept a mix of the older 30-pin SIMMs and the newer 72-pin variety. Fear not, you can mix them and save the old investment. The caveat is threefold:

- If you mix the two types, be sure they're of the same rated speed.

- Be careful about the adapter board you buy for the 30-pin modules—cheap adapters result in dangerous performance and possible system crashes.

- Be sure the memory used on the adapter and the 72-pin modules are either both parity or non-parity.

Failure to observe these three caveats in one form or another has often resulted in the loss of data, and many hours of lost operational time and money trying to find the cause of the system crashes!

I'm not telling you to not use the older 30-pin modules, but be wise when you do. I said before that I do not often specify one vendor over others, but I will this time. The Minden Group makes an adapter for using four of the 30-pin SIMMs in one 72-pin socket, and this adapter has worked beautifully in my servers. The adapter is very simple to use, and I've found them at various computer stores for as little as $35 retail.

So what's this parity business? You gurus hang tight for a minute. For you non-believers, here's the scoop. The old 30-pin modules are nearly all parity types. Parity means that the computer uses an extra data bit to form a type of error-correction code in case the data gets corrupted. Nearly all PCs use odd parity. If you looked at the ASCII representation of the letter "A," its binary equivalent is "01000001," or a hexidecimal 41. If you look at the number of bits that are set, you'll see an even number of them, two to be specific. This letter has even parity, so the parity bit is "1" or said to be set. Parity is used to correct for data loss, and is common in the older systems which were less reliable than current-day systems. Newer motherboards are no longer supporting parity memory because of the significantly increased reliability of all computer components.

This means that if you use one of the adapters for 30-pin memory, make sure the adapter supports these parity memory modules (like the 30 pinners) in a parity or non-parity motherboard. My most recent motherboard purchases were non-parity boards, and they're working wonderfully in my Web servers. I'm also using the Minden adapters for some of the older 30-pin memory. The key here is that if the motherboard uses parity memory (the 9th data bit) then you must use parity memory. If the motherboard uses non-parity memory, you can use either parity or non-parity. As of early March 1996, non-parity memory was $40 to $65 cheaper per 72-pin module, so the per-server savings are obvious.

Cache Subsystem

One more way to expedite your server's performance is by the use of a level 2 (L2) cache system. As I mentioned earlier, the level 1 (L1) cache, shown in Figure 4.4, is built into the internals of the 486, 586, and Pentium processors and acts as a small amount of very fast memory in which a copy

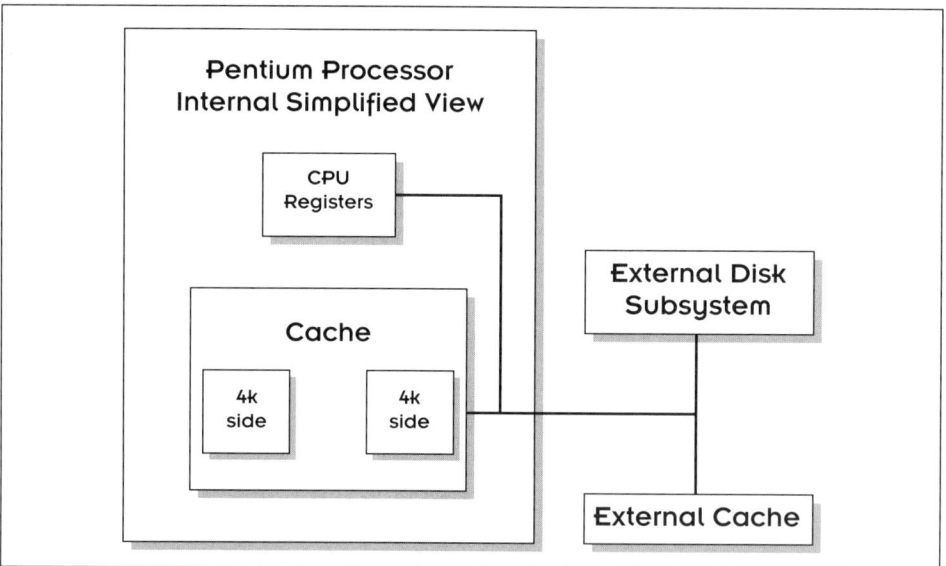

Figure 4.4   An internal L1 cache.

of the most recently used data is stored. An L2 cache, shown in Figure 4.5, is exterior to the processor and installed onto the motherboard itself. For a discussion on cache systems, see the *Processor* section under the heading *Minimum Server Hardware.*

The L1 cache is 8 KB in the 486 series, and 16 KB in the Pentiums. While this seems to be too small to do any good, Intel Corporation has tested and published that this cache delivers a rate of 90 to 95 percent hit rates. A *hit* in cache terms means that the processor has found the desired data 90 percent of the time in the cache, and only 10 percent of the time has had to go back to the disk drive. Hit rates of 80 percent or higher are acceptable and common in Pentium processors.

One of the keys to the performance gains that this cache delivers is that not only is the cache still closer to the processor than the physical disk drives, but it's still electronic data storage, just like the built-in cache inside the processor. The biggest difference between L1 and L2 cache is the size: L1 is 8 KB in 486s and 16 KB in Pentium class, onboard L2 cache is at least 32 KB and up to 1 MB. The L2 cache varies in speed, but a decent cache uses 15 nanosecond chips. The performance difference between 15

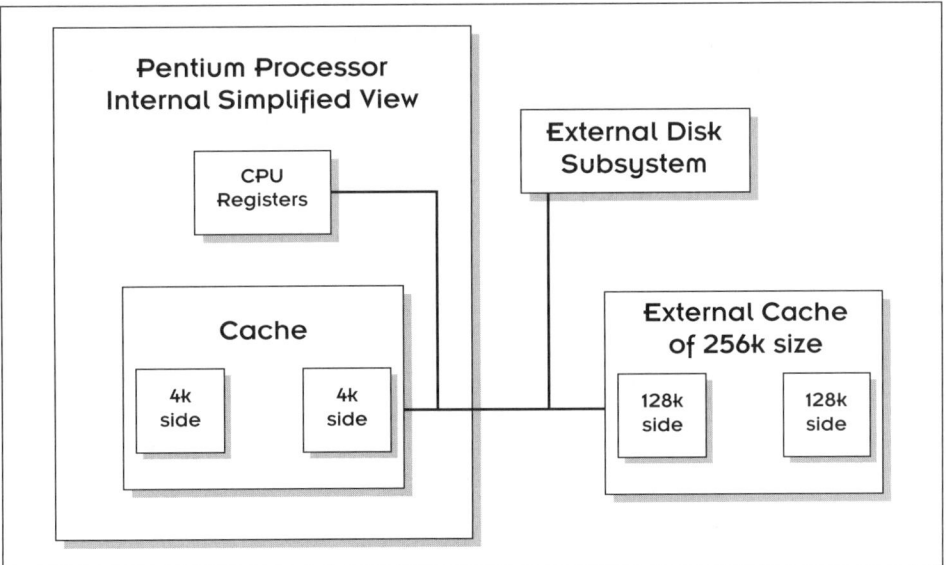

Figure 4.5   An External L2 cache.

nanosecond and 50 nanosecond chips is a factor of 5 and a cost variance of perhaps twice, depending on where you buy the chips.

There's one thing you should keep in mind when installing L2 cache. Keep it to 256 KB or even 128 KB. Larger cache chips frequently result in marginal gains because the increased volume of data in the cache means that the processor has to wade through more information to find what it needs. Now, you may think that because the processor is such a barnburner, this isn't a problem. In fact, it really isn't that big of an issue in terms of a Web server, but if you decide that you want to use your current network server to double as the Web server, then every bit matters. Of course, the increased cost of the larger 1 MB cache chips is a marginal factor, but nonetheless adds to the cost of the server. Another of Intel's tests reported that a 64 KB cache of 20 nanoseconds rating served all but the most demanding of applications. If it makes you feel any better, most vendors of motherboards and completed systems ship with 256 KB cache installed as standard equipment. In these days of huge applications, the old adage "more is better" does not always apply.

Disk Systems

This is another place where server life gets really interesting. By now you've guessed that about all a 16 MB 486DX2-66 is good for is maintaining a bare minimum server for prototype development, so now you've decided that the server needs to grow up into perhaps a minimum Pentium class server. Along with that growth comes, at a necessary expense, the storage system. You've gone to a larger system, perhaps because you've got more users, so why skimp on storage? Likely as not, those few occasional users and prototyping has evolved into a real need for a full server. Alas, the need finally catches up with the expenses.

For the minimum Web server requirements, I stated that an enhanced IDE drive was suitable for storage. This is still true enough for a midrange server, but beware that four EIDE devices is the most you can put in one system and maintain decent performance. Okay, let me restate that. Under normal circumstances, only two EIDE controllers can be used in the system at one time, and maintain decent performance, or even run at all. That may not seem like much, but I said EIDE *devices*, which means a tape drive, or CD-ROM drive, or other such device. Both CD-ROMs and tape drives have become very cost effective solutions these days for storage mediums, and are commonly seen. One variety of CD-ROM plugs directly into the sound card, which is one IDE controller. The system drive obviously needs a controller and one drive. Strike another. This leaves you down to a possible one controller to be added and possibly two hard disks.

That's a lot of maybes and could bes. To ease yourself out of a lot of pain and anguish later on, this midrange Web server could exist using the primary disk controller running one of those really fast EIDE drives, such as the Western Digital 1.65 GB EIDE Caviar drive or a Seagate 1.28 GB Medalist Fast ATA-2 drive. For the system files of Microsoft Windows NT Server, either of these are fine. You're not likely to add much more software that could fill the drive right away, so this should suffice. Both drives have access times as fast as any SCSI-2 drive, so don't let the thought of a fast IDE-style drive keep you from using it as a system drive.

In addition to the system drive, one configuration I prefer for myself and my clients is the use of a secondary SCSI-2 or SCSI-3 controller, in which the tape backup unit and the disk hosting the Web software are stored. If you use a RAID 5 controller, then you can use some of the now-inexpensive SCSI drives of the 2 GB range to form the RAID. I priced these 2 GB drives recently as low as $650 retail! Not bad at all. But, you say you're not interested in RAID just yet? Fine, use a secondary SCSI-2 controller to keep the cost down and use single drives. Just remember to backup often, at least daily. If you use multiple drives on this SCSI controller, you can use a single drive for the Web server software, and another separate drive as the FTP device.

Figure 4.6 is a recap of the disk configuration I favor for the midrange Web server, which walks an even line between the prototype server and the forthcoming best-case Web server. This particular configuration offers a safety net, in that any one device can fail and not take out the other services. Sure, NT itself has been known to self-destruct like any other NOS, but it wouldn't take out the Web software. Why destroy all the configurations?

I/O Devices

The I/O devices won't differ a whole lot from the prototyping system we defined earlier, except that now you're likely to be using serial ports that

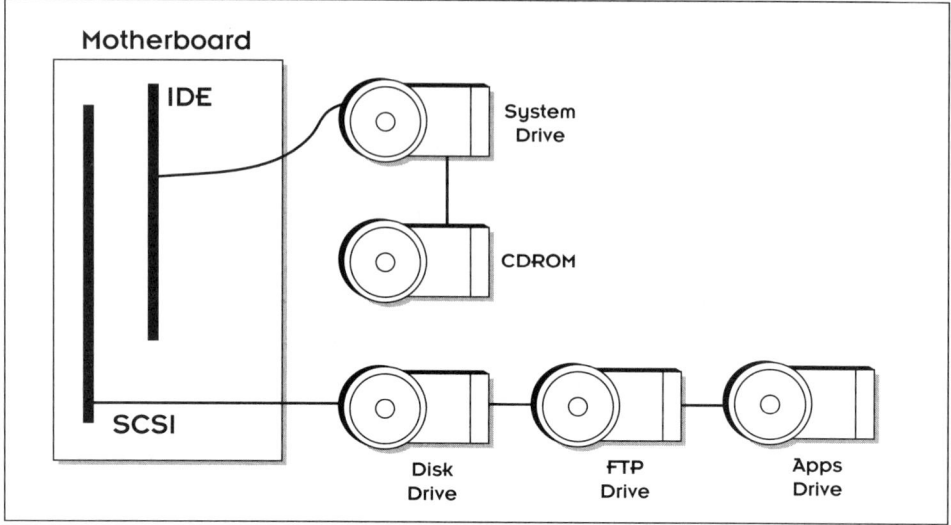

Figure 4.6   Disk configuration of a midrange Web server.

are 16550 style. These are enhanced serial I/O units that buffer data at higher speeds above 9600 baud, and prevent loss of data if the main processor can't get to the data quick enough. In addition, you might consider using four serial ports to provide a little extra access to the server beyond the normal Internet connections. One possibility is to set up a BBS for local customers that don't have an Internet provider handy. Simply have them dialup into your Wildcat NT BBS, as we discussed in the last chapter, and then gateway out to the Internet. Not only is this doable, but it's very practical. We'll get into more detail on the subject in Chapter 12, *Web Server Administration.*

Optimum Server Hardware

Now the time has come to talk some serious money. This is the Web server that separates the kid's game PC from the one that would make the most devout programmer drool. This is also the one system that will serve all but the most demanding of environments. This is surely the last server of any sort that you'll have to buy anytime soon. Wake up and pay attention, because when you put this one in front of the CFO she will definitely have a cow!

Processor

It's time to belly up to the bar and be serious. It's been well established that the Pentium class processors are the king of the hill for Intel-based systems. Just recently (early spring 1996) the 166 MHz Pentium Pro came onto the market with the splash and marketing flair that Intel does so well. This is a killer processor that dwarfs anything the best 486 is capable of, and makes the earlier sub-100MHz Pentiums eat its dust. To build the best Web server so you won't have to go out and upgrade in six months, specify a motherboard or pre-built computer that supports the 166 MHz and also supports multiple processors, either by inserting the processor into another chip socket or adding another card. Microsoft Windows NT Server will use multiple processors with the greatest of ease and split the tasks between the processors.

We've not gotten into any other component yet, and already the cost of the server box has broken $6,000. What you'll gain from this price tag is the ability to simply drop in another processor and relieve the load on the existing system. In the early days of Microsoft Windows NT Server, Microsoft did a test on NT by having over 300 users on one network server. If memory serves me, the processor was a Pentium 90. The overall system performance was dismal, as you may have thought, but not bad for a 32 MB of RAM machine.

The test server had one more Pentium and 32 MB of additional memory added, and the performance jumped to within 90 percent of what two Pentiums would do. In essence, 90 percent of a Pentium 90 was effectively used. Keep in mind that adding memory and another processor was all that was done! Subsequent testing added a total of 12 Pentium processors and 256 MB of memory in a special Compaq server. Overall system performance went up algebraically and more users were supported with less server stress, and with a lot less headaches.

This is a very commanding strength of Microsoft Windows NT Server. Can you imagine having 12 of those 166 MHz Pentium Pro's in one machine? Forget the cost, what about the processing horsepower? What about the heat generated by this system? The case would probably glow in the daylight.

In case you've never played with the likes of a Digital Equipment Corp. VAX/VMS™, a Sun Workstation, or a Silicon Graphics Iris™, these computers are capable of some of the most demanding processing known. One demo that I saw run on the Iris workstation with a 20-inch monitor was four different full-motion videos of four different sets of two fighter jets practicing their dog-fighting skills. The 20-inch monitor was divided into equal fourths so that one set of jets was in each window pane. Ever see "Top Gun" or "Iron Eagle?" Remember those awesome jet fights and how quickly those jets could turn and maneuver? This Iris workstation (back in 1988) was processing all eight of these jets' similar motions flawlessly and without a single discernible glitch in movement! Now *that's* horsepower. Believe me when I say that such processing is astounding to see.

Well, the point is that now the Intel processors have come full circle with high-powered (and high-priced) workstations. They can handle hundreds of user requests in network environments, such as the Internet, on a single 166 MHz processor. Adding a second 166 is like adding a second Iris into the same cabinet. Close enough that you should have the point by now. What's even more amusing about this is that 20 years ago, minicomputers, such as the Wangs and DECs, along with the IBM monsters, handled such matters with ease because they were designed from the ground up as multiuser platforms.

The Intel-based systems were designed initially as a data entry terminal and were enhanced upward to work as servers. As such, it wasn't until the advent of a Unix variant that ran on PCs or NT Server or Netware that the Intel-based machines really got a chance to work in these demanding environments. The PC had to mature into the job, while minicomputers were built for the job from the start. This is one reason that PCs have had such a hard time filling the role of servers, but now the high-end processors, such as the 166 MHz variety, can really do the job with Microsoft Windows NT Server.

Next we'll discuss the most recent evolution in memory designs and variety for your server. Keep in mind that the CFO still hasn't recovered from the multiple-processor system board you bought earlier, and the "sticker shock" will persist all the way to the end of this section! Time for the Maalox.

Memory

Memory has thus far been the single most expensive component of the server. The memory market went absolutely nuts in the spring of 1994 when an overseas plant that makes crucial chemical components of the memory silicon wafers exploded and destroyed perhaps 40 percent of the world's supply of this component. The law of supply and demand jumped right in and drove up the price of a 4 MB 30-pin memory module from an average of $115 to $165 almost overnight. Well, we all know that the supply didn't depreciate that fast, so someone was making a ton of money on a situation that didn't yet exist. Of course, we were all angered at this, but what can a poor systems integrator do?

Memory has stayed in the clouds ever since then, but has started coming down as of early March 1996. Before the pricing came down, a 16 MB 72-pin single module averaged $600 for non-parity and nearly $750 for parity SIMMs. In early March 1996, I bought one of these same modules for $375 and two weeks later the same module dropped to $235 in several places. Two days after that, those same places were selling the module for $285. Suffice to say, the memory market is quite volatile. If you look at the stock market and various aspects of it, the memory market is every bit as topsy-turvy as the precious metals market. At one time, gold was cheaper than memory chips!

I went through this spiel to let you know what to expect when designing your primo server. What you spec out today is likely to be obsolete next week in the memory corner. Hard drives, monitors, keyboards, and the like see no such problem. In fact, nearly every aspect of computers is getting somewhat cheaper, except for memory. There is one respite coming along the road that'll help us. New memory types, designs, and capacities are entering the market, so dealers have to clean out the old models before they can bring in the new. That means better prices for the consumer.

Some of the newest memory types in the market are the 72-pin designs I've mentioned, and are likely to be the only ones you'll put in your server. The 16 MB model is the most commonly used, and its name is usually referred to as a 4Mx32-70. In the 72-pin design, multiply the megabytes rating by 4, and you'll get the capacity—4 multiplied by 4 is 16 MB. The 32 in the name refers to 32 data bits, and designates the non-parity type. The 70 in the name is the speed rating of the module. A 70 nanosecond model is a middle-of-the-road performer, and is the most widely sold unit. So, an 8Mx36-54 memory model is a 32 MB parity model rated at 54 nanoseconds. This module recently sold for $1100, but is fluctuating just as wildly now as the others are.

One more type of memory that I'd like to mention is the EDO, or Extended Data Out, design. This memory is designed to work in servers to provide faster response and better performance under demanding needs. If you know anything about the system boards, you know that various parts of it can be tuned: the bus speed, CPU responses, cache wait states, and more. Well, the memory subsystem is what is called a *slave device* in the system. Its only job is to perform the task it was given, and nothing more. It can't respond back to the processor at all, and dutifully carries out its tasking. EDO will give you better performance out of memory subsystems, but the modules cost a lot more to use. In heavily used Web servers you'll find these modules to be a definite advantage, but be prepared to spend the bucks.

Ideally, our optimum Web server would employ the EDO memory, and would use a pair of the 8Mx36-40 SIMMs. Do you remember the section earlier where I said that usage of memory was dependent on legal memory configurations? I explained that if you used a pair of 16 MB modules and had two memory slots free to give you 32 MB of working memory, adding more memory to this server later meant that you had to use the same 16 MB modules by adding two more of them. If you needed more than 64 MB of memory, then you'd have to remove all four of the 16 MB modules and buy the 32 MB units. In most cases, you can't mix the 16 MB and 32 MB modules on the same motherboard. Sometimes you can, but usually not.

Let's go back to our basic server. This server was installed at 16 MB to test it. The costs were kept to a minimum, and the server proved viable. Fine. Later we jumped it up to 32 MB total using another 16 MB module. Two memory slots used, and two free. These slots were capable of supporting the 32 MB modules as well, but I opted for the cheaper 16 MB units. With 32 MB installed, the Web server was brought online and various software components installed. Performance lagged after awhile, so memory was bumped up one more module to 48 MB. You see the pattern building here. This server has finally made its way up to 96 MB of memory by using three of the 32 MB modules and removing the four 16 MB modules purchased over time. This server now only has one memory slot left, and appears to be headed for a motherboard upgrade soon.

To avoid that problem, start the server with a pair of 32 MB modules right off the bat, and then you can jump up to 128 MB of server memory later if you have to. The cost is likely to run about $2000 to start, but is worth it in the long run.

Disk Systems

Disk drives will be the one area that is likely to please that nervous CFO, especially after that last section. In high-powered Web servers, RAID 5 disk subsystems are the norm. Not only is this for security of the data, but for the increased throughput offered by RAID, which treats all of the physical drives as one logical unit. Because of this scheme, data access is faster due to the RAID controller's usage of the disks that make up the array. Figure 4.7 shows the concept of a RAID system.

This means that if data has to be stored, the controller uses the appropriate disk for the job. If data has to be read, which is perhaps 80 percent of all operations, then the controller determines which disk to use that has the data. It's kinda like rocket science—something that eludes most of

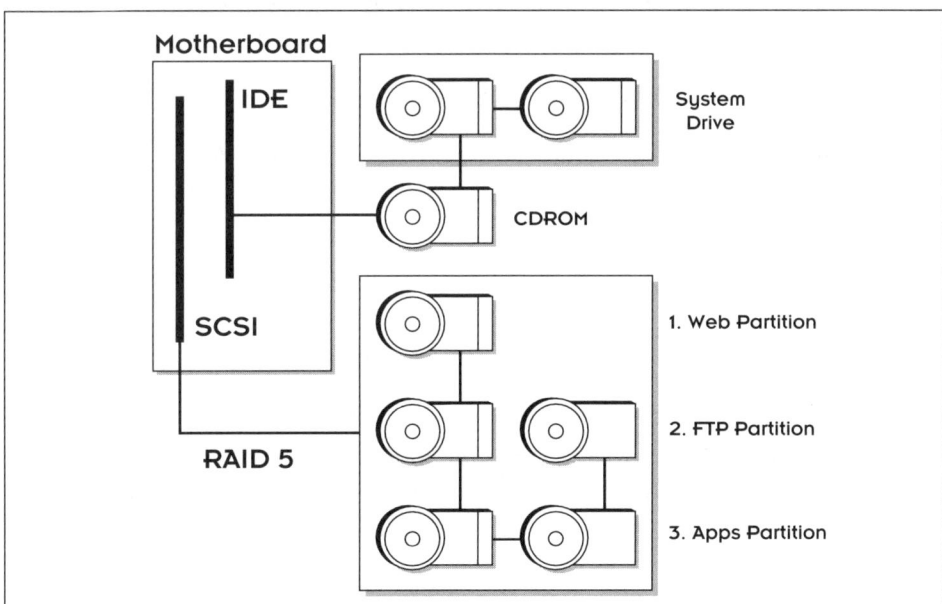

Figure 4.7   Logical definition of a RAID system.

us—but the controller and software make the decisions for us by splitting up the data between physical drives in the logical array. All of the adapters for this server should be either EISA- or PCI-based bus adapters. Nothing else will suffice for this demanding environment.

Some vendors of excellent disk RAID controllers include Adaptec's AHA-3985/3985W RAID adapters for PCI. Here are some of the specs on this adapter:

Host PCI bus data transfer rate:	Up to 133 MB/sec burst rate
SCSI synchronous data rate:	AHA-3985 — 30 MB/sec (10 MB/sec per channel)
Three-channel Fast SCSI-2:	AHA-3985W — 60 MB/sec (20 MB/sec per channel)
Three-channel Fast and Wide SCSI-2	
SCSI asynchronous data rate:	AHA-3985 — 9 MB/sec (3 MB/sec per channel)
Three-channel Fast SCSI-2:	AHA-3985W — 18 MB/sec (6 MB/sec per channel)
Three-channel Fast and Wide SCSI-2	
RAID levels:	5, 1, 0, and 0/1
Drive configurations per array:	
	RAID 5: Min. 3, Max. 8
	RAID 1: Min. 2, Max. 2
	RAID 0: Min. 2, Max. 8
	RAID 0/1: Min. 4, Max. 16

You can find the complete specifications for this adapter at *http://www.adaptec.com/sales/AHA3985Features.html*. I suggest stopping by if you're interested in seeing all of the things that this adapter can do. Another adapter used in the industry is Mylex Corporation's, DAC960. I've used this adapter in Banyan VINES, NT Servers, and Novell Netware systems with no problems. It's fast and easy to set up. You can find more information on Mylex's PCI RAID controllers at *http://www.mylex.com/salemktg.htm*.

Dell Computer Corp. also has a disk array for their servers, but finding specific information on it was fairly difficult on their Web site at *http://www.dell.com*. From that page, you can get contact information for various countries around the world for your particular application.

This should give you a feeling for the products and their capabilities. Now for some pricing. I'll use the Mylex DAC960 as an example. This controller recently was priced at $850 for no cache memory installed. This price is likely to be different when you buy one, so consult with your local vendor for the most current prices. One typical RAID configuration for servers of this magnitude is to run RAID 1 (basic mirroring) on one controller and RAID 5 on a second controller for the data drives. RAID 5 requires three drives minimum, eight maximum, on this controller. RAID 1 requires two drives of the exact same type and geometry, and so does RAID 5. This is where some degree of standardization helps with replacement parts, and in purchasing. For example, if you buy Seagate 2 GB SCSI-2 drives, Model ST32430N, then you'll need six of these drives: two for the RAID 1, three for RAID 5, and one spare. Woe be unto the WebMaster that doesn't have a spare drive handy.

This is the only funny part about RAID—it requires drives of the same geometry. This requirement could put you into a precarious position if the style of drive you buy goes out of production this year, and three months later you need to expand your storage or replace a bad drive. So, many WebMasters purchase several of these drives at once as extras. Table 4.2 tallies up the damage done so far to the disk subsystem.

Getting pretty expensive, isn't it? The memory we used ran about $2400 for 32 MB, now add $5900 for the RAID system. That's $8300 for just the basic core components of the server. Toss in the case, power supply, keyboard, and other odds and ends, and the server can break $15,000 quite easily. And we haven't even added a single piece of software. Take another

Table 4.2 Relative Costs of RAID

Device	Quantity	Price	Total
RAID Controller	2	$850	$1700
Disk drives	6	$700	$4200

gulp of Maalox before you tell the CFO that this primo top-end Web server is still not complete.

I/O Devices

This last section on our best-ever Web server involves some peripheral devices not yet discussed as necessary, because they've been considered optional in the other servers. Tape backup is absolutely necessary. Sure, you say, but what kind? Do we just want to save the data, or truly backup the server? Next, a CD-ROM drive is a must. Because our high-end server uses SCSI, we'll use a SCSI CD-ROM. No problem. How about uploading the huge quantities of files that you may occasionally put on the server? Why not consider a rewritable optical drive that doubles to handle CD-ROM discs?

When your server gets to be as big as this optimum device, SCSI tape backups greater than 4 GB are the only ones that make sense. Not only that, but there's a known problem using IDE tape backups of large capacity—the software won't work under Microsoft Windows NT Server and Workstation. So, SCSI tape drives become mandatory. The drives have come down in price so significantly that it's well worth it. I priced one in March 1996 at $350 with each 4 GB tape costing about $28 apiece. The odd part of this is that a truly full-featured backup program to use Microsoft Windows NT Server and the tape drive costs nearly $700. But, once installed, you can backup the server and any workstations on the network, which is useful if this Web server is going to run any workstations.

Optical disks have come a long way, just like tape drives have, and now you can get a 6x speed IDE drive for $150 everywhere. One distributor I use offered me a Phillips 6x IDE drive for $95! Granted, that's wholesale, but the picture gets better when I tell you that 5½-inch rewritable drives that can handle CDs are now under $1,000. That's the retail price, too. If you find a friend that resells computer equipment, you're likely to find these drives for as little as $700. Why would you want one of these? Well, if your Web site processes large quantities of data, or you have an exceptionally busy Web site, or the Web server is a standalone machine, you need some way to get this data around. The rewritable drive is the perfect answer. At a rated 1.3 GB capacity, it'll solve all but the most demanding needs of your Web site.

One last peripheral device that you may want to explore is the use of a BBS or RAS by way of Microsoft Windows NT Server. This approach provides several solutions to problems that you'll undoubtedly encounter in the course of your Web site. One of these is remote management of the Web site. Another is emergency requests for access to your server for files or messages. Still another is access to the server by users that are not on the Internet and who need to get onto the Internet or to use the Web resources locally.

Microsoft Windows NT Server's RAS handles up to 256 concurrent users. That'd be quite a load for any server, but your primo high-end Web server can handle it. Remember that you built this server to handle large loads, but the standard I/O ports added to computers is limited to four serial ports. Even if you use all four ports for 28.8 Kbps modems, you still wouldn't load down this server. By using a multiport I/O card, you can let plenty of remote users onto the server at once. In fact, this is the premise behind many Internet Service Providers.

Microsoft Windows NT Server excels at this by natively supporting intelligent multi-I/O cards, such as the Equinox SST family of cards. I use a SST-4 on my Web server now for remote access for several users that do not have file transfer capability other than something like Procomm communications software. These users dial in using NT Workstation's and Windows 95's remote access software that comes with each of those two systems, and log into my domain natively to copy files. I haven't fully set up the BBS software yet, but any other users could dial in and get files this way as well, using Procomm or similar software.

Let's not forget one little piece of ancillary equipment that I almost forgot about, and that's a printer. Did you know that if you can log into a domain, you can do anything remotely that you can do locally? Well, anything given the proper rights, and this includes printing to a network printer. When I'm working on some projects, I need to fax information to customers and they respond to it. If I email them a word-processing file, they can use it and mark it up as they see fit. If they then log into my network, they can (and have) printed the file directly onto my network printers and saved the fax cost. This is just another way to save money and expedite the operations of a business using Microsoft Windows NT Server.

A Short Summary

This is the end of a relatively long section on the vagaries of Web servers. I'd like to take a minute to do a short summary with you about what we've covered, why we did it, and what you can expect out of each setup toward the goal of building your Web server.

- **Bare-bones server ($1500)**—Uses existing components around the office; server is comprised of a 486DX2-66 with 16 MB memory, most any hard disk above 650 MB capacity, CD-ROM drive, basic I/O ports. Good for testing theories and running up to 10 users in active usage. Can use a high speed modem to test the site. If it doesn't work out, return the system to the pool of users wanting a decent 486. Nothing lost but a bit of time and someone's salary to do the work.

- **Mid-range server ($5000)**—Uses some existing components around the office; server is comprised of a Pentium 90, CD-ROM, 32 MB memory, a pair of 1 GB drives, or higher storage. Uses basic ISDN lines for low-cost connectivity to support up to 15 concurrently connected users; could support a BBS of up to 5 concurrently connected users at 28.8 Kbps. Needs a bit of time spent with it to continue the prototyping and configuring of the Web software, FTP, browsers, users' home stations, etc. Expect to take a month of testing and evaluation to complete and take public or private for users. Relatively moderate investment that could be used as an in-house network server for up to 50 users if the Web site doesn't fly.

- **Optimum server ($15,000)**—Pentium 166 class processor with 64 MB RAM; RAID 1 and RAID 5 storage for the NOS and data, respectively. Uses all high-end equipment, such as SCSI disks, tape drive, CD-ROM, and optical storage; uses FT1 or full T1 link to support up to 250 users. Seek this level only if the corporate CFO is sure this is a cost effective solution to company business goals. This server could double as an enterprise-wide server, so not something to take lightly. T1 links cost $15,000 to install and up to $3500 a month in fees. Enables processing of a full-fledged Web site with all the abilities thereof.

Next we'll move on to server memory requirements from the application level to see exactly how much memory these applications will use, which will confirm what we've discussed up to this point.

Server Memory Requirements

Now let's get into the heart of the matter—how much memory this thing is really going to require. I know I just went through a complete server build for three different servers, but I think it bears repeating. Memory can affect your Web server's performance in different ways, so let's look at that now.

Just for NT Server

When you built the Microsoft Windows NT Server, you installed it on a machine without any other software running on it. This means that NT had access to all available memory and had to share none of it. This is important! When you have just NT running, and no other applications installed, run the Windows Diagnostics from the Administration Group, and click on the Memory button to show you how much memory is installed, how much is used, and how much is free, as shown in Figure 4.8.

What you'll notice is the resources and the memory load factor placed on the machine by the operating software and required drivers. Of course, if you add more software and drivers, it takes more memory to run them. By using this tool, you can gauge the impact the various pieces of software

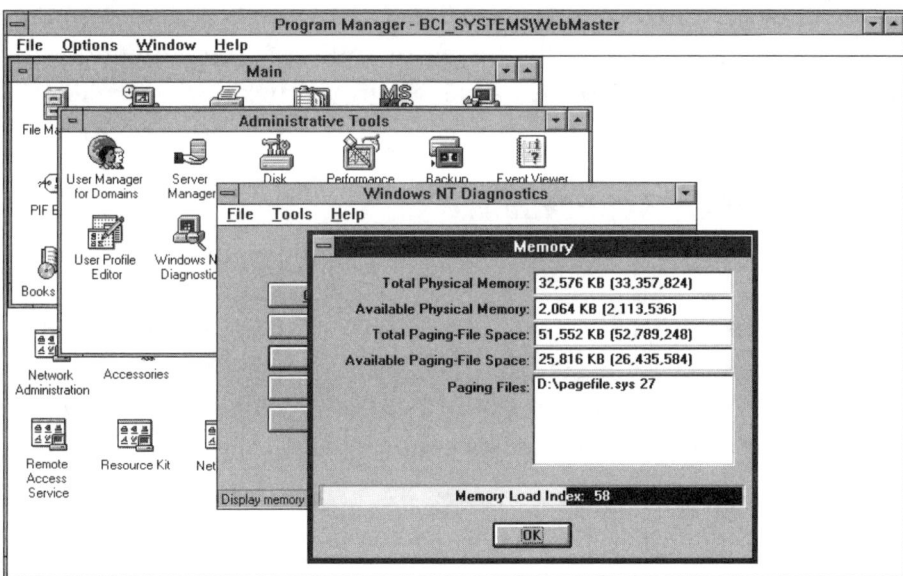

Figure 4.8   Examining system memory.

have on your server, and when you can expect problems caused by them. As a standard rule of thumb, Microsoft Windows NT Server requires 20 MB of memory to completely load itself and run before any other drivers or services are loaded. This is for the virgin installation of NT. Now, earlier I did say that you could run Microsoft Windows NT Server on a machine that has 16 MB of memory—how is that possible?

Microsoft Windows NT Server uses a vulture called *virtual memory* to simulate real memory. Virtual memory is nothing more than disk space converted into a single contiguous file called a *swap file*. This swap file is used when physical memory gets low. At that point the unused, or the least recently used, applications and data are moved off to the swap file and out of real memory to make room for the applications and drivers that need to execute. I called it a vulture because swap files are slower than real memory, and they tend to gobble up applications, even if they're running in real memory. Even if some applications don't need that much real memory to run, Microsoft Windows NT Server sometimes swaps out applications to the swap file anyway, but recalls it back to real memory as necessary.

Because the swap file is fixed, you have to declare a minimum and maximum size for the file. Averages between 25 MB to 95 MB are common for the lower and upper range in the file. Microsoft Windows NT Server adjusts the size of the file dynamically during operations. I recommend setting NT's requirements to 20 MB for a clean setup. You can set the maximum as high as you want.

The Needs of the Applications

The applications you'll use for your server run the gamut from the actual Web server software up to RAS and the CGI applications you may create over time. Something has to perform the task of the Web pages, and that something includes CGI, HTML, and perhaps the Visual Basic applications you wrote for the CGI part of it. I did some experimenting with my server and came up with the statistics shown in Table 4.3.

This table should give you a hint of what your server may or may not need for application support. The memory requirements may not be as important as the processing demand that these applications place upon the processor. In a few sections, I'll introduce you to the Performance Monitor that comes

Table 4.3   Application Demands on Memory

Application	Memory	Demand
VB EXEs	250 KB	High
Perl Interpreter	100 KB	Low
RAS	800 KB	Medium
SQL Server	6 MB	High

with Microsoft Windows NT Server and allows you to watch the server's operational characteristics from a different viewpoint. For now, just know that with these few applications' needs, the Web server has jumped from 20 MB to 27.5 MB of real memory to run its dead-level best without touching the swap file.

Drivers and Your Hardware

Drivers are in a class by themselves when it comes to server memory requirements. This is because if you want to run the device, then you *must* install a driver for it! No questions asked, this is a requirement. Using certain drivers, Microsoft Windows NT Server protects itself from errant applications and utilities. It disallows access, direct access that is, to the hardware on the server like Windows 3.x or Windows 95 does. This protection is called the *Hardware Abstraction Layer*, or *HAL*, for short. Nothing goes in, out, or through the HAL without NT's control. NT regulates the traffic by using protected mode drivers. One perfect example is the venerable QIC tape drive installed from the Windows NT Setup icon in the Control Panel, as shown in Figure 4.9.

While drivers themselves usually don't take over 250 KB to run, once loaded they're running for the duration of the server and can't be removed unless

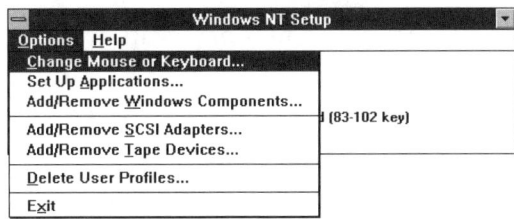

Figure 4.9   Installing a tape drive.

you specifically go to the Control Panel and stop them from running. The main purpose of a driver is as a permanent device in the server, and therefore it shouldn't be removed anyway! If you need to use the device, then it's generally a system-level device like a tape drive, or another disk drive. The memory aside, another performance factor comes into being because NT now has to manage the driver once loaded. Forget the memory, it's something else to manage. Just like crickets crawling on your hand, one or two doesn't matter, but one or two dozen gets to be a pain to manage and takes increasing amounts of your time to take care of. The same is true of NT, as you'll see in a moment.

The Users of the Server

When you think of users on the server, immediately the mind turns to someone logged in at a workstation. However, Microsoft Windows NT Server has many more users than you may have first thought of, and these include silent runners. Of course, when you log onto the server, there's the usual user called *Joe User* that makes the connection. However, there's another kind of user in the system called *InterProcess Communications*, (*IPC*). To illustrate this, I need to explain a few things about multiple processing systems like Microsoft Windows NT Server.

When a user logs onto the server, it creates a number of functional processing subsystems called *processes*. On a Windows 3.x PC, you might have started your favorite word processor. This program is a process. While you were inside this word processor, perhaps you pressed Alt+Tab to flip over to Program Manager to start another program. When you ran the second program, that too started a process. While running the second program, it may have started some add-in utility to help you do something. This started yet another process. Microsoft Windows NT Server is capable of managing and controlling multiple processes and *spawning* other processes from those processes themselves. This functionality causes more efficient usage of the operating system, but it uses more memory to allow the functionality itself. So, if you install and use applications that are specifically written for NT, then chances are that it may, at some time, cause you to need more memory.

So, now you have bona fide users logged in, Web server software operating, Perl scripts and CGI running and doing things for the Internet users, and perhaps an incremental tape backup in progress. If you connected your Web server to the in-house network, and allowed users to use the Web server as a gateway out to the Internet, the server is being used still more by these logged-in users. All of this translates into memory usage by the server, a truly precious commodity. Next, let's talk about how IPCs can affect server performance and memory usage for the users and remote functions.

Interprocess Communications

Interprocess communications (IPCs) are the internal functionality between server processes that communicate and carry out tasks where direct users are not involved. This can occur when two servers are communicating with internal tasking, or if a remote user connects to the server with incorrect settings. This problem causes the server to generate a *Named Pipe* system service call between the connecting user and the operating system via the IPC, as shown in Figure 4.10. Without getting into tons of NT nitty-gritty server stuff, this is yet another "user" in the system, which takes another little bit of memory and another little bit of processor time to handle.

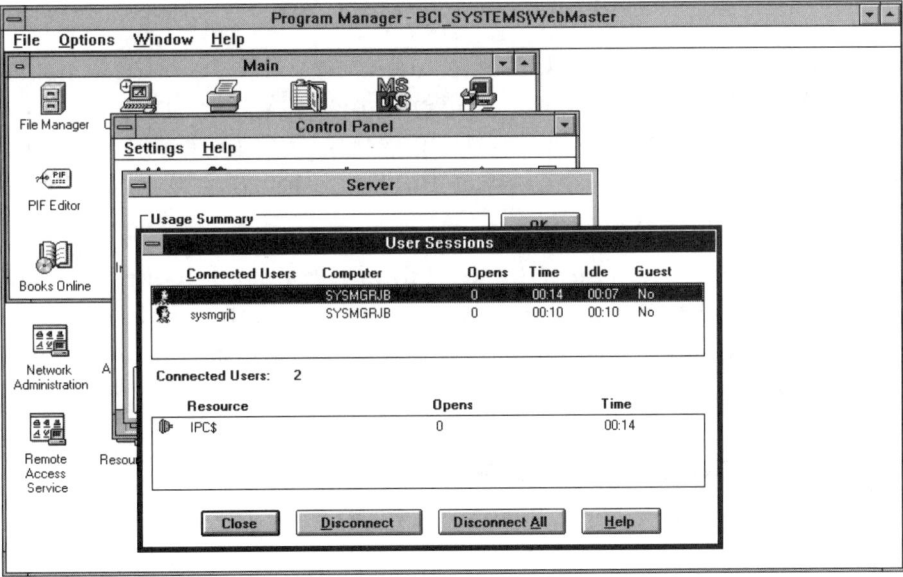

Figure 4.10   IPCs in the server.

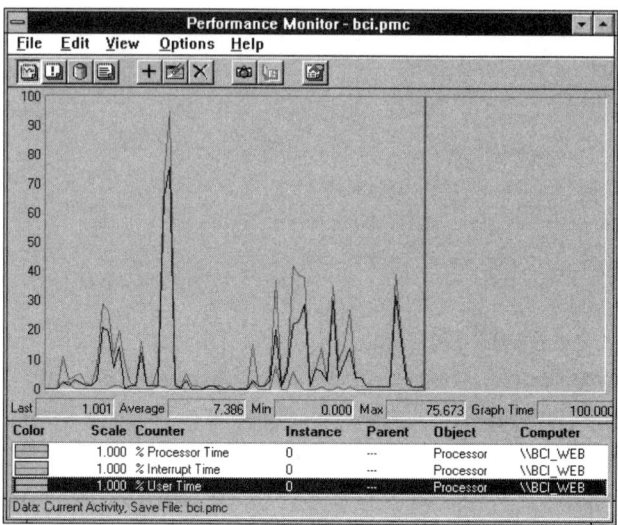

Figure 4.11   Performance tasking.

You can observe the server performance, as shown in Figure 4.11, by opening the Performance Monitor utility from the Administrative Group and choosing the Processor Time, Percentage of User Time menu option, or the interrupts per second processing level.

So now you can see that in even a medium-used Web server, you can count on 32 MB of RAM getting eaten up very quickly. While this will degrade server performance somewhat, you can survive, but for how long is indeterminate. Your best bet is to spend the bucks for 48 MB of memory to start with. You won't regret it.

In the next section, we'll move forward toward connecting our newly completed Web server to the Internet. We'll want to have the server connected to the Internet and PINGing successfully before we step into Chapter 5 with the Web software.

Internet Connectivity Devices

In this section we're going to briefly discuss connecting your server to the Internet by different means. The main goal is to test, develop, and produce a working circuit capable of sustaining data across the link between your Web site and the network users in the business that may be connected to the same Web server. We're assuming that a modem was used to test the Web server's connection to the outside world, establishing that the server's basic communications work fine.

Routers

As I mentioned before, routers perform the task of sending packets of data to the desired destination and preventing undesired packets from getting lost. Users on network A have IP addresses starting with 207.94.233 and users on network B have IP addresses of 207.94.234. Outside users connect to the Web server using IP addresses starting with 207.94.235. Routers say that if data is destined for the user 207.94.233.15 why send it to the Web server on the 235 subnet? Think of the router as a traffic cop in a congested intersection: he sends everyone to their desired location without allowing them to get lost or go down the wrong path.

Routers come in all shapes, designs, purposes, and power levels. There are basic routers that handle Ethernet on thinnet topology for two networks, and that's it. Not much strength to handle beyond 100 users or so, but they don't cost as much, either. Then there are routers capable of handling enterprise-wide solutions of 1000 users or more. Count on paying something on the order of $15,000 for such a router, and they can go up to $25,000 for high-end routers. (I can see the CFO sweating now.)

When I got my Web server online for my business, I had eight users that I needed to connect to the Internet. Four are internal business users, two are dial-in users accessing my BBS and gatewaying to the Internet, and two dial into the server by RAS. For this style of work, I didn't need a lot of horsepower, but I did need it to work on my ISDN link. For this job, I chose the Ascend Pipeline Model 50 ISDN router for the job. It's capable of 128 Kbps data rates, dial-in demand for the internal users, multiplexed PPP links so you can get the full 128 Kbps capacity, and it's incredibly simple to set up and use. Best yet, it's a router as well.

When I installed this ISDN router onto my network and configured it, I did a trial run to a favored FTP site where I get lots of goodies. A file transfer of 500 KB averaged between a 7 Kbps and 8 Kbps per second rate. If you take into account the 10 percent overhead of the data, I was getting nearly 90 Kbps out of the 128 Kbps rates of ISDN! Not too shabby, to say the least. A second test with a second network user doing the same thing caused a drop in data rates for the first user, which was expected, but the second user got 4 KB per second while the first user sustained 5 KB. Cumulatively, this means that the ISDN link achieved a sustained rate of 100 Kbps of the 128 Kbps capacity of multiplexed PPP. This is the reason that smaller sites should take a serious look at ISDN for low capacity-sites. So before we go any farther, let's dive right into ISDN—what it really is, and how it can serve you.

ISDN Equipment

ISDN stands for *Integrated Services Digital Network*, and is a standard by which fax, phone, and pure data can be transmitted over a single line. All three types of data share the bandwidth of the one line, and get separated out by the receiving equipment that you install. These links come in several types relating to style and speed: 32Kbps, 56 Kbps, 64 Kbps, and 128 Kbps. Use 32 Kbps for transmitting just voice, fax multiplexed with voice at 56 Kbps, or pure data running at either of the three speeds. If you use the 128 Kbps rate, then you're actually using a pair of 64 Kbps data channels multiplexed together on one virtual circuit. When you connect to the provider, a single 64 Kbps data channel is started and the second 64 Kbps channel is started only when the first channel fills.

When you plan on ISDN, you'll need to know several things:

- What do you plan on doing with the link? All data? Mixed data and voice? Fax?

- How many users will be on this link? 64 Kbps is recommended for up to 5 users, 128 Kbps for up to 12.

- Will you be hooking this up to an ISDN router? A PC? An external modem?

- How long will the link stay connected when you need to get online?

These things are important because the telephone company provider will need to configure their equipment accordingly. For my Web server, pure data was the only requirement. I wanted the highest bandwidth, so I got two data channels multiplexed on one line. This means that I have a pair of phone wires out back coming in from the telco for the ISDN. They look like any other ordinary pair of phone wires, but they are certified as capable of handling higher speeds and better quality of data delivery.

When you place the initial call for the line, be prepared to wait up to six weeks for the final connection to be made. Most telephone companies will have to do a *loop qualification test* to determine if the currently installed lines are capable of supporting high-quality digital data between your office and the telco's ISDN switch. This takes time for some telephone companies, but nothing for others. My telco, Bell South, took four weeks for the test because my site was only the sixth in the entire county to get ISDN. My requests were way beyond their normal operations, whereas Bell Atlantic has ISDN presence all over Philadelphia and you can get ISDN there within a couple of days.

Once the test is done, and the go-ahead has been given, the installation will be ready for your site. Because I had never dealt with ISDN before, I elected for Bell South to do the inside wiring at our location thinking this was some miracle job. Wrong! They used standard phone wire and standard phone jacks with standard jack screws—and I paid $135 for a 10-minute job that wasn't done right to start with. If you know how to wire a phone jack, you can do it yourself. ISDN isn't a miracle, just a mystic. Imagine the same analog modem traffic across a phone wire, now digitize it, and you've got ISDN. It's called Integrated Services because it's capable of supporting fax, voice, and modem at once.

If you want to learn more about ISDN, try Ascend Corporation's Web site, *http://www.ascend.com/ techdocs/isdnuserguide.html,* where they post lots of technical tips and information about ISDN.

Now let's move on to discuss the ins and outs of the network equipment that you'll need to get your site connected to the Internet.

Network-Specific Equipment

I'm going to break this section out into the three composite parts we discussed earlier: the bare-bones prototype server, the mid-range server, and the optimum Web server. We'll cover how you can connect these server types to the Internet by using a fast modem for the bare-bones server, an ISDN connection for the mid-range server, and dedicated T1 circuits for the optimum server.

The Prototype Server Using a Modem

This isn't too tough to explain, and I won't bore you with too many details. What I will say is that you can use a standard serial port card that most computers come with, but do yourself a favor and get a decent 28.8 Kbps modem such as the US Robotics Sportsters. Most of the major vendors work well with NT, but I have a personal affinity for the USRs. Not much more is required to get this prototype server online for testing, except to make sure you have a serial port that uses the 16550AFN UART. This unit buffers high-speed data transfers and is quite useful under poor quality lines where data has to be retransmitted. You'll need two serial ports, one for the mouse and one for the modem. Beyond that, if you need more than two serial ports, I highly recommend using an intelligent I/O card like the Equinox Super Serial SST-4, which NT uses without you having to worry about all of those interrupt assignments.

The Mid-range Server on ISDN

This is a little bit more complex to set up, but not much. My site uses the Ascend Pipeline 50 ISDN router, which consists of a 10BaseT twisted pair base, a simple 10BaseT hub, and the wiring to our network server. There are two ways to connect to the Web server, and you'll have to decide on one of them for your needs. If you only have a standalone Web server, then forget the network issues. The two schemes are:

- **Indirectly routed path**—All network traffic has to go through the Web server to get to the ISDN router.

- **Directly routed path**—All network users have a direct path to the ISDN router, bypassing the Web server.

Basically, the connections look something like Figure 4.12.

Because I want my business users on the network to have the fastest route possible to the Internet, I chose the directly connected route, where the ISDN router is connected to the hub. If all of the network traffic has to go

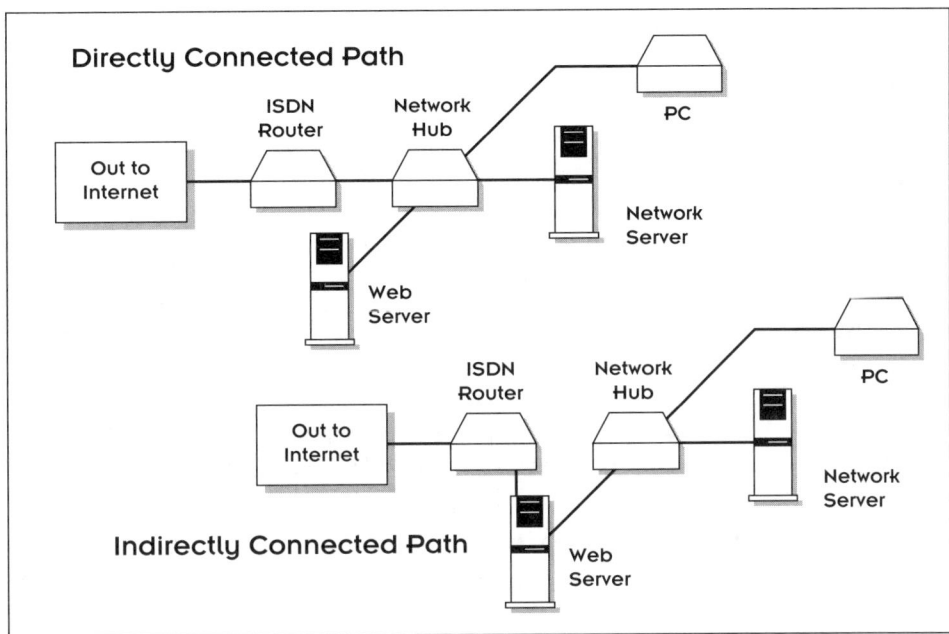

Figure 4.12   ISDN connections to the Internet.

through the Web server first, then the Web server has double duty to perform, causing additional load factors on the server. However, if I send all traffic through the Web server in an indirectly connected route, then I can use firewalls and proxy servers to prevent any unauthorized people from coming into my internal networks. You'll have to decide which method is best for you.

I also mentioned the possibility of having dialup users to your Web server using RAS or connecting via your bulletin board if you have one. These users will connect to the Web server and gateway to the Internet via the Web server, so the Web server will have enough to worry about without additional load factors from these users. This particular Web server was built to handle 20 users connected concurrently, so the additional load of a few dialup users shouldn't affect the server too much.

One other thing to be knowledgeable about is the ISDN adapter that you use. My final bit of advice on this issue is that ISDN requires line termination between the link and your server. The server is digital data, the link is digital data, and the distant end is digital data. So what's the big deal about?

Isn't digital data transferred the same way? Not quite. ISDN uses a different format to move the packets of data, so the digital data coming from your Web server has to be converted to a format suitable for transmission across the link. When the data arrives, the distant end reconverts it back to computereze digital data. This process requires a *line termination* device for the ISDN itself. One way to execute the conversion is to use a *CSU/DSU*, or Channel Service Unit/Digital Service Unit. The CSU adapts and prepares the ISDN line side of the connection to support the DSU, which prepares the Web server side of the connection to connect to the CSU, as shown in Figure 4.13.

Using devices like the Ascend Pipeline does not require a separate CSU/DSU termination because this device, called an *NT-1 Adapter*, does the job in one unit built right into the ISDN router box. Instead of having the Web server connect to the router, which connects to the CSU/DSU, which connects to the ISDN line, we just replace the CSU/DSU and router with a single box—the Pipeline 50.

Our Optimum Web Server on a Dedicated Link

Well, we've connected all of the junior servers, time to spend some bucks for our big server. The server is always operational, now you need to complete the task before loading the Web software. Microsoft Windows NT Server comes with all sorts of useful utilities to test the link, including PING, NSLOOKUP, and others.

To get this guy online, we're going to use a full T1 circuit. This is still a copper wire-based circuit, so don't worry about fiber optics as yet. To make this circuit, we can use an external router like the Cisco 2501, which basically does the same job as the Pipeline 50, but for a lot more users and at

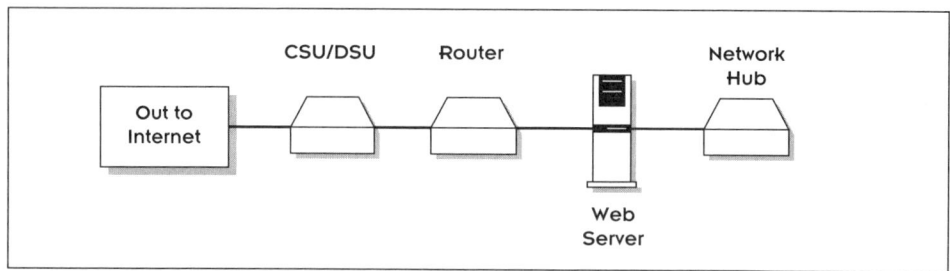

Figure 4.13   CSU/DSU configuration.

higher speeds. The Cisco 2500 serial ports provide up to two dedicated serial port interfaces, operating in DCE or DTE mode, compatible with leased lines and packet-switched services at speeds up to 2.048 Mbps (mega-bits per second). The serial port connectors have a universal design common to the Cisco 7000 FSIP card. This feature enables easy transition to any of the common physical interfaces, including V.35, RS-232, RS-449, RS-530, and X.21, as well as common spares across Cisco's product line.

The Cisco 2500 models 2503 and 2504 also come equipped with a native ISDN Basic Rate S/T Interface (BRI) that replaces an external ISDN terminal adapter (TA). The BRI S/T interface provides one 16 Kbps D channel for ISDN signaling information between the router and the ISDN switch, and two 64 Kbps B channels for user data access to the ISDN network. The Cisco 2500 series supports the NET3 (Euro ISDN) specification in Europe, as well as VN-2 and VN-3 specifications in France, the 1TR6 specification in Germany, and the SITS 92/48 specification in the United Kingdom. In Japan, the Cisco 2500 series supports the current INS-64 signaling specifications, and in North America, it supports the National ISDN-1 specification, AT&T's 5E6 ISDN specification for its 5ESS switch, and Northern Telecom's DMS ISDN specification. This is a good choice to use if you foresee the need for ISDN users, or the need to expand your service between servers at different sites, but don't want to get into the expense of another T1 link.

Connecting the Bulletin Board Users

If you want to run a BBS on the Web server, it is important that you understand the background of this connection approach. I want you to understand that if you run a BBS on the Web server, the potential impact can be severe if you're running a dozen users concurrently with the Internet users. These users gateway out of the BBS software via the Web server to get to the Internet, as shown in Figure 4.14. Notice that some of the connections are through the Web server software itself, and more server memory will be used to allow for this functionality.

Dealing with Your Internet Provider

Your site is spending large amounts of time on this project, and lots of the CFO's budget, so something better work right. In fact, when you hit this

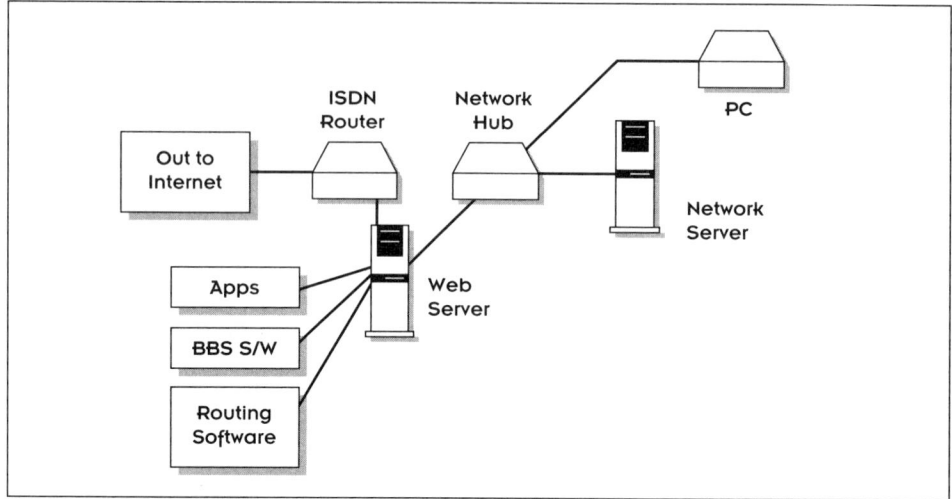

Figure 4.14   BBS users getting to the Internet.

point, most Internet Providers supplying your connections treat you in a completely different light. You've dropped perhaps ten grand to set up the site, and perhaps $3500 a month in connection fees. As such, you'll probably get fairly good service with your provider. Nonetheless, you need to do your own homework so you understand the system, how it works, and what to expect when it goes wrong. I've seen people duped into buying a new router that cost twice the amount of their existing router to fix a supposed anomaly in the system that only required a firmware upgrade to the original router. Now, I'm not saying that your provider will treat you wrong, or try to sell you another router to fix a modem problem, but it's always worthwhile to know what to look for when your site goes down. That way when you call for support, you and your provider will be on the same wavelength, or close, anyway.

This all comes back to how well the WebMaster is trained to support the site. If you tick off your Internet Provider, you'll still get service, but I'll bet that you'll have your share of problems in the shadows. The market is cutthroat right now, but there are plenty of providers around to help you out…and just as many that'll get you into deeper trouble. They're so hungry for your business that some will promise you the moon to get you to sign on. The point here is that the more you know about your site, and how to run it, the better chance you have to have a successful site. However, that doesn't mean that you have to take any crap from them. You sign the checks, and that puts you in the driver's seat. Let's face it, if your provider gives you a hard time, a bit of bad advertising on the Net means disaster for them when word gets around. It's a strange world out there, but the providers know that, too.

What's a Backup?

After you've created this Web server and spent hours to configure it exactly to your designs, how would you like for someone to pull the plug on the server and make it crash? What would you think if a rogue user logged into your server and deleted all the files in the FTP directory? These kinds of threats are all too common on new servers, and even on existing ones. Hardware failure is another ever-present problem. We can never tell when hardware will fail, or what will fail. The best defense from these disasters is a good backup philosophy.

Basic Backup Strategies

There are several ways to backup your server, but only a few wise ones. Over the years, I've learned that the backups are only as good as the equipment and tapes that you use. Avoid the generic tapes and instead purchase the higher-quality tapes from known manufacturers, such as Sony, Maxell, and 3M. Buying the preformatted tapes can save hours of formatting time and server operations. I also recommend using tape drives of 4 GB and higher capacity to start. If you believe that QIC drives are viable in a serious server situation, you're fooling yourself. While QIC has made definitive gains in capacity and speed, when your server matures over the years, the backups are bound to stream over the 2 GB mark and possibly over 4 GB within 3 years.

Use top-quality software that is server based, yet capable of backing up the workstations on the network if you intend to place the Web server onto the internal company network. In this manner, you can use the server-based backup for the critical workstations involved in the server project itself. The backup will also run faster and more efficiently. You'll find centralized control to be a benefit, making security easy to manage. For that reason, SCSI drives in Microsoft Windows NT Server are the only choice above 1 GB.

 While QIC and SCSI drives can both be used on the server, only SCSI drives are supported in high-end backup programs like Arcada backup for NT. Additionally, the backup tape drive must be located on the server itself. This lends further credence to the SCSI-only disk subsystem on the server.

Better Backups by Design

After acquiring the hardware, it's time to decide how you're going to do the real backup. There are several different forms of backup. Let's review the options:

- **Normal**—Makes a complete copy of the server files, including the registry, and resets the archive bit.

- **Incremental**—Copies only the files that have been added or modified since the last normal backup, and resets the archive bit. Incremental backups use the same tape for each backup if append mode is used.

- **Incremental Copy**—Same as incremental backup, but this option does not reset the archive bit.

- **Separate Incremental**—Same as incremental, except you use a different tape each time you backup.

- **Differential**—Copies the files added or changed since the last normal backup, resets the archive bit where applicable, but uses the same tape all the time until it is full or replaced.

You'll have to decide which is best for your server. If not a lot of data changes, say no more than 100 MB, then perhaps an incremental is best. You can use the same tape time and time again until it's full or you change the tape. One server I administered used one 4 GB tape for two weeks, and never used beyond 25 percent of its capacity. The danger here is that if this tape breaks, or gets lost or otherwise damaged, then all of those backups are lost. The benefit is that you can retrieve files based on dates or different needs, such as locating the third oldest copy since you started backing up with this tape.

Differential backups are considered by many to be the way to go. The only difference here between differentials and incrementals is that differentials always use a different tape for each backup, regardless of the volume of data backed up. This assures that if a tape drive goes bad, then only that set is lost. The downside is the volume of physical tapes that are required to support this strategy. Small sites won't see much of a storage problem, but at $20 to $35 a copy, this strategy gets expensive in a hurry.

Practical Backup Systems

When you design your server, backup systems should be in the forefront of the design. Integrating backups into the server from the start shows the CFO that not only do you have your act together in planning, but that you're serious about saving data and money. Of the vendors that make backup systems, a relative newcomer gets my aye vote: the Conner TapeStor 3200 SCSI-2 4Gb tape backup system. It comes with decent backup software and is easy to install and use. Tapes for this system are around $25 apiece in the retail market, and bundles of five can be purchased for just under $100. When I last checked, $700 bought you the whole kit and five tapes to get you started. Now don't get the idea that I'm saying that Conner makes the only good backup, because Hewlett-Packard, DEC, Fuji, and others have really good systems. Seagate's tape divisions are now putting out good products to go with their disk products.

Alternative Backup Systems

One possibility for backups that often is ignored is the use of an optical system. A SCSI device, you can integrate one into Microsoft Windows NT Server very easily, and on the SCSI chain. While backup software may or may not see the optical drive as a valid backup device, you can copy the critical files over to the optical drive instead of backing them up to tapes. This approach has the added benefit of having the files immediately available to users either by disk sharing, or by simply copying the files back to the server's disk drives. These little 230 MB drives are made by vendors such as Fujitsu. The drives are around $500 and the cartridges are priced around $22 apiece.

Toasted and Roasted—The Temperature Demon

Perhaps one of the most neglected topics of any server is one of heat and the degradation it causes on server performance, whether it be a Web server or a regular network server. I feel it is important that you know about heat, its effects on the server, and how you can ease the pain.

Why You Should Worry about Heat

Heat is the number one killer of computer components in a server. A study once suggested that for every 15 degree rise in temperature, the operational life time of electronics components decreases by 5 percent. This doesn't mean that if your server runs at 130 degrees, your server will only last for one year. What it does mean is that prolonged operation at high temperatures causes adverse reactions to these devices. Motors, bearings, plastics, and many other items inside a computer must work harmoniously and for a long period of time, but all of these components are nothing but man-made devices. It took man to make them, and another man-made device (electricity) to break them down. So you see, your server has a defined beginning, lifetime, and ending. It's the ending that we have no firm grasp on until the users start screaming that it doesn't work anymore. Do you remember the proverb "So hot you could cook an egg on it?" and it's implications? Read onward and see the practical examples.

Preventive Measures

One of the easiest and simplest things that you can do to solve the heat problem is to install a $15 fan strategically located inside the case. In the investigation that I spell out later in this section, placement of the fan is not as crucial to success as just installing the fan. Air stagnation between the circuit cards and disk drives causes the worst problems because the air flow is nearly zero. These fans are ideally 12 volt DC 3½-inch fans rated at between 40 to 85 cubic feet per minute (cfm) of air flow. Fans that run over 100 cfm tend to be rather noisy and run at speeds that closely resemble turbo prop airplanes in takeoff mode. Not only that, but DC fans can be installed using the existing power plugs for a floppy drive or a hard drive.

With fans blowing inside the case, one anomaly can arise that defeats the fans and proper cooling. If two fans are installed inside the case, then the case (if tight fitting) can actually pressurize and cause a negative airflow. Nothing moves in the case because the pressure differential causes additional stagnation. In this case, the cure is worse than the ailment. By and large, two fans rated at 30 cfm each do the job fine.

When measuring the airflow or temperature doesn't lend itself to practical help, and the machine is a critical component, then the quickest fix you can do is pull the cover off of the server. This lets the hot air move out of the restricted confines of the case.

A Practical Example

In the course of a computer's lifetime, it, and all components inside, experience both physical and thermal shock hundreds of times over. When a hard drive first has power applied to it, an electrical motor is energized to begin spinning the drive's internal component responsible for holding your data. This device, called a spindle motor, uses direct current as its powering source, and generates heat. This initial surge of power also can be rated as much as 300 percent of the normal running voltage. The same DC current is applied to the various circuit cards installed inside the PC, and thus begins the power up cycle we see when you turn on the PC's power supply switch. This seemingly peaceful occurrence is the hardest hit any PC will incur outside of a power surge, and is the time when many hardware failures occur. Known as the peak inrush current, such a strain on the power supply itself can destroy it. Should you be worried about this fact? No. Modern power supplies are built with internal protection and engineering to withstand a lifetime of on/off cycles. The point is that this is the most stressful time on a PC's components.

In the four computer systems we tested, all were tested from a power off state, and were timed for ranges of 4 to 24 hours after startup. Additionally, two were tested for long-range effects of leaving the system powered on throughout the year as seasonal changes occurred. The temperatures measured were compared with the other systems. The following is a list of the systems and their internal configurations:

System #1
Generic clone desktop PC, large case
12 MHz 286 with 1 MB RAM installed
Standard VGA board
1 serial and parallel port
Floppy controller with two floppy drives

Used as a network workstation
Class B certified

System #2
Same as system #1, but no floppies
Includes network adapter card
Small desktop case
Diskless workstation
Class A certified

System #3
33 MHz 386 small case
8 MB RAM installed
200 MB IDE hard drive, two floppies
Tape drive
Standard AT I/O
SVGA card with 1MB RAM
Additional card
Class B certified

System #4
33 MHz 386 Large tower case
12 MB RAM installed; 8 MB onboard and 4 MB on 32-bit RAM board
Tape drive
Standard AT I/O card
Additional AT I/O card
CD-ROM drive and controller
340 MB ESDI hard drive and ctrl
additional support card
All 8 slots used
Class A certified

It's important to understand that each system has its own characteristics that set it apart from the others. I didn't include the size of the power supplies because that statistic didn't have any bearing on the outcome of the tests. The sizes ranged from 150 watt to 230 watt, and all had single cooling fans. The item that did seem to matter was that the class B certified machines all measured temperatures higher than the class A rated machines. The small desktops also ran at higher temperatures. Changes in seasonal temperature swings simply make the systems run hotter or cooler with respect to the inside temperature of the testing room. Here is a list of the test environment conditions:

- The testing room temperature was set to 68 degrees Fahrenheit.

- Humidity ranged from 35 to 45 percent.

- A temperature probe was placed within two inches of the power supply's air intake screen inside of the PC, and attached so as to remain in open air.

- Where possible, all systems had one empty slot between circuit cards.

Table 4.4 shows the progression of temperature for each system.

From the statistics shown in the table, you can see a wide range of rates of heating, and in general, the systems stabilized by the 2-hour mark. In one system similar to system #3, the system's internal temperature reached 106.3 degrees after the 72 hour mark! So, when you see the moniker of "72 hour

Table 4.4   Comparison of System Temperatures

Time into Test	System #1	System #2	System #3	System #4
15 minutes	68.3	68.8	69.1	68.5
30 minutes	70.5	69.7	70.5	69.8
45 minutes	72.9	71.0	72.3	70.5
1.00 hours	76.4	73.8	75.8	71.0
1.25 hours	78.3	75.1	79.4	72.0
1.50 hours	82.1	76.2	83.3	73.1
1.75 hours	85.5	77.9	85.6	75.2
2.00 hours	87.6	80.2	87.2	77.9
2.25 hours	88.1	81.9	88.2	78.1
2.50 hours	89.9	82.9	89.0	79.3
5.00 hours	92.1	88.7	90.3	82.0
10.0 hours	96.8	94.4	93.6	83.1
18.0 hours	99.4	97.4	95.7	83.3
24.0 hours	103.5	101.9	96.1	84.9

burn-in" that many manufacturers state their systems are put through, then you can tell that's quite a test. Now, expand that test to a one-week-long cycle, and you get a system subjected to a rigor virtually guaranteed to find system faults related to heat.

A word of caution, though. When systems are first assembled, brand new parts tend to withstand this treatment considerably better than a one- or two-year-old system. As part of our reseller program, each system we intend to accept as a trade-in is subjected to a one week long continuous diagnostic test procedure. If it fails any part of this test, the system is not accepted. Due to age, many systems will still run properly in daily usage (one to four hours) but fail when placed in this strenuous test condition.

The solution? After compiling these results, we searched for a suitable cooling fan to be placed in one or two strategic places. The first was to be mounted on the card support cage where all of those seldom-used black card guides are located inside of the system. The second was to be mounted in an unused drive bay immediately above the hard drive, if one was installed, placing a cooling flow of air on the hard drive itself. The first fan placement choice would draw cool air from the outside of the system to inside the system. What we found was that to merely move the air inside the card slots resulted in a marked drop in internal temperatures. Because the power supply's fan could only exhaust the hot air within its immediate reach (8 to 12 inches) of the intake screen, the hot spots in between the circuit cards and hard drive would stagnate, resulting in higher temperatures. Sensor probes were placed around the hard drives of all systems under test, and a remarkable finding was made.

Much to our dismay, every system tested, and a few not listed here, were found to have two major hot spots. The first, and most obvious, was the hard drive. Regardless of drive size and type, each ran up temperatures in the range of 115 to 142 degrees Fahrenheit after 24 hours of continuous operation. The exception was the IDE hard drives, new to the PC computer arena. Those units consistently measured 20 degrees cooler than the rest. The second hot spot was the video board. It reported temperatures in the 95 to 105 degree range. For a general reminder, the circuit board slots, the onboard memory, and the CPU chip on many motherboards are all inline with each other in a four-inch-wide path.

In mounting those cooling fans, we thought of the hard drive first, and the sheer amount of heat it generated after 24 hours of operation. In a normal scenario, however, most users operate their system no more than six continuous hours a day, so instead the video board becomes the major heat generator. Therefore, the first fan was installed on the card guide bracket.

Because heat rises, all of the heat was going to the top of the cabinet but wasn't moving to the power supply's exhaust fan. The card guide fan solved that problem, resulting in a 10 to 15 degree drop in internal temperatures, regardless of the systems detailed back in Table 4.4! System #3, the tightest sealed of the systems, dropped to an average runtime temp of 93 degrees from 103. Furthermore, installing the second fan immediately above the hard drive resulted in an additional 8 degree drop in operating temperature. With the fans installed, the hard drive now averaged 92 degrees, down from 142.

To take this test to further extremes, external cutoff switches were mounted inline with the fans' power so we could control the fan exterior to the system. This way, we could accurately measure the internal temperature without removing the case of the system. What we then found confirmed our earlier observations. Once warmed up beyond the 24-hour mark, stopping the fan above the hard drive resulted in rapid increases in the internal

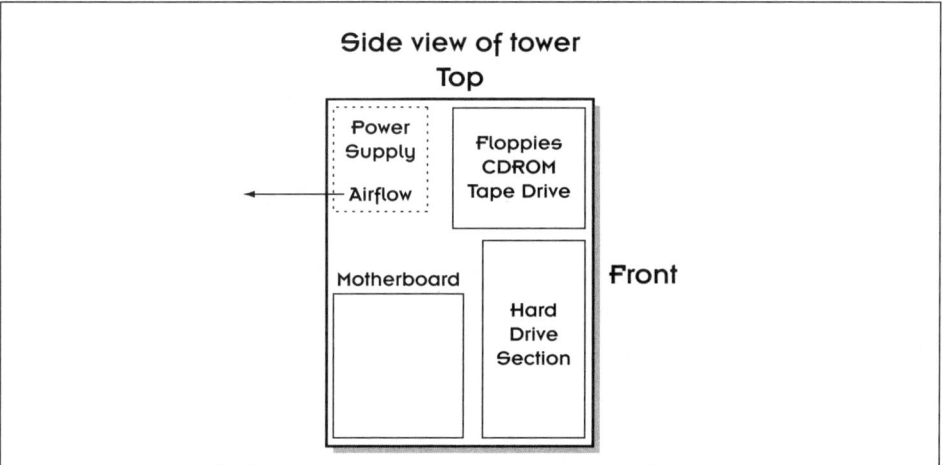

Figure 4.15   General airflow through a case.

temperatures which the card cage fan could not keep up with. All four systems now averaged internal temperatures 8 to 10 degrees above room temperature, about 85 degrees.

The bottom line is this: Cooling your system will inevitably result in longer life span for systems used more than several hours each day. While you won't always be able to install a cooling fan blowing onto each hard drive, perhaps a single fan breaking up the heat around the RAID would be of immense help.

I should note that the fans used were running all the time, so long as the power to the system was on. We then found several fans that could adjust their speed proportionally to the amount of heat sensed. These fans, called closed loop fans, are unique. Their primary feature is a temperature sensor mounted within the fan itself, or an external electrical sensor which senses the average air temperature and adjusts the fan's speed accordingly. Although more expensive, these fans reduce the noise characteristically heard inside PCs. You can mount the sensor either in the exhaust air, intake air, or anywhere else inside the system for maximum effect.

The best benefit is that as the system's internal temperature stabilizes, the heating/cooling effect in the electronic circuits is greatly reduced. One such effect is called "chip creep." This condition causes circuit chips (primarily memory chips) to gradually back out of their sockets. Parity errors, unexplainable operation, or other problems may be caused by "chip creep." Simply reseating the loose chips usually cures the problems.

Power Protection Devices

Let's take a few minutes to go over the most important part of the site, and that's proper power protection. Your Web server should have several forms of power protection, not just a single one. Bad weather and bad power have no worse evil twin cousin than dirty power. One lone lightning strike 20 miles away can show up on your doorstep and wreak havoc on your site. Most often, storms within 5 miles of your site are the prevalent cause of system outages. Let's discuss some of the equipment that is used in the protection of your server. Also, more and more insurance companies are requiring the use of these devices if you want the hardware covered under a data processing policy.

The Difference between a UPS, Filter, and Conditioner

Three types of power protection devices are available to protect your server from power problems sometimes referred to as *dirty power*. Dirty power refers to unstable power or several other types of power problems. Let's take a look at each and evaluate them in terms of our server's needs.

Most MIS types refer to an *Uninterruptible Power Supply* (UPS) as their way of protecting the network server or servers. A UPS is an alternate power supply, nothing more! If you lose primary AC power in the wall from the commercial source, the UPS kicks in to keep the server running. That's all! The batteries of UPSs average 20 minutes of standby power if you use primary commercial power and that primary power fails. This should give you enough time to close all applications and safely shut down the system. Unfortunately, a UPS is a catch-all solution that darkens system administrator's eyes to a larger problem—dirty power.

 If you have a power sag or surge, the UPS is useless to you! Your "protected" equipment is likely to reboot or experience erratic behavior.

A filter is a device that senses very sharp and short duration spikes of power, such as a lightning strike, that only last for a few millionths of a second, but are in the range of 10,000 volts or more. A filter looks at this voltage and runs it off to ground, much like the lightning rod does for the TV antenna on your house. It does nothing for a sag or surge, as those conditions occur relatively slowly with respect to a power spike. The filter is built to respond to these rapid changes in power situations.

This said, the power conditioner is a device that senses the power changes generated by power anomalies such as an air conditioner, refrigerator, or other high power equipment turning on. The line voltage momentarily drops below, or rises above, 120 volts AC to something else, depending on the condition. A power conditioner senses these relatively slow changes in power and compensates by adjusting the output power to the device to a constant steady 120 volts AC. No filtering, just maintaining a steady 120 volts. Figure 4.16 shows the various types of power processing.

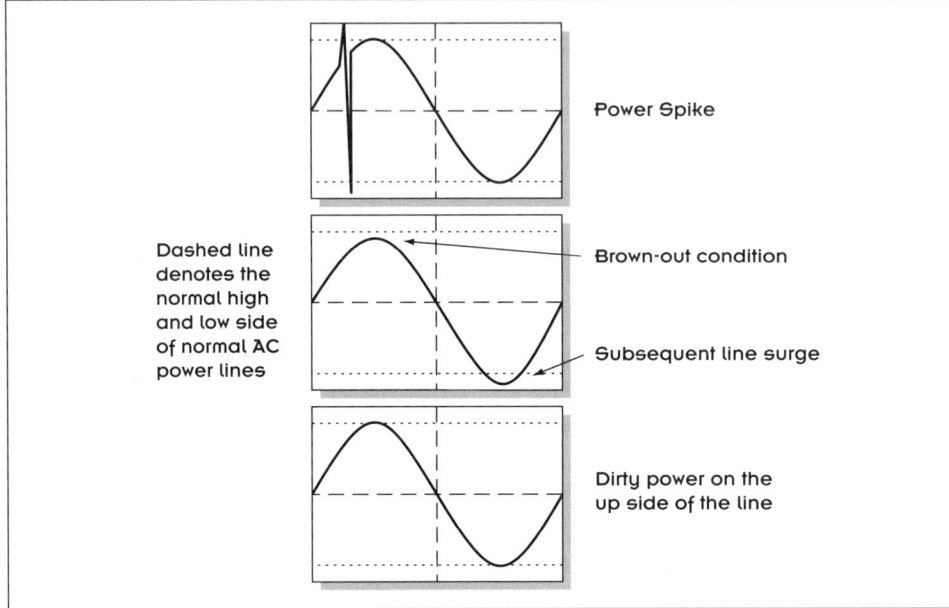

Figure 4.16   Types of power processing.

So, you've been introduced to the three main types of power problems that your site will see. There are others, to be sure, but these are the three that you can buy devices to guard against. Which one do you buy? How will this device help you? First off, changes in the makeup of power protection devices have drastically improved over the last few years. What was once sold as a pure UPS now incorporates several advanced power-protection features. The UPS I use on the workstation on which I am writing this manuscript is a 650 volt-ampere UPS that uses power sag and surge features, but no filtering.

Most commonly, you'll see a UPS with power conditioners built into it, which smooth out the input power in most situations, and buffers those that are beyond normal conditioning. Those beyond the normal situations are called *brown-outs*. In these cases, power is lost for up to a second and you'll actually see the lights dim considerably. It is at this time in low power conditions when servers love to reboot . When the commercial power recovers from the sagging power, a power surge usually occurs. Conditioners prevent this sudden surge from hitting your equipment. If the power drop lasts longer than a second or so, you can almost always count on a *black-out*, which is just that—into the dark you go! This is where a UPS will save you every time! I recently had a brown-out that lasted a few seconds. Neither of my NT Servers missed a beat. Didn't reboot, no harm done, nothing. My own PC has a UPS on it that beeped like a baby missing its bottle, and my fax PC rebooted at the first sign of the brown-out.

Lightning Protection

Few devices incorporate power filters into the UPS because of the inherent problems with a UPS handling such large transient voltages. These filters are usually standalone boxes that are connected to the very first point of input power so any lightning strikes are sent to ground rather than ever making it to the devices. However, this doesn't mean that you don't need other protection. When the lightning strike was shorted off to ground, the devices being protected temporarily lose power. That means a UPS should be installed for them. You're not installing double protection, but rather a layered protection.

There are UPS units that work well concurrently with lightning protectors by using a method called *sine wave power,* in which the commercial input power (which is AC voltage, of course) is converted to DC voltage, and then converted back into filtered AC power for the devices. This double protection ensures that the power being consumed by the devices is as pure as possible. You'll pay through the nose for this kind of specialized protection equipment, but it's worth it if you have $20,000 to protect. Also, this kind of protection equipment has inherent lightning protection built into it by the fact that it takes time for the power spike to make it through the double conversion process. In this time frame, the spike can be filtered off to ground if the protection equipment is built to handle it. In any event, the spike will most likely be drastically reduced to the point that it may not damage anything.

Volume Ratings for Power

When you go to buy these devices, you'll see the rating on the outside of the box. It's nice of the marketing folks to do that, but it's somewhat misleading for your server. That number on the outside is normally the *volt-ampere*

(*VA*) rating, and not the true wattage rating. Let's look at an example of this. I want to purchase a UPS that protects my workstation, which has a 300-watt power supply. What will be the power rating of the UPS that will serve my needs? Take the wattage and divide it by 0.707, which yields 424. This is the volt-ampere-equivalent rating. Current devices usually include a unit of 450 VA, which should do for most any situation. Most vendors of power-protection devices will advise you to purchase a UPS that is rated at 25 percent higher than the maximum load you expect to put on it. This gives a good working margin for the UPS so it doesn't work too hard. If the UPS runs at 90 percent of its rating all the time, it'll wear out faster. In the vast majority of computers, the power supply in it never runs above 50 percent load, so the 300 watt example could be cut in half and the same computer could possibly use a 250 VA unit safely. Personally, I advise my own clientele not to use anything under a 600 VA for a safe margin.

But is the computer base unit the only thing you'll put on it? How about the monitor? Modems? Answering machine? All of these take up power. Most monitors run at an average of 2 amperes of current, which equates to 240 watts of power. Add this to an estimated 150 watts of continuous internal power, and now you have about 400 watts of power needs. Divide that by 0.707, and now you have 565 VA of power. So now? Is the 650 VA enough? You're running this poor 600 VA UPS at 95 percent of its capacity. This isn't a good thing at all. So, you can either get a larger UPS, or don't put the monitor on it.

Estimating Your Volume of Power

To protect yourself adequately, it's important that you are aware of how much power your server uses. To keep it short and direct, let's use Table 4.5 to illustrate the point about estimating power for a Web server.

This should show you that even on an average midrange Web server, a 1200 VA UPS is just barely enough to do the job. It's not unreasonable to jump right up to a 2000 VA UPS and bypass any potential problems with power.

A Word about Extension Cords

Extension cords are one sure-fire way to get your site into trouble with a capital "T." If you really need additional outlets, that's one thing. But, to

Table 4.5   Estimated Power Requirements for a Web Server

Device	Runtime Wattage	Volt-Amperes
Computer	200	283
Monitor	250	353
External Drives	200	283
Sub-Total	650	919
25% Margin	163	230
Total	813	1149

use cheap two-wire extension cords with multiple outlets is not using proper grounding and can result in shorted out power supplies.

The usage of poor-quality extension cords can result in fire or possible electrocution. Multiple-outlet devices should consist of only UL approved cords and outlet devices. Ensure that the total rated power of the devices plugged into the extensions does not exceed the breaker rating of the power source.

There are times when you need more outlets than you have physical wall plugs, and this happens all the time. However, do yourself and the Fire Marshall a favor and use proper extensions. One of the best ones to use is the surge-protected, four- and six-plug multi-outlet boxes. Tripp Lite and APC both make fine devices that solve this need well. *No matter what you do, don't exceed the maximum rating of the wall outlet.* No amount of quality extension devices can replace a burnt down workshop.

Multiple Outlet Control Centers

One really neat device is the power center or controller that resides under your monitor on the desktop itself. These devices are the same thing as one of those rectangular power strips, except that it's a flat pizza box style. The one on my desk is about the size of a small pizza box. It has a switch for the computer box, monitor, printer, modem, and one auxiliary device. It does in fact have a measure of surge protection built into the device, so it makes it nice to have on systems that have no UPS at all. While not a power line filter or UPS, it goes a long way to organizing your power connections, if nothing else, but remember that it's no real replacement for a true UPS or line conditioner.

Backup Generators

The last topic of this section, and the chapter, is one of a power generator. This device actually creates usable power from a motor generator engine. In reality, it's a power generation station. Perhaps only a few thousand watts of power, but it does the job nicely for small volumes. You've undoubtedly heard of someone using a generator when they lost power because of a tornado, hurricane, or other form of natural disaster to keep AC power to critical equipment. Generators are meant to be short term solutions to loss of power, and not long term continued usage. These little "personal" generators come in all shapes and designs, but most notably average 2000 watts of output power on a continuous basis. If you look at the most essential parts of the network and what it would take to keep the site operational, you will see that you need 3500 watts of power for the server, all components of the server, and the router equipment.

One thing that you should keep firmly in your mind is that when you run one of these generators, the output power is not as clean or steady as regular commercial power. To use a generator for a computer, you definitely need a line conditioner and a UPS to keep stable line power going to the server. Also, you may need to turn off the generator at times to let it cool down and refill the gasoline or diesel fuel or whatever is used to power the generator. During this time, of course, the server must come down lest you drain the batteries. Generators have this little thing called a *duty cycle*, which means that the generator is capable of supplying a certain amount of power at 50 percent of the rated speed or capacity of the device. If the duty cycle is exceeded for long periods of time, meaning if you constantly draw 3000 watts of power from a 3500 watt capacity generator for hours on end, then the generator will age very rapidly and produce poor power. Not only that, but such a load factor is not advisable on a temporary power source.

Generators are nice, but have limited outlets. In addition to that, you'll have to run an extension cord from the generator to the devices to be powered. If the distance is beyond 50 feet, then you'll need a power cord of much higher capacity rating than the standard cords you'll see in Kmart or Wal-Mart. Those are fine for normal low power needs, but this is different. Figure 4.17 illustrates the method my company chose for integrating a generator into the power distribution at my office. By doing it this way, I was able to use standard wiring for heavy usage and standard circuit breakers for power isolation.

 Figure 4.17 was approved for our electrical operations. It is meant to provide you with alternative power distribution and redundancy needs. Consult with your electrician to ensure compliance with state, local, and city ordinances before attempting any such power modifications in your office. Failure to do so may render your electrical system unsafe or in violation with your insurance company or local fire regulations.

With this scheme, if we lost commercial power, I could turn off the breaker to the commercial source and turn on the breaker to our generator, thereby

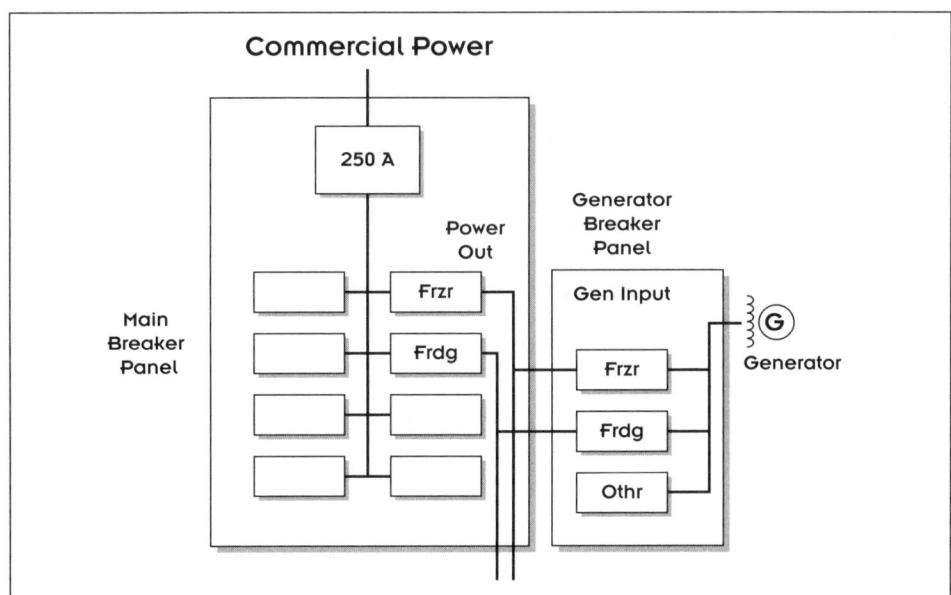

Figure 4.17 Integrating a generator into your power system.

sending power to the desired in-house equipment by selectively turning on or off the breakers in the main power panel.

The real trick to this is to remember when to turn which breaker on or off. If you forget to turn off the breakers to remove the path to commercial power, then the generator and any associated equipment connected to the generator could be destroyed!

Summary

This has been a really demanding chapter, because every aspect of our Web server has been covered to help enhance your understanding of a Web server, and how to build one. Hopefully, you'll take this knowledge forth and build a good server. In reading this chapter, you've learned about:

- Three types of servers and how to apply them

- Various pieces of server hardware to enhance your server's operations and safety

- Connecting your server to the Internet

- What abnormal temperatures can do to your server

- Some do's and don'ts of power protection

In Chapter 5; we'll install the Microsoft Internet Information Server. This server is a native tool of Microsoft Windows NT Server, and ties directly into the operating system in a native form. We'll discuss the many parts of the Web server, and how it can work for you. So stay tuned for another exciting chapter in the saga of the NT Web Server.

Building Your Web Server

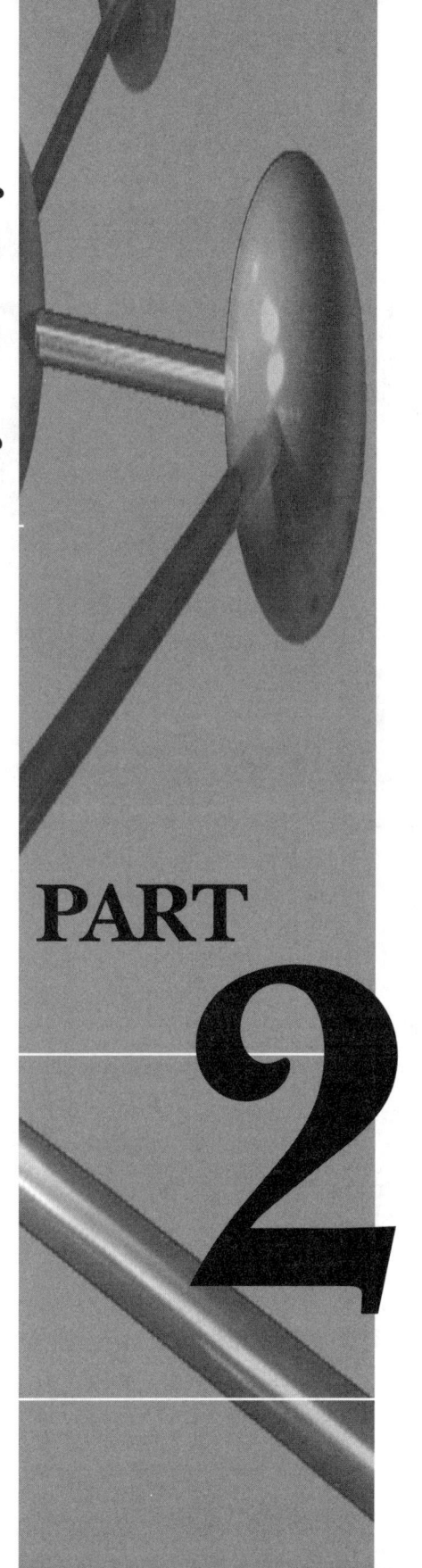

CHAPTER

Microsoft's Internet Information Server

Now that we've covered the basics of Web servers, strategic money-making ventures, and the hardware and software options you have for setting up a server, it's time to get right down to the nitty gritty of Web servers and see how they're used for both personal and business applications. In this and the following three chapters, we're going to preview four Web server packages: Microsoft's Internet Information Server, O'Reilly and Associates' WebSite, Process Software's Purveyor, and Quarterdeck's WebStar. For each server, we'll discuss installation, integration into NT Server itself, administration, and Web page support issues.

An Introduction to Internet Information Server (IIS)

The IIS (as we'll call it) is available for free. Simply stop by the Microsoft home page (*www.microsoft.com*) and select their Web server link. You'll have to fill out a form that asks all sorts of information about you, and why you'll be using IIS, but other than that the download is available at any time. IIS comes with the Web server as expected, but also includes a Gopher and FTP server. Microsoft Windows

211

NT Server includes an FTP server, and the one in IIS is very similar. I'll cover the differences later in the chapter.

IIS is also now a part of BackOffice, Microsoft's integrated family of server software, which Microsoft beefed up as their presence on the Internet broadened considerably. The Microsoft Network, Microsoft's online service, has been successfully running NT and IIS as the core of the system. As you'd expect, IIS's integration into NT Server is the tightest of any server I'll be reviewing. But, is it the best for your application? Let's press onward and find out.

Prerequisites

Before we go any further, we need to discuss the prerequisites to install IIS. To download IIS along with the current Internet Explorer browser, all you need is 13 MB of disk space and about two hours of time (at 28.8 Kbps download rates). Fairly inexpensive to get started, to be sure, and Microsoft wants it that way. As far as experience goes, if you can set up NT Server itself, you'll have no problems installing IIS. In fact, IIS is amazingly simple to set up and is no worse than any network application.

IIS installs in less than 20 MB. Actually, that's not true—IIS is only 12 MB, but you have to install Service Pack 3 to install IIS, which raises the disk requirements slightly. For memory, you'll be pleasantly surprised to hear that I prototyped my IIS server on a 486DX4-100 and 16 MB of memory! Not only did it run, but it ran very well; however, I would have fared a little better if I had 32 MB of memory in it. One of the reasons is that NT itself runs fine in 8 to 12Mb of memory, and the real loading problems don't come to life until more of the Web server options are deployed. In fact, when I did the testing on IIS, adding the second 16 MB of memory let the server, as a whole, run faster, but did little to benefit IIS itself. A little later on I'll be presenting charts to show the performance differences with varying amounts of installed memory.

Installation

Let's begin the installation by presuming you've already built and installed an NT Server using NT v3.51, which is the current incarnation of NT (v4 will debut in Fall 1996). As I mentioned a moment ago, to install IIS, you must also install Service Pack 3 (SP3). This application is nothing more than an update to the operating system; it includes bug fixes, patches, and a few enhancements.

 As always, be sure that you've got a reliable backup of your server before installing SP3. Although the service pack should not cause any direct failures in the NOS after installation, possible glitches in the installation itself due to power failure, hardware failure, etc., could render the server inoperable.

Acquiring and Installing the Service Pack

SP3 is available from a variety of sources, including Microsoft's own Web site SOFTLIB, the Microsoft Developers Network CD-ROM, and sites such as the Beverly Hills Software site at *http://www.bhs.com.* The pack itself consists of eight files—for a total of 15 MB—usually labeled sp3_*x*.exe, where *x* refers to the sequential file number in the pack. I did the SP3 update from my MSDN subscription CD #5, which has the expanded files. Running the upgrade request from the MSDN CD #1, all I had to do was insert the CD #5 when requested, let the files in the winnt35 directory get updated, and reboot the server to make the changes take effect. Pretty simple stuff. The only outward difference you'll see is the very top line when you boot the server. Usually, as soon as the screen turns blue and the kernel of the operating system kicks in, you'll see the message "Microsoft® Windows NT™ Version 3.51 (Build 1057)," but now you'll notice that the words "Service Pack 3" are appended to the startup line.

Performing the Actual IIS Installation

IIS is available on diskette, CD-ROM, or, as I mentioned earlier, from the Microsoft Web site. The installation steps are very similar for all versions of IIS. To avoid some delays, and one or two error messages at the end of the installation, make sure your server is connected to the Internet by whatever means you normally connect. You need to perform the installation at the NT Server console. You can, however, do the installation from any workstation on the network in which you have sufficient rights as a domain administrator. This means that you could actually build a complete IIS server at a customer's site from your home office! Start the setup by running

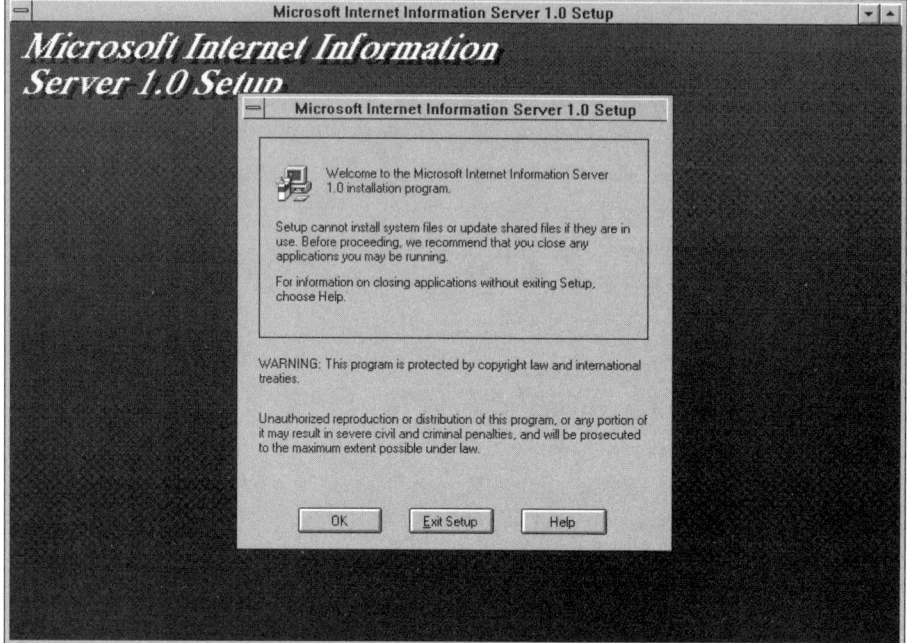

Figure 5.1 Starting IIS installation.

"setup.exe" from the directory containing your downloaded files or from CD or diskette 1. The startup screen is shown in Figure 5.1.

Do yourself a favor and avoid the aggravation of the open files and update problems that Figure 5.1 talks about, and close down all non-essential applications. Click on the OK button and proceed. Next, you'll get to pick the options and software utilities to install with the main product itself. Also, double check the directory where you're installing the server. It defaults to c:\inetsvr, which can cause trouble for some users.

 On many NT Servers, the system builder creates only a small C partition—75 MB—for DOS and critical device drivers. If you accidentally accept the default installation that IIS suggests, then the C partition could fill up during the installation process!

If you're interested in what each of these options does, click once on the text next to the checkbox, and its function is explained in the informational

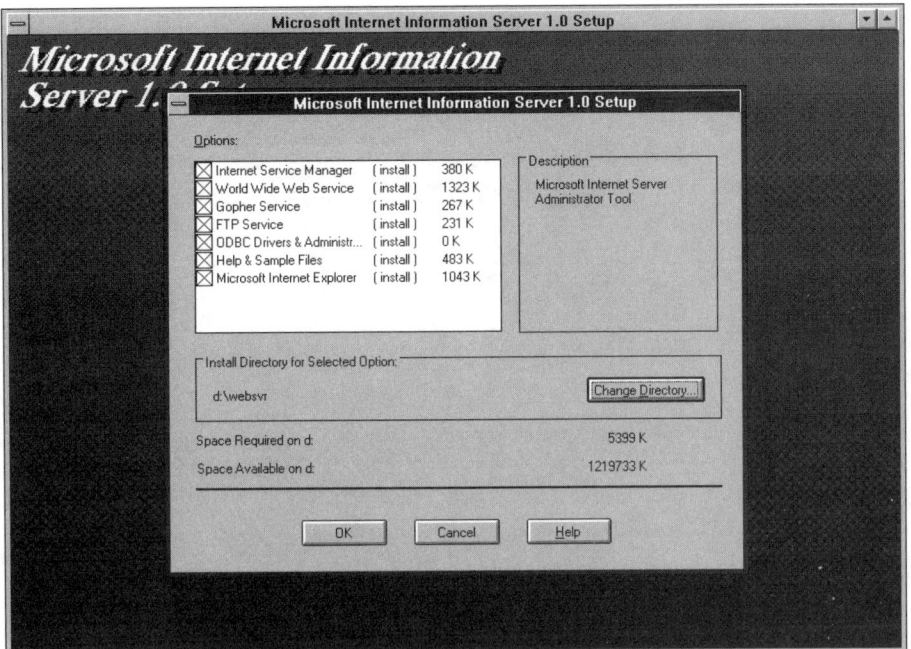

Figure 5.2   Choosing what to install for IIS.

box to the right, as shown in Figure 5.2. After selecting your installation options and verifying the directory, click on OK to proceed onward.

Next, you'll be presented with three options for choosing the main directories for FTP, Web, and Gopher publishing locations, as indicated in Figure 5.3. By default, these directories are created in a subdirectory beneath the main IIS location, but you're free to change that location. I suggest you leave the default locations intact for easier backups.

If the directories you've chosen do not exist, you'll be asked to confirm their creation. The set-up program then copies, installs, and modifies the necessary files, and performs all the rest of the things that IIS needs to do. During the installation, if IIS finds that you've got the NT Server FTP service running, you'll be asked if you want to turn it off. This step is necessary for IIS's FTP service to run properly. If you want to run the IIS integrated FTP, then turn off NT Server's FTP service.

You'll next be offered ODBC (Open Database Connectivity) options for installation, as shown in Figure 5.4. At this time, only the Microsoft SQL

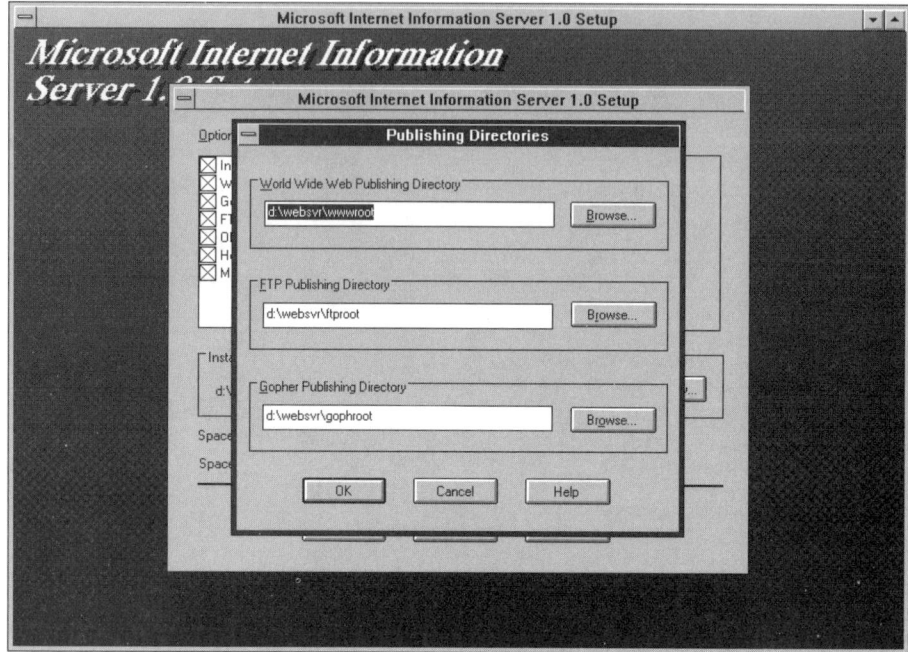

Figure 5.3   Choosing the directory locations.

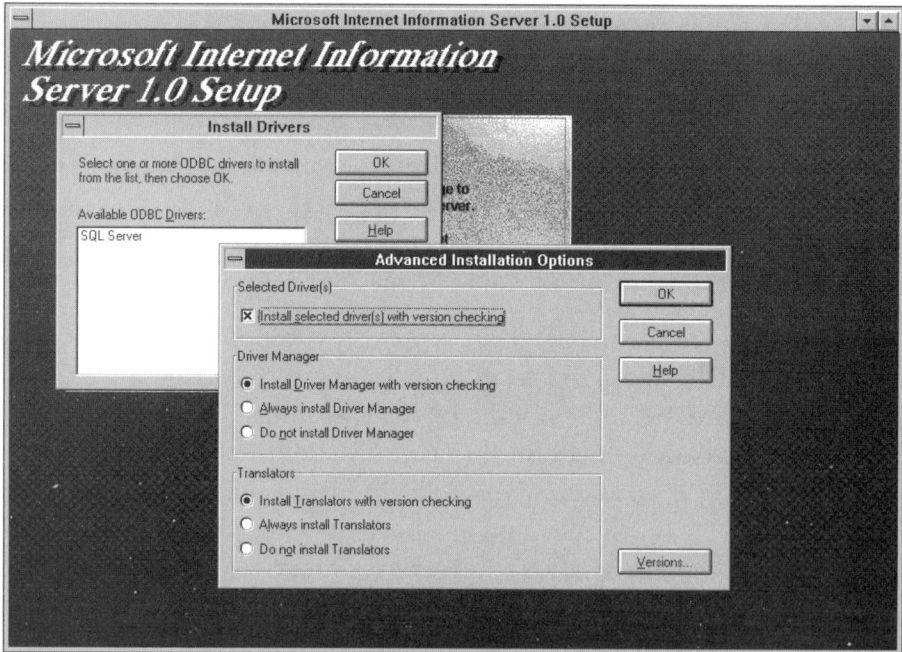

Figure 5.4   ODBC drivers and driver options for IIS.

Server driver is installable. This is probably because IIS has become one part of the BackOffice solution, which Microsoft SQL Server is also a part of. You can define several advanced options for the ODBC drivers if you want, but most people won't need to bother with any of the ODBC at this time.

The remaining files are copied to the server, and the basic configuration is set. Click on the OK button to acknowledge the installation. As I mentioned earlier, Microsoft automatically installs the Internet Explorer for NT browser with the IIS package. Figure 5.5 shows the completed installation screen.

Congratulations! You're done. Now for the good part—making your IIS Web server operational.

Basic Administration

Before people start using your Web server, they must have permissions to use it. We're focusing on using the Web server as a business tool, and will set permissions based on that assumption. As a pseudo-private Web site, all connections can only be made by strictly authorized clients. This means that you'll have to go to the NT Server running the Web services and create the

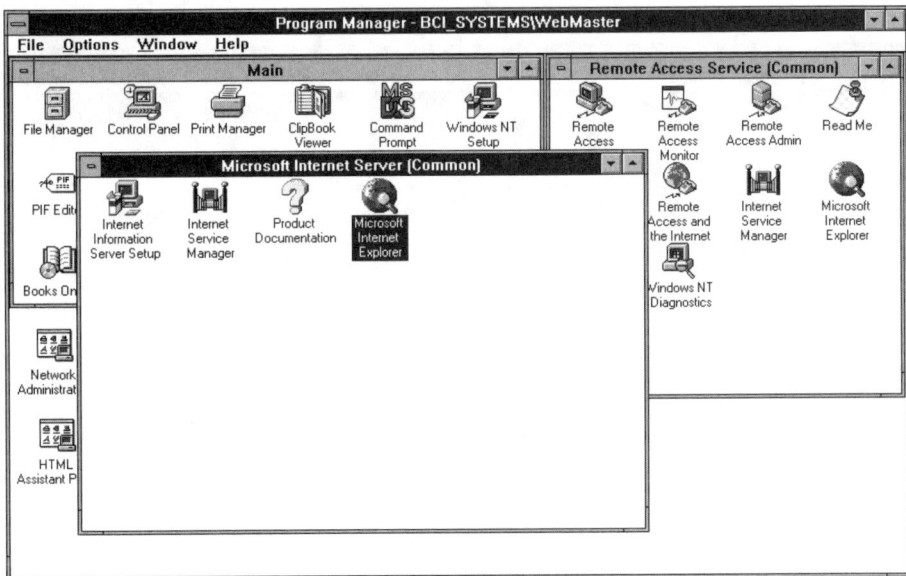

Figure 5.5 The final installed group.

user accounts, rights, permissions, etc., for each client. Once that's done, we can press onward with the Web administration for IIS. If you need any assistance along the way, consult the online IIS manual at *http://www.microsoft.com/InfoServ*.

To start IIS, double click on the *Internet Service Manager* icon, which displays the screen shown in Figure 5.6.

Take a look at the lower-right corner of the screen. It says that *one server* and *three services* are running. Most interesting. This means that IIS is installed as one Web server, but splits out its internal functions as three separate NT services. Each of the three functions—the Web, FTP, and Gopher servers—operate independent of one another, and their individual speed is dependent on the user load factor.

To demonstrate this independence, I started the Performance Monitor in NT Server and initialized the Processor Time, User Time, and Interrupts per second monitors to see how the physical server performs while handling a logged-in user. The results are shown in Figure 5.7.

Four users were on the server when this screen was captured, and the physical server is running only at 40 percent capacity. Not too bad. This server

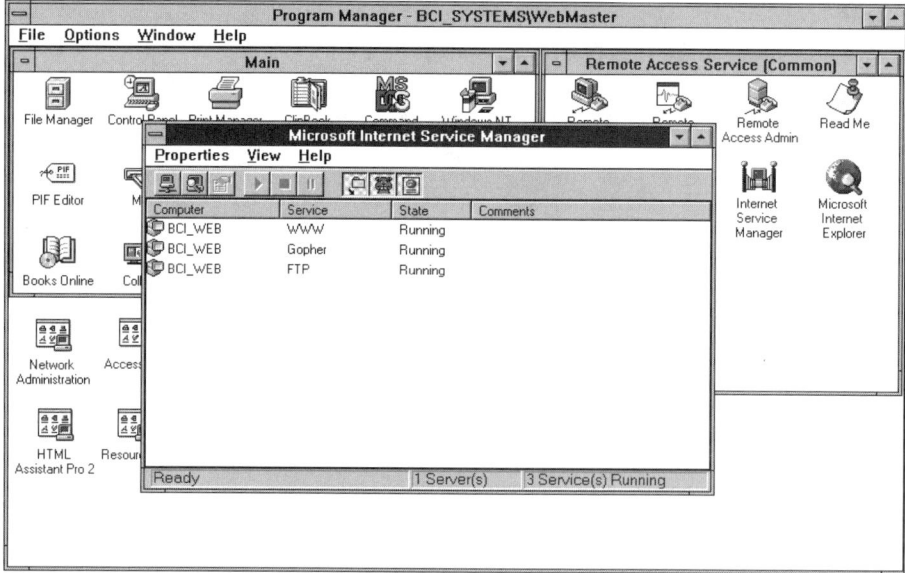

Figure 5.6   IIS's Service Manager.

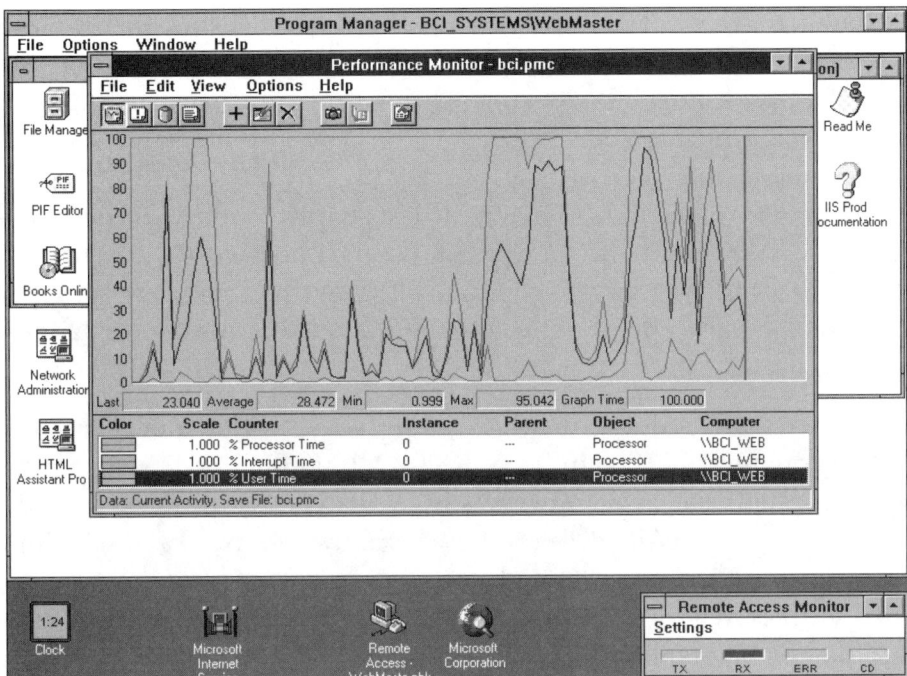

Figure 5.7   Physical server performance of IIS.

could be doing a whole lot more work if it needed to. While testing this setup, I noticed that the physical server appeared sluggish and otherwise slow to respond to tasks. A perfect opportunity to do a little detective work. I ran the Windows NT Diagnostics utility found in the Administrator Group, and found out some interesting things, as shown in Figure 5.8.

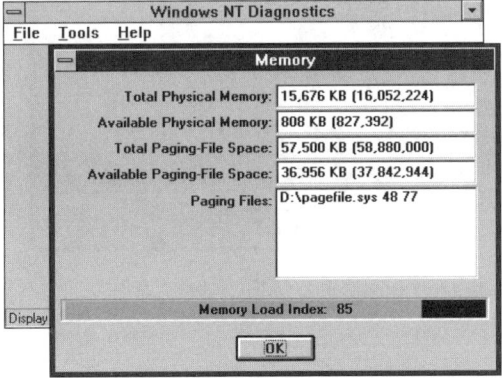

Figure 5.8   Memory tasking diagnostic in 16 MB of memory.

The tasking bar is red and showing nearly 80 percent load factor on the memory subsystem! This means the Microsoft Windows NT Server proper is closely approaching tasks locking up, slow operations, or even the server itself locking up, since the processor now has to do more work with an exceptionally loaded memory subsystem. Why? I'm running this Web server on 16 MB of memory, that's why! In the last chapter when we discussed the relative performance between types of servers, I pointed out that memory is a key factor in Web server operations. I wasn't pulling your leg! Figure 5.9 shows the same operations, only with the server running on 32 MB of memory.

You can see that by adding 16 MB of memory, the free memory went up to 5.2 MB, roughly a 4 MB gain from the 1.2 MB that it was. This means that 12 MB of the installed memory was immediately used for the operating system, all users, and the drivers. How this extra memory was divvied up is a mystery to us, but we saw a slight increase in performance and free system resources. Where the processor was only 40 percent tasked it now is 30 to 35 percent. Not much of a processor gain, but it shows that beefing up one component of the physical server can assist other parts of the server operations. Now let's look at the memory and server performance when we bump the memory up to 48 MB. Figure 5.10 shows boosted performance levels.

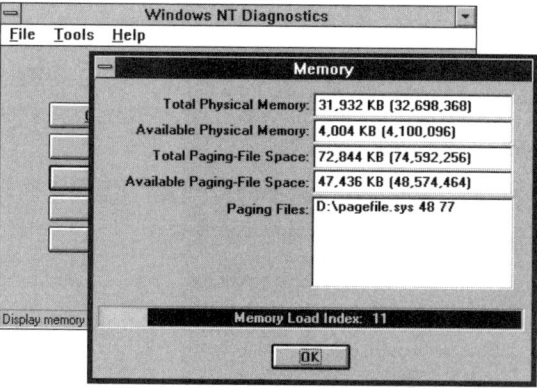

Figure 5.9 Memory tasking diagnostic in 32 MB of memory.

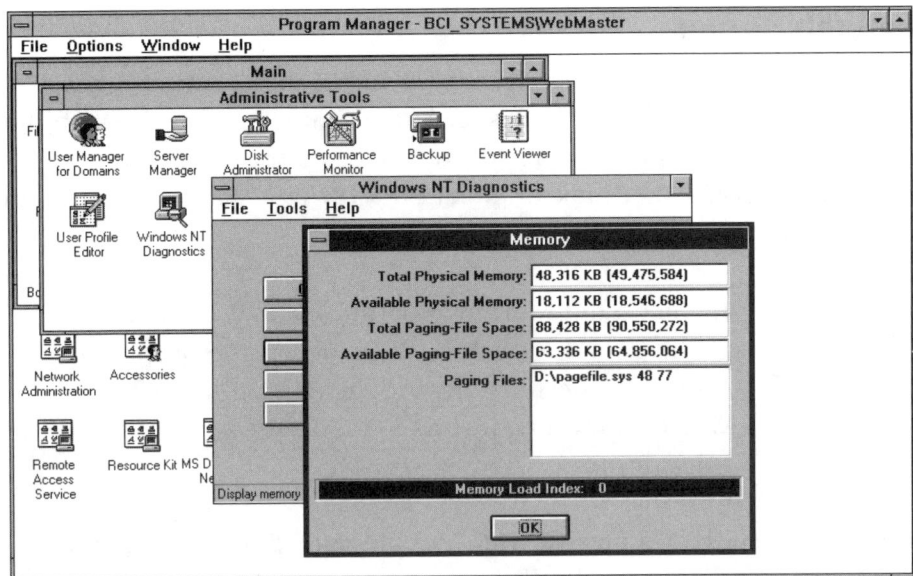

Figure 5.10 Memory tasking diagnostic in 48 MB of memory.

Installing a faster processor won't help memory loss, but it'll speed up what is using memory. Likewise, adding memory provides more "running room" for applications.

As you can see, the server now has 18 MB of free memory after everything is running. When we explored the 32 MB installation, we saw that there was roughly 4 MB of free memory. So shouldn't we have 20 MB of memory (not 18 MB) after adding another 16 MB? No, and I'll tell you why. First, Microsoft Windows NT Server dynamically allocates and manages memory. Second, your free memory is partially determined by how you set the tasking in the NT setup via the Control Panel. In this case, Microsoft Windows NT Server used the additional 16 MB of memory to load more functions and keep the drivers and applications loaded in memory.

This little rendition of server configuration may not have been directly related to the administration of IIS, but I wanted to reinforce the premise that a properly configured server will give you the best performance. Next, let's get right into working with the Web server service of IIS.

The Web Server

There's no doubt about it, the Web server function provides the most visibility of any function of your Web site. And because "surfing the Web" has become the most popular thing to do on the Internet, you want a top-notch server service. Let's take a look at the IIS Web server function and how it can work for us.

 If you do not want to allow anonymous connections to the Web server, then you must set the proper NT rights and permissions for each account you'll provide to the users, just like you do for a normal network setup.

Start the IIS Service Manager if you've not already done so. You'll see the status of all three services. If all the services are not running, go to the Control Panel and start the ones you need. If the services simply won't start up, then it may be necessary to reinstall IIS. From the View menu, select the Services view—the three core services will be displayed. Expand the WWW view by clicking on the plus sign at the left of the window then double-click on the traffic signal, and you'll see a view of the many options that allow you to tune and tweak the installation, as shown in Figure 5.11.

This figure shows the WWW Service Properties window, which includes options for anonymous account selections, password protection, and connection limitations. The options I selected allow for anonymous connections and the use of clear text authentication. If you want to tighten up security, then check the box for NT Challenge authentication. This type of validation is only usable while the clients are using Microsoft Internet Explorer v2.0 or greater, but it ensures the best possible security and lessens the chances of an intruder getting into your site. The NT security is the central point of the server, and you should explore the options here for the Web server. Again, if you have questions, the full manual for IIS is online.

Next, select the Directories tab. This window provides you with options for selecting the location of the scripts and HTML pages, including the default home page that users see when they first log on to your site. If you

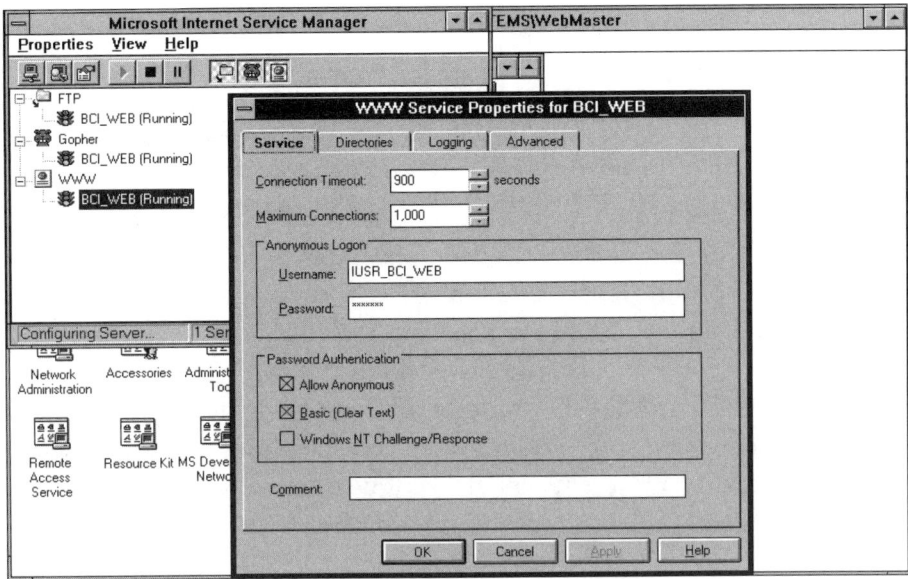

Figure 5.11   Web server options and preferences.

don't modify anything after initial installation, then you'll be presented with the default Web page, shown in Figure 5.12, courtesy of Microsoft.

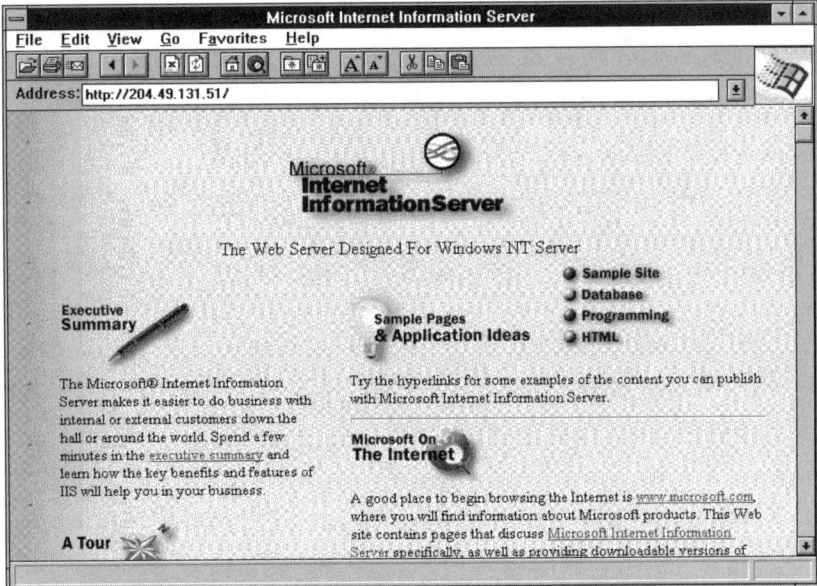

Figure 5.12   IIS's default home page.

Click on the Edit Properties button and take a peek at some important options for your Web server. The highlighted item at the top of the window is the home directory. IIS created this directory by default when you installed the program. If you changed the directory name, your screen will show that name now instead. Right below this selection is a window where you can input an alias directory location in which the users go if no other directory is specified. This is useful to secure part of one directory tree structure and prevent browsing in others. If you specify a virtual directory using the Universal Naming Convention (UNC), such as "bci_web\apps\webserver\iis", then this option for account information is enabled. Do you remember in Chapter 4 when we talked about the topic of named pipes and network access? Well, that's exactly what you're doing when you specify the account information in this block. You're creating a named pipe access to another location on the network with account naming and password protection.

The next thing to consider in this directory information section is the subject of *virtual server,* in which an IP address is assigned to the network card itself (you've already done this, presumably) and assigned to an alias directory. For example, let's say the real server, the Web server, is at 206.139.150.2, which is the NIC. You assign an address of 206.139.150.10 to the virtual server pointing to the "\\bci_web\apps\webserver" directory, and give this directory the alias of www.test.com. When a user from the Internet tries the command *http://www.test.com,* they'll wind up at the specified UNC instead of going to the Web root specified in the IIS setup.

The last part of this properties section is to enable writing if you want to allow users to alter Web pages; reading is enabled by default, of course. The very last item in this section allows you to enable a *Secure Sockets Layer (SSL)* channel, which is a private and public key encryption mechanism to move data across the server to the clients in a secure format. This may be crucial if your business conducts its affairs with financial or privileged data. If you have SSL installed, this option is enabled and you will be able to place an X in the box.

Let's move on to some other options. Click on the Logging tab. The options in this window provide a really neat way to keep an eye on the Web server. On the left side of the window, you can configure the logging function to automatically log server activities for a specified amount of time.

For instance, if you choose the weekly reports option, then the next report will be automatically created at the start of the next week, and the old file will be retained. If you're using SQL Server, then you can log the file to a database instead of a clear text file. This feature is really nice if you need to do analysis of the data in a more automated way. Listing 5.1 shows a sample of the text version of the log functions.

Listing 5.1   Sample Logging File for the Web Service

```
204.49.131.51, TSD_Mgr, 4/4/96, 10:46:20, W3SVC, BCI_WEB, 204.49.131.51,
    1061, 344, 3773, 200, 0, GET, /Default.htm, -,
204.49.131.51, TSD_Mgr, 4/4/96, 10:46:21, W3SVC, BCI_WEB, 204.49.131.51,
    942, 278, 2667, 200, 0, GET, /samples/images/backgrnd.gif, -,
204.49.131.51, TSD_Mgr, 4/4/96, 10:46:26, W3SVC, BCI_WEB, 204.49.131.51,
    4907, 276, 4962, 200, 0, GET, /samples/images/h_logo.gif, -,
204.49.131.51, TSD_Mgr, 4/4/96, 10:46:28, W3SVC, BCI_WEB, 204.49.131.51,
    1472, 275, 1067, 200, 0, GET, /samples/images/SPACE.gif, -,
204.49.131.51, TSD_Mgr, 4/4/96, 10:46:28, W3SVC, BCI_WEB, 204.49.131.51,
    130, 276, 3051, 200, 0, GET, /samples/images/h_exec.gif, -,
204.49.131.51, TSD_Mgr, 4/4/96, 10:46:29, W3SVC, BCI_WEB, 204.49.131.51,
    1512, 276, 2635, 200, 0, GET, /samples/images/h_tour.gif, -,
204.49.131.51, TSD_Mgr, 4/4/96, 10:46:31, W3SVC, BCI_WEB, 204.49.131.51,
    1312, 276, 1047, 200, 0, GET, /samples/images/SPACE2.gif, -,
204.49.131.51, TSD_Mgr, 4/4/96, 10:46:31, W3SVC, BCI_WEB, 204.49.131.51,
    50, 276, 6284, 200, 0, GET, /samples/images/h_samp.gif, -,
204.49.131.51, TSD_Mgr, 4/4/96, 10:46:35, W3SVC, BCI_WEB, 204.49.131.51,
    4306, 278, 3371, 200, 0, GET, /samples/images/h_browse.gif, -,
204.49.131.51, TSD_Mgr, 4/4/96, 10:46:36, W3SVC, BCI_WEB, 204.49.131.51,
    1202, 277, 2982, 200, 0, GET, /samples/images/powered.gif, -,
204.49.131.59, TSD_Mgr, 4/4/96, 10:48:55, W3SVC, BCI_WEB, 204.49.131.51,
    1763, 183, 3749, 200, 0, GET, /Default.htm, -,
204.49.131.59, TSD_Mgr, 4/4/96, 10:48:57, W3SVC, BCI_WEB, 204.49.131.51,
    1873, 229, 2643, 200, 0, GET, /samples/images/backgrnd.gif, -,
204.49.131.59, TSD_Mgr, 4/4/96, 10:48:58, W3SVC, BCI_WEB, 204.49.131.51,
    2744, 226, 1043, 200, 0, GET, /samples/images/SPACE.gif, -,
204.49.131.59, TSD_Mgr, 4/4/96, 10:49:00, W3SVC, BCI_WEB, 204.49.131.51,
    4537, 227, 4938, 200, 0, GET, /samples/images/h_logo.gif, -,
204.49.131.59, TSD_Mgr, 4/4/96, 10:49:01, W3SVC, BCI_WEB, 204.49.131.51,
    5478, 227, 3027, 200, 0, GET, /samples/images/h_exec.gif, -,
204.49.131.59, TSD_Mgr, 4/4/96, 10:49:02, W3SVC, BCI_WEB, 204.49.131.51,
    2724, 227, 2611, 200, 0, GET, /samples/images/h_tour.gif, -,
204.49.131.59, TSD_Mgr, 4/4/96, 10:49:02, W3SVC, BCI_WEB, 204.49.131.51,
    1893, 227, 1023, 200, 0, GET, /samples/images/SPACE2.gif, -,
204.49.131.59, TSD_Mgr, 4/4/96, 10:49:06, W3SVC, BCI_WEB, 204.49.131.51,
```

```
   4005, 227, 6260, 200, 0, GET, /samples/images/h_samp.gif, -,
204.49.131.59, TSD_Mgr, 4/4/96, 10:49:06, W3SVC, BCI_WEB, 204.49.131.51,
   4106, 229, 3347, 200, 0, GET, /samples/images/h_browse.gif, -,
204.49.131.59, TSD_Mgr, 4/4/96, 10:49:09, W3SVC, BCI_WEB, 204.49.131.51,
   2363, 229, 3347, 200, 0, GET, /samples/images/h_browse.gif, -,
204.49.131.59, TSD_Mgr, 4/4/96, 10:49:09, W3SVC, BCI_WEB, 204.49.131.51,
   3825, 228, 2958, 200, 0, GET, /samples/images/powered.gif, -,
```

The log file shows details regarding the following items:

- IP address of the visitor

- Logon name (TSD_Mgr)

- Date

- Time

- Type of connection

- Server name of the connection (bci_web) and the IP address of the server

- Map coordinates of the Web page accessed

- Type of access—in this case, a GET function (or retrieve the Web page)

- Name of the image used to create the map file

Even more important is that the entries are all comma delimited and ready to be imported into just about any database system in existence today.

Moving right along, click on the Advanced tab to see some of the tightest restrictions you can place upon the visitors to your Web site. (Feeling powerful yet?) For example, if you know you want to restrict access to your site based upon a range of IP addresses, you can enter a whole class of addresses such as 206.139.000.000 through 206.139.255.255. Or, you can grant access by leaving the exclusions blank. You can also limit the amount of bandwidth usage per user with the setting at the bottom of the page.

Well, I guess you're wondering what's next, right? Well, that's all! Straight-forward, simple, fast, and easy. What could be better for a budding new Web site? Our next task is to start developing Web pages and grow the site, but we'll hold off on that until the end of the chapter. Figure 5.13 shows a sample directory listing of the Web pages that Microsoft placed in the IIS

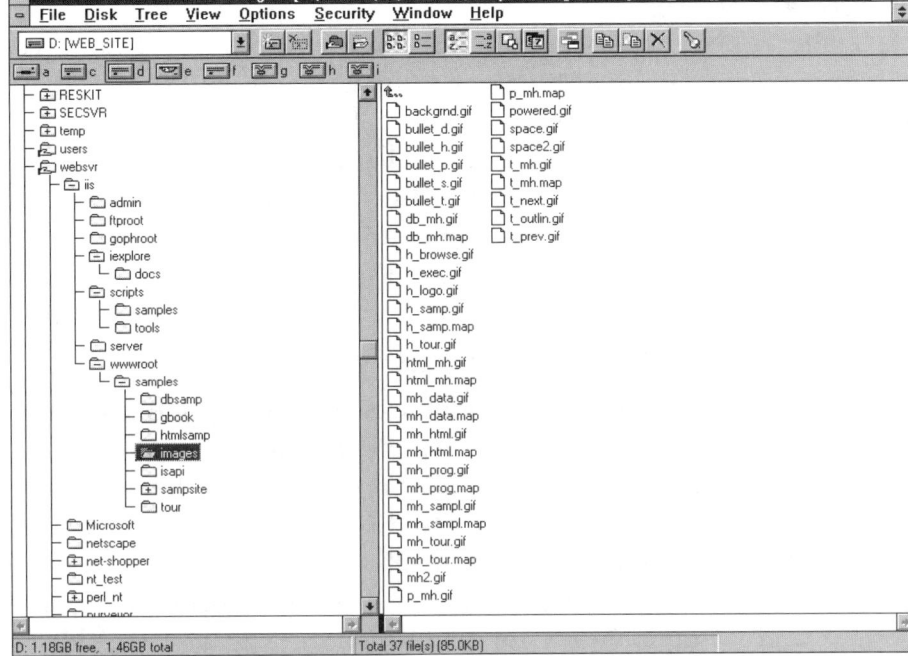

Figure 5.13   IIS's directory structure.

installation. I fully expanded out the directory structure that IIS created during the installation, so you can see everything that's included.

The Gopher Server

Let's presume that the Web portion of your server is installed and operational. You've got some really neat Web pages built and posted. Lots of folks are visiting your Web site, and things are hopping for you. But all at once, you find out that your WebMaster has left you for a better offer and more money and you have a hot request to update a Web page.

No problem. You start up your favorite HTML editor and head off to the location where the Web pages are *supposed* to be stored. Supposed to be because you haven't played with the Web pages in quite a while (that's why you have a WebMaster). Now you discover they're not anywhere close to being in the proper location. Again, no problem. You remember that you can use most any text file to create a Gopher entry. It's quick, painless, and easy. Is this a replacement for the Web server?

What Is Gopher?

No, Gopher is not a replacement for the Web server, but it illustrates the point that Gopher servers are easier to update and maintain than Web servers. In fact, Gophers were around long before Web servers gained widespread use. Although Gophers are easy to handle, they're not as flashy as a Web site, and they are unable to handle the fun stuff like video and sound presentations. However, the advantage to using Gophers is the straightforward and direct informational flow to your users. The Gopher that comes with IIS is fully functional and provides a way to advertise things like descriptions of files, directories, publications at your site.

With IIS Service Manager started, double-click on the Gopher service to bring up its properties. You'll notice that they are quite similar to the Web server properties we discussed earlier. I'm not going into all those options again; you can review the options offered here at your leisure. The one thing I'd like to point out is the Service tab properties. Notice the entries for the system administrator and his or her email address. This option provides a great opportunity for feedback. You can also provide the username for anonymous login if you want to allow that. Aside from this tab, the others tabs in the Property menu are the same as those for the Web server.

We all know what a Gopher is, right? "Go fer this, go fer that." It's the little rodent that scurries around and fetches information for you. But what's a Gopher server? It's where Gophers go to get Gopher data for you! I know, I'm babbling with double-Gopher speak. What is a Gopher server, really? Are you ready for this?

A Gopher server does nothing more than use the Internet Gopher protocol to browse a directory structure on an Internet server, in which the directories on the hard drive appear as Gopher folders and the files in the hard drive's directories appear as Gopher entries inside the folders! That's it! So, if you can create directories and files, know how to use a browser, and can create different file types, then you can build a Gopher server. Plain and simple, it's that easy. I was astounded when I learned that the secrets of Gopher were no secrets at all. This is one reason why running a Gopher server is perhaps the easiest task of the Internet, bar none.

Setting Up Gopher

Figure 5.14 shows my Gopher server, and Figure 5.15 shows one of the files that Gopher can retrieve for you.

Not much to it, is there? But there are a few things that you'll need to remember when you create a Gopher server. When you create Gopher entries, you should use a logical order. For example, you can place accounting issues in one folder, logistics data in another, sales flyers in yet another, and so on. You can create many different types of Gopher files, as identified in Table 5.1.

These are the standard file types of Gopher servers. One glaring problem with IIS's Gopher server is that you can't change these file types or make additions to the server. This is a terrible oversight on Microsoft's part, and I hope they fix it in forthcoming versions of IIS. But don't despair, there is a solution. Head off to the *gopher://gopher.micro.umn.edu* Gopher server at the University of Minnesota. When you get there, take the link "Information about Gopher," then go to "Frequently Asked Questions about Gopher." This link takes you to the FAQ sheets for Gopher. The second question

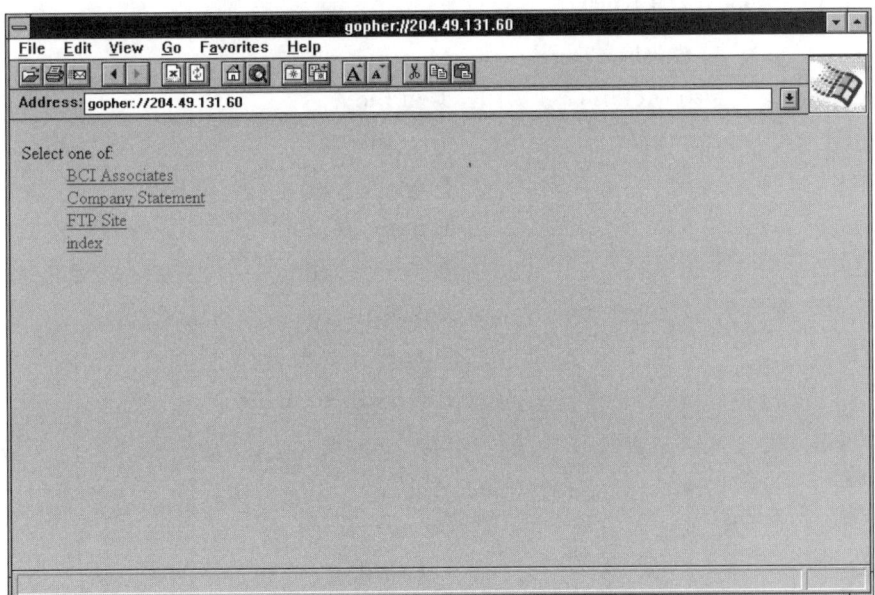

Figure 5.14   IIS's Gopher server in basic form for my company.

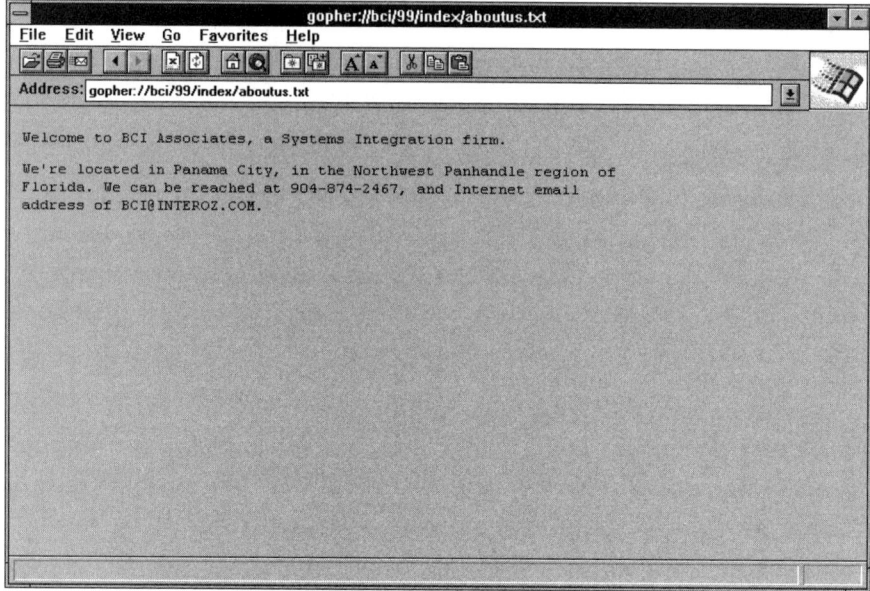

Figure 5.15 File retrieved by Gopher.

Table 5.1   Gopher File Types

Type	Gopher Type	Meaning
TXT	0 (default)	Text file
DOC	1	Text file
ZIP	5	Binary archive
ARC	5	Binary archive
UUE	6	UUEncoded
SRC	7	WAIS index
EXE	9	Binary Executable
DLL	9	Binary Executable
GIF	g	GIF image
BMP	I	Windows bitmap
AU	s	Sound bite
HTM	h	HTML file
HTML	h	HTML file

listed in the FAQ will provide you with a way to get the type of Gopher server you're looking for:

Q1: Where can I get Gopher software?

A1: Via anonymous FTP to *boombox.micro.umn.edu.* Look in the directory /pub/gopher. Or use the locator:

```
<URL:ftp://boombox.micro.umn.edu/pub/gopher;type=d>
```

Or via Gopher itself:

```
<URL:gopher://boombox.micro.umn.edu/11/gopher/>
```

A Customizable Gopher

If you want to see what it means to alter and customize Gopher, download this software and install it on your NT Server. To do so, you must stop the IIS Gopher Server (go to the Control Panel, then select Services). When you expand the Gopher server from UMN, follow the instructions to install and register Gopher with NT. It's amazingly simply. Once you complete the installation process, an icon is added to the Control Panel for the UMN Gopher. Double click on this icon to display the window shown in Figure 5.16.

Notice the file options and settings. In a Gopher server, you're limited to providing links to other sites or using the directory structure on your server to disseminate the information. That's one of the joys of a Gopher server— easy to configure, maintain, and share information.

So, when I said earlier that Web servers did everything under the sun except dance, I wasn't lying. Gophers pioneered the Internet for informational flow and sharing of ideas, but Web servers took over and ran off with the show. When you need a quick and easy way to get data out to your customers, Gopher is the way to "go fer" it!

Error Logging for Gopher

Gopher errors are handled in much the same way as Web server errors— by logging into the system error log and recording to a file as determined

Figure 5.16 A customizable Gopher server.

by you in the Gopher configuration. Listing 5.2 shows a sample Gopher log listing of the accesses to our new Gopher. Notice the exact references to the files and directories accessed, and who accessed them.

Listing 5.2 Gopher Log File Entries

```
204.49.131.74, -, 4/5/96, 8:15:03, GopherSvc, BCI_WEB, 204.49.131.74,
   1122, 2, 206, 0, 0, dir, /,
204.49.131.74, -, 4/5/96, 8:16:21, GopherSvc, BCI_WEB, 204.49.131.74, 30,
   2, 206, 0, 0, dir, /,
204.49.131.55, -, 4/5/96, 10:33:07, GopherSvc, BCI_WEB, 204.49.131.55,
   842, 2, 208, 0, 0, dir,/,
204.49.131.69, -, 4/5/96, 10:52:17, GopherSvc, BCI_WEB, 204.49.131.69,
   1201, 2, 151, 0, 0, dir,/,
204.49.131.245, -, 4/5/96, 10:52:21, GopherSvc, BCI_WEB, 204.49.131.245,
   20, 9, 3, 0, 0, dir, /index/, -,
204.49.131.245, -, 4/5/96, 10:52:24, GopherSvc, BCI_WEB, 204.49.131.245,
   20, 21, 3, 0, 0, dir, /Company Statement/,
204.49.131.69, -, 4/5/96, 10:53:37, GopherSvc, BCI_WEB, 204.49.131.69,
   20, 2, 151, 0, 0, dir, /, -,
```

```
204.49.131.245, -, 4/5/96, 10:53:40, GopherSvc, BCI_WEB, 204.49.131.245,
   40, 9, 46, 0, 0, dir, /index/, -,
204.49.131.245, -, 4/5/96, 10:53:42, GopherSvc, BCI_WEB, 204.49.131.245,
   491, 21, 220, 0, 0, file, /index/aboutus.txt,
204.49.131.55, -, 4/5/96, 11:01:01, GopherSvc, BCI_WEB, 204.49.131.55,
   30, 2, 151, 0, 0, dir, /, -,
204.49.131.60, -, 4/5/96, 11:30:28, GopherSvc, BCI_WEB, 204.49.131.60,
   902, 2, 151, 0, 0, dir, /, -,
204.49.131.60, -, 4/5/96, 11:33:01, GopherSvc, BCI_WEB, 204.49.131.60,
   30, 2, 151, 0, 0, dir, /, -,
204.49.131.245, -, 4/5/96, 11:33:59, GopherSvc, BCI_WEB, 204.49.131.245,
   20, 9, 46, 0, 0, dir, /index/, -,
204.49.131.245, -, 4/5/96, 11:34:02, GopherSvc, BCI_WEB, 204.49.131.245,
   160, 21, 220, 0, 0, file, /index/aboutus.txt,
```

Check out the different IP addresses of our visitors. Lots of different folks are already coming to see what we're about, but there's still a lot more work to be done. We want to share information; after all, that's the primary reason for using Gophers—to point your users to another site of related information. Listing 5.3 shows a sample link file.

Listing 5.3   Gopher Link File

```
Name=BCI Associates
Host=gopher.bciassoc.com
Port=70
Numb=2
Path=
Type=1
```

Let's take this listing apart. The name of the site is BCI Associates, and the host's location is at alias gopher.bciassoc.com. The listing indicates that we're using the standard port number 70 for a Gopher and the number 2 Gopher listing on screen. The path to the link file is always relative to the Gopher data location specified in the configuration, and a Type of 1 indicates an ASCII text file. You can easily build Gopher menus by placing multiple Gopher locations in the same link file, like the one shown in Listing 5.4.

Listing 5.4   Gopher Link File

```
Name=BCI Associates
Host=gopher.bciassoc.com
Port=70
```

```
Numb=2
Path=
Type=1
#
Name=BCI Associates' Primary Customer
Host=gopher.custone.bciassoc.com
Port=+
Numb=1
Path=0\customers\custone
Type=0
#
Name=Gophers in Europe
Host=sunic.sunet.se
Port=70
Type=1
Path=1/Other Gopher and Information Servers/Europe
```

This is an interesting concept for updating and expanding your Gopher server. The "#" sign separates the sites. The plus sign used in the second entry means the Gopher should use the port number on that particular server. The default is port 70, but sometimes that has to be changed, and this is how to allow for that change. In the third entry, the path points to a menu in another Gopher server on another site in Switzerland. Pretty neat, eh? And so very easy to do. Gopher servers have been around for quite some time, and their inner workings have been one of the Internet's best kept secrets.

WAIS Servers by Way of Gopher

What? WAIS from Gopher? You bet, and here's a good example. While the full text of building and maintaining a WAIS server is beyond this chapter, we can take a few minutes to preview the basic steps to using a WAIS server. Let's say that your company has 10 text files that describe various parts of your widgets. As you well know, file names can be very restrictive, often making the file content a big secret. Your customers need to know what's in your files, but they don't want to access each one to find out if it has the information they need. WAIS is designed to allow for searches in databases for information via Gopher. So let's get to it. The first thing you need to do is to build a WAIS database of the documents that you want to be used.

Next, index the database by word and topic to allow users to search your database by keyword or phrase. When you build the database, keep all the documents in the same directory as when you built the database, or you'll have to frequently index them to refresh the locations of the documents in the directory tree. Once that's done, you'll be ready to use your new WAIS server for your users by way of Gopher. The only task left is to install the WAIS server software onto the Web server and link in the databases.

Gopher Conclusion

I hope it's obvious to you just how simple it is to install and maintain a Gopher server. Gopher may not be able to compete with Web servers in popularity, but their sheer simplicity of installation and maintenance certainly deserves consideration and review.

The FTP Server

In all of the Internet, perhaps the most frequently used utility among experienced surfers is the file transfer. Site support technicians use a vast array of Internet tools for troubleshooting, including:

* Email primarily for core communications

* Newsgroups to see how others fix certain problems

* Web pages for service, support, and technical facts

But, when it gets down to the nitty-gritty of fixing problems after installations go wrong, or system compatibility issues crop up, it's the venerable FTP that comes to the rescue. When a technical issue arises, FTP makes updates and information available in the time it takes to simply download a file.

Another way to get files is by way of a bulletin board access. These little file repositories are mostly associated with games, chat sessions, and non-technical issues; however, many BBSs do provide technical support. You generally have to dial long distance to reach the BBS, but more support groups are providing toll-free calls for frequent paying customers. When you get into some of these BBSs, what you'll find is a door out to the Internet and FTP sites! This concept will be explored more fully in a later chapter. But enough on BBSs. Let's press onward to see how the IIS FTP Server can help us with file transfers.

Configuration

Because FTP was installed with the rest of the IIS package, we're going to bypass those installation issues and head right into configuring the system. Before you start any part of the IIS FTP configurations, you need to make sure that you've defined the FTP area in your system by organizing the directories and files the way you want them. As you'll soon see, IIS allows you to define many directories and how you access them, but the permissions need to be completed first on the main server.

Start the IIS Service Manager, if you've not already done so. Double-click on the FTP branch of the tree to bring up the properties of FTP, which are shown in Figure 5.17. As we progress in this discussion, I'll point out some similarities and differences between NT Server's FTP Server and the IIS FTP Server. First, IIS lacks centralized controls for the FTP site if you've got all of the files in one main location. More on that soon enough.

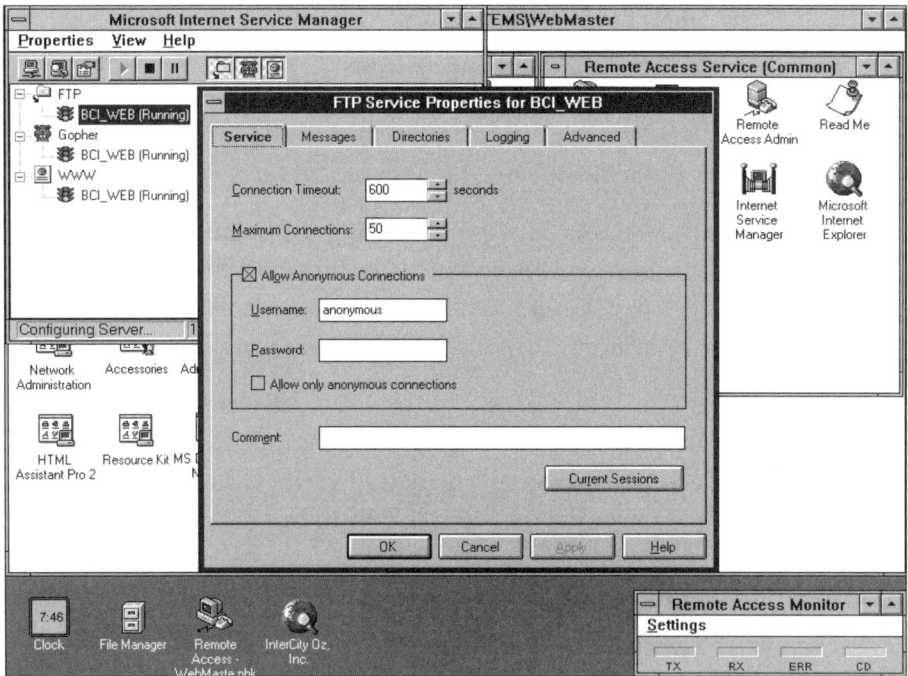

Figure 5.17 IIS's main FTP menu screen.

As with the other servers, the FTP server has five property tabs for setting options: Service, Messages, Directories, Logging, and Advanced. Let's take a minute to explore some of the properties.

The Service tab provides the options for the FTP service itself. Options include connection timeout and maximum connections for this server, anonymous FTP settings, and any comments you may want to put in for this configuration. The Current Sessions button shows you who is connected, their IP address, and the amount of time they've been logged on, as shown in Figure 5.18. In the Logging property tab, you'll see how we can define the server to gather more information on connected users.

The Messages tab allows you to customize messages that the FTP users see when they first connect to the server, when they disconnect and leave the server, and when the server is at its maximum connections as defined in the Service property.

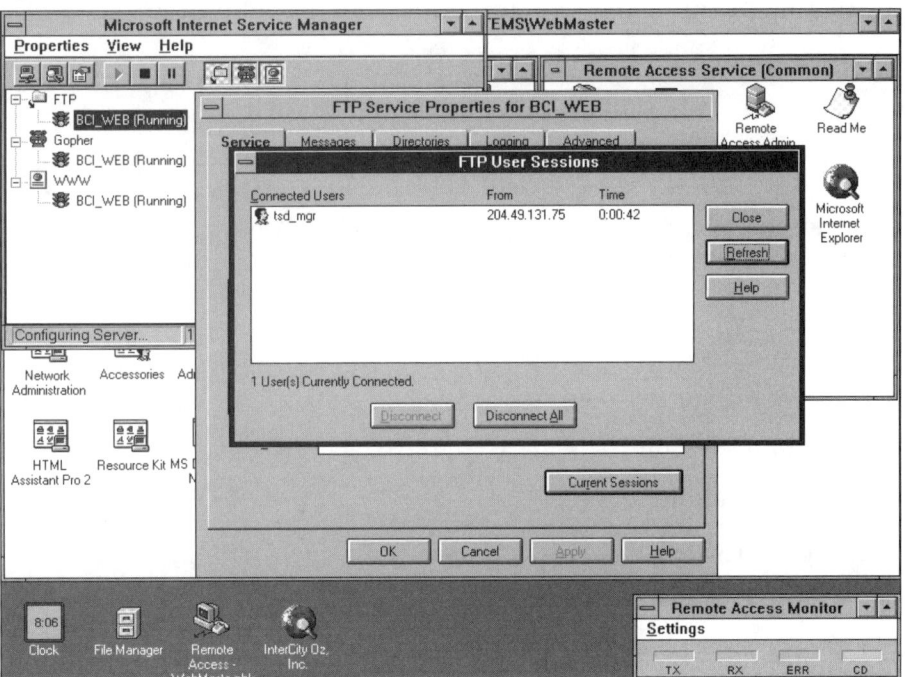

Figure 5.18 FTP user sessions.

The Directories tab is where you define the access locations for the server. My directory structure for the server is four root directories:

/incoming

/outgoing

/private

/pub

You need to enter each directory into the Directories property tab to grant access to them. The only access possible is a global access for any person connecting to the FTP site. From there, use your Microsoft Windows NT Server permissions to regulate directory and file access. No one can get to any other parts of the FTP server without being granted permissions.

One advantage the IIS FTP server has over NT's FTP server is simple security. Let's look at an example first. In Microsoft Windows NT Server's FTP, let's say that the directory structure looks like the following:

/winnt35

/temp

/users

/applications

/other

/other/ftp

/other/ftp/pub

/other/ftp/incoming

/other/ftp/outgoing

/other/ftp/private

/confidential

Refer to the directory listing above. Let's assume you've installed and configured the Microsoft Windows NT Server FTP Server. FTP wants to know where the root directory is for the FTP service itself, so you point it to d:/other/ftp.

You've set Microsoft Windows NT Server's permissions to allow only the FTP users access to this area. But when a user logs into the FTP, they'll be able to traverse the entire directory tree unless you alter the rights of the users group to deny directory traversing. You also need to hide the directory tree for other locations on the disk from the users.

All of this is possible, but very time consuming. Luckily, IIS's FTP server avoids these frustrations. As long as the directory and file permissions are set according to your wishes, then IIS takes care of the rest by simply adding in the directory tree. The completed Directories tab is shown in Figure 5.19.

You can easily change the properties of FTP locations by clicking on the Edit Properties button, or add a new directory by clicking on the Add button. It's all self-explanatory, so I'll leave the little stuff to you. The remaining property tabs, Logging and Advanced, include the same options as in the Web and Gopher servers. Take some time to explore them on your own.

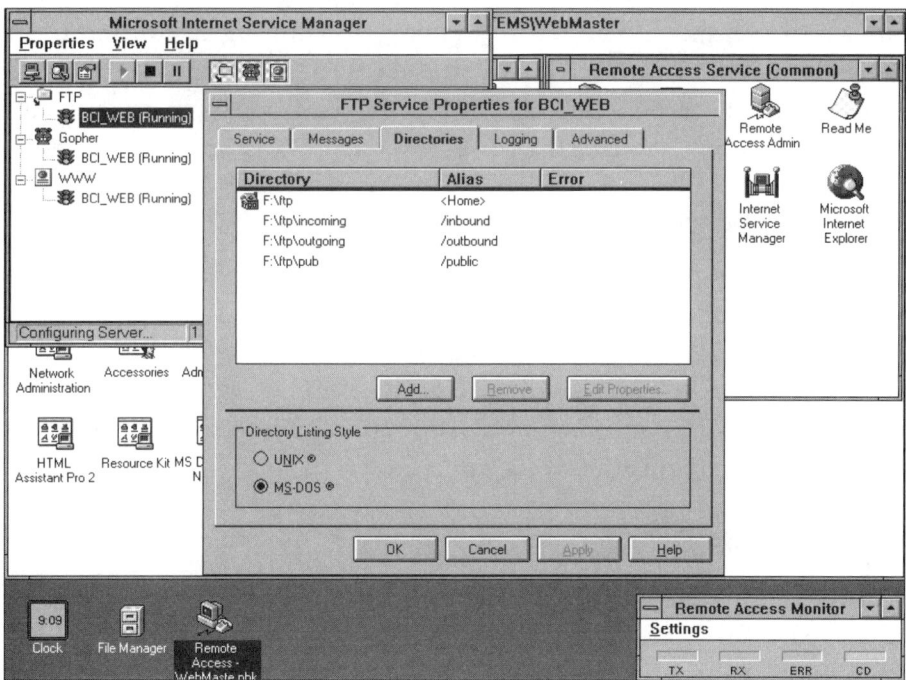

Figure 5.19   Allowing FTP access to specific directories.

IIS Conclusion

That's about it for the IIS work. As you can see, there's not much to it, and it's very simple to administer for all three services. Perhaps the key issue is to have a physical server capable of handling all of the services, tasks, and users that will connect to the server. By the time I was done with the IIS work, I had boosted my physical server up to 64 MB of memory. When this was done, the physical server had 23 MB of free memory and 29 MB free swap space out of 110 MB swap space total.

With five users logged onto the service, spread out among the Web, FTP, and Gopher servers, the physical server had 21 MB free memory and was running at 60 percent processor utilization. The rest of the server statistics reported similar loading indications, which indicate that another five users would have maxed out the physical server. IIS itself showed no indications that it was adversely affected.

When I said that the server was running at 60 percent utilization, I was taking into account the operating system, IIS running five different processes, the Internet connections, and the users dialed in to serial devices on the physical server. This is doing pretty good considering everything that's happening.

Microsoft FrontPage Tools

In February 1996, Microsoft bought FrontPage, a self-contained hypertext markup editor that comes with a personal Web server, from Vermeer Corporation. Most businesses and new Web service providers want to come online to the Internet with a fully developed Web site, which involves building and testing Web pages. With Microsoft's completely self-contained Web development configuration it's a snap.

Requirements

Any piece of software or hardware has certain requirements, and FrontPage is no exception. In the disk space department, you'll give up 20 MB of real estate to get all of FrontPage and the personal Web server installed and configured. Not too shabby, but to run effectively, you'll be using 20 to 25 MB of memory with IIS and FrontPage editor along with the personal Web server running. At this point, you might want to consider going to the Control Panel and stopping the IIS services from running. This approach will save some memory and speed up the processor a bit, but the IIS services will still be in Microsoft Windows NT Server as registered services.

 If you want a snappier system, I suggest you install FrontPage and all of its components on a high-powered workstation on the network or a standalone machine. You can always floppy-copy the HTML pages to the server, or copy across the network when you're done. By using a separate machine, you'll alleviate the severe load factors that exist in the primary servers and avoid disturbing the settings for the TCP/IP and Web server configuration.

Installation

Installing FrontPage is very easy to do. I got my set from Microsoft as part of the Internet connectivity package for IIS at a developers conference.

 As of late April 1996, you could get the v1.1 beta of FrontPage at the *http://www.microsoft.com/frontpage/* site.

On the CD, images for 10 floppies located in the frontpg.win directory are displayed. Change over to the DISK1 directory, and start the setup program. You'll be greeted by a screen that welcomes you to the Vermeer FrontPage setup, and cautions you to close all applications before proceeding. Although I've never had a problem installing with open applications, I suggest you follow their advice.

After closing out all of your applications, click on Continue and you'll be greeted with a screen that asks you to make your choices about location, and what options to install. Choose the appropriate items, and click on Install. Sit back and relax for a while as the files get copied and configured on the disk. When this is done, you'll be prompted to enter an administrative user name and password, as shown in Figure 5.20.

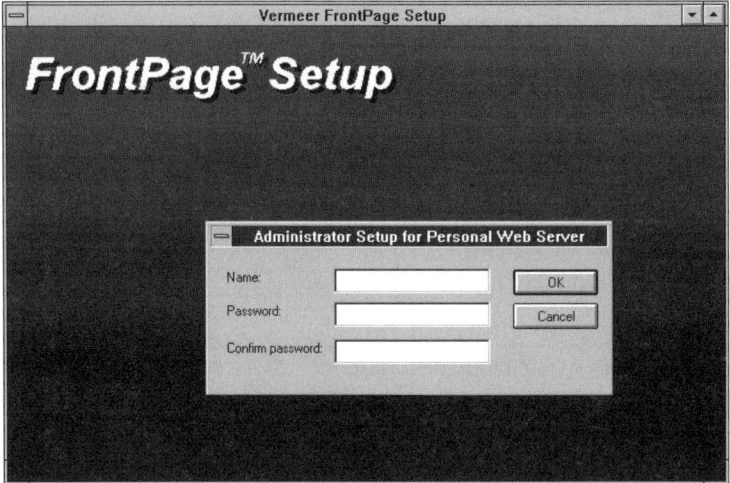

Figure 5.20 Administrative information.

Be sure to safeguard this information! If you lose or forget the data, you'll have to reinstall the product.

The application performs a few more internal configuration settings, creates a Windows group, and that's it! The group contains these six items:

- FrontPage Explorer—Used to create a Web page in all of its glory, including resources

- FrontPage Editor—Modifies the Web page created with Explorer

- Personal Web Server—I'd say this item is self-explanatory

- Server Administrator—Allows you to modify the installation of FrontPage, as shown in Figure 5.21

- Check Information—Verifies that all necessary files to run FrontPage are installed

- FrontPage TCP/IP Test—Verifies the TCP/IP and host server Winsock information

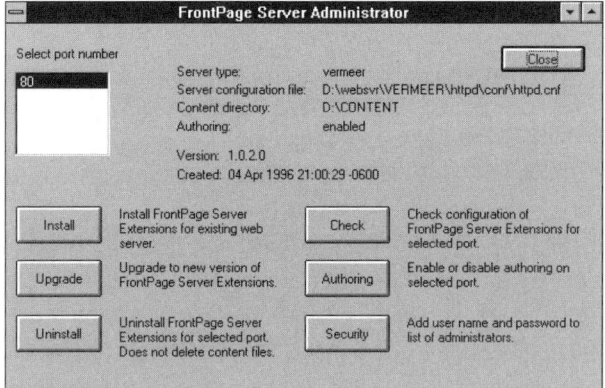

Figure 5.21 FrontPage administration.

The FrontPage Process

Creating a Web page with FrontPage is a two-part process. Even if you've got experience building Web pages, you'll enjoy the tutorial that FrontPage takes you through. It's well worth the trip to see how someone else creates Web pages and enhances your view of the Internet itself. What we're going to do is create the Web home project for my business, BCI Associates. All of the files for this project are included on the accompanying CD-ROM. Because my Web server has been taken offline for more development, I'll be using the Web Server provided with FrontPage. You'll see obvious benefits later as we develop the project.

FrontPage Explorer

Let's take a run through Explorer and make our first Web page. Click on the Help menu, and select Learning about FrontPage. Use the "<<" and ">>" buttons to advance and back up in the tutorial. From the File menu, click on New Web and choose the type of Web page you want. In this case, I'm building a Corporate Presence Web using the wizard shown in Figure 5.22.

Insert the name of your Web server, or the IP address. Enter in the administrator name and password of the Web server, and then let FrontPage create the basic Web page. Now we'll simply follow the wizard to create other parts of the Web. (It's called a Web because several Web pages are created to form a mosaic of all the pages needed to build your site.) We're going to include the following separate pages for our Web:

- What's New

- Products and Services

- Table of Contents

- Feedback Form

The next thing that the Corporate Presence Web Wizard asks for is the topics we want to cover. We're going to put in an introduction, which every business should have, along with a mission statement of what we do here at BCI. We will also create a company profile to illustrate the core values and aspects of our business, and finally, we'll establish a way for my many readers to contact me or my business.

Click on Next and then make your choices for the What's New Web page. I'd like to add Web page changes and press releases for my business. Click on next and then choose the number of products and services you want to create links to. Click on Next again to accept the services selection. Because I don't have an image for my company's logo yet (it's still in the art department), we're going to skip the top option to insert an image into the Web

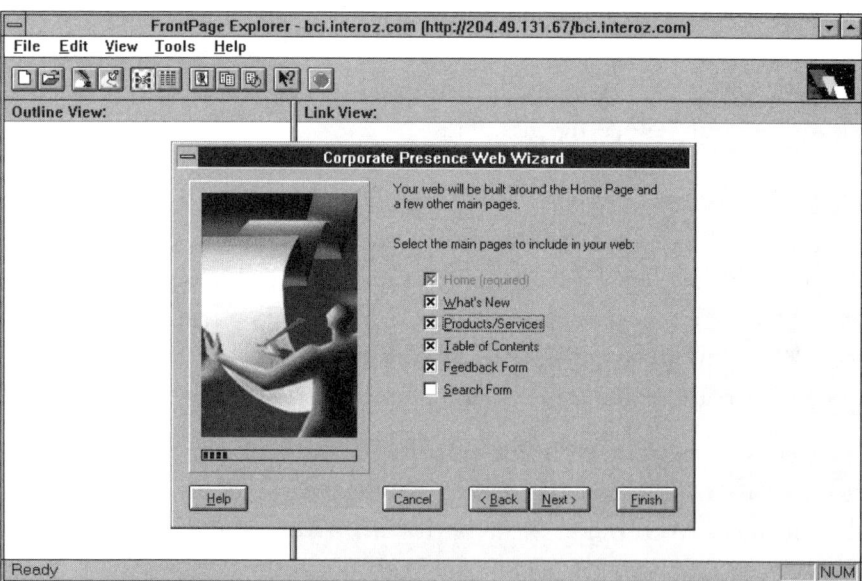

Figure 5.22 Corporate Presence Web Wizard.

page. We'll do that using the editor later on. Click Next and choose all of the options for the feedback form—I want everyone to know how to reach me!

Click Next, and choose the style of exported file for the feedback form. There's a whole series of questions that you'll be asked about the rest of the business. Standard questions like address, email, and phone numbers. Complete that information, and then you'll wind up at the very end of the informational requests. Click on Finish and let FrontPage build the Web. Figure 5.23 shows the completed home page links, while Figure 5.24 shows the links for the Products and Services page of the Web.

Pretty neat, eh? If you wondered where the actual files for the project are stored, look in the c:\vermeer\docs directory, or whatever path you specified in the setup. I wish I could have more flexibility in where the project files are stored because I want to keep all the data files in one area, away from the executables.

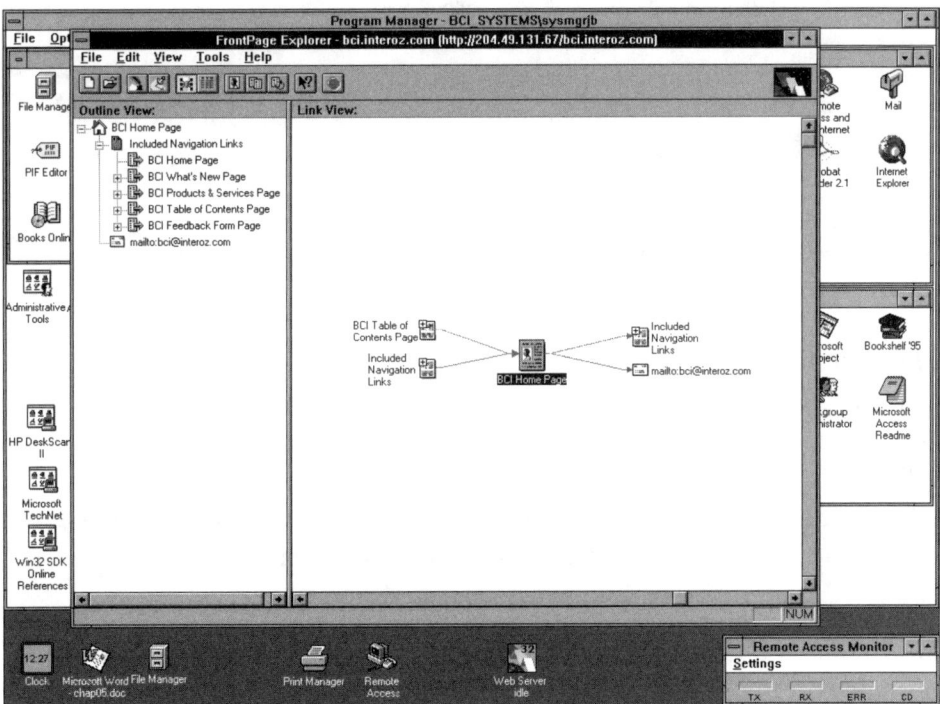

Figure 5.23 The BCI Associates Web home page created by FrontPage.

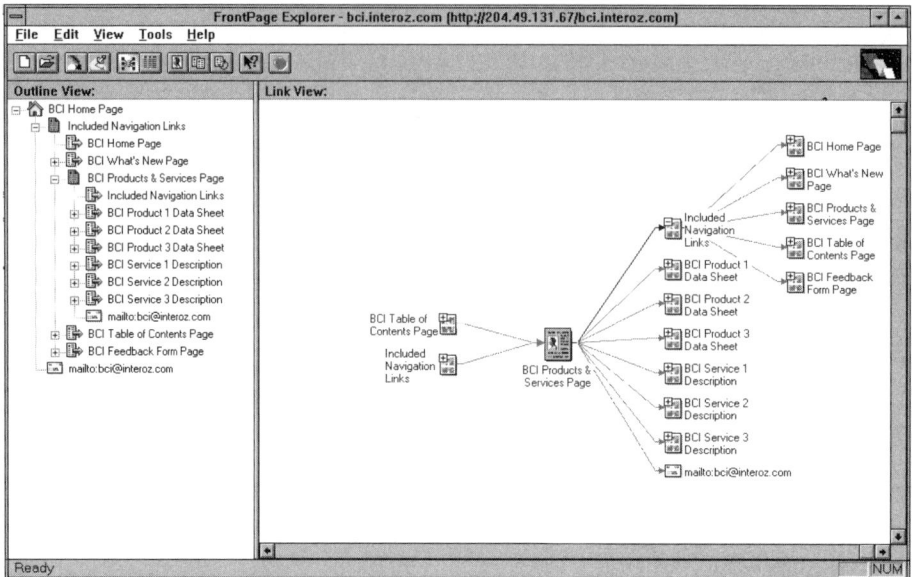

Figure 5.24 Products and services for BCI Associates.

 Notice the plus signs in the upper-left corner of the left column. You can click on this symbol to expand the view and see what is attached to the page. Pretty simple.

Now, how do we edit and change a page in case we made a mistake or need to add something? Let's move on to find out.

The FrontPage Editor

Click on the Tools menu, then click on Show FrontPage Editor to start the editor with a file view of all the project files. Choose a file to edit. The file will look just like a Web page viewed with a browser. We're going to use my home page and add a welcome statement. To do this, select the text at the top of the page. Click on the Edit menu, then click on Properties and change the text. Figure 5.25 shows the modified page.

FrontPage is a great product, and it's very easy and enjoyable to use. I heartily recommend it for full-scale development.

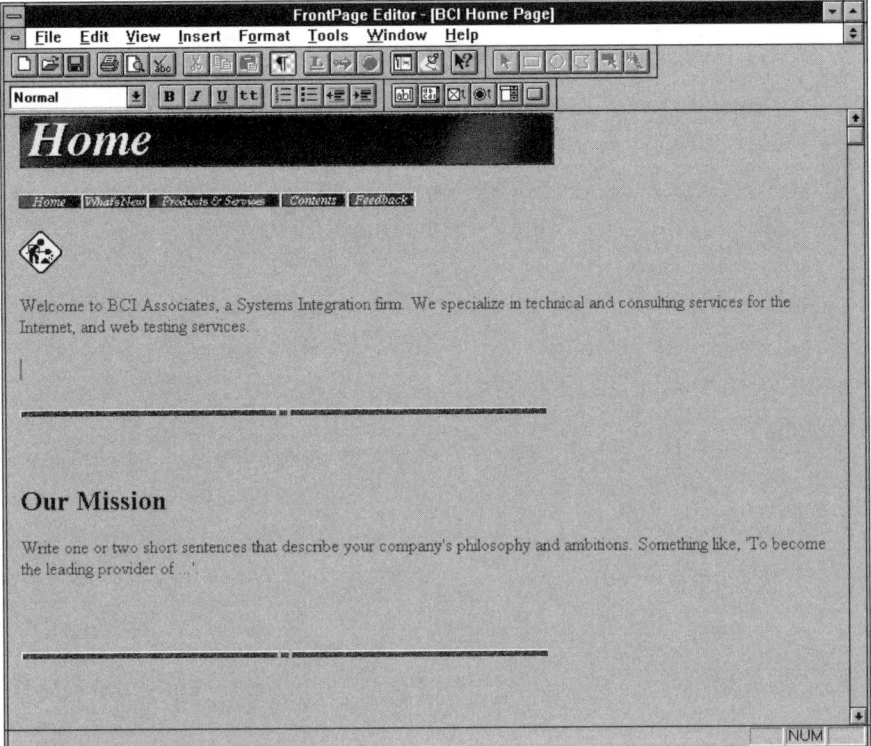

Figure 5.25   BCI Associates' home page.

Summary

This chapter has been the first view of the four Web servers we're going to review. Microsoft has long been dominant in the desktop arena, and the Microsoft Network was their first stab at the online services market. They realized that the future of online services dealt heavily with the Internet, so they not only invested in Vermeer, but the Microsoft Network was the evolutionary process of Microsoft's Internet Information Server. As you can see from IIS, building a Web server is not too difficult—it's the other things involved in maintaining the Web server once the installation is done that can cause you to go prematurely gray. Even so, IIS goes a long way to helping your site get, and stay, operational for the surfing pleasure of the masses. Next, we'll explore the O'Reilly and Associates' WebSite product.

CHAPTER 6

O'Reilly's WebSite

Welcome to the second Web server review in this series of four. O'Reilly and Associates responded to the ever-present competing market for Internet software by presenting this latest version of WebSite. Currently at version 1.1, it truly offers a maze of features, functions, and tools to create and maintain a full Web server. In this chapter, we're going to tackle WebSite's major topics, including:

- WebSite installation and configuration

- WebSite general administration

- The HotDog HTML editor

- Applications development tools

- WebSite utilities

- WebSite troubleshooting techniques

You'll see just how simple and easy it is to create and maintain a Web server. So, without further delay, let's jump right into the WebSite product.

WebSite Requirements

Although WebSite is not very demanding on the physical server, there are several system requirements you must meet. We'll get to those in just a moment. In writing this chapter, I used the 60-day, full-working demo, which I downloaded from the Beverly Hills Software Web site located at *http://www.bhs.com*. This program is a 4.56 MB file that extracts into four component diskette images from which you can make installation diskettes.

Hardware Requirements

Many of the issues we covered in Chapter 5 apply to this chapter as well. As you'll see, the general demands on a Web server are the same no matter what product you choose. For instance, it's important to have the proper physical server hardware installed and running with ample expansion room before starting the server on its trek to success. WebSite says that it can run on a 386 or higher processor, but I think we've determined that to get the best bang for your buck, you really need a fast 486 or a Pentium-class system. O'Reilly recommends 16 MB of memory, but between you and me, 32 MB of memory is your best bet. Although I would recommend this amount of memory regardless of the Web server software, WebSite needs the extra boost simply because more applications come into play. For example, Visual Basic v4 (VB4) is required for some WebSite operations. Although these operations are technically optional, you'll be doing your Web site (and its visitors) a great disservice if you choose not to use them. Another application that you will find useful is Microsoft Access. Both VB4 and Access require a fair amount of disk space, as you can see from Table 6.1.

Table 6.1   Hardware Requirements for WebSite

Name	Memory	Disk Space
WebSite	6 MB	10 MB
VB4	4 MB	45 MB
MS Access	4 MB	15 MB

Software Requirements

As with hardware, software is divided between the requirements and the optional packages. Table 6.2 shows the software required to run WebSite and Table 6.3 shows the optional software that I recommend.

Now we all know that creating and updating HTML pages is the heart of any Web site, which is why an editor is listed as a WebSite requirement. However, WebSite comes with an HTML editor called HotDog Web Editor. We'll discuss HotDog a bit later, but for now, simply understand that you can use almost any editor to create HTML pages as long as you know the HTML tag codes.

As your Web site progresses , you'll find a vast array of other software—for the Web site and for Microsoft Windows NT Server—that you'll be eager to install. Among these are NTFS defragmenters, DNS tools, other browsers, helper applications, and the like. You can redistribute many of these tools as part of your Web site, but make sure that the developer allows redistribution.

Table 6.2   Required Software for WebSite

Name	Use
WebSite	Web server
NT v3.5x	Operating system
HTML editor	Creating/Editing Web pages

Table 6.3   Optional Software for WebSite

Name	Purpose
VB4	CGI programming
Perl	Perl scripts for CGI
C++	Advanced CGI programming
MS Access	Backend databases
Delphi	Borland programming tool

Connectivity Requirements

Although we covered connectivity issues in detail in Chapter 5, I'd like to offer a little refresher because the concept is so important. As you know, a modem and RAS can be used for simple connectivity, ISDN is a decent alternative for low-volume sites (up to 10 users), and a dedicated circuit, such as FT1, is yet another option. No matter what link you use, you'll need to run TCP/IP protocol and know your DNS. In some cases, your Internet provider may maintain your DNS for you, but in case they don't I'll show you how to set up a DNS of your own.

If you're putting your internal business network online to the Internet, then you'll most definitely be interested in erecting a firewall and possibly proxy servers to act as a guard against intrusions. These options allow your users to get outbound to the Net, but limit access inbound to only those you choose. I'll get into those issues later in this chapter and also in later chapters.

Installing WebSite

Installing WebSite is among the easiest processes possible. It's very straight-forward, and I'll present plenty of figures to help you visualize the process and a few of the finer points of interest. Before installing the package, you need to decide where you want the program to reside. Many programs run on the same drive as the Microsoft Windows NT Server itself, but a few place Web software on a separate partition or drive. WebSite offers you both options.

Additionally, you can run WebSite either as an application—just like a Word for Windows application—or as an NT service. The downside to running WebSite as a standard application is that anyone with access to the system console can flirt with the application or mess things up. Also, if WebSite quits or otherwise has problems, then it won't automatically restart. If WebSite runs as an NT service, all those issues disappear, but several other issues crop up. If you're not familiar with how services work, then perhaps your best bet is to run WebSite as an application first until you learn more about it. You can always switch WebSite over to a service later, but you can't switch it back to an application.

Prelude to an Installation

Okay, enough lead-in, let's get into the installation. Go to your system console and open the package you received. It should contain four 3½-inch high-density floppies, the manual, and associated papers. My package also came with a T-shirt which my wife promptly stole for another nightshirt.

Before starting the installation, I suggest that novices (and those that just want a refresher on Web servers) read Chapters 1 through 3 to learn a little bit about the processes. You might also consider reading the manual at this point. I know, reading the manual is for greenhorns, but it's a good idea. Also, this is a good time to install Visual Basic v4 and MS Access v2.0 if you have it. WebSite will need it for some of the test functions that will be used after installation.

Performing the Installation

Insert diskette 1 into the drive, and double click on the SETUP.EXE program. After WebSite heartily welcomes you to the world of WebSite, choose the destination directory, and then click on the Next button. Figure 6.1 shows the screen that allows you to choose the WebSite components that you want to install.

If you have an existing Web site defined on the destination drive, you can tell WebSite and use those files for the Web pages. Otherwise, indicate where you want to have these files stored, or press Next to accept the defaults. Your next choice is to determine how you want to run WebSite—as an application or as an NT service—as shown in Figure 6.2. The default selection is as an iconized service, which is the one I chose.

Enter in the domain name of your Web site. This must be a fully qualified domain name of a registered site, and should be registered in the DNS process of whomever maintains your DNS files. Click on the Next button. Enter the site administrator's email address into the next block. Have you ever been at a Web page and needed to send email to the WebMaster with a question about the site? Well, you've just entered in your *mailto://* address so people can ask you questions about your site! You'll see later on how to use this feedback mechanism.

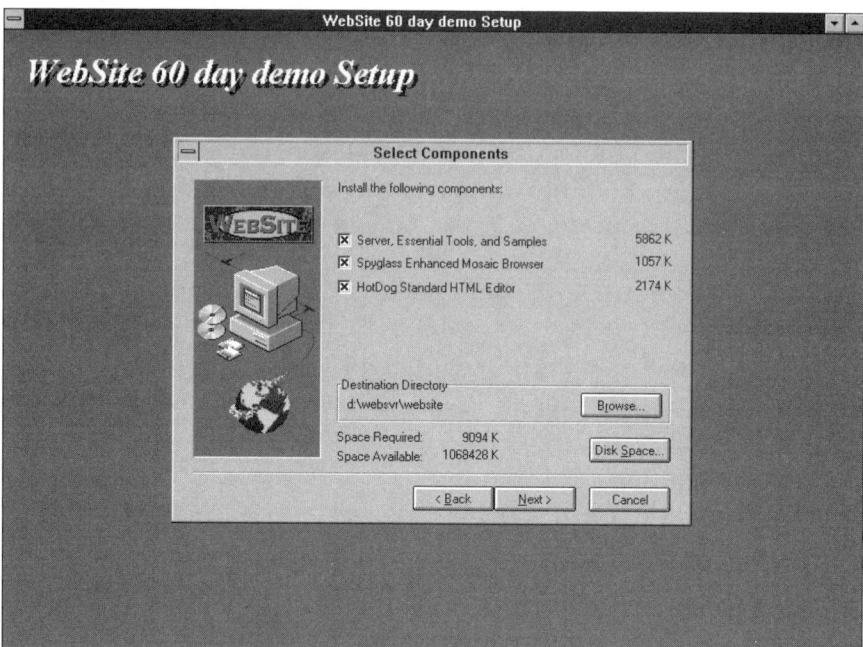

Figure 6.1 Choosing the installation options.

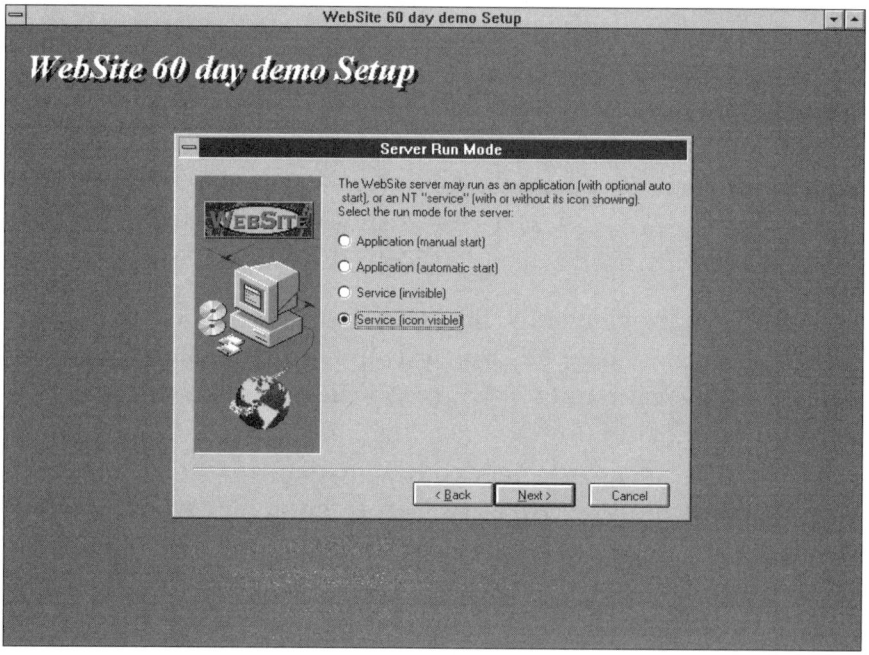

Figure 6.2 Choosing how to run WebSite.

Click on Next and choose the program folder name for WebSite and all of its tools. It defaults to "WebSite 1.1." When you've finished, click on Next. Setup is going to copy all of the files and make the necessary configuration changes to the system, as shown in Figure 6.3. Follow the instructions on the screen to complete the installation. When the installation is complete, the program group will be created.

The default is a service installation. If you set it as a service originally, the only way to change it back to an application is to stop the Web server and change the operating mode via Server Admin. This step renders the Web site inoperative until you restart the server as an application. Your users will not have access to any production services during this time.

The next screen shows you the WebSite performance monitor options for Microsoft Windows NT Server, which are just like those we discussed in

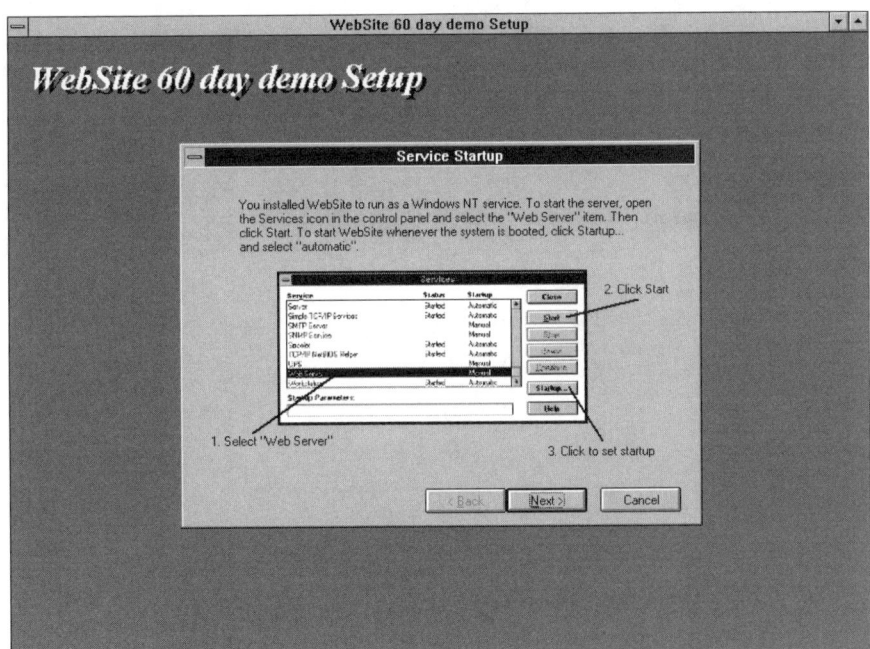

Figure 6.3   Making the Web server operational.

Chapter 5. I set these two options during development, and I can attest to their usefulness. Click on Next and the system registry will be updated for WebSite. You'll next be asked if you want to read the Read Me file and start the server. Accept both options and click on Next. The Read Me file has some neat information that wasn't available when the manual was printed. Nothing earth-shattering that causes problems with WebSite, but some informative goodies.

The installation completes and starts WebSite immediately if you chose that option. Exit the Read Me file if you read it, and everything is ready to go! WebSite should be running and in full operation. Figure 6.4 shows the WebSite program group that displays when you exit the Setup program.

Validating the Installation

Let's see what we've installed. Connect to the Internet and issue the commands to reach the newly created Web server. You can do this from either the system console or from any one of your workstations. You can use the

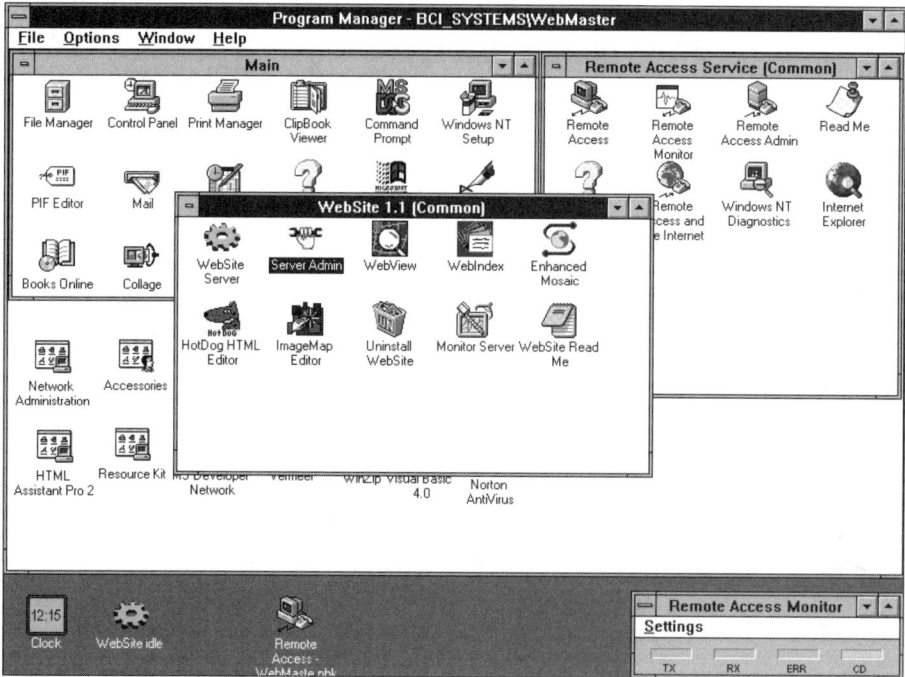

Figure 6.4   The program group for WebSite.

alias for the server, or just the IP address if you know it. Keep in mind when you connect that this is the brand new view without any customization or Web pages, as shown in Figure 6.5. We'll adjust this view when we use HotDog to create Web pages later in the chapter.

I'd like to point out the major functions shown on this screen:

- Release notes of extra information that didn't make it in the printed manual

- A server self-test to validate operations

- Hints on fixing problems with the server

- CGI sample programs (requires VB4 and MS Access)

Running the Server Self-Test

Before actively using WebSite, let's make sure it's working correctly. I know we just accessed the server, but let the self-test be the final authority. You can start the self-test from the Server Admin icon or link from the default

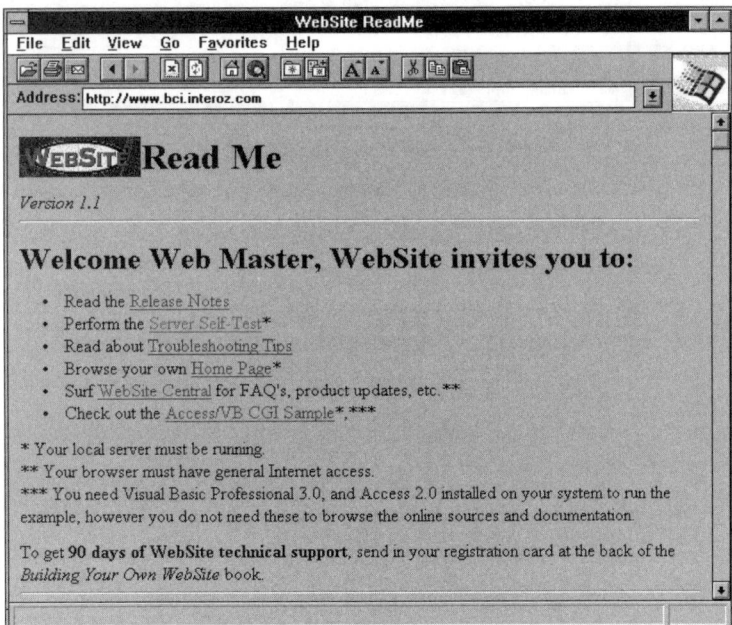

Figure 6.5   Initial logon to WebSite.

Web page. For our test, click on the Server Self-Test link on the Web page, which will take you to the Self-Test and Demonstration Web page. When you get there, scroll down until you see various functions that the server can do for you. Before executing any of these tests, it might be informative to scroll through the entire page to examine all of the tests that can be performed.

Actually, they're not tests but rather sample CGI scripts and Visual Basic programs that demonstrate the functions of Web servers in general. Click on the sample order entry application link, which is one of the primary forms used by Web sites to gather information and process requests. When the sample entry form displays, click on the order-entry service link. Figure 6.6 shows the results.

As I mentioned, order-entry forms are commonplace among Web sites and can be especially useful for fielding questions, registering for training classes, sending email with extra information using the *mailto://* protocol, placing new orders for customers, and much more.

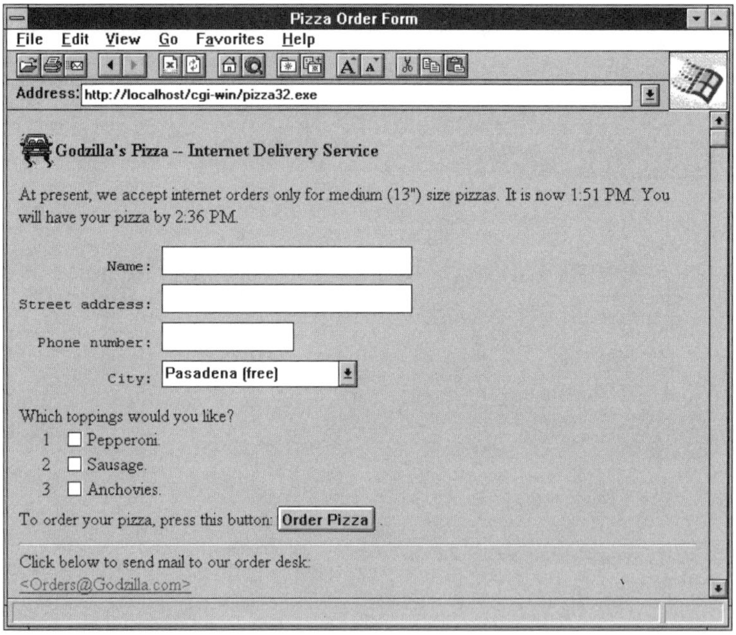

Figure 6.6   Sample order-entry form.

Now, back up one page and then scroll down to the "Sample Search form." This form is used to search a database or other parts of the server to find specific information. Look at the parameters of the search options. The first one allows you to search by name, title, and department. I bet you're wondering what could this be used for. Let's say that one of the business' traveling sales representatives connects back to the Web server and needs to verify that a special order went out on time. The sales rep enters in the particulars, and hits the "search." Voilà! Immediate results.

In the next section, we're going to take a look at the administrative options for WebSite and some of the techniques for the general care and feeding of this product.

Basic Administration

WebSite comes with more tools than you could ever imagine. WebSite provides you with the ability to perform general administrative functions, manage users, manage the Webs you'll create, and more. Any server administration function you can think of is handled in one package.

The Server Admin Menus

Let's first review the nine menu property tabs for the Server Admin functions. Double click on the Server Admin icon in the WebSite program group. When it starts up, the General tab displays, but you can quickly access any of the other tabs: Identity, Mapping, Dir Listing, Users, Groups, Access Control, Logging, and CGI.

Let's examine each tab in order so you'll have a firm understanding of what they can do for you.

General

The General properties are split into two sections—Server and Network—as shown in Figure 6.7.

The server settings are the most fundamental to the Web server's operation. We'll start from the top of the window. The two directory listings are self-explanatory. *Admin Addr* is the email address of the person that your clients should send mail to if they have questions or problems about the

Figure 6.7 General Properties Tab.

site. This address goes into the *mailto://* function. *Run mode* specifies the way that WebSite runs. Figure 6.7 indicates the default setting, "System Service (show icon)", which is how I installed WebSite. Click on this pull-down menu to see the other options—"Desktop Application" and "System Service (hidden icon)".

 **NT SERVER TIP** If you decide to change WebSite's mode of operation, this is the place to make the change.

Moving right along, the Network option *Normal Port* refers to the HTTP protocol port number that is used to receive requests from the users. If you entered *http://www.bci.interoz.com* to connect to my server, then port 80 is the default port that your browser expects to connect to and use. If, on the other hand, you really wanted to secure the server, you could use non-standard port settings for everything, say port 91. In that case, your request would have to be *http://www.bci.interoz.com:91* to make the connection. The *Timeout(s)* values indicate how many seconds before WebSite reports connection failure. *Maximum Simultaneous Connections* is another no-brainer. Does your NT Server have a 50-user license? Here's where you place restrictions on Web access to correlate to NT's licensing of clients. Lastly, the

Winsock information is nothing more than an informative box that let's you know what Winsock the NT Server is running.

Identity

The Identity property sheet, shown in Figure 6.8, is seemingly short, but don't let your eyes fool you! The first block is a check box called *Multiple Identities*. Click on this box, and a small screen comes up asking you to check the IP addresses that have been added to the Web server. Click on OK, and verify that the added addresses are correct. If the addresses are incorrect, then take this opportunity to correct them. Remember back in Chapter 2, when we discussed DNS and the mapping of multiple identities? Well, this is where you map multiple identities for WebSite. Once you turn on the *Multiple Identities* checkbox, the *IP Address* drop-down box is enabled. Before you turn on multiple identities, take note of the *Server Name* in the box immediately below it. Mine has *bci@interoz.com* in it right now. Clicking on the drop-down box will then display more IP addresses, as shown in Figure 6.9.

If you want the same IP address to apply to two different aliases, here's where WebSite allows you to do it. This flexibility is a very convenient feature for Web server administration! Table 6.4, which is a copy of Table 2.6 from Chapter 2, shows a sample DNS resolution file.

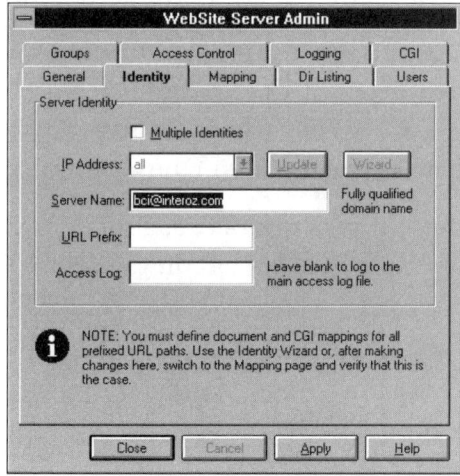

Figure 6.8   Identity property sheet.

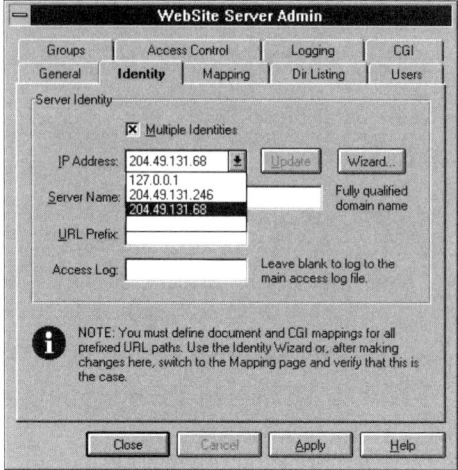

Figure 6.9   A look at multiple identities.

Notice how the table shows the same IP address mapped to different aliases. Why would this be useful? The IP address is that of the network interface card inside my server. The card itself is attached to the router which has the Internet connection on it. When someone comes into the server, they only map to the server network card and not any other possible IP addresses on the internal network. It's not a foolproof security measure, but it works 99 percent of the time for basic security. NT Server provides other security features that you can also implement to tighten up overall server security.

Next, enter in the server name for the IP address. One technique is to use different IP addresses for virtual servers, and map each to a directory on the Web server's hard drive. Basically you could map d:\websvr\website\shoes to 206.139.150.110, and make that the alias of the www.shoes.bci.com virtual server.

I wanted to point these things out because some of your favorite sites on the Web could be multiple sites hosted on the same physical server. All of

Table 6.4 Sample DNS Resolution File	
Name	**IP Address**
BCIASSOC.COM	204.49.131.245
BCIASSOC2.COM	204.49.131.245
TEST.SERV.COM	204.49.131.245

the sites have different aliases and different IP addresses, but reside on the same physical server in different directories. Companies with high-powered Pentium 166 servers find this appealing because it offers the possibility of a lucrative return on their investment, which could easily have exceeded $50,000 just to build. Again, we'll discuss this topic more in *Virtual Servers*.

Next, click on the little button in the upper-right corner of the Identities screen to activate the Identity Wizard. In a nutshell (because we'll discuss the topic more in *Virtual Servers*), this option allows you to create Virtual Servers for the aforementioned multiple Web sites on your server. It requires very little to operate, so I'd like to defer explanation for a few minutes. Actually, I just wanted to keep you hanging.

Mapping

This set of properties is quite simple, so I'll keep it brief. As Figure 6.10 shows, this is the place where you map the directories for the CGI scripts, applications, and redirected tools, and define the application associations. Not too much to it, but very important nonetheless.

Dir Listing

Directory listing properties, shown in Figure 6.11, determine how WebSite handles HTML when no other definitions for these tags are made. For instance, if you connect to the site *http://www.bci.interoz.com* without specifying

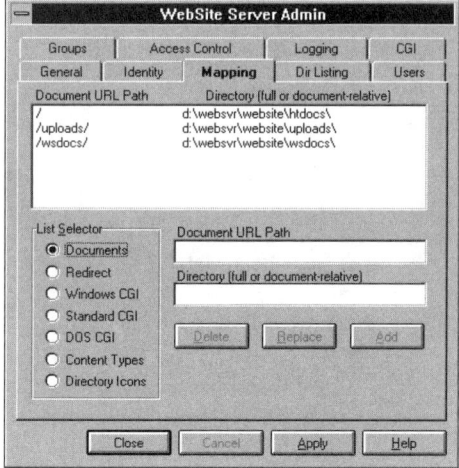

Figure 6.10   Directory mapping.

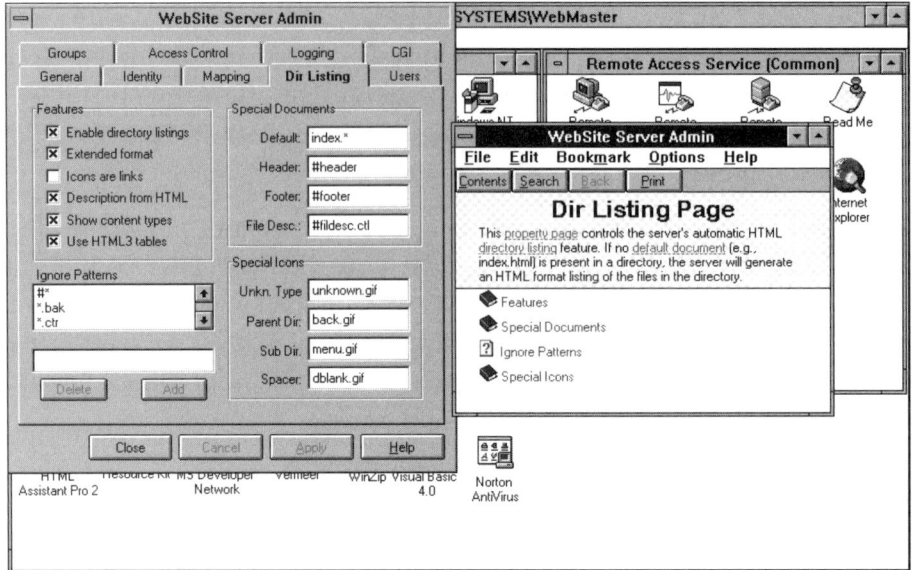

Figure 6.11 Dir Listing properties.

any root listing, then index.html will be used by default. The *Features* section determines how HTML is handled by WebSite. The *Special Documents* section defines how documents that are indexed and placed into the generated listing are handled. The default names use the special character "#" to hide files from normal view.

Users

The Users properties, shown in Figure 6.12, allow you to add specific users to access the Web for a variety of situations. There are several options for users that merit discussion:

* **Authentication Realm**—Segregates users and groups into topical areas much like territories.

* **User**—Allows you to manage individual users.

* **Group Membership**—Provides for group management within WebSite itself, not NT Server; however, the similarity between NT groups and WebSite groups is obvious.

Figure 6.12 Users Properties.

 Passwords are case-sensitive but user names are not.

This is a good place to discuss security a bit more in depth. As you know, NT Server has security right down to the file level of all accesses. WebSite's security is in no way related to NT's security, nor is it related to Windows 95. Since Windows 95 has no object level security, but rather directory level, WebSite employs its own security, and has its own user and group administration.

Groups

Okay, so I let the cat out of the bag just a little bit. Earlier, I said that groups under WebSite have no direct bearing on NT Server, and I didn't lie to you. However, when you start using the Groups administration, you'll surely see the similarity to NT. For example, take a look at Figure 6.13, which shows the "Web Server" realm (the default realm) and the user group called "Users" selected. Notice that the only members of this group are "mom" and "sysmgrjb;" "Admin" is not listed as a user. This omission is because the system administrator has global privileges, and is not required in the

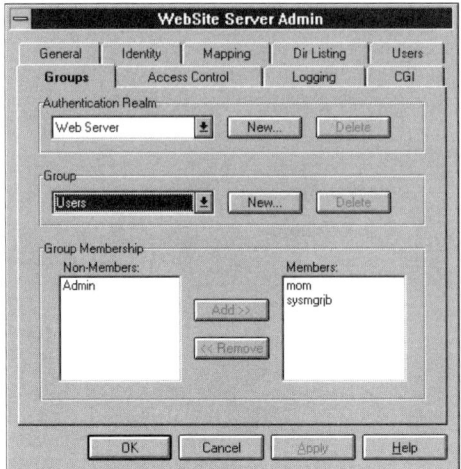

Figure 6.13 WebSite group administration.

Users group. Sounds a lot like NT groups, doesn't it? If you know NT, you know WebSite!

Now, let's take a look at the core controlling function of WebSite and see how it handles lower level controls of file and directory access to your Web.

Access Control

The subject of access control is often viewed as a time-consuming and aggravating necessity of networks and Web servers. This is true to an extent, but WebSite makes it fairly easy to get a grip on it. Figure 6.14 illustrates the basic access control options.

Notice the entry called "URL Path or Special Functions." If you open this pull-down menu, you'll see a list of directory options in which users can be granted or denied access. Figure 6.14 shows the default access setting which is the root level for WebSite. If I ever had a bone to pick with anyone, this would be it. In my not-so-humble opinion, global access should not be granted on a default setting!

Of particular interest is the security that you can set using the options in this menu. It involves a weird but effective set of controls called the *Deny/ Allow* function, which is found under Class Restrictions, and shown in Figure 6.15.

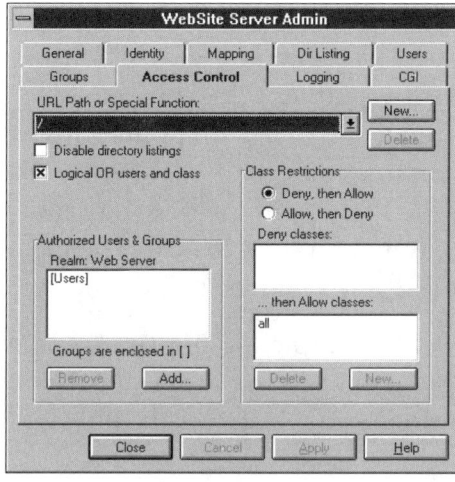

Figure 6.14   Access control options in WebSite.

Figure 6.15   Deny/allow security.

Using this function, WebSite first denies access, then grants access to specific areas of the Web, based upon criteria you set. Figure 6.15 shows that
WebSite first denies access to all users, and then grants access to a specific
class of users in the domain starting with 199.182 IP block of addresses.
This is handy for excluding an entire range of users for tighter security. If
you wish to deny access to a specific user, you'd first allow all users access
and then deny the one user.

Logging

The logging functions of WebSite are quite extensive and involved. The Logging properties menu is rather self-explanatory, as indicated in Figure 6.16, and I won't go into detail except to point out three pretty neat functions. You can set the names and path of the log files to nearly anything you want under Log File Paths, and the Tracing Options are many. If you need to zero out everything, hit the Clear All Tracing button in the lower-right corner. You can use any standard text editor to look at the log files.

Next, let's take a look at a sample log file run from WebSite. Listing 6.1 shows the log file. This is only a sample run for the "access" portion of a log. Looks amazingly similar to the Microsoft Internet Information Server log listing, doesn't it?

Listing 6.1   Access Control Log Run

```
204.49.131.58 bci@interoz.com - [11/Apr/1996:13:41:53 -0600] "GET / HTTP/
   1.0" 200 1224
204.49.131.58 bci@interoz.com - [11/Apr/1996:13:41:55 -0600] "GET /
   wsdocs/images/Website-sm.gif HTTP/1.0" 200 981
127.0.0.1 bci@interoz.com - [11/Apr/1996:13:50:57 -0600] "GET /wsdocs/
   32demo/ HTTP/1.0" 200 32065
127.0.0.1 bci@interoz.com - [11/Apr/1996:13:51:04 -0600] "GET /wsdocs/
   images/wstile.gif HTTP/1.0" 200 4158
127.0.0.1 bci@interoz.com - [11/Apr/1996:13:51:13 -0600] "GET /wsdocs/
   images/Website-sm.gif HTTP/1.0" 200 981
127.0.0.1 bci@interoz.com - [11/Apr/1996:13:51:14 -0600] "GET /wsdocs/
   images/rfinger.gif HTTP/1.0" 200 194
127.0.0.1 bci@interoz.com - [11/Apr/1996:13:51:54 -0600] "GET /wsdocs/
   32demo/images/pizza.gif HTTP/1.0" 200 271
127.0.0.1 bci@interoz.com - [11/Apr/1996:15:22:53 -0600] "GET /wsdocs/
   32demo/windows-cgi.html HTTP/1.0" 200 22942
204.49.131.57 bci@interoz.com - [14/Apr/1996:16:34:38 -0600] "GET / HTTP/
   1.0" 200 1224
204.49.131.57 bci@interoz.com - [14/Apr/1996:16:34:46 -0600] "GET /
   wsdocs/images/Website-sm.gif HTTP/1.0" 200 981
204.49.131.57 bci@interoz.com - [14/Apr/1996:16:34:58 -0600] "GET /
   wsdocs/relnotes.txt HTTP/1.0" 200 1388
204.49.131.69 bci@interoz.com - [15/Apr/1996:20:31:25 -0600] "GET / HTTP/
   1.0" 200 1224
204.49.131.69 bci@interoz.com - [15/Apr/1996:20:31:28 -0600] "GET /
   wsdocs/images/Website-sm.gif HTTP/1.0" 200 981
```

```
204.49.131.69 bci@interoz.com - [15/Apr/1996:20:31:46 -0600] "GET /
    wsdocs/trouble.html HTTP/1.0" 200 11874
204.49.131.69 bci@interoz.com - [15/Apr/1996:20:31:48 -0600] "GET /
    wsdocs/images/Website.gif HTTP/1.0" 200 2765
204.49.131.51 bci@interoz.com - [15/Apr/1996:20:33:27 -0600] "GET / HTTP/
    1.0" 200 1224
204.49.131.51 bci@interoz.com - [15/Apr/1996:20:33:29 -0600] "GET /
    wsdocs/images/Website-sm.gif HTTP/1.0" 200 981
127.0.0.1 bci@interoz.com - [15/Apr/1996:20:33:37 -0600] "GET /wsdocs/
    32demo/ HTTP/1.0" 200 32065
127.0.0.1 bci@interoz.com - [15/Apr/1996:20:33:42 -0600] "GET /wsdocs/
    images/wstile.gif HTTP/1.0" 200 4158
127.0.0.1 bci@interoz.com - [15/Apr/1996:20:33:47 -0600] "GET /wsdocs/
    images/Website-sm.gif HTTP/1.0" 200 981
127.0.0.1 bci@interoz.com - [15/Apr/1996:20:33:47 -0600] "GET /wsdocs/
    images/rfinger.gif HTTP/1.0" 200 194
127.0.0.1 bci@interoz.com - [15/Apr/1996:20:33:48 -0600] "GET /wsdocs/
    images/question.gif HTTP/1.0" 200 229
127.0.0.1 bci@interoz.com - [15/Apr/1996:20:33:49 -0600] "GET /wsdocs/
    32demo/images/imapdemo.gif HTTP/1.0" 200 5382
127.0.0.1 bci@interoz.com - [15/Apr/1996:20:33:55 -0600] "GET /wsdocs/
    32demo/images/file-imap.gif HTTP/1.0" 200 486
127.0.0.1 bci@interoz.com - [15/Apr/1996:20:33:57 -0600] "GET /wsdocs/
    images/note.gif HTTP/1.0" 200 275
204.49.131.53 bci@interoz.com - [15/Apr/1996:21:33:33 -0600] "GET / HTTP/
    1.0" 200 1224
204.49.131.53 bci@interoz.com - [15/Apr/1996:21:33:34 -0600] "GET /
    wsdocs/images/Website-sm.gif HTTP/1.0" 200 981
204.49.131.53 bci@interoz.com - [15/Apr/1996:21:33:42 -0600] "GET /
    wsdocs/relnotes.txt HTTP/1.0" 200 1388
204.49.131.53 bci@interoz.com - [15/Apr/1996:21:34:02 -0600] "GET /
    wsdocs/trouble.html HTTP/1.0" 200 11874
204.49.131.53 bci@interoz.com - [15/Apr/1996:21:34:03 -0600] "GET /
    wsdocs/images/Website.gif HTTP/1.0" 200 2765
204.49.131.84 bci@interoz.com - [15/Apr/1996:21:55:30 -0600] "GET / HTTP/
    1.0" 304 162
204.49.131.84 bci@interoz.com - [15/Apr/1996:21:55:30 -0600] "GET /
    wsdocs/images/Website-sm.gif HTTP/1.0" 304 162
```

CGI

This last property tab contains the functions of the Common Gateway Interface (CGI). These are advanced options for those already familiar with the what, how, when, where, and why aspects of CGI. Notice from Figure 6.17 that you can specify the command shell, executable templates, and

Figure 6.16 WebSite logging functions.

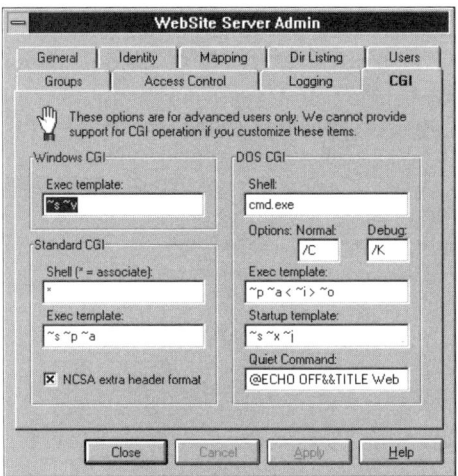

Figure 6.17 CGI options.

runtime options. While this is a neat way to extend the Web, be careful that you know how and why you're adjusting these settings.

Automatic Directory Listings

Automatic Directory Listings (ADLs) are a product of user interest and necessity. ADLs are generated—in URL format—when you browse an FTP site in which there is no index file. Go into the self-test section of the WebSite default Web page and look for the "Look Here First" URL. Locate the "directory tree" link and click on it. What you'll see is an ADL, which is shown in Figure 6.18.

Controlling Access to Your Server

This is one of the most important parts of Web server administration, and surely one of the easiest in WebSite to manage. The possibilities for WebSite server security include user, directory, Web, and domain-naming security. These options provide you with a definitive level of authentication and control. ADLs, which we just discussed, can be disabled for more security. ADL indexes are created when a user browses a directory for which no index exists, and presents the index in such a way that a Web browser like Netscape can see the directories.

WebSite has about 20 pages of documentation on the topic of security. Because you can read as well as I can, I won't bother to discuss everything included within those pages; instead, I'll concentrate on the points that I

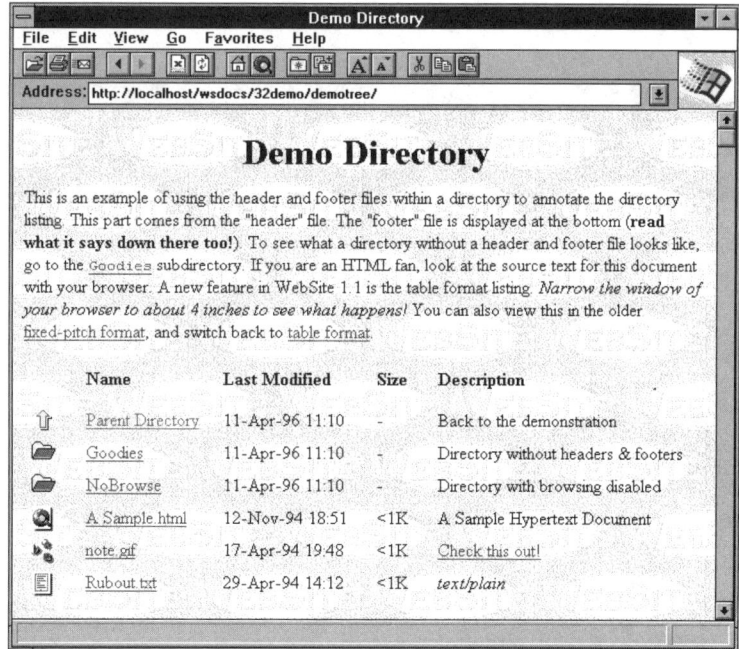

Figure 6.18   A generated ADL listing.

found to be the most important. When you apply security, you do so using what WebSite calls *control points*. This is nothing more than a reference to places in directories where permissions have been placed. Assume that your directory structure is like the structure shown in Figure 6.19 (which happens to be my temporary FTP site).

This is a view of the Microsoft Windows NT Server FTP Service location. Notice the little hand out under the FTP directory. This is NT's way of indicating this is a shared directory. I also have the Microsoft Windows NT Server permissions set so that only the appropriate users get to the appropriate data. In each of the subdirectories beneath the \ftp\pub directory, I set the Microsoft Windows NT Server permissions, limiting access to reading and writing for those specific locations.

If you know how to administer Microsoft Windows NT Server, then you can administer WebSite. In WebSite, the standard way to limit access is to use username and passwords, which is easy enough to do. The next level of security falls under the umbrella of groups and realms: groups, as I mentioned earlier, are very similar to Microsoft Windows NT Server groups; realms can be likened to an NT domain. One of the primary uses for user

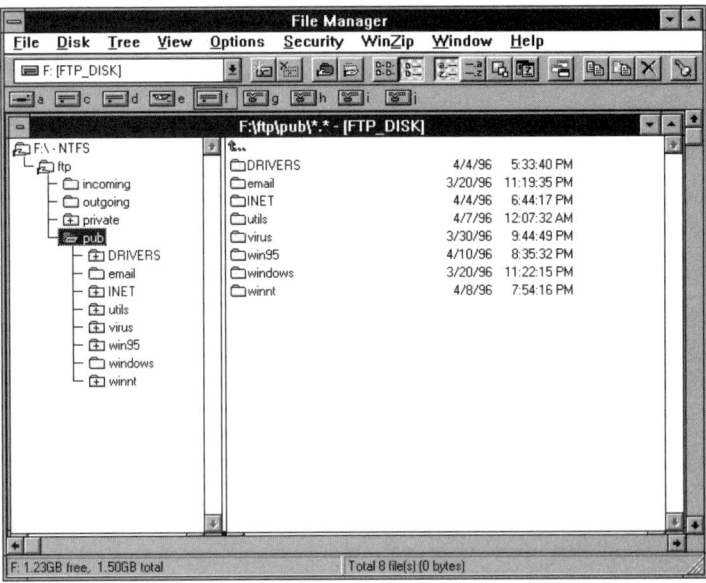

Figure 6.19   Security permissions for FTP.

authentication is to deny access to unauthorized users attempting to connect to WebSite by browsing. WebSite responds to the client that the authentication failed, and tells the user of the browser to please enter the required username and password. Once entered, the browser sends the HTTP data back to WebSite for further authentication. This is the basic process for HTTP security.

 Because the parallel is so close between WebSite and NT, administrators often believe that WebSite ties directly into NT security. This is *not true* but rather reflects how WebSite has made life easier on the WebMaster by having similar functions.

I could go on for pages and pages, but I can't spare the space. Suffice to say, WebSite administration and security is more than sufficient to secure WebSite, and close enough in operation to NT to alleviate many headaches that the WebMaster doesn't need.

The next section provides an overview of the HotDog HTML editor and how you can use the provided tools to build your Web presence. You'll create a basic home page plus a few other associated documents to see how this tool works with WebSite.

HotDog HTML Editor

HotDog is the standard HTML editor provided with WebSite v1.1. HotDog is a very capable editor and tool set, but the version provided is limited to creating HTML files up to only32 KB in size. If you plan on creating larger files, then you need to upgrade to the HotDog Pro version or get another editor. HotDog has many of the standard tools for forms, HTML, CGI, and processing scripts. Here's a rundown of HotDog's main features:

- Supports Netscape's HTML extensions

- Finds duplicate links and converts files to Unix-ready format where applicable

- Edits CGI and HTML files

- Uses Windows 95 style of user interface under Windows 3.1 and NT Workstation

- Has tons of options for customizing HotDog's behavior

This list only covers the main features of HotDog. You'll find plenty more and will have a great time while you're exploring HotDog. Figure 6.20 shows a sample untitled HotDog document.

HotDog is just like many other editors. You'll instantly recognize the HTML tags and functions. Many of the standard HTML tags are prewritten into the file to get you ready to roll your own Web pages.

Features and Functions

HotDog supports all of the HTML v2 standard and most of the forthcoming HTML v3 standard, whenever that gets adopted. The menu functions are mostly standard Windows types for file manipulation, editing tools, font characteristics, and the like. One notable exception is the Tags menu, which is shown in Figure 6.21. This menu contains all the features necessary to help us build a home page, including:

- **Document**—Creates all the core document attributes for the HTML file

- **Body**—Defines the characteristics of the body of the document, including background and text color

- **Content**—Works with the data inside the document

- **Headings**—Defines six heading levels

- **Attributes**—Allows text formatting

- **Graphics**—Works with the imbedded graphics

- **Font**—Sets the text characteristics

- **Lists**—Provides information and options for creating lists in HTML

- **Forms**—Allows you to create custom forms

- **Tables**—Provides table generation tools

- **Miscellaneous**—Allows you to place comments in the code and access page-breaking tools

- **Custom**— Only available in the professional version

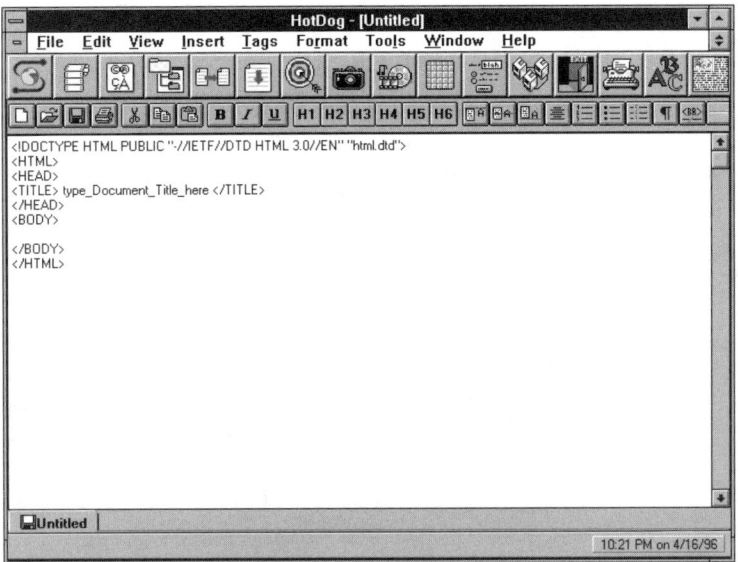

Figure 6.20 HotDog's default HTML page.

The other interesting menu option is the Tools, Options menu. Open this menu to display six other useful options. These options are shown in Figure 6.22 I'll let you go through them at your leisure, as most of them are self explanatory. HotDog's tools are very simple, yet quite functional.

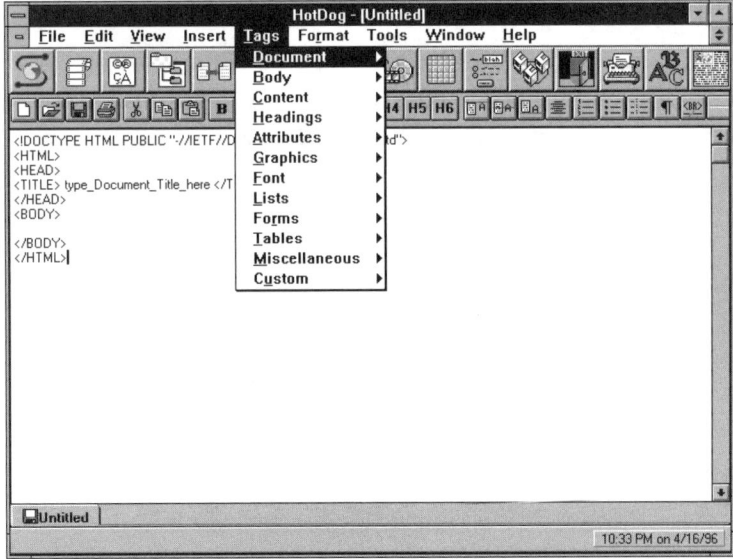

Figure 6.21 The Tags menu options.

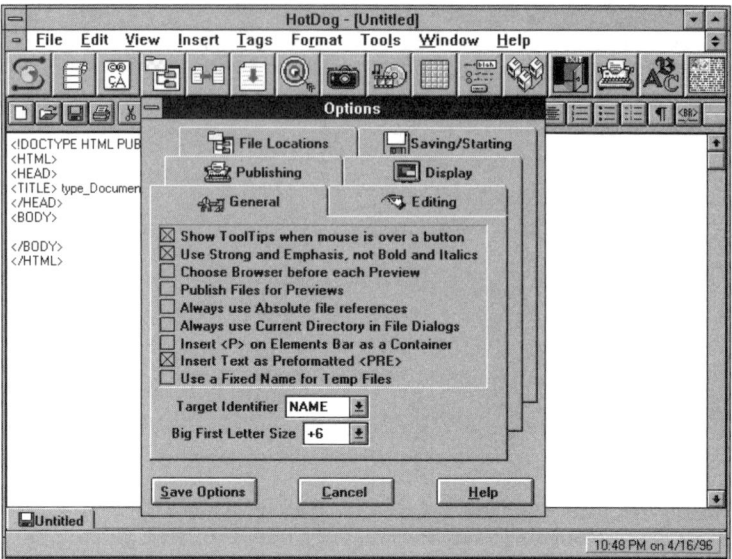

Figure 6.22 HotDog's other options settings.

If there's one thing I don't like about HotDog, it's the online Help file. Some topics don't even have help. HotDog's authors could have put a little more effort into the online Help because novice HTML authors often rely on this source of information.

WebSite Utilities

WebSite contains some of the best server tools and utilities I've found in a single package. In this section we'll look at how WebSite allows you to watch the server and make adjustments to the operations of WebSite. Additionally, we'll review tools like WebIndex, which allows you to index your documents on the server for easy perusal.

WebView

WebView is a tool that not only allows you to view and manage the Web you created, but also provides some authoring capabilities. Every Web server needs to be fixed from time to time, and WebSite is no exception.

Start WebView from the WebSite program group to display the screen shown in Figure 6.23.

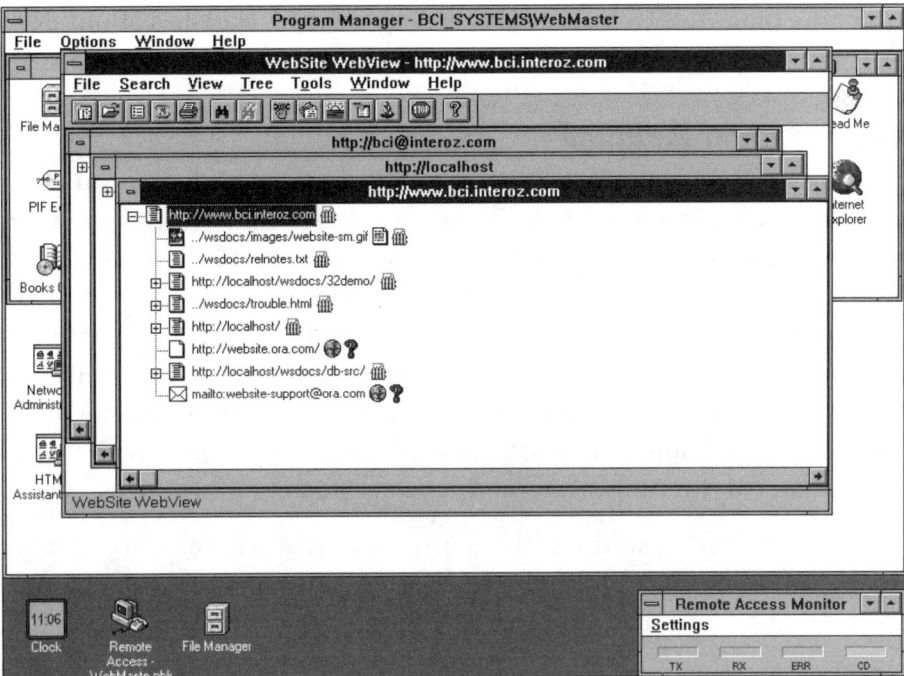

Figure 6.23   The WebView administration tool.

Notice that this screen is a representation of the Identity property tab, which we discussed in *The Server Admin Menus.* If you change the Server Admin setup, then this display will change to match it. I won't bore you to tears with the menu options themselves—WebView is simple and non-taxing in its understanding. The screen represents your Web sites in a tree structure linking all of the necessary documents and URLs that compose the site. This is a quick and easy way to see what is connected to what. Double click on any of the items in the tree to associate the item with the appropriate application—for example, text files (*.txt) are normally associated with the Windows application NOTEPAD.EXE. Page 62 of the manual has a very clear layout of the file representations and what they mean to you.

Click on the Tools menu to display its options. *Server Admin* is a link back to the individual program for server administration that we used earlier. *WebIndex* and *Image Mapping* are both discussed shortly so I won't go into these options here. *QuikStats* provides a really neat way to see how your server is being used. Click on QuikStats to display a small screen showing how many times the Web server has been accessed, statistics about file usage, CGI calls, and more.

WebIndex and WebFind

Indexing your documents on the server doesn't seem like a fun job, or maybe even a necessary one, but trust me, it is absolutely necessary. Suppose you have 500 documents in a directory. All the files are help files of some sort, or perhaps tech notes that your company representatives use to help clients find the appropriate widget for their needs. Searching such a directory would be an extraordinary task with a text editor. This is why indexing is so important. Indexing based on words inside the documents is a keen way to build rapid access to the data, especially if the data is accessed across the Internet using a slow modem.

The WebIndex utility in the WebSite program group helps you index your documents in a rather painless manner. Start WebIndex to display the three tab selections shown in Figure 6.24.

In the Create Index option, you'll notice that all of the URLs and files are excluded from indexing by default. You need to add the items that you desire to index. If you want to index all documents regardless of the actual type, simply press All>>. In the field at the bottom of the screen, type in the name of the index. When you click on OK, the index is created and

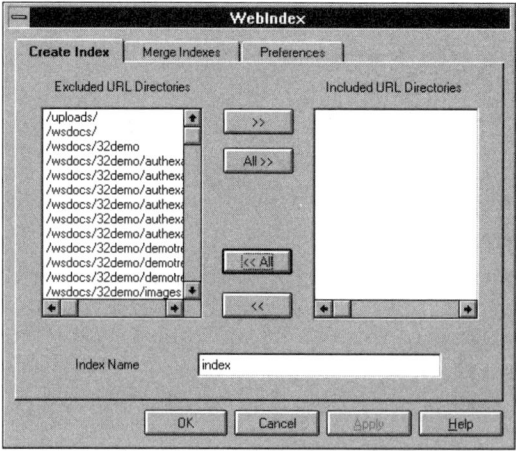

Figure 6.24 WebIndex options.

WebIndex is exited. I find this annoying. If I wanted to create multiple indices, I have to restart WebIndex each time.

The Merge Indexes tab allows you to merge multiple indices to form larger ones. The original indices are left intact after the operation is complete. The Preferences properties include options for deciding which file types to include in the index process, the percentage of common words in the files to define, and the maximum number of files to index. If you create or update many indices, then you may want to save the preferences for each index process into separate selections.

Once the index is created, you should search the index to make sure everything is in working order—kind of like an index self-test. That's where WebFind comes in. WebFind, which is located in the /CGI-SHL directory, is used in conjunction with CGI and Perl programming to support a wide variety of search and retrieval functions. More on this topic in Chapter 10.

Image Maps

The last item we need to address before winding down the chapter with troubleshooting techniques is image mapping. Image maps are those fun little tools that WebMasters use to present the browser with a range of options to select, and then carry out a task based on that selection. For example, imagine looking at a Rand McNally roadmap of the United States. If you didn't know that the states were arranged in alphabetical order, you'd have to go to an index to find a particular state's page. However, if you are viewing an image map of the United States on your computer, finding a particular state would be as easy as clicking your mouse on the state in question.

So basically, an image map is a single image file that can be used to represent a larger idea or set of functions. However, each topic on the overall image map is broken down by a range of choices. For instance, consider a square that is 10 units wide by 10 units deep that is used to represent ten topics. Starting at the 0,0 position, any mouse movements from 0,0 to 9,9 fall within the range of the first topic. The range of 10,10 to 10,20 (still on the first row) is the second topic. This sectioning of the map delineates the range of coverage of a map.

Troubleshooting Server Problems

Fixing a broken Web site can run the gamut of problems from broken physical links, to broken logical links, to broken outside links on the Internet. Finding and resolving these problems can bring you to the forefront of success or the forefront of the line at the loony bin, depending on the situation. All of the preparations you painstakingly made to get your site up to speed are useless if you can't fix a broken server. I've made it quite clear in this chapter that Microsoft Windows NT Server's permissions and security are distinctly different and separate from WebSite's security and access rights.

That's still true, but when your server breaks, you've got to consider both as problem areas. If NT rights and permissions change, I guarantee you that WebSite will act up as well. WebSite will apparently be broken, but it isn't, and you need to find that out. Lucky for us, WebSite provides the server self-test to help us see how things are working, including general access to the server. You can start the process by going to the server and starting your browser from the server console, or start the Enhanced Mosaic from the WebSite program group. This is a version of SpyGlass written for O'Reilly and Associates for distribution with WebSite. When you open the server, you'll automatically go to the Read Me file for the server.

Before you select the Server Self-Test link, notice the requirements for the test. You'll need to have VB4 and MS Access v2 installed to perform certain tests. Without these two, the self-test won't run, so don't even try it. You'll be able to browse the many topics of the root page here, so let's jump right into the main topic.

Server Self-Test

Click on the Server Self-Test link which goes to the main server screen. As you can see, WebSite covers all the bases as far as possible glitches in server operations, as shown in Figure 6.25. It's best to go through all the testing areas to verify proper operations before calling anyone. There are five core testing areas:

- Information Retrieval
- Using CGI Programs

- Testing the CGI Interfaces

- Security Features

- Miscellaneous Features

Getting you through all of these tasks should keep you busy for the next two hours or more, so let's do a few of the critical ones. If you suspect the Web server itself is broken, try using SpyGlass running from the system console to see if you can access the Web server. As always, you can run PING to see if you can see the physical server from both the system console and from a workstation on the network.

Try things like the basic document retrieval and server side "includes." The sample Visual Basic applications with forms is another good one to use. All of these simple tests show that the Web server is capable of operating to some degree. Next, try the simple document retrievals from a workstation on the internal network, not from the Internet itself.

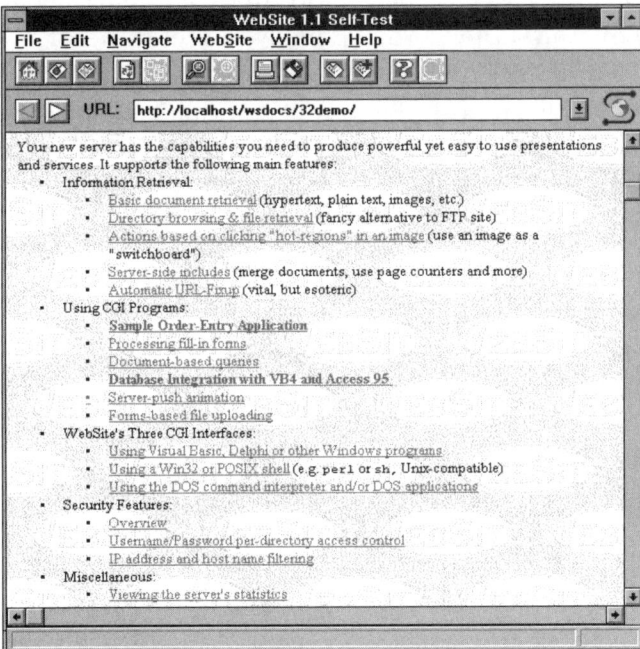

Figure 6.25 Server Self-Test.

Security Issues

As always, suspect the WebSite configuration first but hold true to your suspicions of NT itself as a possible candidate for trouble. Use the NT tools to see if the proper permissions are still in place for the users, or groups of users, if required. Double check access rights for consistency. It's possible that someone has been accidentally given access to an area through WebSite and not through NT. Check with your coworkers to see if someone has changed anything or added someone to the users groups.

Summary

This concludes our discussion of WebSite. This server, with all its tools, functions, and features has proven itself to be very capable and easy to use. Don't let the seemingly daunting number of options scare you away—the manual is clearly written and the help files are equally useful. My only major problem with this server was HotDog's limitations. I would have expected a more-substantial HTML editor with such a powerhouse as WebSite. However, HotDog proved to be a more than adequate HTML editor for the majority of WebMasters. You're likely to feel some of the limitations when you get into more advanced work, but that may be a while away. In the meantime, you'll have your hands full enjoying WebSite as much as I did.

Process Corp's Purveyor Web Server

Welcome to the third in our series of Web servers for Microsoft Windows NT Server: Process Corporation's Purveyor Web server. As you will soon see, Purveyor is a very easy server to install, maintain, and manipulate for your users and visitors.

In this chapter, you'll learn all about Purveyor, but specifically we'll cover:

- Installing and configuring Purveyor

- Managing the Web server

- Securing the Web server

- Performing basic Web server operations

- Troubleshooting Web server problems

Before getting into the meat and potatoes of Purveyor, let's take a minute to preview some of the reasons why you might want to consider Purveyor as your Web server. This server is quite capable of performing as a proxy for HTTP, Gopher, and FTP servers, keeping all functions rolled up into one neat operation. It supports server side includes (predefined procedures that execute on the server instead of at the client's browser) for faster operations, and multiple virtual servers and paths for multiple home pages. You'll find this last feature very helpful if you sell processing time on a powerful machine and want to use it as a Web site for many businesses.

Purveyor also works under DEC Alpha servers and Intel-based processors. The DEC (Digital Equipment Corp.) Alpha processor is a RISC (Reduced Instruction Set Computer) that is several times more powerful than the hottest Intel CPU. Of course, this added power comes with a price tag to match! Purveyor integrates very tightly into the NT operating environment, as well, to give you very fast file I/O. It uses the NT event logger to store the errors and events as they happen.

For our review, we'll be using v1.2 of Purveyor, which comes on ten 3½-inch high-density diskettes. The package ships with the following three manuals, which, in combination with the precise online help, will guide your every affair with Purveyor:

1. *User's Guide*—Provides instructions for handling the core operations and functions

2. *Programmer's Guide*—Provides help with CGI and other programming tasks

3. *Guide to Server Security*—Provides instructions for securing Purveyor

So, without further delay, let's see what Purveyor has to offer our Web site.

Installing Purveyor

You always need to know what physical server requirements must be met before you can install any software, and Purveyor is no different. Let's jump right in and take a look at Purveyor's requirements.

System Requirements

Before installing Purveyor, your systems must meet several conditions:

- TCP/IP must be installed and fully configured on the physical server

- Your processor must be at least a 386; a 486 is recommended, and a Pentium is desirable

- At least 16 MB of *free* memory

- At least 12 MB of disk space for Purveyor; more for HTML and CGI work

- Microsoft Windows NT Server v3.50 or greater

- An Internet connection

- The installer must have administrator privileges

As I mentioned earlier, Purveyor comes on ten floppy diskettes, so obviously you'll need a floppy drive. Just as in the other Web server installations, you should have already decided on the directory structure for the Web server before you begin. This structure includes the CGI scripts, any programming tools, and the HTML source. If you're re-installing Purveyor, the installation process will find the existing location and handle the necessary file operations. Another convenient feature is the handy uninstall process that takes care of everything should you decide to remove Purveyor.

Performing the Installation

At the physical server, insert the first diskette into the appropriate drive and start the Setup program. You'll get a warning screen reminding you that you must have administrator privileges on the server to perform the installation. If you forgot, then this is the time to bail out and correct the rights problem. If everything's okay, click on the Continue button. Enter the name and company of the owner. The name is required, but the company is not. Enter in the serial number of the software, which is provided on the cover sheet that came with the books. Figure 7.1 shows the owner information screen.

Next you will enter the directory for the server files. There's no Browse button, so you'll have to know the full path by heart. If you can't remember where you decided to install the files, press Alt+Tab to switch to the Program Manager and run the File Manager to determine the destination directory.

To give you an idea of some of the Microsoft Windows NT Server functions that Purveyor will use, I captured the screen shown in Figure 7.2, which informs you of the NT services that must be shut down in order for Purveyor to install. I had File Manager opened in the background to generate this message box.

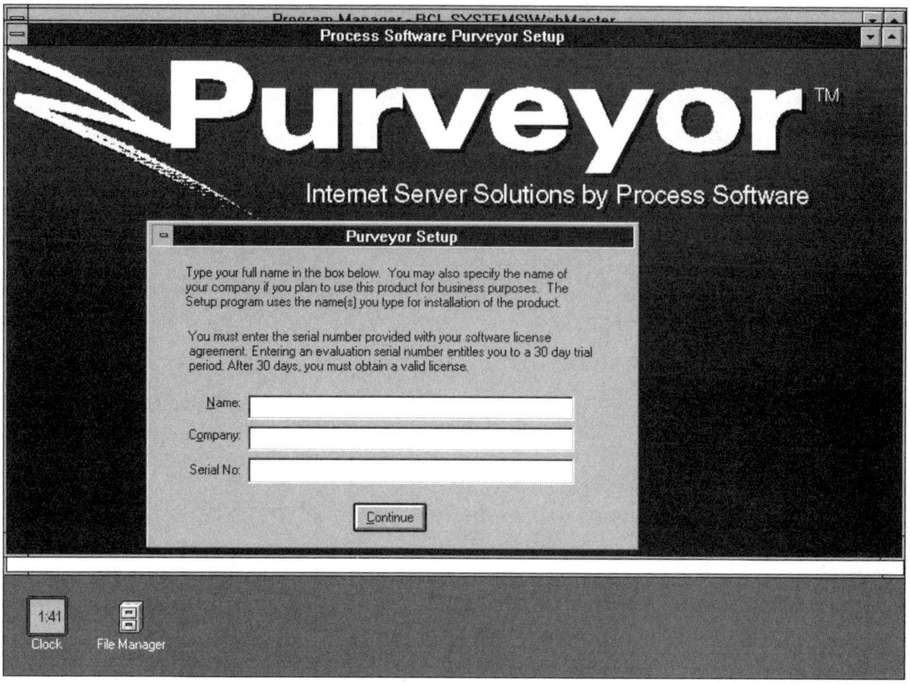

Figure 7.1 Enter the owner information in this dialog box.

Click on Continue and let Purveyor install the required files by inserting the appropriate disk when asked. When Purveyor has completed installation, click the Start button to configure the application.

Configuration Property Sheet

Purveyor offers you thirteen property options:

- Main Settings
- Realms
- Users
- Groups
- Virtual Servers
- Virtual Paths
- CGI Mapping

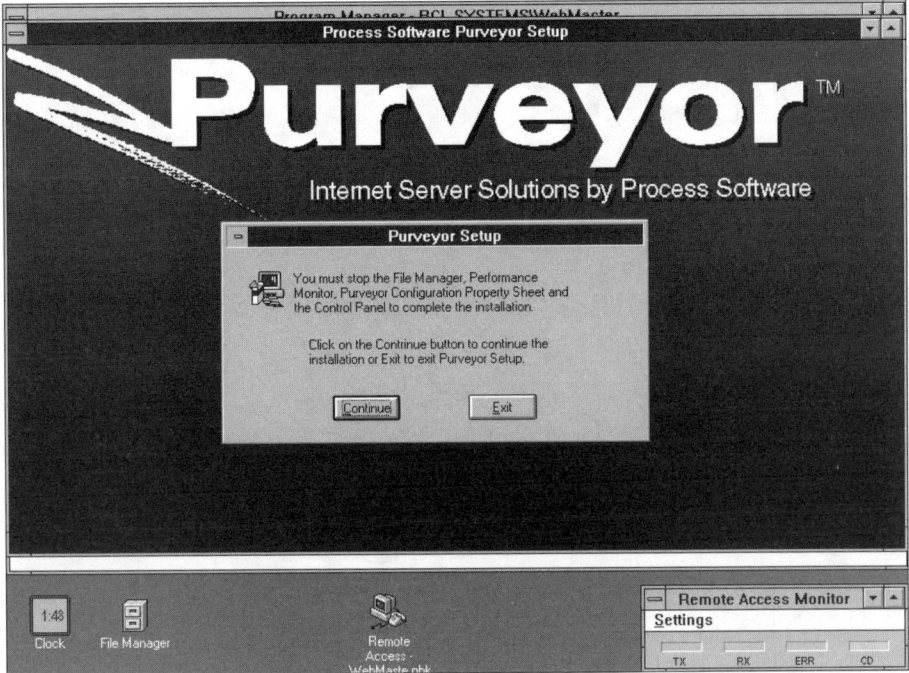

Figure 7.2   NT functions used by Purveyor.

- Logging

- Logging Templates

- Proxy

- MIME Types

- MIME Icons

- About

Let's discuss each of these options, and how they affect Web server operations.

Main Settings

The Main Settings property sheet, shown in Figure 7.3, is the focal point for controlling the server. Notice that the default TCP/IP port for Internet operations is 80. If you want to throw your users a real curve ball, change this port setting to anything other than 80, and I guarantee they will not be able to find your site.

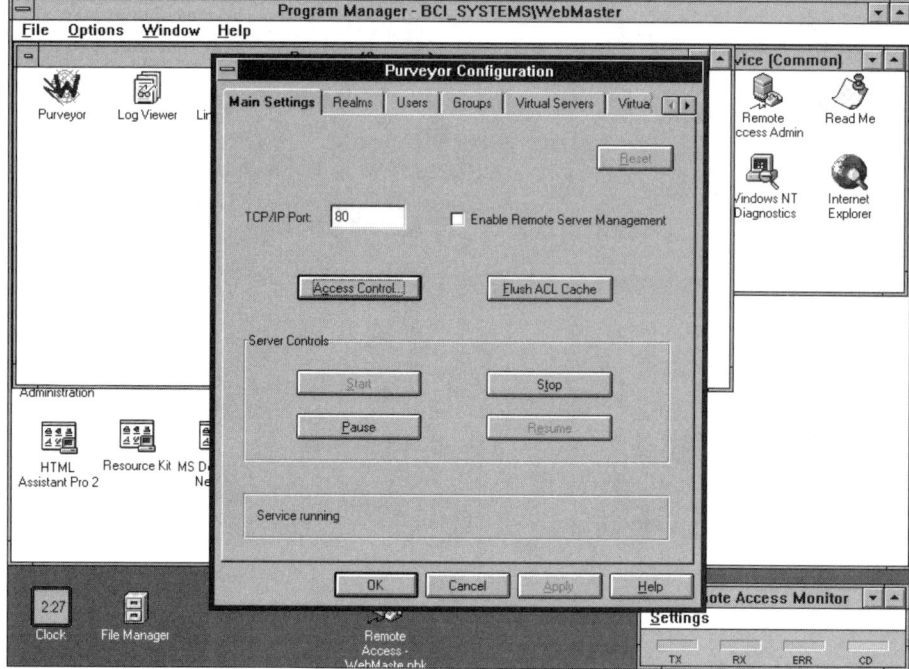

Figure 7.3   The Main Settings properties.

One really nice aspect of Purveyor is its integration with the Microsoft Windows NT Server File Manager. Simply click on the Access Control button to access the NT File Manager, as shown in Figure 7.4. Once there, click on the new Purveyor menu item to display access control options particular to Purveyor. I can't think of an easier way to integrate Web server security and make the WebMaster's life easier than this.

Realms

Realms are like territories—or in NT terminology, like domains. Realms allow you to group users for one virtual server. Providing your systems is capable—some can support upwards of one thousand concurrent users— you can run several realms and several virtual servers on the same physical NT server, but keep all of the users separate. This is one way to earn a good profit from your investment.

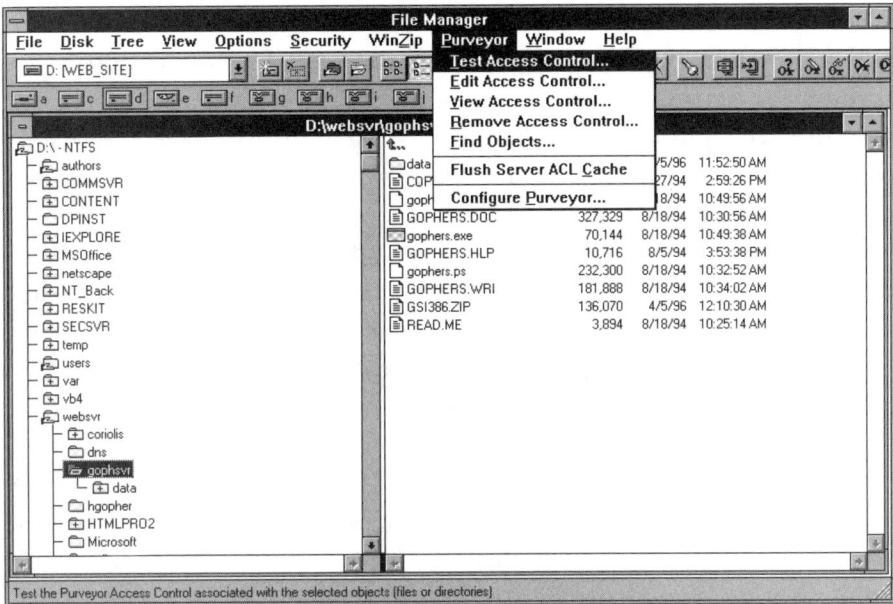

Figure 7.4 Purveyor's integration within the NT File Manager.

Users

The Users property tab is used to add Purveyor Web users to the setup; these properties have nothing to do with the NT user base. However, Purveyor does register the user with the NT Registry functions for users on the Web server. Adding a user to the system is very simple, but the change does not take effect until you click on the Apply button, which has the effect of protecting changes until you're sure you want them to become effective— a nice safety feature.

Groups

The Groups setting allows you to group together common users with common needs, using realms to form the commonality and security. The only drawback to this feature is the inability to move a group from one realm to another. That is, if you create a group in one realm, and find later that it really belongs in another realm, you'll have to create a new group in the other realm and then manually add the users into that new group from the old group.

Virtual Servers

As I mentioned before, virtual servers provide a way for one set of software—Purveyor, for example—to operate many different simulated Web servers, giving the appearance that your business has multiple Web sites when in reality there's only one. A virtual server is another thread running under Microsoft Windows NT Server, and is a separate resource under NT and Purveyor. The virtual servers use different data directories, realm names, and Web pages. Virtual servers are easy to create and run. If your site has more than just a few users and your business is growing with multiple major areas of interest, then you'll do well to explore virtual servers. Figure 7.5 shows the default server that is created to get you started.

Virtual Paths

Virtual paths are nothing more than a representative name for a drive and directory on the physical server disk. If you've ever used the ancient SUBST command, then you already know how and what a virtual path is. If not, here's a brief example. Imagine that the following list is a partial directory structure for your site:

```
D:\WEBSVR\PURVEYOR\VIRTUAL\SERVERS\DATA
D:\WEBSVR\PURVEYOR\VIRTUAL\SERVERS\DATA\accounting
D:\WEBSVR\PURVEYOR\VIRTUAL\SERVERS\DATA\engineering
D:\WEBSVR\PURVEYOR\VIRTUAL\SERVERS\DATA\engineering\plans
```

Let's say that you created a virtual server, called ENG_HOME, for the engineering department. This virtual server references the "plans" subdirectory. Now, only the engineers, not the accountants, need access to the engineering plans for the site. To set this up you simply open the Virtual Paths property sheet, enter the virtual path name of ENG_HOME in the "Name" field and the fully qualified path into the "Path" field. Simple and secure!

CGI Mapping

This property sheet does nothing more than allow you to establish an association between a file extension and a program in much the same way that NT Server's File Manager allows you to associate a TXT file with Notepad. If you associate pl files with the Perl interpreter, then any action on a pl file automatically runs Perl. The same association can be created with any other program that you need for Web server operations.

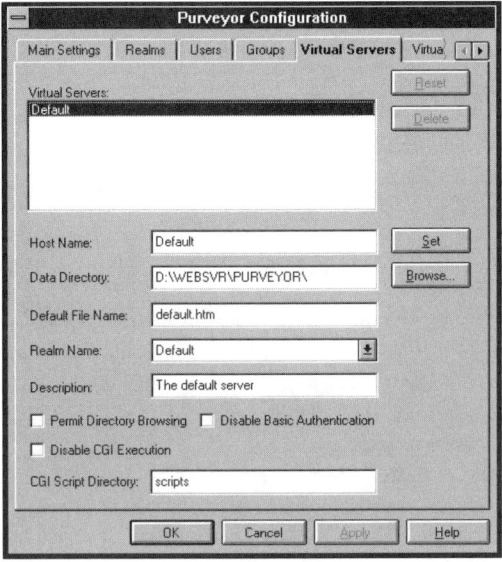

Figure 7.5   Virtual servers allow you to have the illusion that you are running multiple Web sites.

Logging

Logging Purveyor actions and reactions ranks right up at the very top of administrative tools necessary for troubleshooting server problems. The logging feature, shown in the upper-right corner of the Logging property sheet in Figure 7.6, is turned off by default. I checked the box so you could see the logging options more easily.

You'll need to choose such options as how often the log should be renewed, what to log, where the log file should be stored, and if you should use URL paths to work with the log file. Another option is the use of *tracing,* in which detailed information is gathered on each access to your Web server. Listing 7.1 shows the detail of Purveyor's logging operations. This logging is a part of NT itself at this point.

Listing 7.1   Trace Listing for a Detailed Error Log

```
15:33:17:449 Thread 0001-Creating new thread - System thread id 185
15:33:17:639 Thread 0001-REQUEST INFO: Request from: 204.49.131.55 to
   204.49.131.245(gulf245.interoz.com)
15:33:17:639 Thread 0001-REQUEST INFO: Requested url: GET / HTTP/1.0
15:33:17:649 Thread 0001-REQUEST INFO: Request Headers:
```

```
If-Modified-Since: Thursday, 18-Jan-96 16:29:34 GMT
User-Agent: Mozilla/1.1 (Windows; U; 32bit)
Accept: */*
Accept: image/gif
Accept: image/x-xbitmap
Accept: image/jpeg


15:33:17:659 Thread 0001-OBJECT INFO: Path to the object requested:
   D:\WEBSVR\PURVEYOR\
15:33:17:669 Thread 0001-AUTH. INFO: Performing global authentication
15:33:17:669 Thread 0001-AUTH. INFO: No user name in request
15:33:17:679 Thread 0001-AUTH. INFO: Global authentication verified.
15:33:17:689 Thread 0001-OBJECT INFO: Fetching object D:\WEBSVR\PURVEYOR\
15:33:17:689 Thread 0001-OBJECT INFO: Fetching object
   D:\WEBSVR\PURVEYOR\default.htm
15:33:17:699 Thread 0001-AUTH. INFO: Performing file authentication
15:33:17:709 Thread 0001-AUTH. INFO: Could not find ACL file
   D:\WEBSVR\PURVEYOR\$HTTPS$.ACL\default.htm
15:33:17:709 Thread 0001-AUTH. INFO: File authentication process
   completed. Access granted
15:33:17:729 Thread 0001-SOCKET INFO: 27 bytes sent on socket
15:33:17:739 Thread 0001-SOCKET INFO: 36 bytes sent on socket
15:33:17:749 Thread 0001-SOCKET INFO: 22 bytes sent on socket
15:33:18:400 Thread 0001-Ending thread - System thread id 185
15:33:18:931 Thread 0002-Creating new thread - System thread id 199
15:33:19:281 Thread 0002-REQUEST INFO: Request from: 204.49.131.55 to
   204.49.131.245(gulf245.interoz.com)
15:33:19:321 Thread 0003-Creating new thread - System thread id 192
15:33:19:351 Thread 0004-Creating new thread - System thread id 208
15:33:19:361 Thread 0005-Creating new thread - System thread id 128
15:33:19:382 Thread 0002-REQUEST INFO: Requested url: GET /purveyor.gif
   HTTP/1.0
15:33:19:392 Thread 0002-REQUEST INFO: Request Headers:

If-Modified-Since: Wednesday, 30-Aug-95 16:36:34 GMT
Referer: http://204.49.131.245/
User-Agent: Mozilla/1.1 (Windows; U; 32bit)
Accept: image/gif
Accept: image/x-xbitmap
Accept: image/jpeg


15:33:19:402 Thread 0003-REQUEST INFO: Request from: 204.49.131.55 to
   204.49.131.245(gulf245.interoz.com)
```

```
15:33:19:402 Thread 0004-REQUEST INFO: Request from: 204.49.131.55 to
   204.49.131.245(gulf245.interoz.com)
15:33:19:412 Thread 0003-REQUEST INFO: Requested url: GET /selmap.gif
   HTTP/1.0
15:33:19:422 Thread 0002-OBJECT INFO: Path to the object requested:
   D:\WEBSVR\PURVEYOR\purveyor.gif
15:33:19:442 Thread 0004-REQUEST INFO: Requested url: GET /ball.gif
   HTTP/1.0
15:33:19:442 Thread 0005-REQUEST INFO: Request from: 204.49.131.55 to
   204.49.131.245(gulf245.interoz.com)
15:33:19:462 Thread 0002-AUTH. INFO: Performing global authentication
15:33:19:462 Thread 0003-REQUEST INFO: Request Headers:

If-Modified-Since: Tuesday, 12-Dec-95 21:42:58 GMT
Referer: http://204.49.131.245/
User-Agent: Mozilla/1.1 (Windows; U; 32bit)
Accept: image/gif
Accept: image/x-xbitmap
Accept: image/jpeg


15:33:19:472 Thread 0005-REQUEST INFO: Requested url: GET /psc-icon.gif
   HTTP/1.0
15:33:19:482 Thread 0002-AUTH. INFO: No user name in request
15:33:19:502 Thread 0003-OBJECT INFO: Path to the object requested:
   D:\WEBSVR\PURVEYOR\selmap.gif
15:33:19:502 Thread 0004-REQUEST INFO: Request Headers:

If-Modified-Since: Monday, 22-Jan-96 19:10:38 GMT
Referer: http://204.49.131.245/
User-Agent: Mozilla/1.1 (Windows; U; 32bit)
Accept: image/gif
Accept: image/x-xbitmap
Accept: image/jpeg


15:33:19:532 Thread 0005-REQUEST INFO: Request Headers:

If-Modified-Since: Tuesday, 17-Jan-95 21:38:38 GMT
Referer: http://204.49.131.245/
User-Agent: Mozilla/1.1 (Windows; U; 32bit)
Accept: image/gif
Accept: image/x-xbitmap
Accept: image/jpeg
```

```
15:33:19:542 Thread 0003-AUTH. INFO: Performing global authentication
15:33:19:542 Thread 0002-AUTH. INFO: Global authentication verified.
15:33:19:552 Thread 0004-OBJECT INFO: Path to the object requested:
   D:\WEBSVR\PURVEYOR\ball.gif
15:33:19:562 Thread 0005-OBJECT INFO: Path to the object requested:
   D:\WEBSVR\PURVEYOR\psc-icon.gif
15:33:19:582 Thread 0003-AUTH. INFO: No user name in request
15:33:19:582 Thread 0004-AUTH. INFO: Performing global authentication
15:33:19:592 Thread 0002-OBJECT INFO: Fetching object
   D:\WEBSVR\PURVEYOR\purveyor.gif
15:33:19:592 Thread 0005-AUTH. INFO: Performing global authentication
15:33:19:612 Thread 0004-AUTH. INFO: No user name in request
15:33:19:612 Thread 0003-AUTH. INFO: Global authentication verified.
15:33:19:622 Thread 0004-AUTH. INFO: Global authentication verified.
15:33:19:632 Thread 0002-AUTH. INFO: Performing file authentication
15:33:19:632 Thread 0005-AUTH. INFO: No user name in request
15:33:19:642 Thread 0003-OBJECT INFO: Fetching object
   D:\WEBSVR\PURVEYOR\selmap.gif
15:33:19:662 Thread 0005-AUTH. INFO: Global authentication verified.
15:33:19:682 Thread 0004-OBJECT INFO: Fetching object
   D:\WEBSVR\PURVEYOR\ball.gif
15:33:19:682 Thread 0002-AUTH. INFO: Could not find ACL file
   D:\WEBSVR\PURVEYOR\$HTTPS$.ACL\purveyor.gif
15:33:19:692 Thread 0003-AUTH. INFO: Performing file authentication
15:33:19:702 Thread 0005-OBJECT INFO: Fetching object
   D:\WEBSVR\PURVEYOR\psc-icon.gif
15:33:19:712 Thread 0004-AUTH. INFO: Performing file authentication
15:33:19:712 Thread 0003-AUTH. INFO: Could not find ACL file
   D:\WEBSVR\PURVEYOR\$HTTPS$.ACL\selmap.gif
15:33:19:702 Thread 0002-AUTH. INFO: File authentication process
   completed. Access granted
15:33:19:732 Thread 0003-AUTH. INFO: File authentication process
   completed. Access granted
15:33:19:742 Thread 0005-AUTH. INFO: Performing file authentication
15:33:19:742 Thread 0004-AUTH. INFO: Could not find ACL file
   D:\WEBSVR\PURVEYOR\$HTTPS$.ACL\ball.gif
15:33:19:762 Thread 0002-SOCKET INFO: 27 bytes sent on socket
15:33:19:802 Thread 0004-AUTH. INFO: File authentication process
   completed. Access granted
15:33:19:812 Thread 0002-SOCKET INFO: 36 bytes sent on socket
15:33:19:822 Thread 0003-SOCKET INFO: 27 bytes sent on socket
15:33:19:832 Thread 0002-SOCKET INFO: 22 bytes sent on socket
15:33:19:842 Thread 0003-SOCKET INFO: 36 bytes sent on socket
15:33:19:842 Thread 0005-AUTH. INFO: Could not find ACL file
   D:\WEBSVR\PURVEYOR\$HTTPS$.ACL\psc-icon.gif
```

```
15:33:19:852 Thread 0003-SOCKET INFO: 22 bytes sent on socket
15:33:19:862 Thread 0004-SOCKET INFO: 27 bytes sent on socket
15:33:19:872 Thread 0002-SOCKET INFO: 19 bytes sent on socket
15:33:19:872 Thread 0005-AUTH. INFO: File authentication process
    completed. Access granted
15:33:19:882 Thread 0003-SOCKET INFO: 19 bytes sent on socket
```

Even Microsoft Windows NT Server core system information is provided by way of the thread name and system ID created to support the call to Purveyor. This is the kind of information that can help you find the source of errors in user requests, such as a GIF file that can't be transferred on a Web page. Notice the sixth line from the bottom of this listing in which an ACL file couldn't be found. Actually, the GIF file is missing, but Purveyor reports it as an access problem. Purveyor is right…it can't access what isn't there.

Logging Templates

One other logging property you'll find useful is Logging Templates, which allows you to specify attributes of what information is listed in the log file and how it is listed. Purveyor adheres to the NCSA and CERN log file standard, but offers the administrator the ability to customize the log files using standard templates furnished with Purveyor, as shown in Figure 7.7.

Figure 7.6 Purveyor Logging operations.

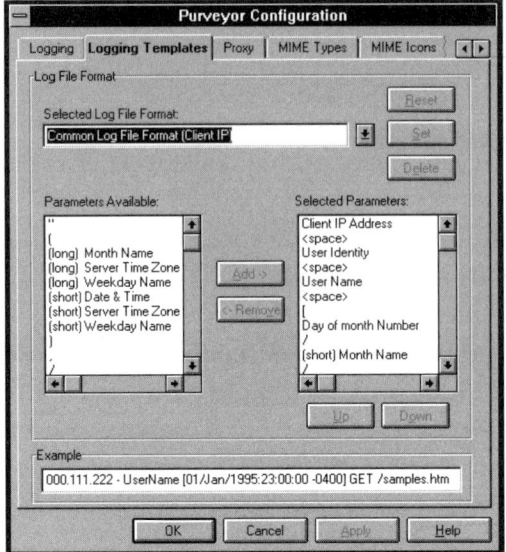

Figure 7.7 Purveyor's templates for logging.

Proxy

A proxy server is used to point users to another location on the Purveyor server that hosts different operations. Take a look at Figure 7.8 and see how I've configured my proxies to host all three common Internet functions. Notice the functions (Proxy Cache, Cache Lifetimes, Gopher Icons) in the property tab that appeared when proxies were enabled.

Assuming I configured the LAN card through NT Server so that the three IP addresses listed in Table 7.1 are bound to the TCP/IP protocol for this physical server, when a user enters one of the IP addresses listed in Table 7.1, he'll come to the corresponding server.

If these IP addresses are registered with a DNS, then I could just as easily perform the associations.

 If you enable certain functions, then additional property sheets appear in the Purveyor menus, allowing you to further customize Purveyor.

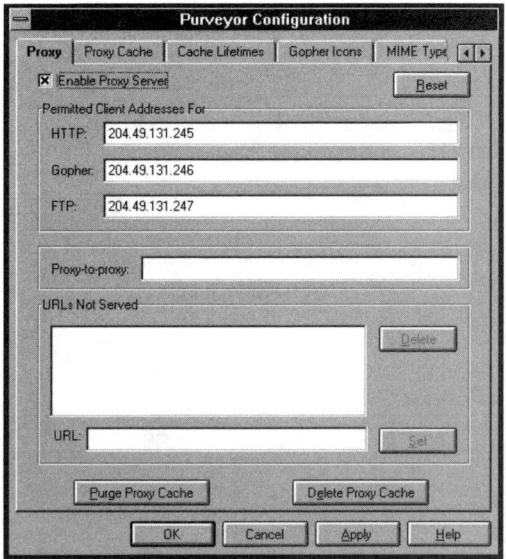

Figure 7.8   Configuring the Purveyor server to host different operations.

MIME Types

MIME, *Multipurpose Internet Mail Extensions*, is how the Internet associates files, functions, and message flow with various files. Every piece of data that crosses the Internet is a different format and type. MIME specifies the associations and type of data so that the receiver and sender handle the proper type of data, as shown in Figure 7.9. For example, a MIME type of JPEG would be used to handle an image type.

MIME Icons

MIME icons are used to associate a MIME type with an appropriate picture. As you can see from Figure 7.10, each of the MIME types has a corresponding GIF file. You can use a GIF viewer to see the icons.

Table 7.1   Proxy Server Associations

IP Address	Function
HTTP	www.bciassoc.com
Gopher	gopher.bciassoc.com
FTP	ftp.bciassoc.com

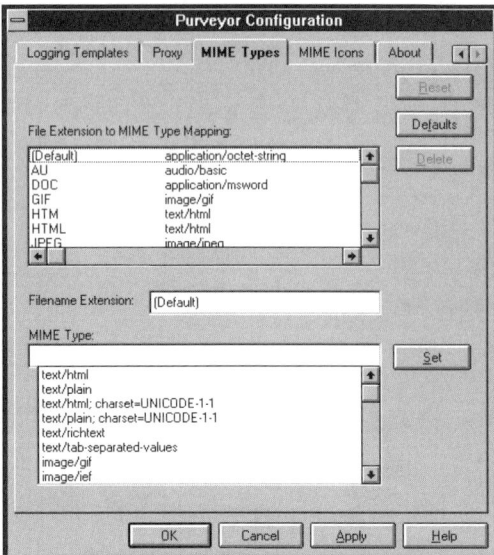

Figure 7.9   MIME types and associations.

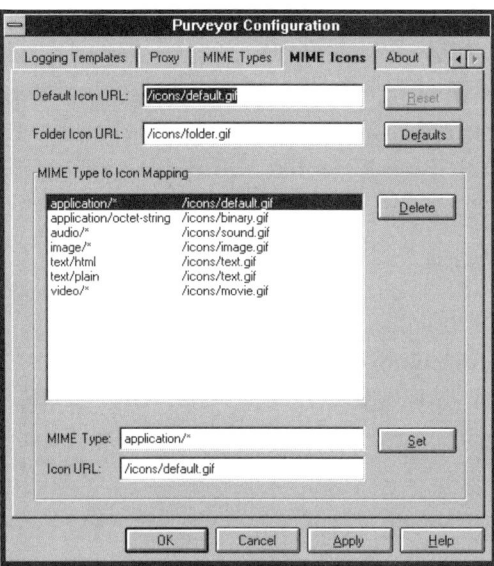

Figure 7.10   MIME icons and associated MIME types.

About

The last property sheet, which doesn't include any configuration information, shows the registration information, owner, and serial number of the registered Web server.

Basic Administration

After you've completed the installation, you'll have gone through a number of options for setting up Purveyor for nominal operations. However, there's still plenty of work to be done. Space constraints prevent me from doing Purveyor full justice, but I'll hit the high points for this Web server in the rest of the chapter.

Enabling Directory Browsing

Directory browsing allows Web users to look around and retrieve files based on rights and access permissions that you give. However, you must explicitly grant the right to do this in the Virtual Servers configuration property sheet. Check the box titled "Permit Directory Browsing" to enable this option. Once done, the MIME icons take effect to identify the files in a visual manner.

Within each virtual server, you'll identify directories for the browsers. You'll need to create and copy all of the icons from the default browser into each of the virtual paths' root level for the icons to be used properly.

In Figure 7.11, the icons are all the same type and color (although you can't identify color in the figure). These are the default types as viewed by Netscape's client browser.

Figure 7.12 shows the difference in the directory browsing with the Purveyor icons stored in the icons directory, which is created in the data directory.

If you don't like the icons or their colors, you can use any standard GIF file editor and change them, as shown in Figure 7.13. I used Hijaak v3.0 running inside Microsoft Windows NT Workstation v3.51 to open the GIF files. I then saved the files as Windows bitmap BMP files and used the standard

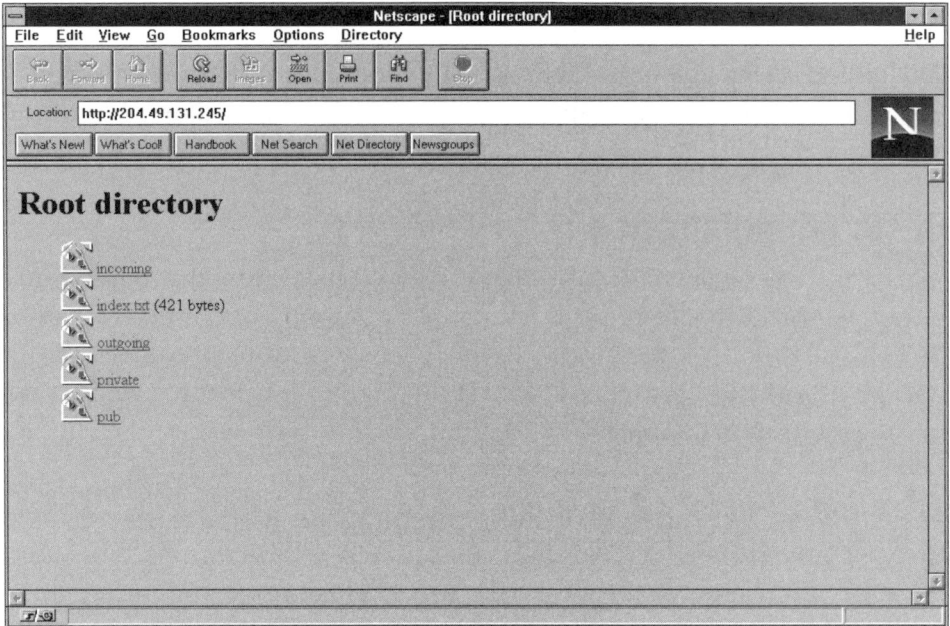

Figure 7.11   Default icons in Purveyor.

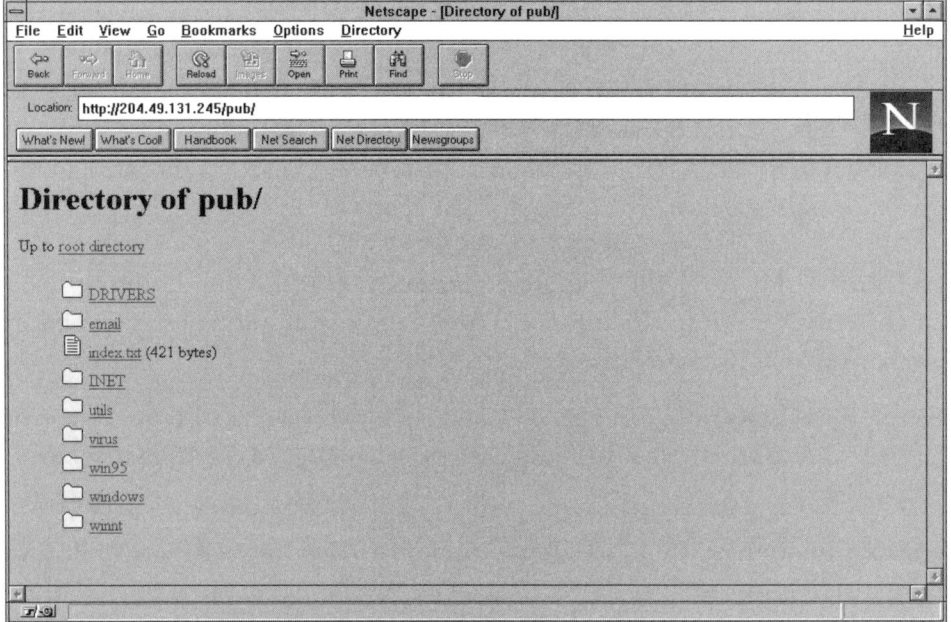

Figure 7.12   Purveyor icons in the same browser.

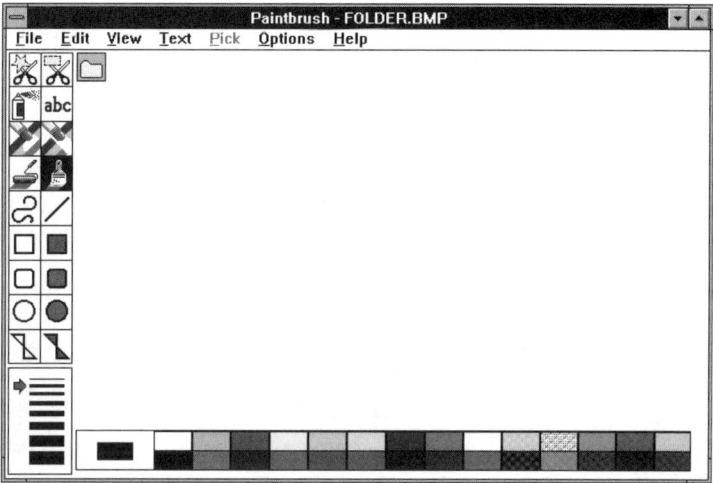

Figure 7.13 Creating your own icons.

Paint program inside Windows to open the resulting files. Pay attention to the file size when you are creating or modifying icons. If you go much bigger than 48k with BMP files, the icon will be massive and will take forever to download with a browser. It'll also severely distort the directory browsing view.

If there's a directory beneath the data directory that you don't want the users to browse, create a text file called NOBROWSE in the respective directory. When Purveyor sees this file, this directory becomes invisible to the users.

Virtual Paths

I touched on the concept of virtual paths in the last section, but there's one more thing we need to cover. For this discussion, we'll use the same directory structure as we did earlier, assigning the virtual server ENG_HOME to the plans directory:

```
D:\WEBSVR\PURVEYOR\VIRTUAL\SERVERS\DATA\engineering
D:\WEBSVR\PURVEYOR\VIRTUAL\SERVERS\DATA\engineering\plans
```

When a user wants to access the Web server's HTML home page (let's use the default index.htm) for my site, he would enter:

```
http://www.bciassoc.com/~plans/index.htm
```

Notice the tilde (~) character, which tells Purveyor that the requested Web page is a virtual one. Purveyor recognizes this character and can then interpret the client's HTML request.

Purveyor's Guide to Server Security

Purveyor's Web server security is better than most of the security included in server packages. Security involves a lot of issues, and this section will look at the most important ones. However, I recommend that you consult the documentation for a more detailed explanation of the security.

Access Control Lists

Purveyor maintains access control by way of an ASCII text file, in a protected location on the server, in which the users' names and IP addresses are used to form groups. You may think that an ASCII file is not that secure, but Purveyor provides a special protection mechanism to prevent unauthorized viewing. The access control lists, commonly referred to as ACLs, within the file are assigned names with the prefix $http$. Because this prefix is not recognized as a valid URL, users are prohibited from gaining access to these files.

One oddity exists with Purveyor's use of ACLs. The sequence of the listings inside ACLs are very important, and determine access to the site. Purveyor grants or denies access based upon the order of the entries within the ACL file. For example, let's say that user Acct_01 is a member of the groups Accounting, Logistics, and Users. In one of the ACLs used to control access to a special manufacturing directory listing, the Users and Accounting groups do not have access, but Logistics does. Although the user name Acct_01 is allowed access, if the name is located *after* the group Accounting, which is denied access, then the user is denied access because the user is a member of a denied group.

Managing Access Controls

Purveyor provides three types of ACL controls:

- **Global Access Control**—Controls access to everything within the Data directory

- **File and Browse Access Control**—Same as Global, but for individual files or directories

- **Virtual Path Access Control**—Same as File and Browse, but for virtual paths

Administration for each of the three controls is performed using Microsoft Windows NT Server's File Manager. Simply locate the directory you wish to place the controls in, click on the Purveyor pull-down menu, and select the functionality you wish to use. It's that simple.

The ACL Editor

Starting with page 17 of the *Guide to Server Security*, the topic of "Managing Access Control Entries" takes you through an 18-page run with all of Purveyor's security settings, and how to implement a secure server. Even if you've been an accomplished NT server administrator for some time, I highly recommended that you take a good hard look at this part of the documentation. All too often, software documentation is best relegated to the restroom reading rack, but these documents from Process Corporation are a gem to read and understand.

Take a look at Figure 7.14, which shows the Access Control Editor. It is here that you get to play God and allow or deny access to the Web site—parts of it, all of it, or none of it. Luckily, access is applied dynamically when you make the changes, so you don't have to restart the Web server or reboot the Microsoft Windows NT Server for the changes to take effect. The Access Control Editor is really quite easy to use. The functions shown in the figure are mainly self-explanatory, so I'll just describe a few notables.

Access control to your Web server is perhaps the single most important part of running a Web site. I've harped on this issue many times, and it bears repeating. The primary grouping function in Purveyor is the realm. You can create all of the realms you could possibly need for your business, but what happens if you create the wrong groups within the realm? Or, worse yet, put the users all into the wrong realm?

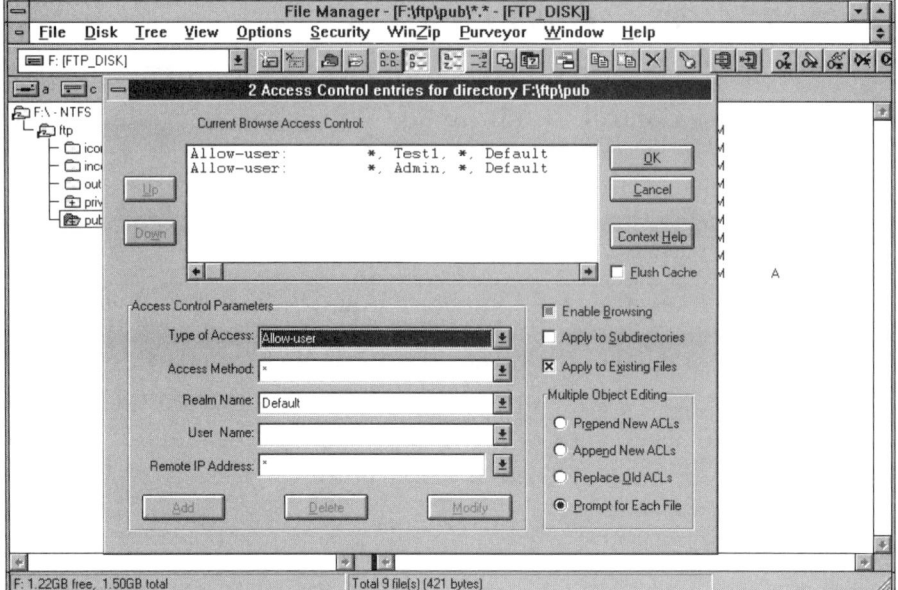

Figure 7.14   The Access Control Editor.

Purveyor makes this problem a non-issue by allowing merging and reorganization of the ACLs. What happens if you forgot which directories or files were listed for the various groups or realms? Not to worry, because Purveyor has a neat tool to search any part of any drive on the physical server and find the objects that have ACL object rights assigned to it. Almost any security issue that you can imagine as usable on a Web server is served by Purveyor's excellent security modules. I'd love to stay here and chat with you all day about the many ways Purveyor can assist you in security, but I'll direct you to Purveyor's documentation instead.

Web Server Operations

In this section we'll go over some of the finer points about general Web server operations within Purveyor. Of course, I can't cover every topic, so I'm limiting my discussion to the everyday use issues.

Realms

Turn to page 139 of the Purveyor manual, if you purchased the product, and follow along as we move through this discussion. As I mentioned before, a realm is nothing more than an abstract concept of placing related users, and groups of users, into one common entity. This draws some parallel to the Microsoft Windows NT Server Domain Model in that likeminded users and groups are gathered into one common place; not only for organizational purposes, but also to control these users with rights and permissions. But that is where the similarities end.

By default, Purveyor maps user entries into the NT registry, which causes administrators feelings ranging from casual disgust to complete dismay that the registry would be used for user database entries. To this end, the programmatically minded have the ability, courtesy of Purveyor, to store the user lists into some other database such as Microsoft Access. To do this, open the Realm property sheet from Purveyor's configuration menu, check the box titled "Use External Authentication DLL," and then enter the fully qualified path to the DLL that controls this process. If you're not to sure about this external DLL process, see the *Programmer's Guide* for the particulars about it.

Perhaps the key to realms is that they are indelibly tied to a virtual server. Although you can create users and groups using only the standard default realm where all users are initially stored, I encourage you to take some time exploring this concept because separate realms can be very advantageous. But, like the workgroups or domains of NT, you'll have think out a strategy for who goes where in the domain. The realm, on the other hand, allows you to have a free form movement of users between realms. The external DLL concept frees up registry entries and keeps that part of Microsoft Windows NT Server clean.

Remote Server Management

It happens to everyone at least once. The Web server is down and the WebMaster is enjoying a relaxing vacation in a rustic cabin, alongside a pristine lake. What now?! Any true WebMaster will never be far off from technology. Relaxing to these folks is simply a matter of getting down to work in a place where no one can disturb their fun. With a laptop computer, cellular phone, and adapters, the WebMaster can connect back to the physical Microsoft Windows NT Server by way of NT's RAS product. With RAS, the WebMaster simply logs into the NT Server as an administrator to start, stop, or change the Web server's configuration.

Purveyor's Remote Server Management (RSM) performs tasks just as if you're sitting in front of the NT server console administering Purveyor. The trick is to set it up properly so that just the WebMaster has access to the Web server. Here's a summary of the things to do for RSM to be active:

• Configure the user database so that the proper access rights have been granted

• Enable basic authentication

• Enable the Virtual Path controls specifically created by Purveyor for the administrator

• Start RSM by using the Web page of *http://host.domain.name/~rsm/ main.htm*

If you enable RSM, and do not enable authentication, *any user can access your site remotely in unprotected access!* This effectively allows someone wide open entry into your Web site.

This setup allows the administrator to access the RSM functions remotely from the Internet. In case you're wondering, RSM displays the same property sheets as those shown in Figure 7.3, with only a slightly different style. The functions are identical.

ODBC Wizard

ODBC, or Open Database Connectivity, is a Windows standard by which programmatical methods can be used to access data on the server side during normal Web operations. This is a nice feature because businesses can not afford to sit idle while they surf the Web in search of other toys, when this Web server is supposed to be serving them!

Purveyor installs ODBC drivers for MS Access and MS SQL Server tools. You'll need to have a toolset such as Visual Basic, Borland's Delphi, or for the rough and rugged, C++. And you'll need to run the ODBC Wizard before you integrate the ODBC platform with whatever toolset you use. From the Purveyor program group, double click on the ODBC Setup icon,

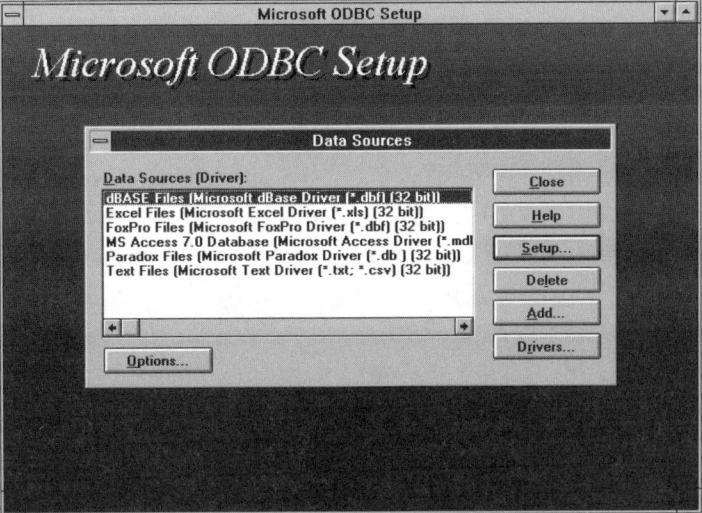

Figure 7.15 My ODBC setup.

and follow the instructions for setting up the drivers. I selected the FoxPro driver. Figure 7.15 shows what is currently set up on my Web server to support ODBC.

Link Browser

When the site is in a heavy state of flux with many changing customer needs, you're bound to end up with broken links, which can cause a myriad of problems, including loss of business. Don't worry. Again, Purveyor comes to the rescue with Link Browser.

Link Browser is a tool that searches your Web looking for mismatched associations of Web pages. It looks for missing HTML files, graphics, databases, and more, and displays a tree to show the structure of directories and files in the HTML picture. This shows you in an instant how your site's links are doing. Page 203 of the *User's Guide* has a good view of the links and representations of the link status.

Document Management with Purveyor's Verity Tools

Purveyor includes a host of tools that are used to create an index and expedite the retrieval of documents stored on the Web server. These *Verity* tools perform three basic functions:

- Creating the index by using the DOS utility MKVDK

- Using CGI and HTML forms to customize a search tool

- Running a search of your existing database by using HTML Web pages

To see these functions in action, I suggest you stop by the Yahoo Web site, which performs this very set of basic functions for the Web. The only real difference between a site like Yahoo and your site is the size of the databases that these search engines operate. For instance, you would probably use these functions to create an index of sales documents, technical support bulletins, or any similar documents where the user needs to get to the data without a hassle or worrying about how to find the data. Chapters 9 through 11 will lead you into this realm of Web operations.

Troubleshooting Server Problems

You know it will happen, it's just a matter of when. Fixing your Web server can be a troublesome task, especially because the timing of such problems can be critical to the business. When the time comes, bite the bullet and put Purveyor to work. Purveyor includes tools to track down problems you are having and to help you keep a record of such failures. Logging errors is important because repetitive failures can indicate a much larger problem.

Transaction Logging

Transaction logging is used to show who is accessing the server, what locations of the Web server are being accessed, and what methods are being used to respond to the user's requests. Listing 7.2 shows a sample log file in Purveyor.

Listing 7.2   Sample Transaction Log

```
#!PARAMETER logtemplate = %r %i %u [%d/%b/%Y:%H:%M:%S %O] "%q" %s %n
204.49.131.81 - - [22/Apr/1996:02:38:09 -0500] "GET / HTTP/1.0" 200 455
204.49.131.81 - - [22/Apr/1996:02:38:12 -0500] "GET /icons/folder.gif
   HTTP/1.0" 404 -
204.49.131.81 - - [22/Apr/1996:02:38:22 -0500] "GET /pub/ HTTP/1.0" 200
   881
204.49.131.81 - - [22/Apr/1996:02:38:24 -0500] "GET /icons/folder.gif
   HTTP/1.0" 404 -
204.49.131.81 - - [22/Apr/1996:02:40:49 -0500] "GET / HTTP/1.0" 200 561
```

```
204.49.131.81 - - [22/Apr/1996:02:40:50 -0500] "GET /icons/folder.gif
   HTTP/1.0" 404 -
204.49.131.81 - - [22/Apr/1996:02:42:41 -0500] "GET /icons/text.gif
   HTTP/1.0" 404 -
204.49.131.81 - - [22/Apr/1996:02:42:41 -0500] "GET /icons/folder.gif
   HTTP/1.0" 404 -
204.49.131.81 - - [22/Apr/1996:02:46:27 -0500] "GET /icons/text.gif
   HTTP/1.0" 404 -
204.49.131.81 - - [22/Apr/1996:02:46:27 -0500] "GET /icons/folder.gif
   HTTP/1.0" 404 -
204.49.131.81 - - [22/Apr/1996:02:46:45 -0500] "GET / HTTP/1.0" 200 1534
204.49.131.81 - - [22/Apr/1996:02:46:47 -0500] "GET /icons/image.gif
   HTTP/1.0" 404 -
204.49.131.81 - - [22/Apr/1996:02:49:25 -0500] "GET /icons/folder.gif
   HTTP/1.0" 200 144
204.49.131.81 - - [22/Apr/1996:02:49:25 -0500] "GET /icons/text.gif
   HTTP/1.0" 200 161
204.49.131.81 - - [22/Apr/1996:02:49:24 -0500] "GET /icons/image.gif
   HTTP/1.0" 200 160
204.49.131.81 - - [22/Apr/1996:02:51:57 -0500] "GET / HTTP/1.0" 200 455
204.49.131.81 - - [22/Apr/1996:02:51:59 -0500] "GET /icons/folder.gif
   HTTP/1.0" 404 -
204.49.131.81 - - [22/Apr/1996:02:54:08 -0500] "GET /icons/folder.gif
   HTTP/1.0" 304 -
204.49.131.81 - - [22/Apr/1996:02:54:18 -0500] "GET /pub/ HTTP/1.0" 200
   881
204.49.131.81 - - [22/Apr/1996:02:54:44 -0500] "GET /pub/ HTTP/1.0" 200
   991
204.49.131.81 - - [22/Apr/1996:02:54:46 -0500] "GET /icons/text.gif
   HTTP/1.0" 304 -
```

To generate this log, I performed a simple browse across the FTP location into a few directories. Of course, this type of tracking repeats itself automatically wherever the user goes on the Web server. This kind of detailed logging is crucial to finding problems on the Web server, and are worth their weight of bytes in gold.

Log Viewer

The Log Viewer is a really neat utility that gives you the graphical look and feel of a transactional log file. As you can see from Figure 7.16, a picture is truly worth a thousand words. I realize there's not much to this little sub-section, but what else can be said? Purveyor makes it this easy!

Remote_Host	Logon	Auth	Date/Time	Request	Status	Bytes
204.49.131.73	-	-	4/23/96 3:56:11 AM	GET / HTTP/1.0	401	
204.49.131.73	-	sysmgrjb	4/23/96 3:56:42 AM	GET / HTTP/1.0	401	
204.49.131.73	-	SysAdmin	4/23/96 3:56:50 AM	GET / HTTP/1.0	401	
204.49.131.55	-	-	4/20/96 8:33:17 PM	GET / HTTP/1.0	304	
204.49.131.55	-	-	4/20/96 8:33:19 PM	GET /purveyor.gif HTTP/1.0	304	
204.49.131.55	-	-	4/20/96 8:33:19 PM	GET /ball.gif HTTP/1.0	304	
204.49.131.55	-	-	4/20/96 8:33:19 PM	GET /psc-icon.gif HTTP/1.0	304	
204.49.131.55	-	-	4/20/96 8:33:19 PM	GET /selmap.gif HTTP/1.0	304	

Figure 7.16   Log view of the transaction log file.

Microsoft Windows NT Server's Event Viewer

Although Purveyor maintains a separate identity from NT, this is one place where the two merge; Purveyor uses NT's event platform to register happenings and events within NT. I've secured my Web server so that only those with an account and password can be validated into the server and therefore have access to other parts of my networks. If you want to run a secure operation, this becomes a necessary evil.

Figure 7.17 shows you that even Purveyor uses some of NT's best utilities to keep an eye on things as they transpire. What you're looking at is the Security Log entry showing that I successfully logged on to the server, and with what rights.

Performance Monitoring

Microsoft Windows NT Server has performance tools that monitor all aspects of the physical server itself. With Purveyor comes an integration into these same tools that assist the WebMaster to see how well, or how rough, things are going with respect to data throughput with the Web server. Let's see how this works.

In the NT Administrative group, start Performance Monitor. I have my own customized monitor settings for an array of views of my server, and I was pleased to see that Purveyor continues to make life easy on my daily

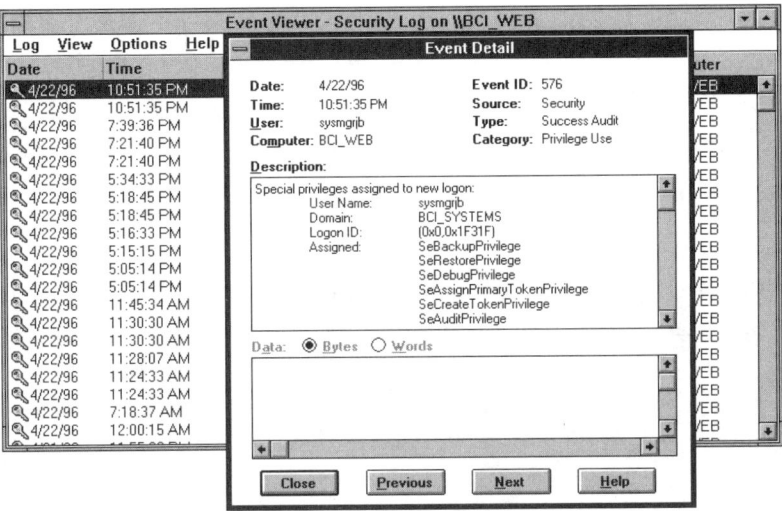

Figure 7.17 Microsoft Windows NT Server's event logon listing.

routines. Click on the Edit menu option, then select Add to Chart to display the basic options to add to a monitoring chart. Figure 7.18 shows Purveyor's Monitor log options. Click on the Object drop-down menu,

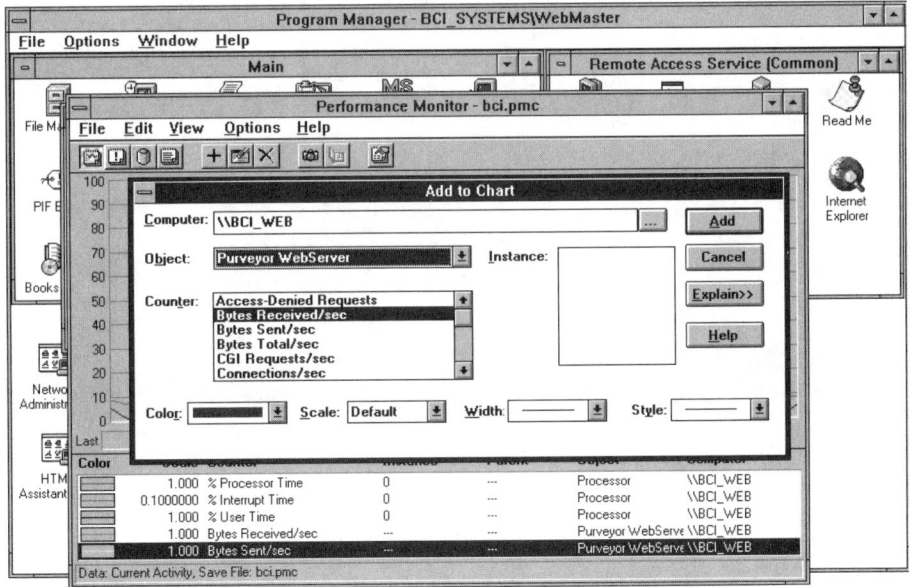

Figure 7.18 Purveyor's Monitor log options.

and select the Purveyor entry to display the many items that Purveyor operates inside of the Microsoft Windows NT Server to perform its functions.

Use the Add button to select the things you want to see in operations, then return to monitoring the server's operations. When a user accesses the site, you will be able to monitor the functions you selected, as shown in Figure 7.19.

I chose the Bytes Read and Bytes Sent options to monitor how much data is moved. There's plenty of things that can be viewed, and I urge you to explore the rest of the monitor options. Once you see how many there are to use, you'll soon see how the integration of Purveyor into NT's monitor makes perfect sense.

Summary

Although I was unable to cover all the aspects of this server package for you, I can honestly say that I found Purveyor a joy to use, understand, and maintain. This chapter has shown you:

*   How to install Purveyor

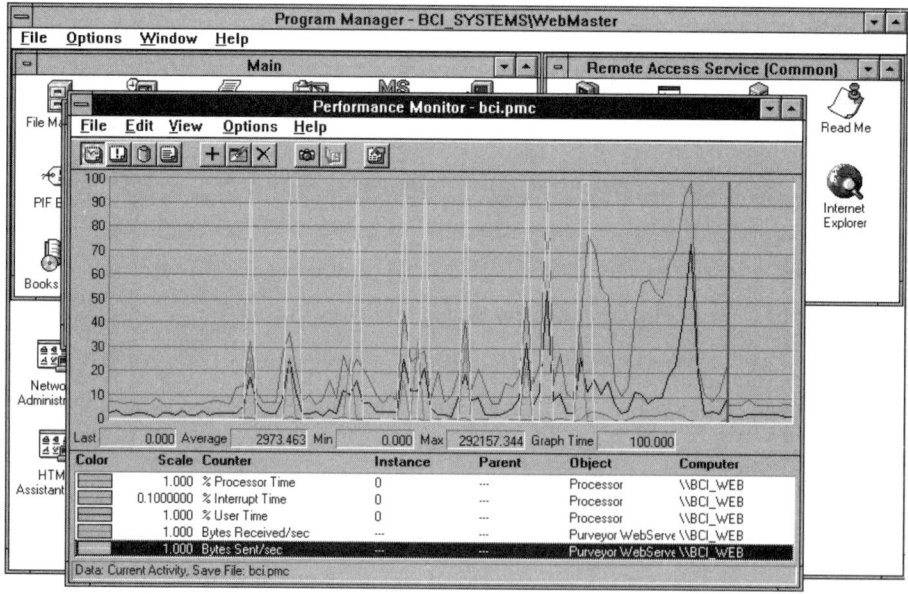

Figure 7.19   A sample monitoring of two Purveyor functions.

- How to configure Purveyor for open and private access

- Basic Purveyor maintenance techniques

- Troubleshooting tools native to both Purveyor and NT Server

As we start Chapter 8, Quarterdeck's WebServer, let's keep in mind that serving our customer base is the prime motivation for our actions. You should continue to keep an open mind on these Web servers, yet be aware of what each has to offer your Web. See you on the next page.

Quarterdeck's WebServer

Welcome to our fourth and final review of Web server packages: Quarterdeck Office Systems' WebServer. Quarterdeck, best known as the developer of QEMM, the memory manager that provides significantly better memory management than its contemporaries, has entered the exploding Internet marketplace with a real bang. In this chapter, I'll be presenting the same core instructional material for WebServer as I have with the packages in the previous three chapters. We'll cover the installation, configuration, and administration processes of this product, as well as troubleshooting techniques if you should find yourself in a bind.

Quarterdeck offers three products that form the core functionality of their Internet capabilities:

- **WebServer**—The Web server product itself

- **WebAuthor**—An HTML add-in for Word for Windows v6, somewhat reminiscent of the Microsoft add-in for WinWord

- **InternetSuite**—A suite of tools, including Quarterdeck Mosaic for browsing, Quarterdeck Message Center for Internet newsgroups and email, and Quarterdeck FTP and Qterm for FTP and Telnet capabilities.

315

At the time of this chapter's development, the only product I had available was WebServer, so let's jump right in and explore its installation and use.

Installing WebServer

Installing WebServer is a simple process involving just two floppy diskettes. WebServer dispenses with many of the options found in Purveyor and WebSite; WebServer is strictly a hard core server, and that's it. If you want to write some HTML pages, you'll have to find an HTML editor because WebServer doesn't install one. Quarterdeck does have an HTML editor, as you saw earlier, but a version for Windows 95 or Windows NT Workstation wasn't available at the time of this writing.

Performing the Installation

Go to the system console for your Web server, and insert diskette one. Enter the command a:\install, or use File Manager to begin the operation. Figure 8.1 shows the opening screen welcoming you to WebServer's installation program.

Aside from the usual welcoming messages, you'll notice that WebServer requires either a Winsock compliant interface or the LAN WorkPlace TCP/IP package normally found with Novell Corporation's Netware LAN WorkPlace interface. To give you a little background, Microsoft Windows NT Server and client products like Windows for Workgroups and Windows 95 have TCP/IP built into them, whereas the basic Windows 3.1 running as a client on a Netware NOS does not. If these Win 3.x clients want to access the Internet, they need a TCP/IP product to provide this additional set of capabilities.

This is the purpose of LAN WorkPlace. If the system on which you're installing WebServer doesn't have TCP/IP, then WebServer offers to install it for you. This is not the full version of LAN WorkPlace, but rather the core TCP/IP functions to maintain Winsock compatibility. Quarterdeck is one of the first vendors to directly support Novell Netware servers as a base for Internet activities.

Click on the Continue button to go to the next screen. If you have TCP/IP installed (and you most certainly should because previous chapters required

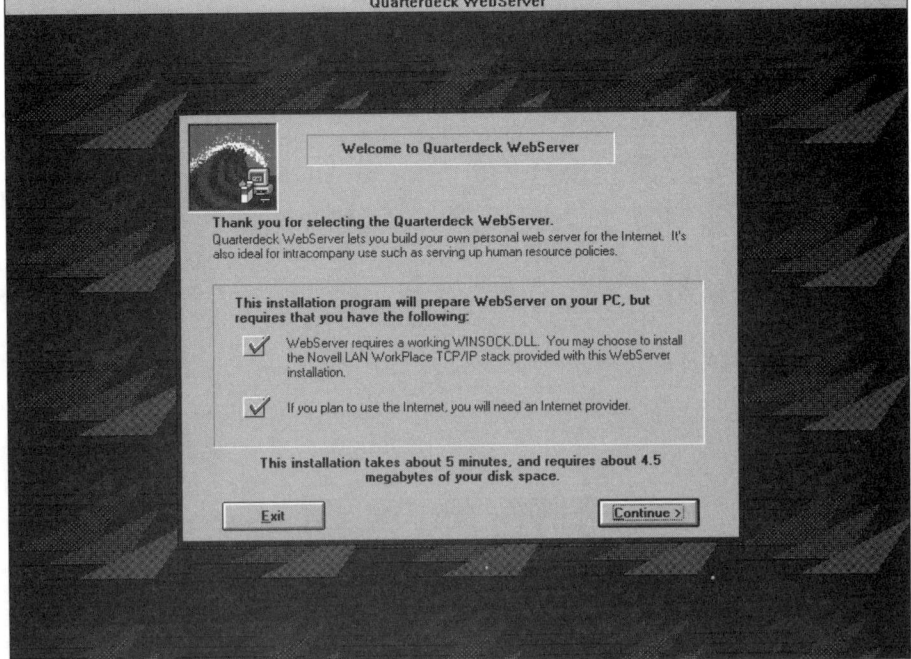

Figure 8.1 WebServer installation welcoming screen.

it!), you'll be presented with Figure 8.2 letting you know that Winsock compatibility was found. The checkbox for "Install LAN WorkPlace" is cleared now for you.

At this point, you'll be prompted to enter in the company's data for the owner, as shown in Figure 8.3. Most likely, you'll type in the MIS group's information or something to that effect. Make sure that the registration card matches the data you enter here.

The Install program then provides you with choices of locations for the placement of the WebServer files on your server, as shown in Figure 8.4. Notice that the default location is the C drive. When I build servers, I always create a 75 MB C partition that stays as a DOS FAT partition and not an NTFS. This step gives me the ability to boot up to the C prompt during difficult times when I need to perform some drastic troubleshooting. I recommend that you make a habit of this procedure as well, but the advantage to the default installation location is that WebServer's installation takes up so little disk space that the problem is negligible.

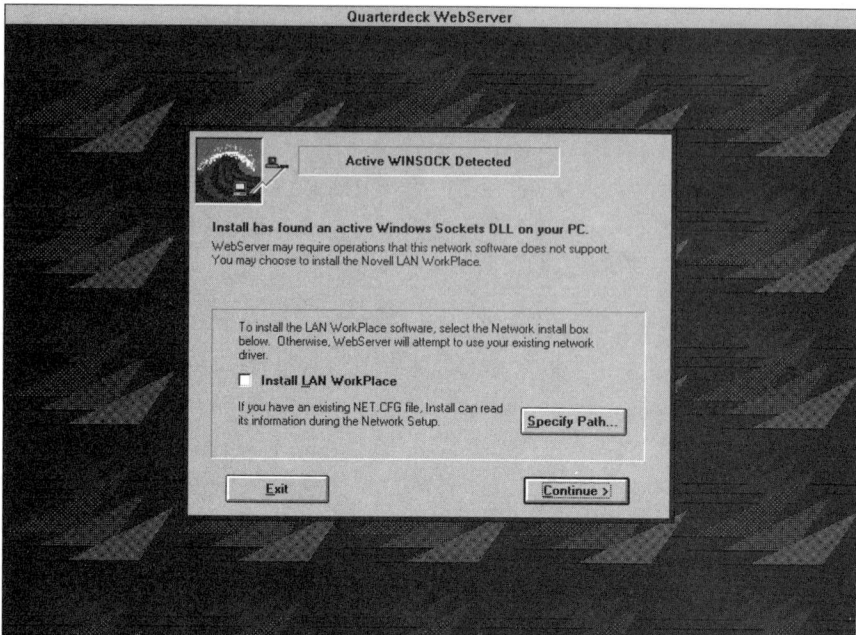

Figure 8.2 WebServer has detected Winsock.

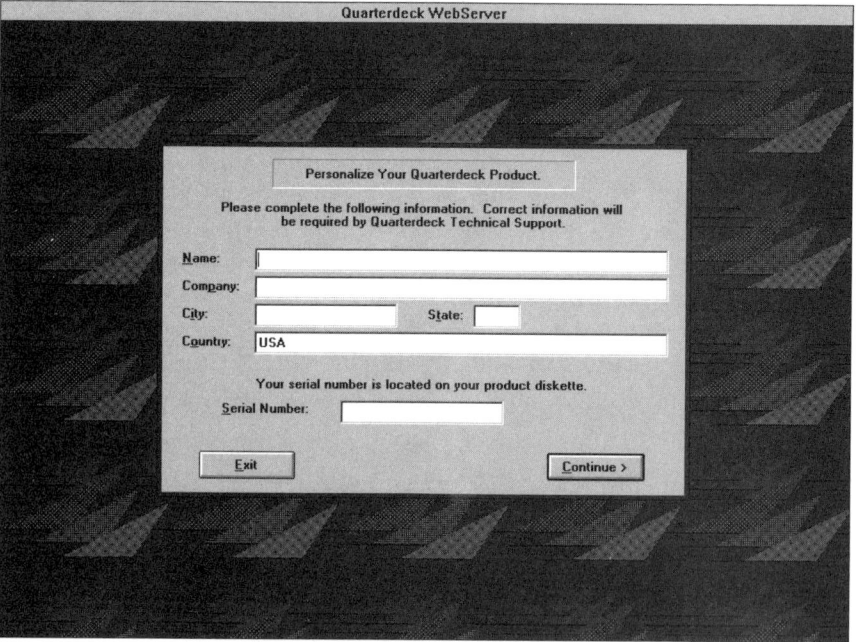

Figure 8.3 Filling in registration information.

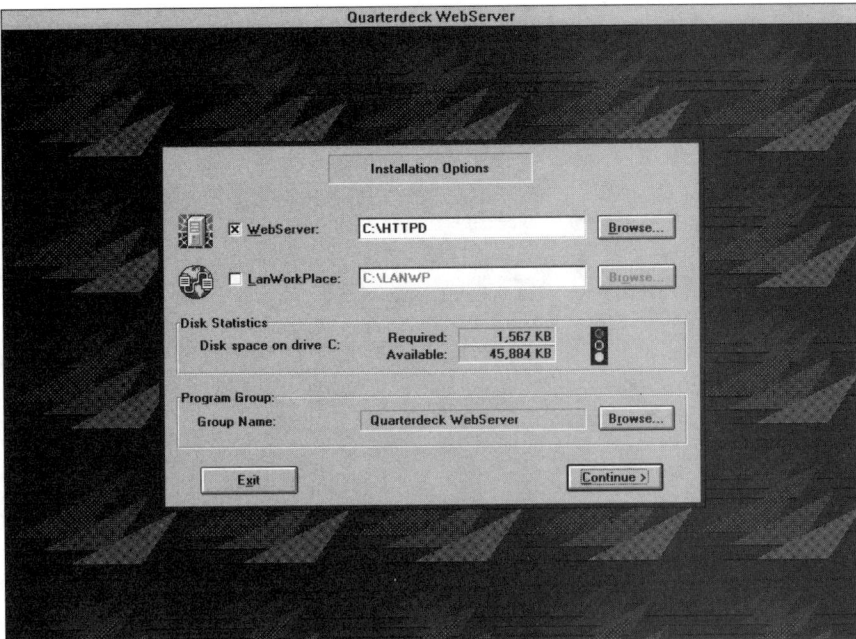

Figure 8.4   WebServer installation options.

The next screen, shown in Figure 8.5, allows you to enter the email address of the WebMaster, and to also set the time zone of the server, which is particularly helpful for email.

After you've completed these few settings, let WebServer continue the remainder of the installation, inserting the second floppy when requested. The screen shown in Figure 8.6 displays when the installation is complete, and advises you to reboot for the time zone environment variable to take effect.

Reboot the server and you'll be presented with the WebServer program group, shown in Figure 8.7. Don't jump to the conclusion that WebServer is not hearty because only a few items reside in the program group. WebServer is powerful indeed. Quarterdeck purposely lets you make your own selection for an HTML editor and other tools to use with WebServer, even though they supply WebAuthor and InternetSuite. Personally, I applaud this move towards independence.

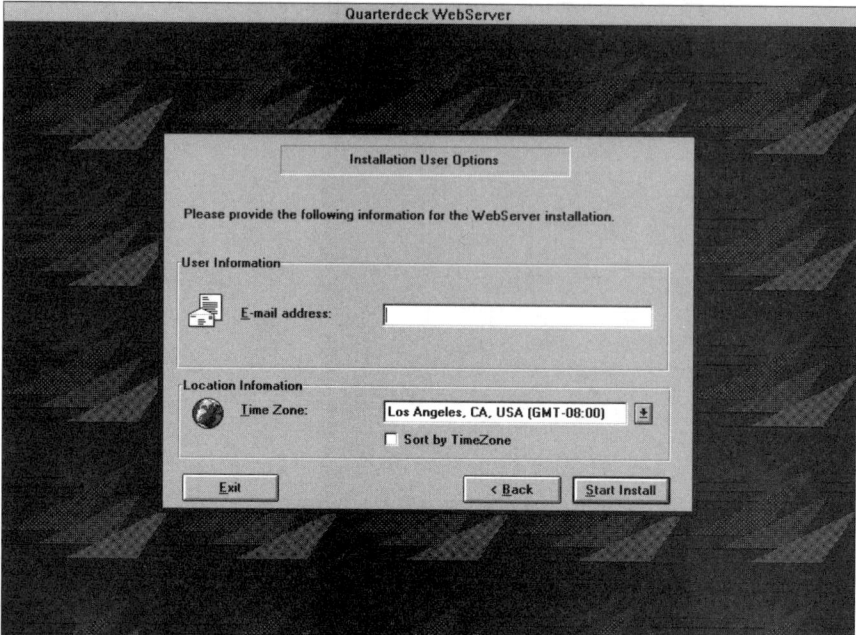

Figure 8.5 User installation options for the WebMaster.

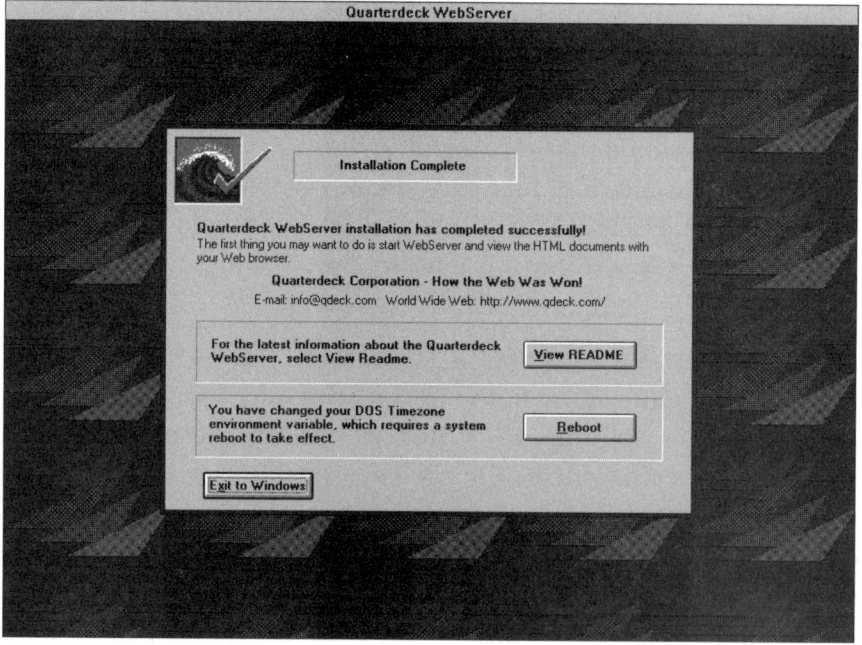

Figure 8.6 Installation complete!

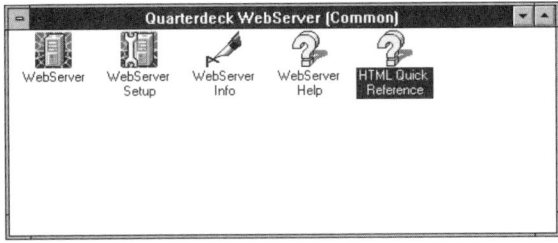

Figure 8.7   Program Manager group for WebServer.

Basic Administration

With the installation completed, let's turn our attention to the administration options and matters of the user, shown in Figure 8.8, by double clicking on the WebServer Setup icon. It is these options that will prove to you just how powerful WebServer truly is.

The core functions of WebServer are:

- Administration and Logging
- Directory Listings
- Aliasing and Redirection

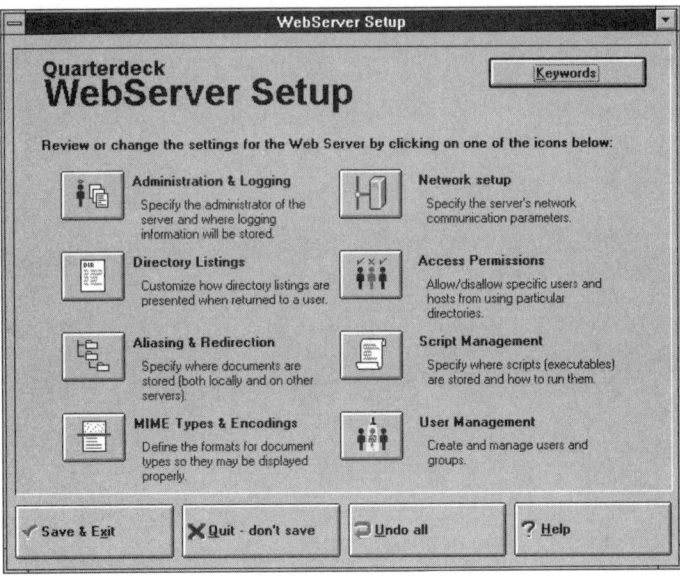

Figure 8.8   WebServer Setup main menu

- MIME Types and Encodings

- Network Setup

- Access Permissions

- Script Management

- User Management

You access each of these functions by clicking on the corresponding button on the main administration screen. Let's go over each of these functions and see what they do for WebServer.

Note: If you make a change to any of the functions in the following sections and then change your mind, you can undo the change or abort the operation to preserve your old settings.

Administration and Logging

The Administration and Logging option, shown in Figure 8.9, allows you to identify where you want the root level of the Web server HTML stored, where you want the documents stored, and where you want the two log files stored.

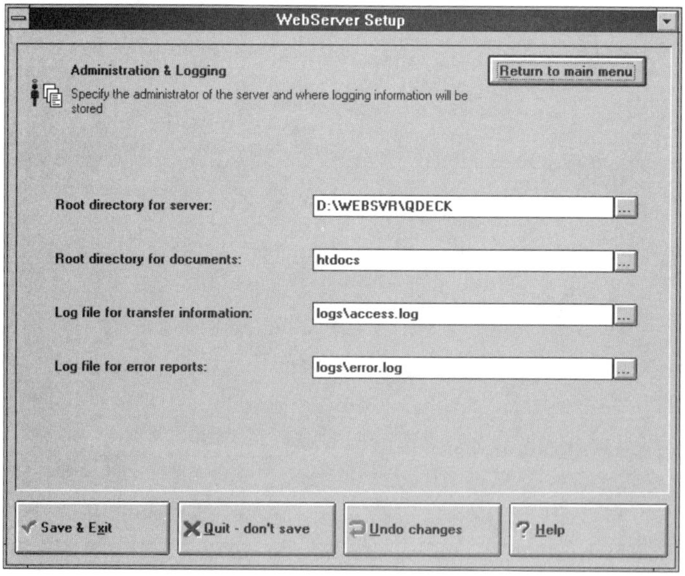

WebServer Setup

Administration & Logging
Specify the administrator of the server and where logging information will be stored

Return to main menu

Root directory for server: | D:\WEBSVR\QDECK |

Root directory for documents: | htdocs |

Log file for transfer information: | logs\access.log |

Log file for error reports: | logs\error.log |

✓ Save & Exit   ✗ Quit - don't save   ⤺ Undo changes   ? Help

Figure 8.9 The Administration and Logging options.

Directory Listings

The Directory Listings options allow you to set the defaults for handling HTML pages as well as the many file types and associations like sound, video, and more, as shown in Figure 8.10. You can create your own extensions to customize the server for most any occasion by using the Extensions function.

Aliasing and Redirection

Simply put, the Aliasing and Redirection option, shown in Figure 8.11, allows you to create virtual directories, which use an alias of a physical directory path. We covered this topic in the previous chapter when we created the alias "ENG_HOME," which we then routed to the path f:\depts\eng\data\plans. This step makes it possible for any user who wants to get to the data directory for the Engineering department to use the alias "ENG_HOME" instead of keying in the full path. For more information, refer back to Chapter 7. You can also link a URL on your Web server to one of these aliases, providing access to data or programs on your Web server.

MIME Types and Encodings

MIME comes into play for nearly all of the Internet functions, and WebServer makes it easy to accommodate any of these types. Take a look at

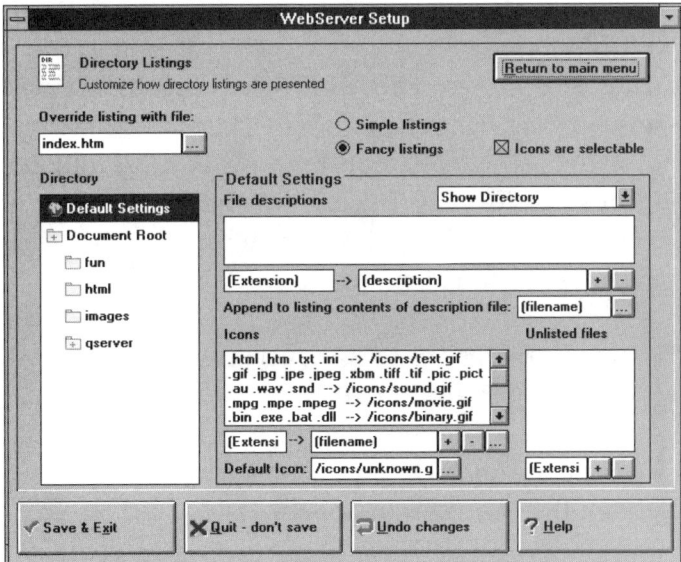

Figure 8.10 Directory listings and file associations.

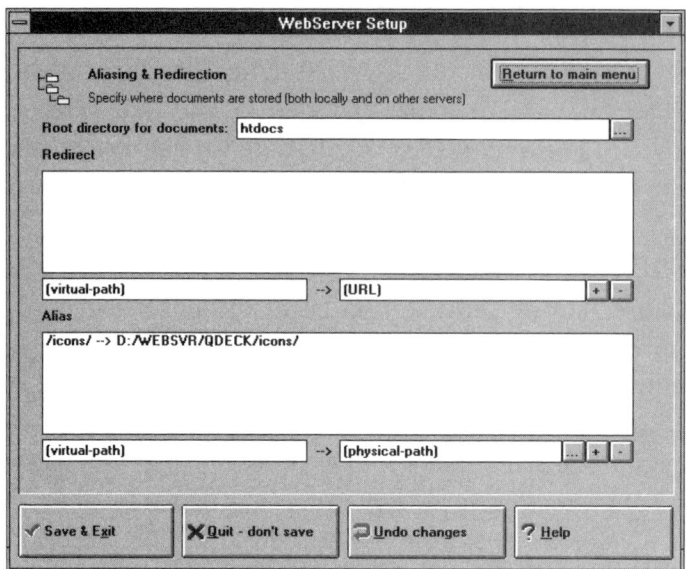

Figure 8.11   The Aliasing and Redirection option.

Figure 8.12 and you'll see how easy it is to make these changes and associations with MIME types. All you have to do is click on the plus sign (+) to add an association, or highlight the current association and click on the minus sign (–) key to remove one.

Network Setup

The Network Setup option screen, shown in Figure 8.13, is where you customize the server by entering the host name of your server, typically something like www.your-server.com, and then registering your server's name with the DNS of your site. This is a crucial step in getting your server operational, so remember to do this! Also, you can change the port number from the default to anything you might need it to be.

 If you do not register your server with a DNS, then your users must know the IP numerical address of the site to reach it. Not registering servers in this way is a major cause of Internet servers not being found on the Internet. Don't let this happen to you!

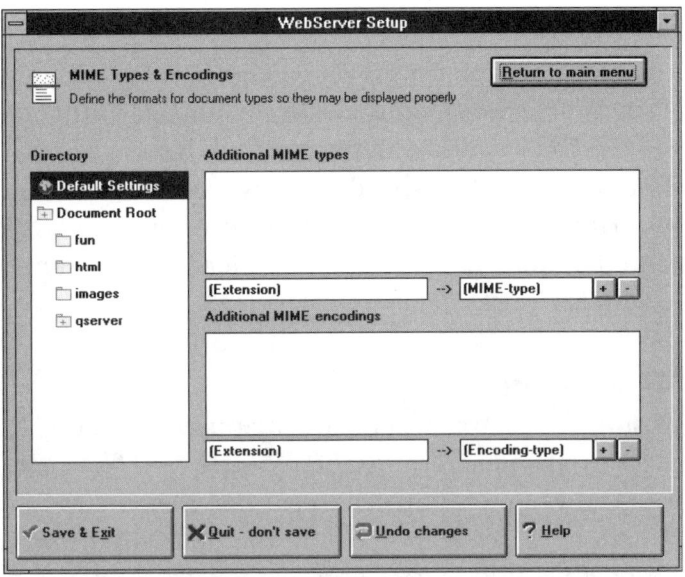

Figure 8.12   Setting MIME types.

Figure 8.13   Network settings.

Access Permissions

Access permissions, which are shown in Figure 8.14, are another important part of the WebServer operations. By default, all visitors are allowed to reach the server. You can allow all hosts, which is the default setting; deny all hosts; allow only some hosts; or deny only some hosts. You can get really tight with security here as you further customize your server. It's important to understand that none of the users listed here, or added here, have anything to do with NT's user databases.

Script Management

Figure 8.15 shows locations where the scripting programs for DOS and Windows are stored when you installed WebServer. Normally, there's no need to change any of the settings here, although you may find it easier to set a virtual path to these locations while you build up the server. Clicking on the Advanced Shell Processor Options button yields a number of settings strictly used for the WebServer shell. If you're not sure how these options work, don't touch them!

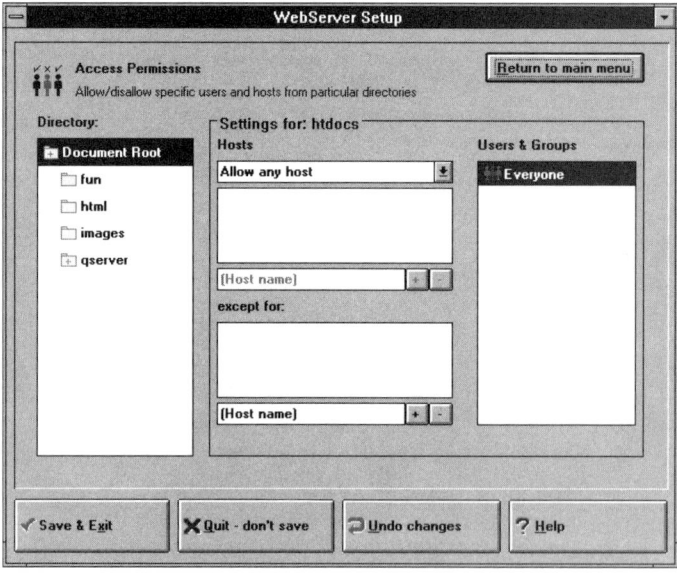

Figure 8.14 Access permissions.

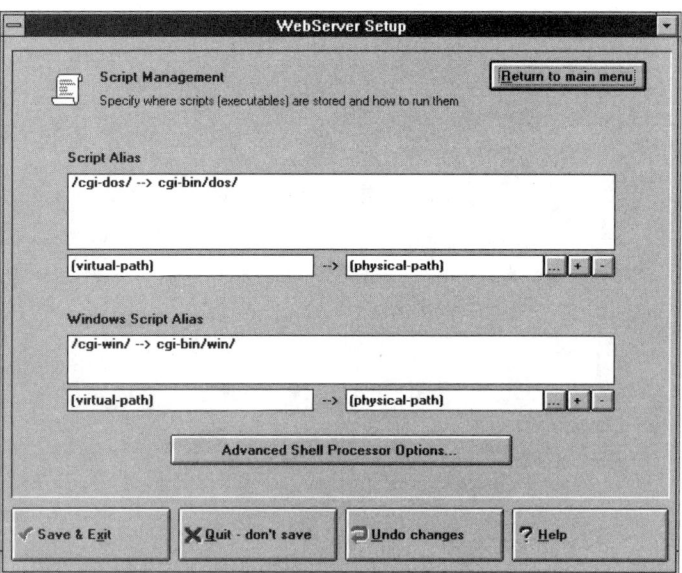

Figure 8.15   The Script Management dialog box.

You should be knowledgeable in the shell environment before making any changes to the Advanced Processor Options.

User Management

The set of options in this section are the User Management options, which are shown in Figure 8.16. Actually, "Users and Groups" would have been a more appropriate name because these options allow you to create or change your user and group setups. If you know the concepts of NT Server groups, then you've got it made. This is pretty straightforward stuff. Like users are placed into like groups of functions. If you have to install and create a new Web server from scratch, then you'll have to create each user and group just like the other Web servers that we've covered.

That's about it for the WebServer settings. Not too bad, eh? Now let's take a look at the operations and general characteristics of WebServer.

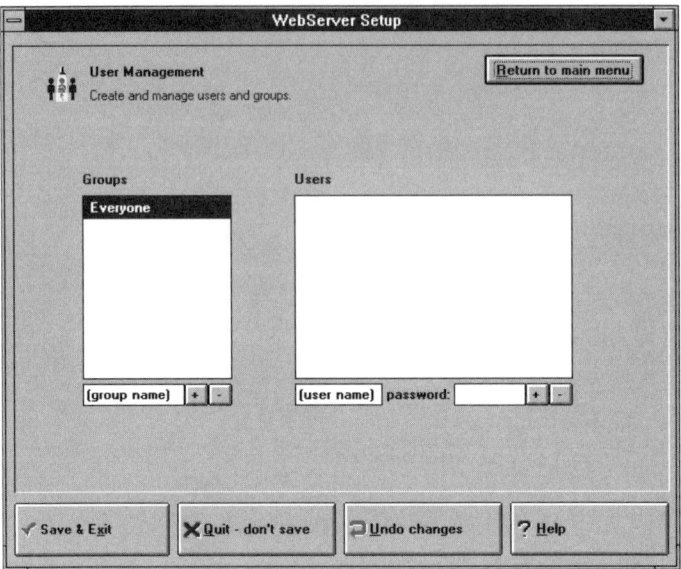

Figure 8.16 Creating and maintaining users and groups.

WebServer Operations

When you consider purchasing any Web server, think about what the server is supposed to do for you. Specifically, you need to consider speed, security, ease of maintenance, and upgradability. Luckily, WebServer is easy in all of these departments.

Running the Server

Go to the NT Server console and double click on the WebServer icon in the WebServer program group. WebServer starts, initializes, and then iconizes itself to run minimized. That's it! WebServer is operational as far as Microsoft Windows NT Server is concerned, but what about the clients?

Using your favorite Web browser, type in the URL of the new WebServer installation. You can either use the IP address or the alias, but remember that you should get the site registered into a DNS if you want the world to see the site. WebServer responds to the http request and presents you with the default HTML page installed with WebServer, as shown in Figure 8.17.

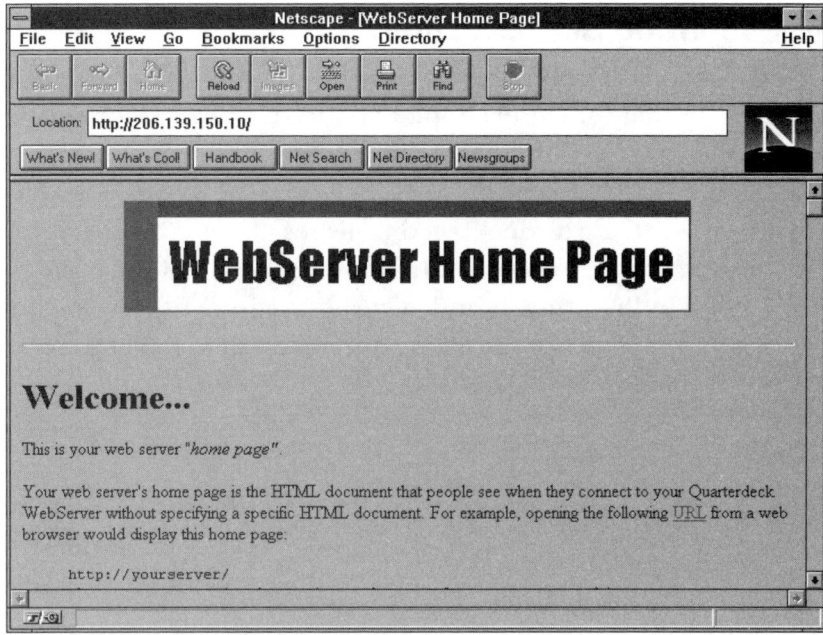

Figure 8.17　WebServer's default home page.

Validating the WebServer

It doesn't look like much, but scroll down the page so you can see everything that's included. You'll find a demo program for using WebServer, fun sites to visit, a short lesson on HTML if you need it, and, most importantly, a program to test the Web server and make sure its operational.

Click on the link "Quarterdeck WebServer Demonstration" and follow it along while the Web server is validated. You'll have the opportunity to test document-based queries, form-based queries, Windows CGI applications, directory and tree navigation, and hotspot edited regions.

Once you've completed the testing, WebServer can largely be considered operational. The things that you may have to alter include the user base and groups definitions, along with directory assignments for the virtual paths. Other than this, all you'll have to do is create your HTML pages and graphics using a product such as Front Page (discussed in Chapter 5) or HTML Assistant.

Troubleshooting Server Problems

Alas, no Web server is complete without having a problem from time to time. One thing that I sincerely hope I've shown is that a Web server does not necessarily have to come packaged with tons of documentation, third-party or customized products, or anything else to be a complete and powerful Web server. Quarterdeck accomplishes this by providing a pure http-driven machine in WebServer. It accomplishes all of the basic tasks of http protocol handling, users, and security assignments leaving the secondary tasks of the Web site—creating and maintaining HTML pages—to you or your WebMaster.

Log Files

I mentioned earlier that WebServer has two log files for keeping tabs on users accessing the server. Listing 8.1 shows the access.log file which is stored in the \LOG directory beneath the directory where you installed WebServer.

Listing 8.1   WebServer Log File for Web Accesses

```
206.139.150.51 - - [30/Apr/1996:22:22:07 +-600] "GET /HTTP/1.0" 200 1876
206.139.150.51 - - [30/Apr/1996:22:22:13 +-600] "GET /images/homepg.gif
  HTTP/1.0" 200 2126
206.139.150.51 - - [30/Apr/1996:22:59:00 +-600] "GET /HTTP/1.0" 304 150
206.139.150.51 - - [30/Apr/1996:22:59:05 +-600] "GET /images/homepg.gif
  HTTP/1.0" 304 150
206.139.150.51 - - [30/Apr/1996:23:02:04 +-600] "GET /qserver/index.htm
  HTTP/1.0" 200 6518
206.139.150.51 - - [30/Apr/1996:23:02:10 +-600] "GET /qserver/images/
  qsrvr.gif HTTP/1.0" 200 16323
206.139.150.51 - - [30/Apr/1996:23:03:43 +-600] "GET /qserver/demo.htm
  HTTP/1.0" 200 8948
206.139.150.51 - - [30/Apr/1996:23:03:49 +-600] "GET /qserver/images/
  check.gif HTTP/1.0" 200 149
206.139.150.51 - - [30/Apr/1996:23:04:27 +-600] "GET /qserver/images/
  question.gif HTTP/1.0" 200 232
206.139.150.51 - - [30/Apr/1996:23:05:12 +-600] "GET /qserver/images/
  shapes2.gif HTTP/1.0" 200 3864
```

Just like any other Web server log file, the basic (and most important) information is provided in the IP address of the user, date/time of access, what was accessed, and the path to the files accessed. This information is usually all the WebMaster cares about for the daily chores of Web life. Of course, there's more to it than that—but we'll leave that to the HTML products.

Can't Find the Server?

Can't find the server, you say? Is security set properly for the user or group? One of the things you can do to check this problem is to use another computer and see if you can access the Web server. If you have one handy, try dialing into another ISP and http down to your site.

 If you're performing this test from a computer attached to the same network as the Web server, then you'll likely get bad results because the same packets of data trying to get out to the Internet are also going to the Web server. This can be a source of confusion for new WebMasters.

As always, the easiest things in life can have the easiest solutions. PING is one of them. Using PING to check servers can save your bacon in a two-fold approach. First, use the IP address to see if the server responds. If it does not respond, then there's either a routing problem or a hardware issue, or possibly a Web server software problem. If it does respond, try using the alias. If the alias doesn't resolve into an IP address, then the DNS entry is fouled. If the alias works, then there's likely congestion on the network where resolution occurs at sporadic rates and times.

Summary

Chapter 8 has been relatively short in comparison to the other Web server package chapters, but it's painted a surprising picture of Web servers. The most pleasing aspect we've uncovered is the speed at which a Web server is capable of responding, and the simplicity of its operations. No extra tools, nothing to complicate matters; just raw http serving. If you need an FTP server, there's always the FTP server that comes with Microsoft Windows NT Server itself. If you need a Gopher server, try the one at the University of Minnesota. It's clean, straightforward, and powerful. Most of all, the FTP and Gopher servers are free, which allows you to create a Web site that's sure to cover all of the Internet bases with a relatively small price tag.

Extending
Your Web
Site

PART

3

The Power of Scripting

It's time to dig in and create your own Web pages, and I'll take you through all the steps that are required to make your Web site both useful and easy to use. I'm assuming that you know the basics of Hyper Text Markup Language, or HTML, which is the basic language for all Web pages. In this chapter I'll explain how to create forms, using CGI and VB4 scripting, so that you can interact with the people who are reading your pages. Forms can provide a vital link between you and your customers.

A myriad of tools are waiting on the Internet to assist you in building your Web pages and to get your Web site up and running quickly. With all these tools it's possible for you to build Web pages and forms without ever laying an eye on the HTML code in raw form. And there are even tools that help you create the forms themselves, like Form-Gen or WebSite's HotDog, all without your having to learn scripting. But you guys are past that, right? You can't wait to get your hands dirty.

And that's just what we're going to do. In this and the next few chapters we're going to be covering HTML, forms, and CGI to create complete applications without the aid of helper tools. Don't get me wrong; these tools are important and can be used to speed up your Web site production, but they may also limit your page design capabilities.

Always be on the lookout for new ideas; and the best place to find them is right in your own backyard. Let's face it, we can get a lot of good ideas for our Web site by surfing the Internet and noting how other sites are constructed. You can take new information and incorporate it into your own applications and improve on an existing design. (Unfortunately, not all of the new techniques we see on the Internet can be used on a Web site.) Keep in mind how your Web site appears and is used by your staff, as well as your customers. Your Web site should be designed with an audience in mind—Internet or intranet—and how they connect should be of consideration. Modem connections from the sales staff in another state or the casual connection from a home user will have a much slower response time than a high-speed business, government, or university connection.

So without any further delay, roll up your sleeves and let's do a little catching up with our not-so-distant past and present technology.

Getting Your Bearings

The Internet has been defined and described in a vast number of ways. You can call it the Net, Internet, Web, WWW, W3, World Wide Web, the Net of networks, or whatever else you want. When it comes right down to it, the Internet is most simply and best defined as, "The world's largest and most up-to-date multimedia encyclopedia." And you never have to buy the new version like you did with the old World Books. The Internet is a complete wealth of information on subjects ranging from technology to movies and everything in between. The real challenge of today's technology is finding or generating the information and providing better management solutions. How are we able to see, not to mention *use*, so many different information pages, business applications, and useful Web sites?

The Internet is built upon different existing protocols, as well as future technologies. It may help to remember that a protocol is simply a set of standard instructions; it is not machine, nor is it platform specific. Let's get a few specifics on the table. The HTML pages are transported using the HTTP (HyperText Transfer Protocol) of the Web site. The CGI (Common Gateway Interface) is a method used by the HTTP to transfer information to and from a Web site and to make extensive use of the resources available at that site. The end user (customer, client, or staff) uses their Web browser to see your Web pages and request specific information. Your Web server receives the request through the HTTP that then passes it to/ through the CGI to process the information through the necessary applications. That's a lot of information moving about, but it really isn't as confusing as it sounds. Take a look at Figure 9.1 and you'll see what I mean.

Don't confuse the protocol transfer method, HTTP, with the page layout language of HTML. HTML coding is possible because it is an application of SGML (Standard Generalized Markup Language).

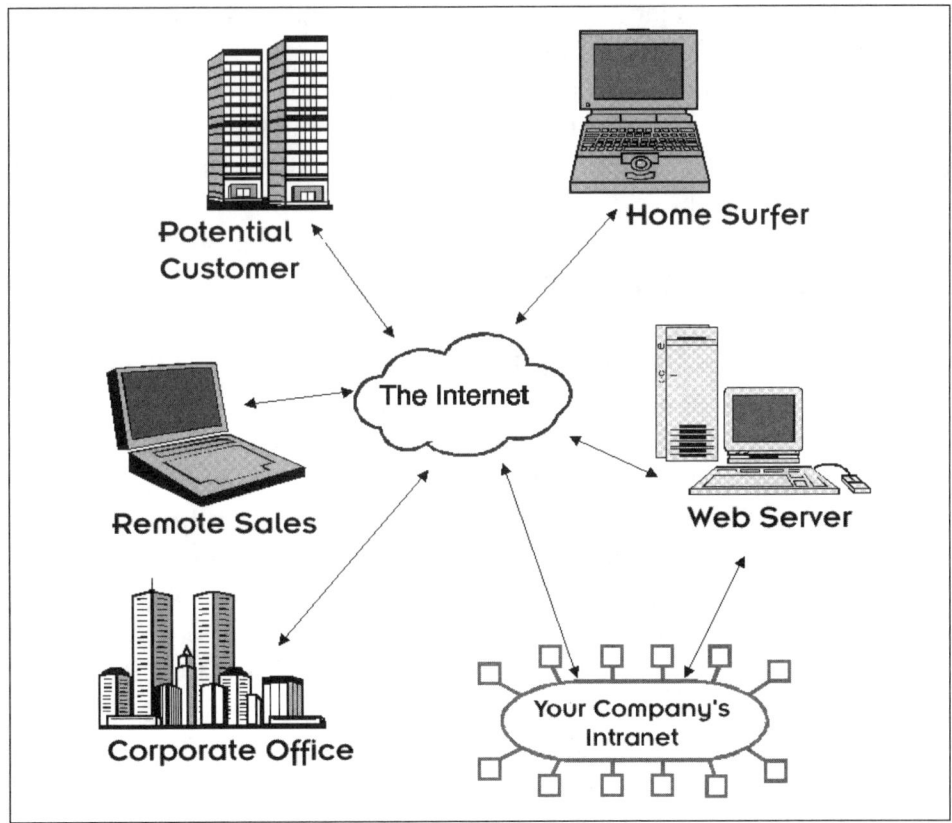

Figure 9.1   A pictorial representation of an Internet/intranet process.

SGML is an international standard used for definitions of devices, systems, and electronic text applications. It was designed to help define a form of language description or a description of each document part. The interpretation of the descriptors and the appearance of the document is handled by the browser. Today, markup is sometimes referred to as *encoding*, which is a way of presenting a body of text in a specific format. SGML was originally designed to allow someone else to read your SGML application and vice-versa. SGML even has an ISO (International Standards Organization) designation: ISO-8879-1. Because of this standardization, many institutions—sectors of U.S. government and industries—have adopted SGML as a standard in their document construction. To find out more about SGML take a look at the SoftQuad sponsored page at *http://www.sil.org/ sgml/sgml.html.*

A descriptive markup language uses codes, or *tags*, to describe the document elements to a browser. The description allows the browser to display documents differently without changing the original content. Because SGML has become an almost international standard for defining documents, it was used to create HTML, which was designed specifically with the Internet in mind.

Which HTML Standard Should You Use?

There's one more question you need to answer before you start building your company's Web site: Which HTML should you adopt and follow? There are currently three standards: the IETF (Internet Engineering Task Force) HTML 2.0, the WWW Consortium HTML 3.0, and Netscape's 3.0 enhancement. The not-yet-established HTML 3.0 and the Netscape enhancements offer powerful functions, but not all browsers accept all the extensions. HTML 2.0 is the current standard for the Internet community and would be the safe bet for a new Web site. All of the applications found in this section follow the HTML 2.0 standard with some of the more advanced features clearly pointed out. If you want to get a feel for HTML 2.0, take a look at the example tutorial included in the accompanying CD-ROM. To keep yourself abreast of the current status and features of HTML 3.0, surf on over to *http://www.w3.org/hypertext/WWW/.*

Creating Forms with HTML 2.0

In a nutshell, *forms* are Web pages that are used to collect and pass information to and from the browser. We'll be creating forms using HTML 2.0 and also using Visual Basic 4.0 (but we'll hold off on that portion until a bit later in the chapter). By now, you are probably familiar with most of the basic elements (or tags) of HTML 2.0. However, before we proceed, take a look at Listing 9.1, which shows the basic structure of an HTML 2.0 document. To be able to use the Internet and your Web site you will need to be able to read and write HTML.

Listing 9.1   Required Components of the Standard HTML Document

```
<HTML>
<HEAD> Title on the WWW Browser </HEAD>
<BODY>
The Information
and
Really Cool Stuff
</BODY>
</HTML>
```

There are only three necessary sections to an HTML document: the declaration (**<HTML> ... </HTML>**), head (**<HEAD> ... </HEAD>**), and body (**<BODY> ... </BODY>**). Notice that two tags are required for each section, an opening **<TAG>** and closing **</TAG>**.

Understanding How Forms Work

Web pages can do more than simply provide a one-way flow of information. As I mentioned earlier, Web pages can be designed to collect and pass information to and from the browser using forms. Forms pass information to a Web site using an *action statement* that specifies the name of the program that will process the form's information. Forms also include a *method attribute* to specify how the data requested in the form is sent back to the program. The two methods are **GET** and **POST**. The **GET** method is the default value for the method attribute. The syntax is:

```
<FORM METHOD=how_to_send ACTION=where_to_send>
```

Unfortunately, the **GET** method will choke if too much data is submitted at one time (more than a few hundred bytes). This situation happens because the server is passing the data to the form-processing program via a shell command line, which has a fixed length. This problem does not exist with the **POST** method. We'll explore this in detail later on.

Designing a Form

Let's begin by designing a useful form that is simple to construct and understand. We will be able to view the form with our browser, as shown in Figure 9.2, to see if our formatting is correct. Later in the chapter we'll change the form to collect information for our Web site database using Visual Basic 4.0.

This is what we would like our customers to see when they take a look at our home page on the Internet. Keep in mind that this is just the first example of a form and it does not have all the bells and whistles of hidden images and background images, *yet*! We will take an in-depth look at form

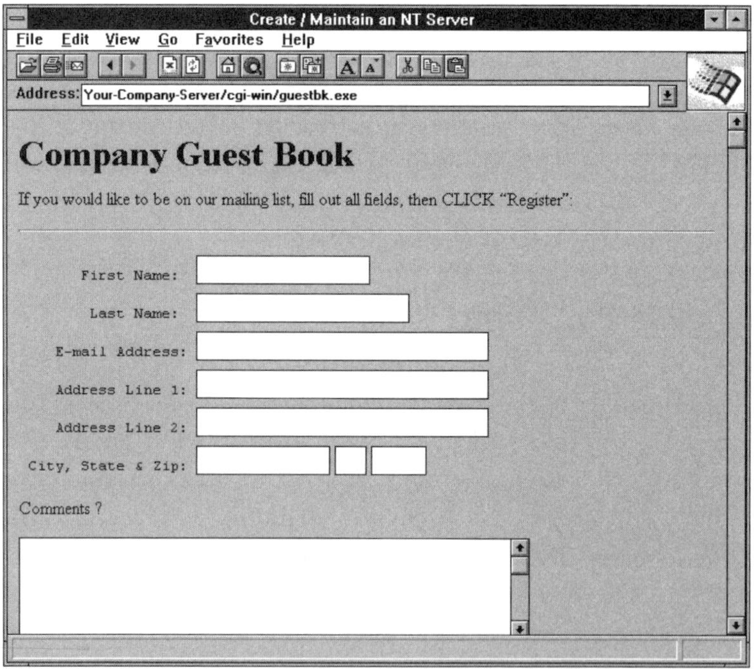

Figure 9.2 Our Guest Book example viewed through Netscape.

construction in Chapter 10, but for now, this explanation should suffice. Listing 9.2 shows the HTML code used to generate the form from Figure 9.2.

Listing 9.2 HTML Script for Our Guest Book Example

```
<!-- GUEST BOOK Example --!>
<HTML>
<HEAD>
<TITLE>Create / Maintain an NT Server </TITLE></HEAD>
<BODY BGCOLOR = FFFFAA>
<H1> Company Guest Book </H1>
<P> If you would like to be on our mailing list, fill out all fields,
then CLICK Register:</P>
<HR>
<FORM METHOD=POST ACTION="http://WEBSERVER/cgi-win/guestbk.exe">
<PRE>
   First Name:       <INPUT  FNAME="fname">
   Last Name:        <INPUT SIZE=25 LNAME="lname">
   E-mail Address:    <INPUT SIZE=35 ENAME="email">
   Address Line 1:    <INPUT SIZE=35 ADDR1="addr1">
   Address Line 2:    <INPUT SIZE=35 ADDR2="addr2">
   City, State & Zip: <INPUT SIZE=15 CITY="city"><INPUT SIZE=2
STATE="state"><INPUT SIZE=5 ZIP="zip">
</PRE>
Comments ?<P>
<TEXTAREA ROWS=5 COLS=65 NAME="comments">
</TEXTAREA><BR>
<P><INPUT TYPE="submit" VALUE="Register"><BR>
<INPUT TYPE "reset" VALUE="Clear this Form"></P>
</FORM><HR>
</BODY></HTML>
```

 Forms are not automatically set apart from the rest of a document. Try using the **<HR>** (horizontal rule) tag before and after a form to cleanly differentiate it from surrounding text and/or other forms.

Let's take a close look at the HTML script for our Guest Book example. We'll begin with the standard header information, which is followed by the line:

```
<FORM METHOD=POST ACTION="http://WEBSERVER/cgi-win/guestbk.exe">
```

The **\<FORM\>** tag is an action tag that uses the **POST** method to send the information to the URL *http://WEBSERVER/cgi-win/guestbk.exe.* Because we are writing programs in Visual Basic 4.0 (32 bit) to run in a Windows environment, the program that processes the information the **FORM POST** statement sends is stored in the CGI-WIN subdirectory. The program that will process all of the information from our guest book HTML form is titled guestbk.exe.

Because these programs were written for WebSite v1.1, which creates and sets up the CGI-WIN subdirectory, we can't just create this subdirectory with the File Manager and expect it to work. This is true with all of the server software that can be used for your Web site—specific directories are created for specific CGI programs. We are writing programs in Windows (32 bit) environment, so all of our programs will be saved into the CGI-WIN subdirectory. If you have questions please refer to the help files inside the 60 Day Test Drive of WebSite ver. 1.1 (which you can download for free from *http://website.ora.com*) or the manual if you purchased the product.

The **\<PRE\>** tag is used because we want the text and input boxes to line up in a specific format. The next line uses an **\<INPUT\>** tag to place the user's information into the field "fname", which will be used to hold the value of the First Name. On the **\<INPUT\>** tag for fname we used the *default* box character size, but in the following lines of code we set the **SIZE** option. This is because a person's last name and address tend to need more input space.

Your first priority in designing a Web page is to make it easy for the casual surfer to use. Long gone are the days when we designed the program and made the user learn our software. Just remember, if your Web site is difficult to use, no one will use it! And word *does* get around.

The next line sets **SIZE** to 25 to give our input box a longer look than the previous line. The browser takes care of the characters that the user enters; if they exceed the length of the input box the browser scrolls to accommodate the additional text. The same is true for the **<TEXTAREA>** tag; we set the input size for columns and rows to make it easier for the user. The **<TEXTAREA>** tag is used to record any comments the user wants to make at the bottom of the form. Each **<INPUT>** tag takes the user's information and places it into the corresponding field, such as "fname" for their first name, "ename" for their email address, etc. The information is then sent to the Web site with the following lines:

```
<P><INPUT TYPE="submit" VALUE="Register"><BR>

<INPUT TYPE "reset" VALUE="Clear this Form"></P>
```

We use the first **<INPUT>** tag above to allow the user to send the information in our form back to the Web browser specified in the **<FORM POST>** statement. A Register button is provided on the HTML page to start the **POST** process and pass all of the information the user has input into each option. Yes, we could instead use an image for the user to click on, but we won't get to that until Chapter 10. The next line is used to clear or reset all of the inputs the user has entered on the HTML page.

This type of form is a standalone HTML document and could be linked from the Web site home page using the hyperlink anchor like this:

```
<A HREF="http://WEBSERVER/home_docs_dir/guestbk.htm"> Enter our Guest
Book </A>
```

The form shown back in Figure 9.2 would be sent to the browser making the request, and the information would then be routed to the Visual Basic program we wrote to process the data. We could generate the form "on-the-fly" by adding the same script into our Visual Basic 4.0 program.

Understanding Form Tags

To create quality forms that work, you need to have a solid understanding of the HTML code you'll need to use. Inside a form you can have anything except another form. Once you've created a form using the **<FORM>** tag, you can then specify elements of the form using the **<INPUT>**, **<SELECT>**, and **<TEXTAREA>** tags.

The <FORM> Tag

Let's begin with an example of a **<FORM>** statement:

```
<FORM ACTION="URL" METHOD=POST>
```

The **<FORM>** tag specifies a fill-out form within an HTML document. More than one fill-out form can be in a single document, but forms cannot be nested. Let's take a look at the attributes of **<FORM>**:

- **ACTION** is the URL of the query server to which the form contents will be submitted; if this attribute is absent, then the current document URL will be used.

- **METHOD** is the method (either **GET** or **POST**) used to submit the fill-out form to a query server. Which method you use depends on your server, but I strongly recommend using POST:

  - **GET** is the default method and causes the fill-out form contents to be appended to the URL as if they were a normal query. When the user presses the submit button on a form when the **GET** method is used, the contents of the form will be assembled into a query URL that looks like this:

    ```
    action?name=value&name=value&name=value
    ```

  - **POST** causes the fill-out form contents to be sent to the server in a data body rather than as part of the URL. The contents of the form are encoded exactly as with the **GET** method, but rather than appending them to the URL specified by the form's **ACTION** attribute as a query, the contents are sent in a data block as part of the **POST** operation. The **ACTION** attribute (if any) is the URL to which the data block is **POST**ed.

The <INPUT> Tag

Inside the **<FORM>** ... **</FORM>** tags, any number of **<INPUT>** tags are allowed, mixed with other HTML elements (including **<SELECT>** and

<TEXTAREA>) and text. The **<INPUT>** tag is used to specify a simple input element inside a form. It is a standalone tag; it does not surround anything and there is no terminating tag. **<INPUT>** tags have many attributes, most of which we referenced in Listing 9.2. Let's take a closer look at the attributes for this tag. All of the attributes in the **<INPUT>** tag are shown in the line below:

```
<INPUT TYPE="text|password|checkbox|radio|submit|reset" NAME="symbolic
name" VALUE="on|off or name on button" CHECKED(use only if box should be
checked) SIZE="number" MAXLENGTH="maximum number of characters accepted">
```

- **TYPE** indicates the type of input you are requesting on the form. **TYPE** can be any of the following:

  text—Text entry field; this is the default

  password—Text entry field; entered characters are represented as asterisks

  checkbox—A single toggle button; on or off

  radio—A single toggle button; on or off

  submit—A button that causes the current form to be packaged up into a query URL and sent to a server

  reset—A button that causes the various input elements in the form to be reset to the default values (more on this in Chapter 10)

- **NAME** is the symbolic name (not the name displayed on the screen— **VALUE** or standard HTML within the program is used for that) for this input field. This must be present for all types except "submit" and "reset," because it is used in the query string that is sent to the remote server when the form is submitted.

- **VALUE** is used in a text or password entry field to specify the default value of the field. For a checkbox or a radio button, **VALUE** specifies the value of the button when it is checked (unchecked checkboxes are disregarded when submitting queries); the default value for a checkbox or radio button is on. For types submit and reset, **VALUE** can be used to specify the caption for the button.

- **CHECKED** (no value needed) specifies that this checkbox or radio button is checked by default.

- **SIZE** is the physical size of the input field in characters in text and password entry fields. If this attribute is not present, the default is 20. In our first example (guest book), we used both default and custom values. You can specify multiline text entry fields as **SIZE**=width, height.

The **SIZE** attribute should not be used to specify multiline text entry fields now that the **<TEXTAREA>** tag is widely used in current browser programs.

- **MAXLENGTH** is the maximum number of characters that are accepted as input in single-line text entry fields and password entry fields. If this attribute is not present, the default will be unlimited. The text entry field is assumed to scroll appropriately if **MAXLENGTH** is greater than **SIZE**.

The *<SELECT>* Tag

Inside **<FORM>** ... **</FORM>**, any number of **<SELECT>** tags are allowed. **<SELECT>** creates a pulldown menu of choices for the user. Unlike **<INPUT>**, **<SELECT>** has both opening and closing tags. Inside **<SELECT>**, only a sequence of **<OPTION>** tags, each followed by an arbitrary amount of plain text (no HTML), are allowed. Listing 9.7 shows how to use the **<SELECT>** tag properly.

Listing 9.7   Using the <SELECT> Tag

```
<SELECT NAME="my select menu">
<OPTION> First option.
<OPTION> Second option.
</SELECT>
```

Let's take a closer look at the **<SELECT>** tag's attributes:

- **NAME** is the symbolic name for this element, and must be present because it is used in the query string for the submitted form.

- **SIZE** if SIZE is 1, or if the **SIZE** attribute is missing, **SELECT** will be represented as an option menu. If **SIZE** is 2 or more, then **<SELECT>**

will be represented as a scrolled list with the value of **SIZE** determining how many items will be visible.

- **MULTIPLE** specifies that the **<SELECT>**tag should allow multiple selections. The presence of **MULTIPLE** forces the pulldown menu to be represented as a scrolled list, regardless of the value of **SIZE**.

The <OPTION> Tag

The attribute for **<OPTION>** is **SELECTED**, which specifies that this option is selected by default. In some instances, multiple options can be specified as being selected.

The <TEXTAREA> Tag

The **<TEXTAREA>** tag is used to place a multiline text entry field with optional default contents in a fill-out form. The **<TEXTAREA>** element requires both an opening and a closing tag. A **<TEXTAREA>** tag with no default contents looks like this:

```
<TEXTAREA NAME="Text Here" ROWS=4 COLS=40></TEXTAREA>
```

A **<TEXTAREA>** tag with default contents looks like this:

```
<TEXTAREA NAME="Text Here" ROWS=4 COLS=40>
Default contents go here.
</TEXTAREA>
```

Let's take a closer look at the attributes for **<TEXTAREA>**:

- **NAME** is the symbolic name of the text entry field.

- **ROWS** is the number of rows (vertical height in characters) of the text entry field.

- **COLS** is the number of columns (horizontal width in characters) of the text entry field.

<TEXTAREA> fields automatically have scrollbars; any amount of text can be entered in them.

Using Visual Basic 4.0 to Generate a Form and Process the Information

You should have already installed Visual Basic 4.0 (VB4) using the 32-bit option, so let's start it now. Open the File menu and use the Remove File option to remove FORM1 from our program, temporarily. Because we are writing this VB4 program for a server using WebSite v1.1, we have to add the CGI framework to our program. WebSite comes with a set of routines called the *framework model* that takes care of most of the interface work. This module handles communication between the browser and server software for us. Open the File menu, select Add File, and select cgi32.bas from the WebSite\cgi-src subdirectory.

This framework module defines the main routine for your CGI program and defines the variables to use. It also defines a number of functions with error handling and establishes a global exception handler to catch runtime errors and produce browser error messages that can be used to debug your program. I suggest you take some time to look at the routines in the framework module so you can get a better understanding of some of the CGI variables and utility routines. Table 9.1 shows some of the more common variables.

Most of the variables have intuitive names. And, as I'm sure you can tell, these variables can come in pretty handy. If the browser sends us information back in a form, we may want to gather some demographic information to use for our Web site design. Remember, a system administrator's work is never done! For example, it might be useful to file away the number of times a browser from a sub-Net address comes into our Web site. We can get information from that browser and the user to help better construct our server.

The cgi32.bas module also has a large array of utility functions that we can use in building our Internet/intranet Web site. Table 9.2 lists the more common functions.

The utility functions all use the syntax *name = value*, where the value is passed into the name provided in the form and in the VB4 program. In our first form example, we get the email address sent to our program from

Table 9.1   Some Common Variables in WebSite's CGI Framework

Variable Name	Description
CGI_ServerSoftware	Version of the server HTTP
CGI_ServerName	Server's network host name
CGI_Server	Admin email of the server's administrator
CGI_Version	Version of CGI spoken
CGI_RequestMethod	Method is POST or GET
CGI_RequestKeepAlive	Client connection reused (yes/no)
CGI_Referrer	URL of the referring document
CGI_From	Email of the browser (if set)
CGI_UserAgent	Browses software of the "surfer"
CGI_RemoteHost	Browser's network host name
CGI_RemoteAddr	Browser's network address
CGI_AuthUser	User's name
CGI_AuthPass	User's password

the **<INPUT>** tag that saved the *value* in the variable email. In VB4, the code to accomplish this task looks like this:

```
sEmail = GetSmallField("email")
```

It is good programming practice to use names that have meaning and also adhere to the standard naming convention recommended for VB4 functions and routines (refer to your Visual Basic users manual).

There are a few things we need to do before we can turn our HTML code into VB "script" that can be inserted into VB4 code. Open the Insert menu

Table 9.2   Some Common Utility Functions in WebSite's CGI Framework

Function Name	Description
GetSmallField()	Retrieves the contents of a named **<FORM>** field
FieldPresent()	Tests for a preset value (used in checkboxes)
Send()	Sends the "string" to be spooled (back to the browser)

and select Module, which will allow us to write some routines. We'll begin with the CGI_Main routine, shown in Listing 9.3, which is called by the CGI framework to check if the CGI request is passing information to be processed or requesting that an HTML form page be generated.

Listing 9.3   CGI_Main

```
Sub CGI_Main()

If CGI_RequestMethod = "POST" Then
      Enter_Data
   Else
      Send_Form
   End If

End Sub
```

The first line of code does a check to see if the request method was from a **<FORM ACTION=POST>** tag. If it was, then we have data that we need to process and we call a routine called Enter_Data (more on this routine in a bit). If the request method is null or empty, then the program was called from inside an HTML document and we need to generate a form and send it to the requester via Send_Form. The coding for Send_Form is shown in Listing 9.4.

Listing 9.4   The Send_Form Routine That Uses Coded Script to Produce the HTML Form

```
Sub Send_Form

Send ("Content-Type : text/html")

Send ("")

Send ("<HTML><HEAD><TITLE>Create / Maintain an NT Server </TITLE></HEAD>")

Send ("<BODY><H1> Company Guest Book </H1>")

Send ("<P> If you would like to be on our mailing list, fill out all _
      fields, then CLICK "Register":</P>")

Send ("<HR><FORM METHOD=POST ACTION=""http://WEBSERVER/cgi-win/ _
      guestbk.exe""><PRE>")
```

```
Send ("        First Name:  <INPUT   FNAME="""fname""">")

Send ("         Last Name:  <INPUT SIZE=25 LNAME="""lname""">")

Send ("     E-mail Address: <INPUT SIZE=35 NAME="""email""">")

Send ("     Address Line 1: <INPUT SIZE=35 ADDR1="""addr1""">")

Send ("     Address Line 2: <INPUT SIZE=35 ADDR2="""addr2""">")

Send (" City, State & Zip: <INPUT SIZE=15 CITY="""city"""> _

      <INPUT SIZE=2 STATE="""state"""><INPUT SIZE=5   ZIP="""zip""">")

Send ("</PRE>")

Send ("Comments ?<P>")

Send ("<TEXTAREA ROWS=5 COLS=65 NAME="""comments"""></TEXTAREA><BR>")

Send ("<P><INPUT TYPE="""submit""" VALUE="""Register"""><BR>")

Send ("<INPUT TYPE="""reset""" VALUE="""Clear this Form"""></P>")

Send ("</FORM><HR>")

Send ("</BODY></HTML>")

End Sub
```

This code is almost as simple as HTML code! Refer to the HTML form example and you'll see that the only changes we have to make include the spacing on each **<INPUT>** line so the VB coded script produces the same format for our **<INPUT>** boxes. You may also notice that I've included a space followed by an underscore on lines that continue. It looks like this: "_" (without the quotation marks, of course). This technique makes code easier to follow and read.

One other routine we need to write is Inter_Main, shown in Listing 9.5. If the CGI executable is started from the File Manager on the Web server, this routine is used to display a message indicating that the program cannot be executed in that manner.

Listing 9.5   Inter_Main

```
Sub Inter_Main

msg = "CGI Program for Create / Maintain an NT Server"

MsgBox  msg

End Sub
```

This code will produce a simple message box that informs the user what this program is and will then exit. If this program is executed from the File Manager, the user will see the screen shown in Figure 9.3.

Figure 9.4 shows the entire guestbk.mak project. You can type the code yourself or load the program from the CD included with this book.

> *Note: For the remainder of this section, I will refer to HTML text that is sent from inside a VB4 program as coded script.*

If CGI_Main's check for the **POST** method resulted in a true value, then we need a routine to save the data into our database and route a simple "Thank You" document back to the requester. There are several different methods to use to communicate with a database. One of the simplest is to create a new form in VB4 (using Insert|Form) and then add the DataBound control to link our program with an existing database. In our example, we'll only be placing information into the database, so we won't need any other controls. Figure 9.5 shows the DataBound control on the VB4 form.

Using a VB4 form may not be the best solution for our task because of the length of time it takes to execute a routine or an entire program. Numerous other ways exist to add, delete, or query information in a database through VB4, but they all have their limitations, as well. We will go into

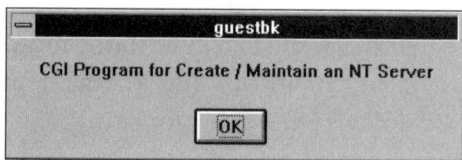

Figure 9.3   guestbk.exe executed from the File Manager on the NT Server.

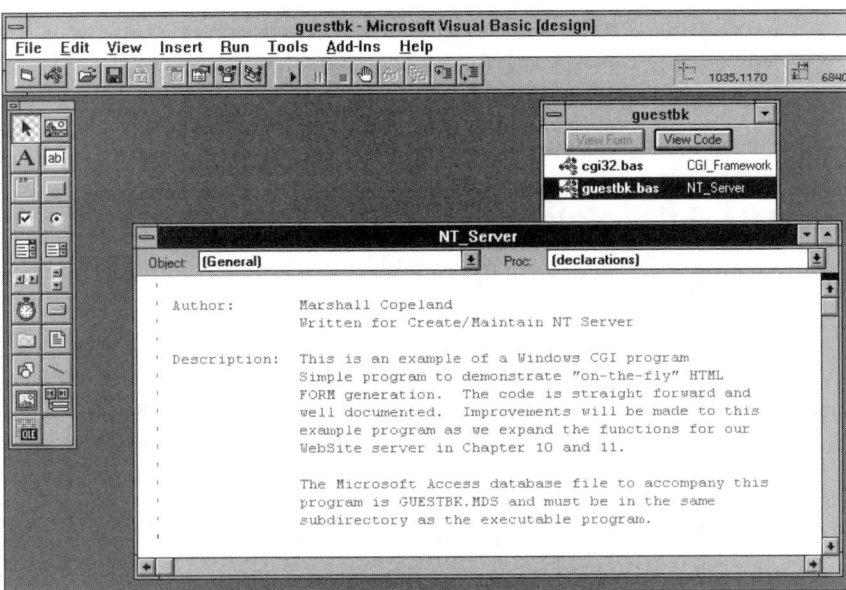

Figure 9.4 The guestbk.mak project as it appears in VB4.

greater detail in Chapter 11, but for now let's look at another, more elegant way that we can use a VB4 form to enter information into our database using SQL commands.

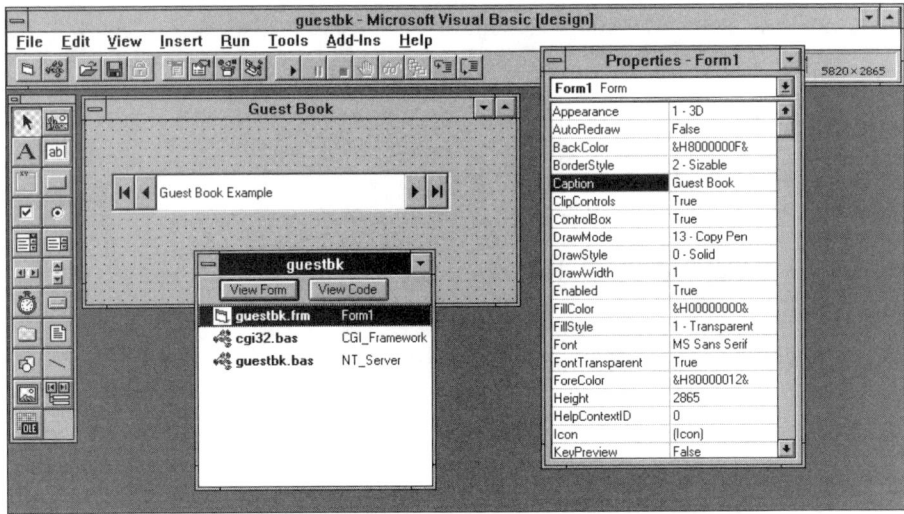

Figure 9.5 Guest book example using a DataBound control in a VB4 form.

The routine Enter_Data, shown in Listing 9.6, allows us to enter information into the database without using a DataBound control, by setting up the necessary dimensions so we can read the values from the browser and prepare them for storage in our database.

Listing 9.6   Enter_Data Receives Data from the Browsers for Our Database

```
Sub Enter_Data()

'This routine stores the values passed by the
'browser software

    Dim sFname As String
    Dim sLname As String
    Dim sEmail As String
    Dim sAddr1 As String
    Dim sAddr2 As String
    Dim sCity As String
    Dim sState As String
    Dim sZip As Integer
    Dim sComments As String
    Dim sDate As String
    Dim sBrowser As String
    Dim fn As Integer

    'Since the POST command was used we can read the data
    'that is passed from the browser

    sFname = GetSmallField("fname")
    sLname = GetSmallField("lname")
    sEmail = GetSmallField("email")
    sAddr1 = GetSmallField("addr1")
    sAddr2 = GetSmallField("addr2")
    sCity = GetSmallField("city")
    sState = GetSmallField("state")
    sZip = GetSmallField("zip")
    sComments = GetSmallField("comments")


End Sub
```

This procedure collects the information passed from the browser, and stores the data into the variables that we set up for our database. We will stay with

Microsoft's VB4 naming conventions by using s=String on all of the values used to store information. Keep the naming conventions understandable and logical so that you won't get confused when you use the same variables in both the VB4 coded script and the VB4 code. Our next step is to write a routine to open the database, write the record, update the database, and close the file. We will see how to set up a Microsoft Access database and become more familiar with the methods to edit and query fields in Chapter 11.

Summary

This chapter has given you the necessary background to create basic interactive Web pages using HTML 2.0 and VB4. We learned that generating HTML documents inside VB4 increases the flexible services that we can offer our customers and staff from our Web server. Understanding the process of passing information to and from an Internet/intranet browser program provides you with the essentials for building powerful "back-end" programs and routines that could cross platform boundaries to accelerate your company's growth.

The next chapter continues with our discussion of forms and the use of HTML and Visual Basic. I'll provide multiple examples to demonstrate methods for receiving and interpreting users' responses, dealing with multiple forms to produce the information the client requests, and designing better user interfaces. Server programs are used to demonstrate connectivity methods with other office software, such as email, spreadsheets, and databases, and I'll explain how these methods can continue to enhance solutions for your company's Web server. You'll soon realize that the more you do to make your Web server easier for your customers/clients to use, the more your company will excel.

CHAPTER 10

Forms of the Web

Now that you have the basics of HTML snugly in your pocket, we can expand our discussion to include some of the more interesting elements currently proposed for inclusion in the HTML 3.0. Of course, you must keep in mind that the goal of your site is to serve your customers, which requires staying on top of the latest market trends. For example, Netscape has earned over $400 million in the first quarter of 1996. From this information, you can see that the Netscape browser enjoys a large market share of total Internet browser sales. Developing HTML pages, then, without considering the use of Netscape extensions could be potentially damaging to your Web site.

In this chapter, we'll take an advanced look at creating forms using HTML 3.0—including the addition of text entry and password security

Creating Forms

In this section, we'll build on your knowledge HTML Level 2.0 to incorporate the advanced features of HTML Level 3.0 into your forms—both standalone documents and those you generate inside VB4.

As you know, we use the **<FORM>** tag inside the HTML document to submit a set of responses to a Visual Basic program or to generate the form itself. Inside the form we can have any other HTML tag—except another **<FORM>** tag—which allows us to produce a more in-depth selection of user inputs to retrieve information. We can use this information in our database to help with marketing, to help the user specifically select the query information, or both. Of course, our first priority is to understand the intricate uses of the various HTML tags so that we can design our pages to be user friendly—not intimidating or frustrating to the users. We can even design our form to request a password before access is granted to a specific section of our Web site.

Using the <SELECT> Tag

We briefly reviewed the **<SELECT>** tag in Chapter 9, but there are a few more uses for this tag that I'd like to cover here. We're going to build on the Guest Book form from the previous chapter; if you need to refresh your memory, refer back to Chapter 9. We're going to implement some changes to provide the user with some options. We'll begin by asking a few "marketing" questions in the form to collect information about our users.

We can provide a list of options from which the user can select one or more items. Using the **<SELECT>** tag requires the use of the **<OPTION>** "attribute" tag for each item in the list. I call it an "attribute" tag because it is used only with the **<SELECT>** tag and does *not* require a closing **</OPTION>**. As with other HTML tags, you can use the name and size arguments to define the field variable. The general syntax for creating our list of options is

```
<SELECT attributes> </SELECT>
```

where *attributes* can be:

- **NAME**="*VariableName*" where V*ariableName* is the name of an input field

- **SIZE**=*n* where *n* is the number of options

- **MULTIPLE**, which allows multiple selections using the **<OPTION>** tag

The **<OPTION>** tag itself has several possibilities:

- **<OPTION>** *VariableName1*

- **<OPTION>** *VariableName2*

- **<OPTION SELECTED>** *VariableName3*; this selection is the default

The **<SELECT>** tag's attributes help us not only in designing the form, but also when we pass information to the server. Because the server receives this information as raw data, we need to choose logical name variables to aid the "flow" of information. Listing 10.1 shows the **<SELECT>** tag added to an HTML document.

Listing 10.1   Using the <SELECT> and <OPTION> Tags

```
How did you see/hear about our Web site? <BR>
<FORM method="POST" action="http://webserver/cgi-win/PROGRAM.EXE">
<SELECT name="RequestArea">
<OPTION SELECTED>Internet
<OPTION>Magazine
<OPTION>Radio
<OPTION>Television
<OPTION>Other
</SELECT>
</FORM>
```

We provide a prompt for the user followed by a break (the **
** tag), and select the default value with the line **<OPTION SELECTED>** Internet. We could have selected any item in the list as the default, it does not have to be the first item. When viewed through a Web browser, the user will see the label, the word "Internet" in a text box, and a down arrow used to indicate more options. Figure 10.1 shows the listing as it appears in a browser.

As you can see, this is a fairly straightforward form. There are a number of different variations that you can use to change the design of the form page. Let's look at one more example. We'll use the same variable names but change the "look" by using more attributes. The **MULTIPLE** attribute defaults to a text box that displays four variables at one time; the remaining variables can be viewed using the scroll bars. To change our form just a bit more we use the **SIZE** attribute to reduce the display of attributes to three. These modifications are shown in Listing 10.2.

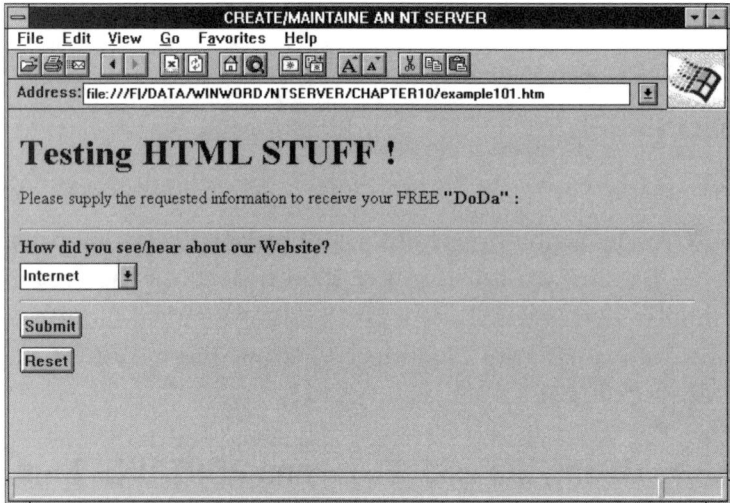

Figure 10.1 Providing multiple choices for your users by using the <SELECT> tag.

Listing 10.2   Using <SELECT> with the MULTIPLE and SIZE Attributes

```
How did you see/hear about our Web site? <BR>
<FORM method="POST" action="http://webserver/cgi-win/PROGRAM.EXE">
<SELECT name="RequestArea" MULTIPLE SIZE=3>
<OPTION>Internet
<OPTION>Magazine
<OPTION>Television
<OPTION>Radio
<OPTION>Other
</SELECT>
</FORM>
```

Something to keep in mind is that when you use the **MULTIPLE** attribute you can no longer select the default variable with the **<OPTION SELECTED>** tag. This may change in the future. Figure 10.2 shows the modified form.

Adding Text-Entry Capabilities

The **<TEXTAREA>** tag provides you with another way to get helpful information from your users. This approach allows users to enter specific information into the form—personal information about them, or feedback about your site. The general syntax for creating a text entry option is

```
<TEXTAREA attributes> </TEXTAREA>
```

where the *attributes* can be:

- **NAME**="*VariableName*" where V*ariableName* is the name of an input field

- **ROWS**=*n* **COLS**=*n* where *n* is the number of rows across and columns down; ROWS = 4 and COLS = 30 are the default values

Listing 10.3 shows how to incorporate the **<TEXTAREA>** tag into your form, and Figure 10.3 shows the form with the added text-entry capability.

Listing 10.3   The <TEXTAREA> Tag

```
Leave a comment about our Web site? <BR>
<FORM method="POST" action="http://webserver/cgi-win/PROGRAM.EXE">
<TEXTAREA NAME="comment" ROW=5 COLS=70>
</TEXTAREA>
</FORM>
```

One thing you need to consider is the amount of text users will enter in this section of your form. Currently, the amount of text that can be received in the **<TEXTAREA>** tag is unlimited. To make sure you collect everything the user enters, be sure to define a memo field in your database

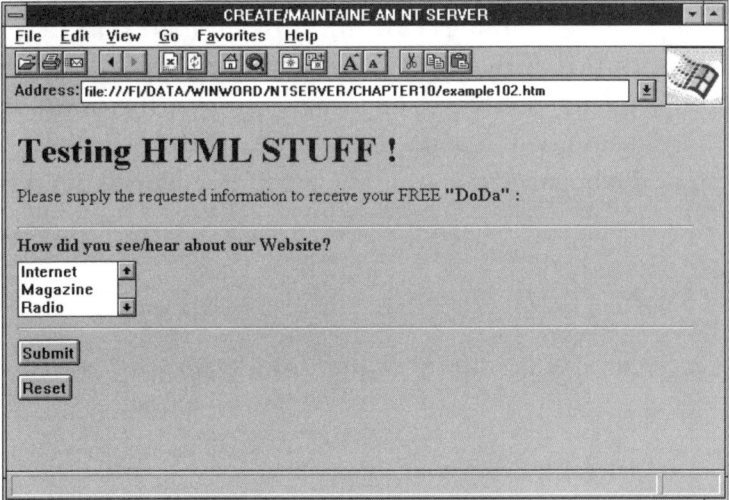

Figure 10.2   Displaying multiple options for the user.

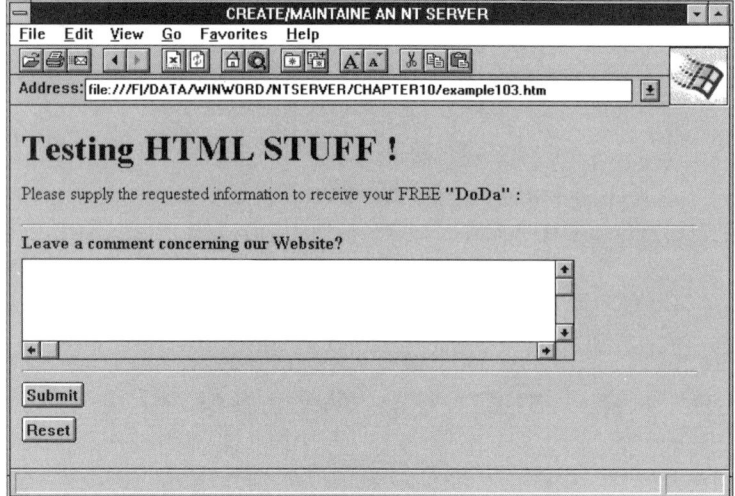

Figure 10.3   Requesting more information from users.

to store this information with the rest of the record. Of course, our example shows only one way to use the **<TEXTAREA>** tag. You can use it anytime you want users to enter text.

Modifying Your Forms with <INPUT>

If you remember from our brief discussion in Chapter 9, one of the most important tags we use in our HTML form is the **<INPUT>** tag. It has attributes that provide us with options for text entry, security, quick response to our questions, and submitting or resetting the form. As you'll see, the **<INPUT>** tag is very versatile and can be used in several different sections of our form by mixing and matching the attributes. The general syntax for the **<INPUT>** tag is

```
<INPUT attributes>
```

where the *attributes* can be the following input types:

- **TYPE=TEXT**
- **TYPE=CHECKBOX**
- **TYPE=RADIO**

- **TYPE=IMAGE**

- **TYPE=SUBMIT**

- **TYPE=RESET**

- **TYPE=PASSWORD**

- **TYPE=HIDDEN**

The input types can be further defined by using the following attributes:

- **NAME**=*"value"* to supply the name of the field

- **CHECKED** to set defaults via checkboxes or radio buttons

- **SIZE**=*n* to set the box size in characters for the TEXT attribute

- **MAXLENGTH**=*n* to limit the user input TEXT attribute size

- **VALUE** =default value of the field if no other is specified

The **<INPUT>** tag uses variables that have a specific variable *name*, which uses a defined input field *value*. This field value must be of a specific data type that corresponds with the possible values of the field. For instance, if you used a numeric field, you wouldn't want text characters in it. One example of the **<INPUT>** tag can be found near the end of Listing 10.4, where the input types of mail vendors are listed.

Creating Text Fields

Single-line text fields **<INPUT TYPE=TEXT>** are used for entering short text strings, such as names, numbers, and dates. The visible width of the field in characters can be set with the **SIZE** attribute. The **MAXLENGTH** attribute can be used to specify the maximum number of characters permitted for the input string. If the **TYPE** attribute is missing, the **<INPUT>** tag is assumed to be a single-line text field. The **NAME** attribute is used to identify the field when the form's contents are converted to the **NAME**=*value* list.

Checkboxes and Radio Buttons

Checkboxes and radio buttons provide an alternative to using the **<SELECT>** tag, and provide benefits for both the end user and the server administrator. End users can select the options quickly, which is helpful to entice them to provide information to subscribe. And administrators receive far more detailed information for the profile database. The **CHECKBOX** and **RADIO** types are toggle fields; that is, they either *are* selected or *are not* selected.

 The Windows environment has existing conventions for input on a form. For example, Tab and Shift+Tab are used to navigate among fields, and Enter is used to submit the form. These conventions stem from the days before the mouse became popular, and are still implemented for those users who are "rodent impaired."

Each field normally is given a distinct name. However, several **<INPUT>** tags with the **TYPE=RADIO** attribute can share the same name to specify that they belong to the same group. If you use this naming technique, understand that only one button in the group can be selected, or *active*, at one time. Unselected checkboxes and radio buttons don't appear in the submitted data, but we can initialize **CHECKBOX** to a preselected state by using the **CHECKED** attribute. Only the selected radio button in the group generates a **NAME**=*value* pair in the submitted data, and both **NAME** and **VALUE** are required for radio buttons.

Listing 10.4 shows a typical form that uses menus and radio buttons to obtain data from users, and Figure 10.4 shows the form as it appears in a browser.

Listing 10.4   Using <SELECT> and <INPUT TYPE=RADIO> Tags

```
<HTML>
<!--This is a comment Field -->
<HEAD>
<TITLE>CREATE/MAINTAIN AN NT SERVER</TITLE>
</HEAD>
<BODY BGCOLOR=FFFFA0>
<H1>Testing HTML STUFF !</H1>

<FORM method="POST" action="http://WEBSERVER/cgi-win/PROGRAM.EXE">

<CENTER>
<STRONG>Choose an AREA and a DATE to "Calculate" a delivery charge for
   Your Purchase!</STRONG><BR>
```

```
</CENTER><HR NOSHADE>

<CENTER><PRE><B>AREA       MONTH       DAY</B></PRE></CENTER>

<CENTER>
<SELECT name="RequestArea">
<OPTION> Canada
<OPTION> South America
<OPTION SELECTED> North America
<OPTION> Europe
<OPTION> Asia
<OPTION> Africa
<OPTION> Japan
<OPTION> China
<OPTION> England
</SELECT>

<SELECT name="Month">
<OPTION>January
<OPTION>February
<OPTION>March
<OPTION>April
<OPTION>May
<OPTION>June
<OPTION>July
<OPTION>August
<OPTION SELECTED>September
<OPTION>October
<OPTION>November
<OPTION>December
</SELECT>

<SELECT name="Day">
<OPTION>1
<OPTION>5
<OPTION>10
<OPTION SELECTED>15
<OPTION>20
<OPTION>25
<OPTION>29
<OPTION>30
<OPTION>31
</SELECT>
</CENTER>

<HR>
```

```
<CENTER><STRONG>What Vendor would you prefer?</STRONG><BR>
<INPUT TYPE=RADIO name="MailVendor" Value=UPS>UPS
<INPUT TYPE=RADIO name="MailVendor" Value=FedEx CHECKED>FedEx
<INPUT TYPE=RADIO name="MailVendor" Value=Courier>Courier
<INPUT TYPE=RADIO name="MailVendor" Value=US Mail>U.S. Mail <BR>

<HR>
<STRONG>How would you like it Sent? </STRONG><BR>
<INPUT TYPE=RADIO name="MailSpeed" Value=Gnd>Ground
<INPUT TYPE=RADIO name="MailSpeed" Value=ON>Overnight
<INPUT TYPE=RADIO name="MailSpeed" Value=Second CHECKED>2nd Day Air

</CENTER>

<HR NOSHADE>
<INPUT TYPE=SUBMIT Value="Request Estimate">
Send your choices for an "Estimate"<BR>
<INPUT TYPE=RESET Value="Clear FORM">
Clear your "options" and try again
</P>
</BODY>
</HTML>
```

As I mentioned earlier, time is of the essence when it comes to getting users to fill in forms (and simplicity doesn't hurt either!). The **<INPUT**

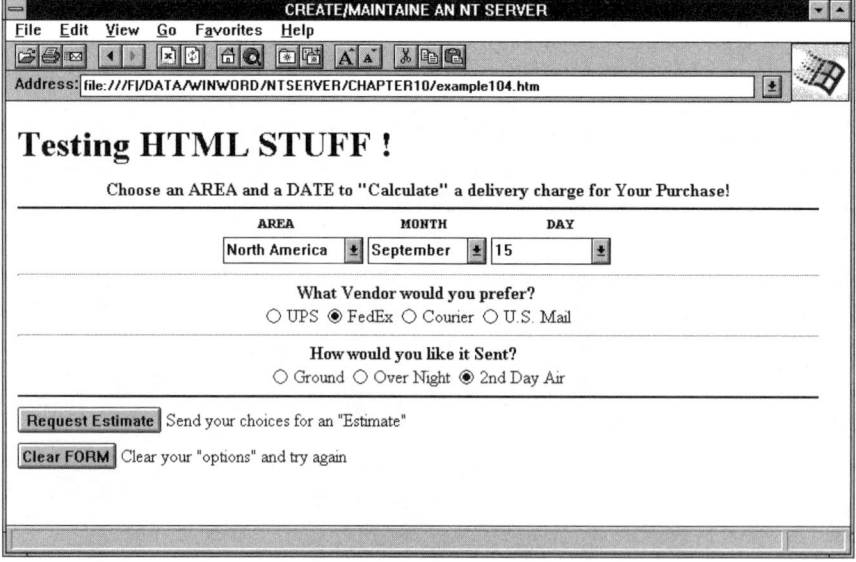

Figure 10.4   Creating a form with menus and radio buttons.

TYPE=RADIO> tag provides a method for making quick choices and avoids the "clutter" of drop menus used in the **<SELECT>** tag. Another way to get readers to sit up and take notice of your form is to add a little flash. This is exactly what we did with the line **<BODY BGCOLOR=FFFFA0>** at the beginning of the document. This tag statement changes the background color, which we hope will catch the users' attention. Very simple, but very effective.

Polishing Your Form Design

When it comes to attracting users, a good form relies as much on its ease of use and functionality as it does on general appearance. *A professional-looking form is a form that gets responses!* The Internet provides the ability for any business or company—no matter how small—to give the appearance of a large well-established business. Your forms and other HTML documents will speak for themselves.

We're going to make a few changes to the form shown in Listing 10.4 to help in your understanding of the **<INPUT>** tag attributes and to add an artistic flair. We'll begin by adding an eye-catching image instead of the Request Estimate button to get users' attention. We'll also change the background by choosing a GIF for the **<BODY BACKGROUND**="URL"> tag. These changes, shown in Listing 10.5, are simple but add a polished look to the document, as shown in Figure 10.5.

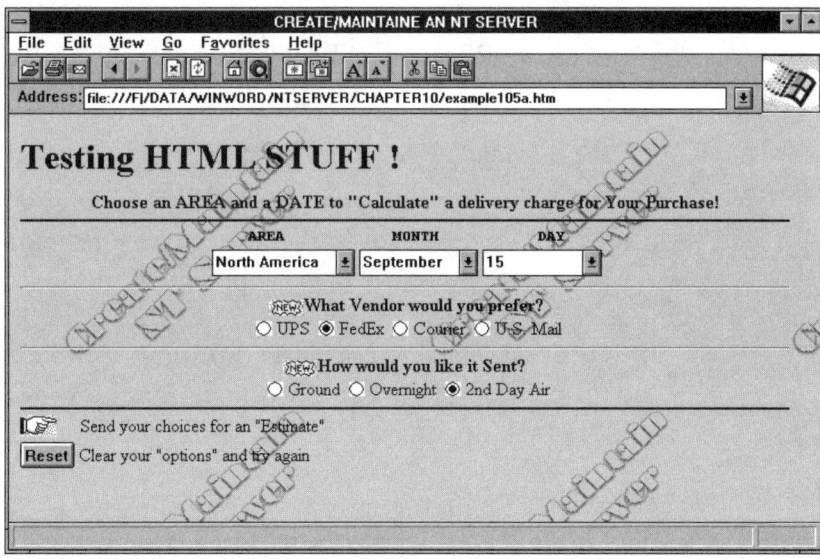

Figure 10.5 Using GIFs to create a more eye-catching form.

Listing 10.5 Polishing the Form Design

```
<HTML>
<HEAD>
<TITLE>CREATE/MAINTAINE AN NT SERVER</TITLE>
</HEAD>
<BODY BACKGROUND=bkgnd.gif>

. . .

<HR><IMG SRC="new.gif">
<STRONG>How would you like it Sent? </STRONG><BR>

. . .

</CENTER><HR NOSHADE>
<INPUT TYPE=IMAGE  SRC="rfinger.GIF"><IMG SRC="space.gif">
Send your choices for an "Estimate"<BR>
```

Here we used a simple image for the background of the form to produce different overall feel. The image background was made transparent so the edges would not be so apparent and also to provide a more seamless method of combining text and images in the same HTML document. We also used various small images to add color and text to the document. For example, we added the word "new" to an option by inserting the NEW.GIF image, and we replaced the Request Estimate button with an image. When the user moves the mouse pointer on top of the image, it displays the familiar hypertext link pointer to indicate an action for the image.

 There are many dazzling features that you can add to your HTML documents, but many require lengthy downloads. Many sites have an option, for the users who prefer to get information quickly, that allows them to view text only. This option displays a duplicate set of HTML documents without all of the extras. Of course, this means you have to create two sets of HTML documents.

There are only two possible command button functions for forms: Submit and Reset (**<TYPE=SUBMIT>** and **<TYPE=RESET>**). Submit, of course, submits the contents of the form to the WebServer\cgi-win\VBprogram.exe. Reset causes the contents of the form to be reset to the default values. Each command button can use a label or a graphic to describe its function.

 Use a small, transparent GIF image to add space in you HTML documents, or place the GIFs into an HTML table without a border. Either of these options will provide necessary spacing to produce a polished look.

Adding Security to Your Forms

Sometimes it might be necessary for a user to view sensitive information at your Web site, but you don't want everyone to have access. For example, you might want a large distributor, and not an individual buyer, to see your wholesale price list. HTML has responded to this need with the **<TYPE=PASSWORD>** attribute. This attribute restricts users from "classified" information by requiring a password to view it. Listing 10.6 and Figure 10.6 show password protection in action.

 Do not let this lead you to believe that HTML security will fully handle your Web server's security issues. Any serious hacker will breach right through HTML-generated password files, so you should refer to the NT Server security manual or your Web server's manual.

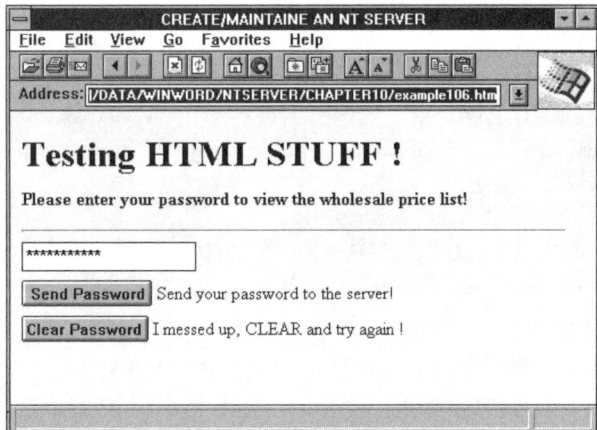

Figure 10.6   Using a password to help restrict site access.

Listing 10.6   Adding Security to Your Forms

```
<INPUT TYPE=PASSWORD name="RegistedUser" MAXLENGTH=11> <BR>
<INPUT TYPE=SUBMIT Value="Send Password">
Send your password to the server!<BR>
<INPUT TYPE=RESET Value="Clear Password">
I messed up, CLEAR and try again !
```

Here we used the **<TYPE=PASSWORD>** and **MAXLENGTH** attributes to require a password from the user. As the user enters the password, an asterisk character (*) is displayed in the text area for each character typed. The user can see how many characters have been typed but not *what* was typed.

 Even though the data being entered to the password field is hidden from the user on the screen, there are no security features to protect the information when it is transferred over the Net. Therefore, the password field alone is insufficient to protect the confidentiality of private information passed over the Internet.

MAXLENGTH is set to 11 because of the old "eight-dot-three" (eight characters plus a three-letter extension) DOS filename limitation, but you can change the setting.

Controlling Access to Your Server with HTML

You can restrict access to specific documents or subdirectories on your server with an HTML form that requests a username and a password before access is granted. Your server software will dictate the type of security you can use, but most restrict through either IP connections, filters, or URLs.

WebSite 1.1 restricts users by URL (or control point). When a browser tries to access a document that is below a particular control point, the server sends a form to the Web client requesting a username and a password. If the username and password are authenticated, the information is returned to the Web browser. The username and password are needed only once for each control point. In other words, as long as the Web browser is not closed, then the access is granted once the proper username and password have been provided. Once the client software is closed and re-opened or a different control point is encountered, the server will send another message requesting authentication.

 If you need greater security for your Web server for functions such as credit card transactions, you may want to use encryption-based security. Two methods that are designed for high-level security are: Secure Sockets Layer (SSL) and Secure HTTP (S-HTTP).

If you want to learn more about secure operations for Web servers, try the Netscape's Web site at *http://home.netscape.com.*

Summary

Chapter 10 has supplied you with a brief overview of forms on the Web and how they can work for you. It included key topics of interest in creating forms using HTML. While the examples here may seem simplistic, they're meant to show you how much information you can generate by placing forms on your site. Whether you want simple demographic information or online ordering—simply decide what information you need from your site's users, and there's a way to receive it, using forms and HTML.

CHAPTER
11

Internet/Intranet Resources

In Chapters 9 and 10, we learned the basics of designing, developing, and implementing HTML forms for our Web server. Now it's time to apply that solid foundation to some specific business applications. In addition to supporting the topics we've covered so far, the example applications will allow us to further explore such issues as the preparation of the overall design, business challenges, support software issues, database queries, and connectivity methods.

A Word about Web Project Management

Before we get into the example project, I'd like to take a moment to discuss the most important component of any Web development—management. Effectively managing projects requires you to allocate the right personnel, and enough time and resources to get the project done right. In theory, this system is foolproof. But in practice, we all know that things don't always work according to the system. Every day, managers face the task of setting priorities, but *how do you identify the priorities when everything is important?* One method that is proven to help set priorities in business-based Web development is called the FAST track, which helps to generate the Focus, Agreement, Schedule,

373

and Tracking of the project—that is, who will do what by when. Let's take a look at the steps involved in this system:

1. *Define the goal of the Web project.* Before any work is started, make sure everyone involved in the project has a clear understanding of what the project is all about. This step will help you to gain valuable insight from the project personnel, and avoid delays and changes in requirements.

2. *Assign the Web project coordinator.* The coordinator may not even contribute to the project other than coordinating the parties involved from the beginning to project close.

3. *Assign the Web team members.* Assign team members based on the goal of the project (see step 1). Don't be afraid to solicit help outside of your department if other areas of the business have the talent to contribute to the project.

4. *Use all available resources.* The project coordinator should request a meeting with specific division representatives of the business (not the project team members) and ask for their input. Gathering ideas can be helpful even if solutions to issues are not immediately obvious.

5. *Obtain constant feedback.* You should always perform a routine confidence check with the "customer" who will use the site. How will the project serve the customer, and is the project currently focused on the customer's needs? Keep in mind that the customer can be business employees or bona fide clients of the business. A customer is really anyone who can derive information from the site.

Project Killers

There are five ways to kill an HTML Web project and prevent it from moving through the necessary steps to completion:

- **Clutter**—Too much paperwork (red tape) or too much control can interfere with a project. Keep the project moving and don't add to the problem. This can be a big concern when dealing with sensitive or classified materials.

- **Unclear Communication**—When requesting support or sending email for response, be concise, simple, and direct. The respondent may not need highly technical details to answer your (the developer's) request.

- **Procrastination**—Plan, commit, and break down the tasks into smaller more manageable tasks to prevent a delay to the overall project.

- **Indecision**—Avoiding decisions until you "have all the facts" can kill your project. Make the best possible decisions (team member availability, time frames, etc.) based on your current information. You can always tweak things later on if necessary.

- **Closed Ears**—Listen to everything your team members have to say, and provide verbal feedback. Every idea is worth the few minutes it takes to hear it.

Automating an Office

Now that you understand how to successfully approach a project and avoid mishaps that can derail its progress, let's take a look at an example. We're going to automate an office by implementing a backend program that uses Microsoft's Visual Basic 4.0 on your Web server. (For our example, we'll be using WebSite 1.1, but any of the Windows-based programs will work fine.) This example is designed to give you a basic set of development code that you can easily change for a particular design solution for your office Web server. Before we go any further, we need to define the goal of the project.

Defining the Goal of the Project

Many off-the-shelf solutions exist to help businesses with their daily office tasks. Unfortunately, most of these products are not "network aware," which means that the sharing of information can be hazardous at best. Here's the problem: Suppose your company submits a price list to all your customers. If the price list is updated frequently—even daily—you need to get the updated information to your customers in a timely manner. Without the luxury of network sharing, the price list needs to be printed out and faxed or sent to your customers, who then need to compile the updated information for their own purposes. This approach not only takes time, but also increases your cost for labor hours, paper resources, and facsimile or postage expenses.

Our goal for this project, then, is to create a program that allows you to take advantage of your Web server to share information with your customers electronically, making updates and new information available at a click of the mouse.

Filling in the Details

Our task is to write a Visual Basic 4.0 (VB4) program that reads data in a file (like the price list) and serves the information up on our Web site so we can share the information with the end user. The first thing we need to do is to save the data file into a format that will be easily readable by VB4. Most application software includes a comma-delimited text file (CDT) format option in the Save As dialog box. This format is an ASCII text file that contains only raw data with commas between every column.

For our project, we'll use a spreadsheet file that provides work schedule information for a production company. The file contains seven columns with several rows of information, including projects in the schedule, their start and end dates, and their priority. The actual number of rows may change, depending on the volume of information, so we need to adjust our computer array to accommodate a varying number. Listing 11.1 shows the VB4 code to read the input file into an array.

Listing 11.1   Reading a Comma-Delimited Text File into an Array

```
Dim EventDate(1000) As String, Tbegin(1000) As String, Tend(1000) As String
Dim Event(1000) As String, Priority(1000) As String, Style(1000) As String
Dim Note(1000) As String
                            ' Setup the array

Dim schedule As Integer     ' Declare variables
   Dim J As Integer

Dim NL
NL = Chr(10)
comma = Chr(44)
Blank = Chr(32)

For I = 1 To 1000           ' Clear the array

    EventDate(I) = ""
    Tbegin(I) = ""
    Tend(I) = ""
    Event(I) = ""
```

```
      Priority(I) = ""
      Note(I) = ""

Next I

Open "C:\DirectoryName\SCHEDULE.CDT" For Input As #1  ' Open to read file.

J = 0                           ' Initialize line counter
Do While Not EOF(1)             ' Read lines until EOF

      J = J + 1
      Input #1, EventDate(J)  ' fill arrays with the file data
      Input #1, Tbegin(J)
      Input #1, Tend(J)
      Input #1, Event(J)
      Input #1, Priority(J)
      Input #1, Note(J)

   Loop
                                ' J now has the value of EOF
Close #1                        ' Close input file
```

This portion of the program code demonstrates the basic steps to produce more than simple HTML pages of information for your customers. The first part of the code initializes the arrays and memory variables that will be used in the code. Next, the looping routine initializes the arrays to empty. The program will then open and read in the file until the end of file has been reached.

You can set the number of columns and rows when you save the CDT file. If there is an unknown default value for rows and columns, then read the file into an ASCII text editor and manually count the number of columns and rows.

After the CDT file has been read into the array, we need to save it as an HTML file to give it a little more structure and to make it easily displayed in a Web browser. Listing 11.2 shows the **For** loop that is used to complete this task.

Listing 11.2   Saving the CDT File Information as an HTML File

```
Open "C:\Directory\schedule.htm" For Output Access Write As #2

    Print #2, "<HTML><HEAD><TITLE>DevelopMental Systems schedule
      </TITLE></HEAD><BODY BGCOLOR= DDDDFF>"
    Print #2, "<HR><CENTER><H1> DevelopMental Systems Hourly Schedule
      </H1><HR>"
    Print #2, "<H4><FONT COLOR=BLUE>Last Up-Date "; sTime; " <BR>"
    Print #2, "On "; sDate; "</FONT></CENTER></H4>"

    Print #2, "<TH>"; "<CENTER>"
    Print #2, "<TABLE BORDER>"
    Print #2, "<CAPTION><H3>DevelopMental Systems SCHEDUEL</H3>
      </CAPTION>"
    Print #2, "<TR><TH> Date <TH> Start Time <TH> End Time <TH> Event
      <TH> Note"

    For N = 1 To J

    Print #2, "<TR><TD>"; "<BR>"; EventDate(N); _
      "<TD>"; Tbegin(N); "<TD>"; Tend(N); "<TD>"; Event(N); "<TD>"; _
      Note(N); "</TR>"
    Next N

    Print #2, "</TABLE>"; "</CENTER>"
    Print #2, "<BR>"
    Print #2, "</PRE><H4> <A HREF=""mailto:add@thisPlace""> _
      Questions and comments !</A>"
    Print #2, "<HR></BODY></HTML>"

Close #2
```

In the **For** loop, we simply print each item in the field to the file; then the loop advances to the next row of fields. The entire file is read into the array and will print until the end of the file is found. The variable that holds the end of the file integer is defined in the earlier section of code when the input file was read.

So far, our program is a little sparse. Using VB4's built-in functions, we can add a polished look. We'll use the **Now** function to return the computer system's time and date, which we can change to provide a date and time in our HTML document, as shown here:

```
sTime = Hour(Now) & ":" & Minute(Now)
sDate = Month(Now) & "/" & Day(Now) & "/" & Year(Now)
```

Because updates can be crucial to customers, we should run the Visual Basic program each time a change is made. We can do this by adding a timer to our program to run the EXE (executable) file as often as needed. To add a timer to our program, we have to create a form and place a timer on the form. You can set the timer to run at whatever interval is best for your situation, as shown here:

```
Form1.Timer1.Interval = 64000
```

Take a look at Figure 11.1 to see the HTML file that our VB4 program has produced.

Our next step is to add several rows of information to a single date entry. For this task, we'll be using the HTML tag **<TABLE ROWSPAN=**n **COLSPAN=**n**>**, which spans a number of rows or columns over a redefined number of entries. To perform a **ROWSPAN**, we count the number of items in a single row before we write to the output file in HTML format. This step takes a little more setup code, but it allows our output file to change "on-the-fly" as the input information changes. Listing 11.3 shows the code we'll use.

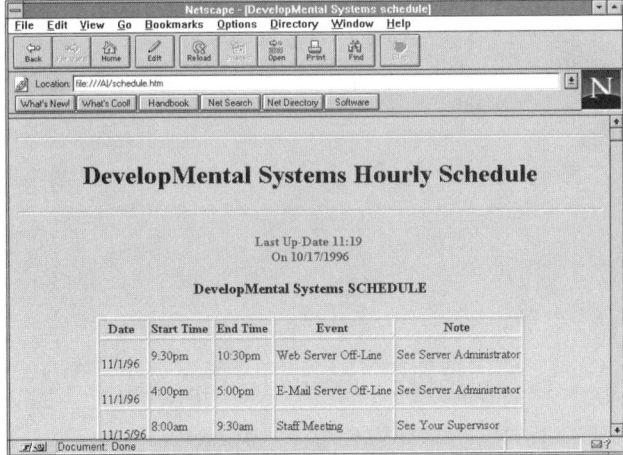

Figure 11.1 The HTML file produced by our VB4 program.

Listing 11.3   Calculating the Number of Rows to Span for HTML Tables

```
{more code above here}
Print #2, "<TR><TH> Date <TH> Start Time <TH> End Time <TH> Event"

        N = 0

    For K = 1 To J

            Count = 1


                N = N + 1

            For m = N To (J - 1)
             TempDate = EventDate(m)
             NextDate = EventDate(m + 1)
             If TempDate = NextDate Then
                Count = Count + 1
             Else
                 Exit For
             End If
          Next m

        Print #2, "<TR><TD ROWSPAN="; Count; ">";  " EventDate(N); _
        "<TD>"; Tbegin(N); "<TD>"; Tend(N); "<TD>"; Event(N); "</TR>"

        Do While Count > 1
           Print #2, "<TR><TD>"; Tbegin(N + 1); "<TD>"; Tend(N + 1); _
           "<TD>"; Event(N + 1); "</TR>"
           N = N + 1
           Count = Count - 1
        Loop
        If N = J Then Exit For

    Next K

   Print #2, "</TABLE>"; "</CENTER>"
{more code below here}
```

Now that you have the basics you need to automate an office, let's look at more specific tasks within an office environment that could use the help of a Web server.

Automating Office Tasks with an Access Database

In most office environments database programs play a large part in performing such daily tasks as ordering products for customers, sending out new product information, and updating customer information. For this example, we're going to use the Microsoft Access database program to set up three different tables—customers, products, and orders—which can be accessed via the Web. Our database will take on a rather simple design for demonstration purposes, but we can modify the record fields and the Visual Basic code to add needed functions. Figure 11.2 shows the tables inside our database.

NT SERVER TIP In a fully integrated office Internet/intranet environment, you could include more information for employees, sales staff, suppliers, and shippers. The options are endless.

Communicating with the database is easy using standard VB4 code with some built-in functions. When we initialize our database connection through VB4, we'll work with a workspace function to allow multiple use of the same database. Because our application is going to be an Internet-wide solution, we need to be able to perform several queries from different

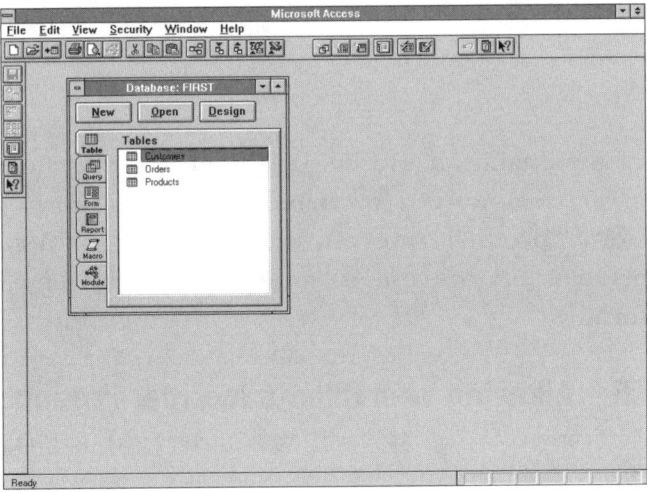

Figure 11.2 Access database tables.

Web clients at the same time. The workspace function we are going to use allows us to set up a Workspace which is similar to VB 3.0 DynaSet. Listing 11.4 shows the code to open the database.

Listing 11.4 Opening an Access Database

```
Sub main()

Dim TempWorkspace As Workspace, TempDatabase As Database

Dim dbFileName As String

dbFileName="d:\Website\cgi-win\test.MDB"        ' Define database name

Set TempWorkspace=Wordspaces(0)

Set TempDatabase=TempWorkspace.OpenDatabase(dbFileName)

Set TempTable=TempDatabase.OpenRecordset("TABLE NAME")

   TempTable.AddNew      ' We are going to add information to the database

   TempTable![INFORMATION]=Variable-that-was-passed      ' Variable name

   TempTable.Update         ' Save changes

   TempTable.Close          ' Close the table

TempDatabase.Close          ' Close the database

End Sub
```

Any or all of these tables could be expanded to include access from/to your Web server. We now need to expand our code to allow a Web client or customer to order products from our Web site. Listing 11.5 shows the code that allows us to set up this type of connection with a Web client through an HTML form.

Listing 11.5 Allowing Web Clients to Order Products Online

```
Function SendDbCommand(hConn As Long, ByVal query_str As String, _
   get_results As Integer) As Integer

   Dim db_success As Long, result As Long
```

```
       MsgBox "In DB Send Command"
       If MiExec(hConn, query_str, 0) = MI_ERROR Then
           SendDbCommand = 0
           Exit Function
       End If

       ' Check the results of the command
       db_success = 1
       result = MiGetResult(hConn)
       While ((db_success = 1) And (result <> MI_NO_MORE_RESULTS) And _
           (order_index <= 500))

          Select Case result
             Case MI_ERROR
                db_success = 0

             Case MI_ROWS

                If (get_results = 1) Then
                   db_success = read_query_results(order_index)
                Else
                   db_success = 1
                End If

             Case MI_DML, MI_DDL
                ' We only get these messages after the query has returned all
                ' its rows
                row_count = MiResultRowCount(hConn)

             Case Else
                db_success = 0

          End Select

          result = MiGetResult(hConn)

       Wend


       ' Flush the query and check for an error
       If MiQueryFinish(hConn) = MI_ERROR Then
          SendDbCommand = 0
       Else
          SendDbCommand = db_success
       End If

End Function
```

Two nice features to add to any form are a header and a footer—standard bits of information sent to the customer after a request has been processed in the database. These items add a professional touch with a small amount of code, as shown in Listing 11.6.

Listing 11.6   Header and Footer Coded Script

```
Sub SendHeader(title As String)

    send ("Content-type: text/html")
    send ("")
    send ("<HTML><HEAD><TITLE>" & title & "</TITLE></HEAD>")
    send ("<BODY>")

End Sub


Sub SendFooter()

    send ("<HR>")
    send ("Click below to send mail to our registration desk:<BR>")
    Send ("<A HREF=""mailto:userName@Address.SomeWhere"">")
    Send ("<ADDRESS>&lt;????&gt;</ADDRESS>")
    send ("</BODY></HTML>")

End Sub
```

After our information has been passed on to the client or Web user, we can send a thank-you HTML form to let the user know the results of the request, as shown in Listing 11.7.

Listing 11.7   Confirmation Form

```
Sub SendOrderConfirmation()

    '
    ' Notify user that order has been processed and must be reviewed.
    '
    SendHeader ("Order Confirmation")
    send ("<H1>Order Confirmation</H1>")
    send ("Your order has been received, and entered into the database.")

    ' Send confirmation info
    send ("<PRE>")
```

```
    send ("         Name: " & full_name)
    send ("Ship Address: " & street1)
    If (street2 <> "") Then
        send ("               " & street2)
    End If
    send ("               " & city & ", " & state & " " & zip)
    send ("  Work Phone: " & wphone & "        Home Phone: " & hphone)
    send ("        E-mail: " & email)
    send ("         Media: " & media_type)
    send (" ")
    send ("         Cubes: " & cube_files)
    send ("</PRE>")

    send ("<B>The system administrator will notify you after the order _
        request has been reviewed.</B><BR>")
    send ("<P>")
    send ("<A HREF=""/DIRECTORY/filename.html""> Return to previous _
        page.</a><BR>")
    send ("</P>")
    SendFooter

End Sub
```

Summary

This chapter concludes Part 3, in which you learned all about integrating a programmatical approach to solving Web server customer issues. In this case, Visual Basic was used as the tool of choice. You can use C or C++ if that's your native language, or Borland Delphi if you want. The main issue is serving your Web clients in the most efficient manner, and the methods shown here should help get you started.

Building your Web site over time will be both personally and professionally rewarding if you follow these tips and suggestions. The next chapter starts Part 4, in which you'll learn about everyday Web site administration, care and feeding, and adjustments of all types. Just because you're transitioning from this programmatical section to administration, don't forget about what you learned in Part 2, since many parts of Web administration may indeed affect your forms and programs. It's all part of the fun of the Web.

Maintaining Your Web Server

PART

4

CHAPTER

12

Web Server Administration

Although the previous chapters have focused on specific products or applications of ideas, we haven't yet completely dissected the ins and outs of Web server administration. It's been apparent for some time that administration takes up where the installation leaves off, but to what degree? What are your options for managing the Web server? How can you or your business benefit from the different types of administration? These are some important questions, deserving of some detailed answers.

In this chapter, I will present answers to these questions and discuss several other ideas, including:

- Normal Web admin practices

- Emergency actions when the server goes haywire

- Preventive medicine for your Web server

- Other forms of remote Web access

When Web servers run fine, they're great to have around. When they have problems, it can be a terrible nightmare. Problems happen; it's part of a normal course of server life, but arming yourself to combat those problems can

389

make a huge difference in lessening the nightmare. As you read onward, understand that the solutions we'll discuss are not all encompassing, but rather present some of the easiest and most proactive methods of Web server administration.

NT's Remote Access Server

Microsoft Windows NT Server includes one of the most welcomed communications packages around in the form of a standard PPP (Point-to-Point Protocol) connection. This is the protocol used by most Internet servers to allow dialup connections from Joe User who wants to surf the Internet. The other protocol, called SLIP (Serial Line Interface Protocol), is the most commonly used for Internet clients; however, PPP improves on SLIP by offering more security, better error correction, and better streamlining of data movement by reducing overhead slightly. All in all, PPP is the way to go if such a connection is available.

Server Considerations

If you're contemplating using your newly completed Web server machine for Internet access for your customers, there are several things to consider. You've already seen how running the Web server software affects performance of the physical server itself. Allowing anyone to connect to the Microsoft Windows NT Server by way of dialup modems puts pressure on server resources in an incremental manner. Although RAS doesn't reduce the strain on a server's ability to serve the users, configuring your physical server with RAS in mind is key to a successful site.

Each user will take up approximately 600 KB of server memory in normal operations. When high-speed modems are being used, the server must be able to handle the increased data throughput of the users. At one site where I consulted and assisted in the planning of the site, a Pentium 133 MHz system running 64 MB of memory was sufficient to handle 48 concurrently connected users at speeds of 28.8 Kbps. The processor was "clocked" at approximately 75 percent utilization with memory utilization around 65 percent.

Obviously, this server could accommodate a few more users, but one thing remains to be said: Even if 48 users were connected to the server at the same time, it's doubtful that every user was getting full 28.8 Kbps bandwidth out of the connection—the phone lines could be terrible, the modems themselves may not match up the speeds completely, and the list goes on of possible irritants to the server. In a real-world setting, these and other factors not controllable by the WebMaster can affect the operations of the user dialup lines. Your best bet is to use error-correcting modems on the RAS connection, and employ the use of the PPP options, which we'll discuss later in this section.

Installing RAS

Installing RAS couldn't be easier, but we need to discuss a few decisions that you'll need to make. In the Microsoft Windows NT Server world of networking and connectivity, the NetBEUI protocol has long been the Microsoft standard for connectivity. Over time, however, Microsoft began to use the IPX (InterPacket eXchange) protocol more often for networking connectivity. And the world standard for network connectivity is TCP/IP, which Microsoft Windows NT Server can use as well.

You'll have to decide which protocols you want to allow the users to request for the connection:

- NetBEUI is the network protocol specific to Microsoft operating systems such as Windows for Workgroups and NT Workstation.

- IPX accommodates Netware clients and Microsoft clients using IPX identifiers.

- TCP/IP is the Internet standard.

Go to the server where you'll install RAS. You'll need the NT Server CD-ROM for this operation. The remainder of this section assumes that your Microsoft Windows NT Server is already operational with TCP/IP installed for the normal network operations, and that you're adding RAS as a side element of operations. Install RAS using the instructions found in your server manual.

Configuring RAS

RAS has a few simple configuration options. We'll begin with those that weren't covered in the installation of RAS. Open the program group for

RAS, and then double click on the Remote Access Admin icon to display the main screen for RAS functions that control access to the server. From the menu bar, select Users|Permissions to display the user permissions options shown in Figure 12.1.

In the list of users section on the left, note the "Grant dialin permission to user" checkbox. If this option is not turned on, then the user will never be able to connect to the server. Period! The other options just below this checkbox deal with the ability to dial into, or out of, the server by calling back to validate the call. *Callback functions* are commonly used in a secure environment to prevent unauthorized access. Make sure these last two options are set, and then exit the administrative part of RAS.

Now that we've set permissions for the user, we need to configure RAS so users can connect properly. Let's take a few minutes and go over the process in which a RAS-enabled client will be connecting to the Web server. Start RAS by clicking on the RAS button in the RAS program group. Because you've just installed this component, no entries exist in the phone book, so we'll add one in just a moment. Also, the RAS monitor will start

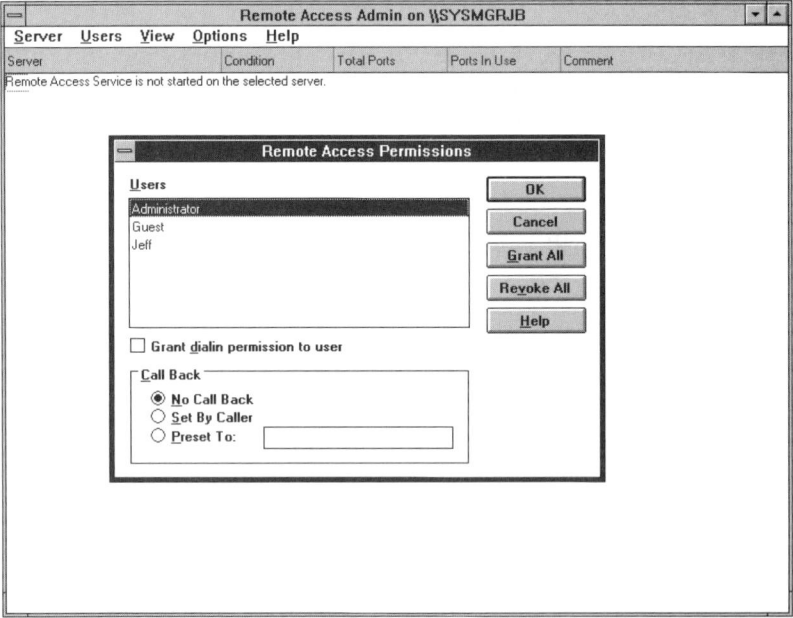

Figure 12.1   RAS user permissions options.

up automatically. The monitor is a graphical representation of what is happening to the modem line: received and transmitted data, errors in transmission, and carrier detection. Each option has a corresponding light. All of the lights are green except for the error light, which is red as you might expect.

To add a phone book entry, click on the Add button, and fill in the blanks for the Entry, Description, and Phone Number. Clear the Authentication checkbox because we're not using the NT registry of users to validate the user. Click on the Advanced button to show the network settings that must be configured. Click on the Modem button and set the required parameters for your modem, then click on OK.

Some modems will not work properly on a dirty phone line if the Compression option is checked. If you experience problems connecting or maintaining connections, clear this option.

The next two buttons, X.25 and ISDN, pertain only to those settings requiring these items—for example, when you've got an ISDN adapter connected to the server. While ISDN is taking off in a big way, you don't need to worry about it in this context. Skip these options, and click on the Network button to display the options shown in Figure 12.2. It is here that you need to begin making your protocol choices. The first choice you'll make is deciding between a SLIP and a PPP connection. Windows clients can use either, but when presented with the options, you should always choose PPP.

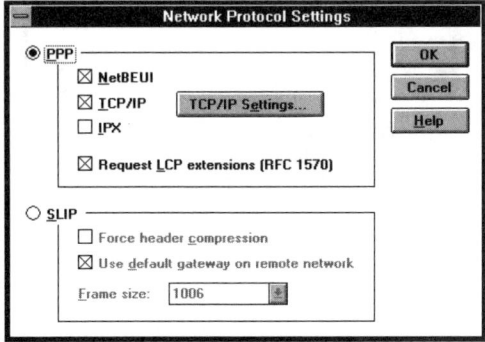

Figure 12.2   RAS network options.

Select the appropriate options for your connection types. NT binds the protocols you select to the RAS Server; the more functions you choose to offer, the more physical server resources are used. For most settings, TCP/IP is the only protocol required. Notice in Figure 12.2 that I selected the NetBEUI protocol as well as TCP/IP. I did this to allow WFWG computers to connect to the server when the user has no knowledge of how to configure TCP/IP. I'll explain why I did this after you take a look at the TCP/IP settings shown in Figure 12.3.

If you're using RAS to connect to an ISP, then the ISP will generally assign you an IP address. In this case, the "Server assigned IP address" checkbox should be selected. Likewise, the "Server assigned name server addresses" checkbox should also be selected, which allows the ISP to define the DNS server. The user-defined options in both sections are therefore greyed out. In the case of my network, I defined all of the parameters for each workstation on the network. For my traveling laptop users, I also have them follow the above two settings so they don't have to worry about assigning IP addresses to their computer. Using the NT Resource Kit IP Configuration utility, I assigned each of these settings to my workstations as indicated in Figure 12.4.

We'll keep the default Security settings. Normally, the ISP handles the security authentications. In a purely Windows environment like this, you can tighten up security by selecting Microsoft encryption as the most secure

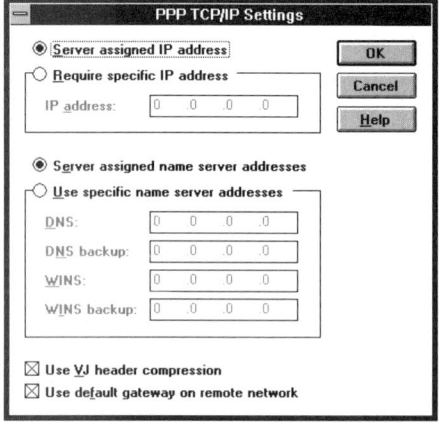

Figure 12.3　TCP/IP settings in RAS.

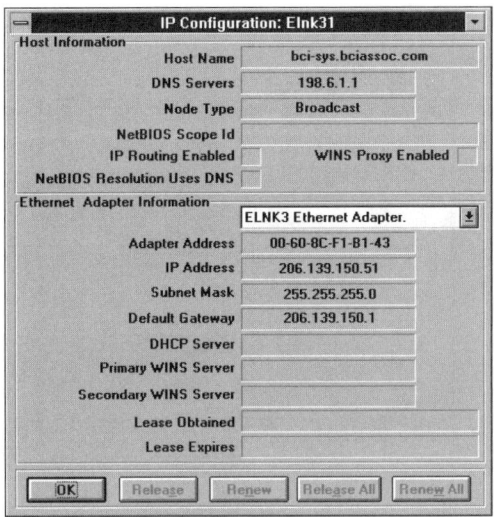

Figure 12.4 Network assigned settings.

form of connections. Close this section; now it's time to test accessing the server!

Using RAS for the Web Server

Now that we have RAS fully configured, we can test access to the server. Open the RAS program group from the computer you configured to connect and click on the Dial button to connect to the server. Despite the settings that you entered earlier, RAS insists that you enter the username, password, and domain. Type in your username and password, clear the domain entry, and then click on OK to connect. When RAS connects for the first time, a dialog box appears asking if you want the program minimized upon connection, displays the type of protocol that successfully connected with the server, and also asks if you want such messages suppressed in the future. Select all the options, and then double click on the minimized icon and bring the RAS dialer back up on screen. Click on the Status button to display connection information, as shown in Figure 12.5.

This screen shows the IP address you were assigned by the server, the connection settings of the modems, and more. You are now considered a full user of the server to which you've connected! If you have the privileges set on the remote server, you can map to directories, send or receive email,

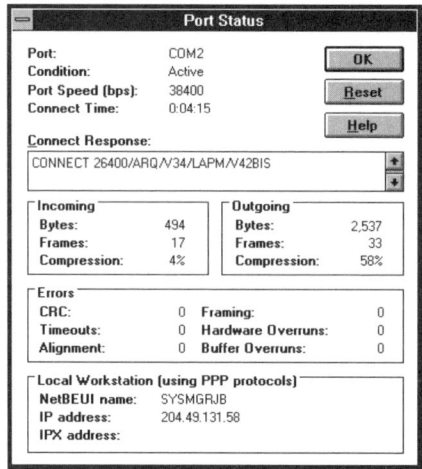

Figure 12.5 RAS connection information for the link.

move files, and do anything else that you could do if you logged into the server locally. The same goes for your customers. Once they've connected, they can have access to all the things they normally would, including printing.

Setting Up a Bulletin Board System

With all of the explosive growth of the Web and Internet in general, it's hard to imagine why a bulletin board system (BBS) would be of any value to you in your quest for the perfect Web server. BBSs generally bring to mind games, shareware, product support, software testing, and a place to chat with friends, but for some users they provide a whole lot more than this—BBSs provide the crucial link to accessing your server. Here's why. The business environment here in Northwest Florida is one of a growing and learning computing world. In many parts of this area, a 9600 baud modem is considered a luxury, and a 386 processor of any type is an upscale user! Many of the communications infrastructures in this region are still part of what King Arthur left behind when he upgraded The Round Table. As a result, many businesses have no reliable communications. Only within the last year has this situation been addressed, and poorly addressed at that. We have one Internet provider to service an area of a quarter million people that largely view the Internet as a figment of some dream. A dream it is when all of these potential users must dial long distance from town to town, and the towns are 45 miles apart.

This may sound like the ranting and raving of a poor old country boy, but, unfortunately, this situation exists for many small towns and cities across the U.S. that are striving to expand their telecommunications abilities to help their own businesses, large and small. When the lack of Internet presence is partially caused by a lack of business infrastructure such as remoteness or stymied technological growth, the only other solution is bulletin boards. This is one of the major reasons that BBSs have survived to this point, but largely for personal usage.

In this section, I'll show how a BBS package from Mustang Software and an outstanding hardware product from Equinox Corporation team up to provide your Microsoft Windows NT Server with superb Internet connectivity for your users. BBSs provide several advantages over RAS:

- Even though RAS connects users to your server just like the BBS does, RAS forms a pure NT Server connection from user to server. Functions like email or chat aren't available directly from RAS. The BBS offers both email and chat, as well as connectivity, which allows you to bypass purchasing expensive email server software.

- No Internet presence exists in the local area, requiring a long distance call to the closest ISP for your users and customers to connect to your site.

- Your Web server is connected to the Internet, but your customers and some users have to call long distance to connect to the Web server.

- Your business has traveling users with diverse platforms such as OS/2 or Macintosh laptops that do not natively connect to NT Server using RAS; the BBS connects virtually anyone.

- BBSs offer conferencing so that online discussions can take place in real time.

These are compelling reasons to consider a BBS system on your Web server if the situation warrants it. Although I've said that I avoid promoting one vendor over another, when I find a total solution to a problem I just have to endorse it—and this is one of those clean and efficient solutions. I'll begin by discussing the hardware, and then I'll discuss Mustang Software's Wildcat! for Windows NT.

Equinox's SuperSerial Multi-I/O Processor

When I was checking the marketplace for the solution to this issue, I came across the *SuperSerial Technology* (*SST*) intelligent processor made by a little-known company called Equinox. This card is a souped-up version of a PC's serial port built onto one card, with several ports on the card operating as highly enhanced serial ports. This card comes in several models that run in Unix, Netware, NT Server, DOS, and Windows 3.x or 95. Bus structures included are ISA, EISA, PCI, and Micro Channel. If you have the slots, you can add 8 ports at a time until you run out of slots, or hit the limit of 256 ports.

Not feasible, you say? How about running a 20-slot passive backplane server with a single board computer. That leaves 19 slots free, so 16 of these cards could be added. Equinox has cards running 2, 4, 8, 64, and 128 ports. If I had any one bad thing to say about the SST line, it'd be that I'd like to see a 16- and a 32-port model to minimize the number of cards to be installed. The 16-port model is a common installed item with BBS systems. In fact, the Digiboard, which is a competitor to Equinox, has a 16-port model, but a comparable SST out-performed the Digiboard by as much as 25 percent in our testing. If you want more information on this card, call Equinox at 954-746-9000 or fax them at 954-746-9101. Their email address is *info@equinox.com.*

Installing the SST

The first thing that you've got to do is know what hardware you have installed in the server now. The ISA card requires a unique I/O port address, and you'll have to select one. PCI, EISA, and Micro Channel cards have no such requirement. You'll need to shut down the Microsoft Windows NT Server itself, and power it off. Install the SST card into a spare slot, and restart the server.

Failure to observe proper safety precautions can cause loss of life. Ensure that all power is turned off before installing the SST card. The technician performing the installation of the card should be using the proper electrostatic protection devices to prevent destruction of the circuit cards.

Configuring the SST

After restarting the server, NT knows nothing about the card until you install the driver for the respective device. In the *Software Installation and Reference Manual* locate the NT section. The installation instructions for the driver are incredibly simple. When you're done, reboot the server to initialize the card. In the Control Panel, double click on the Networks icon. You'll see the installed Equinox card, as shown in Figure 12.6.

Click on the Equinox card, and then select the Configure button to see the settings for the card. The SST has two settings—First COMPort and ISA Memory Block—as shown in Figure 12.7. Click on the First COMPort drop-down menu, and you'll see that the first port that the SST can use is highlighted by default. On my server, I already have two serial ports, so COM 3 is selected. If you scroll down to the end, you'll see that 256 ports are possible, which is the maximum that one RAS server can use. Click on the ISA Memory Block drop-down menu and you'll see the various memory ranges possible for the card. If you only use one ISA card, I suggest you leave it set to "auto" and let NT handle the matter.

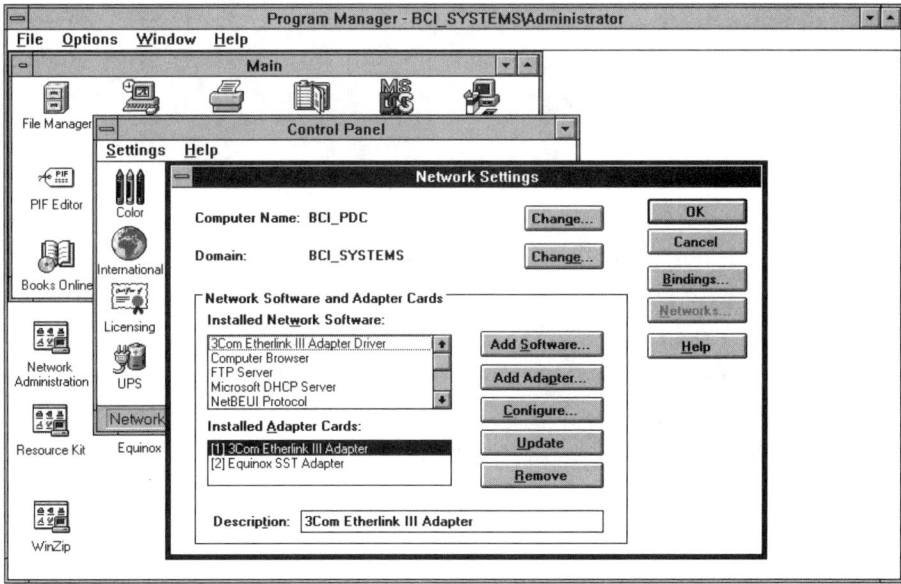

Figure 12.6   Equinox card installed.

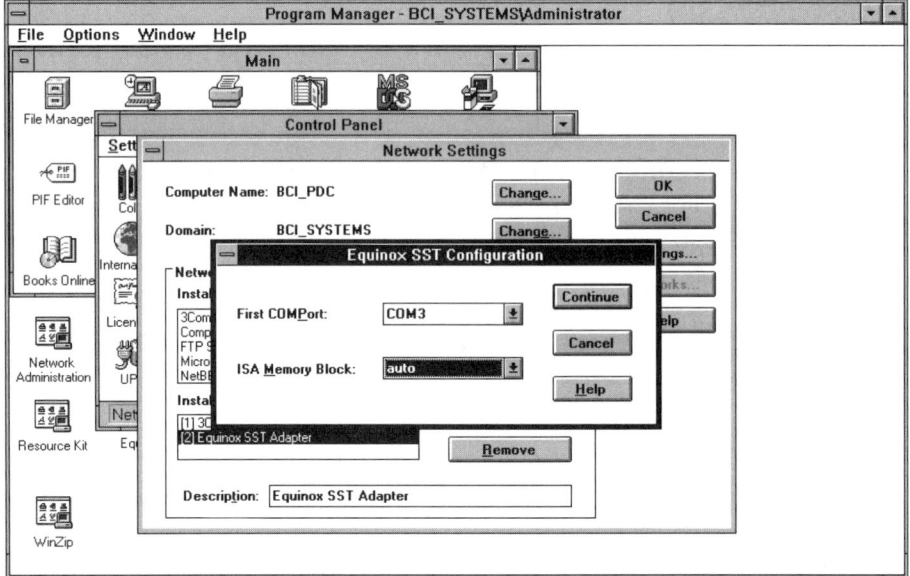

Figure 12.7　SST's settings.

That's about it as far as the Equinox settings go. Now, you can use the additional ports for any function that NT supports, including RAS. In fact, you can mix and match RAS users on half of the ports and BBS users on the other half. NT takes care of the intricacies of port management.

Wildcat! for NT

Now that the hardware is set up properly, the next thing we need to do is to install the Wildcat! software. Wildcat! comes suitably equipped to handle a large numbers of users, but Mustang Software saw fit to further enhance Wildcat! with a variety of functions and extensibility. These tools include *wcCode Plus Pack* if you want or need to add additional customized functions, *Internet Connectivity Pack* for the BBS to Web integration, and *wcExchange* for Microsoft Exchange integration.

Installing Wildcat!

Open the packages and insert the CD. Start the installation by running the SETUP.EXE program. You'll be presented with a really neat installation screen with three options, as shown in Figure 12.8.

- Install Wildcat!

- Install Navigator Web browser

- Review other Mustang products

We, of course, need to install the software. Take some time to look over the other options when you get a chance.

Click on the Wildcat! icon and follow the instructions on the following screens. The install wizard then installs Wildcat!. When the installation is complete, you'll be presented with an option to either upgrade an existing configuration, or create a new one. Select the option to create a new configuration (we'll modify the configuration in the next section), and exit the installation program. A program group that is created for all of the Wildcat! tools is shown in Figure 12.9.

Configuring Wildcat!'s Basics

The first thing you'll need to do is to start the Wildcat! server by double clicking on the wcserver icon. The server activates and then minimizes itself. Next, double click on the wcConfig icon to display the configuration options shown in Figure 12.10.

Figure 12.8   Wildcat!'s installation program.

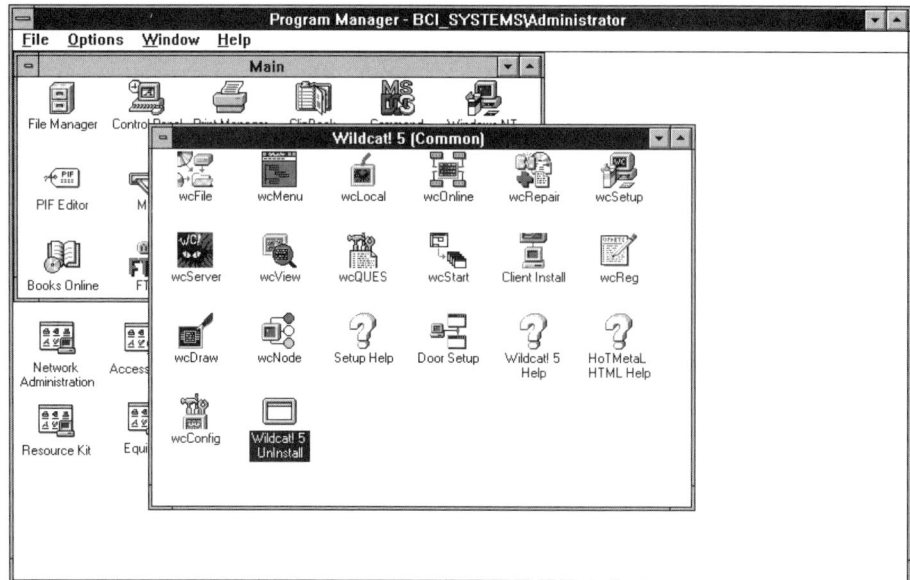

Figure 12.9 Wildcat!'s program group.

Figure 12.10 Configuration options for Wildcat!.

The first thing you need to do is configure the modem(s) attached to the Equinox card or to the NT server's serial ports. You can attach virtually any external modem to the ports, and you can customize the connection settings and result codes to match any of them. Double click on Node Settings to see the configured modems, as shown in Figure 12.11.

And that's all there is to activating a modem. The next most important thing to do is set the system operator's (sysop's) information. Double click on the Configuration icon, and enter in the requested information. Click on the System Security icon and define the parameters for the BBS. By default, the BBS is open to any new user. A common practice in private BBSs is to have potential users fill out a questionnaire to evaluate the merits of a request to access a BBS.

Secondary Configurations

After you've completed the basic configuration options, several other Wildcat! functions are available to customize the BBS to fit your needs. The most important of these is the menu structure that the users see when they connect to the BBS. From the Wildcat! program group, double click on the

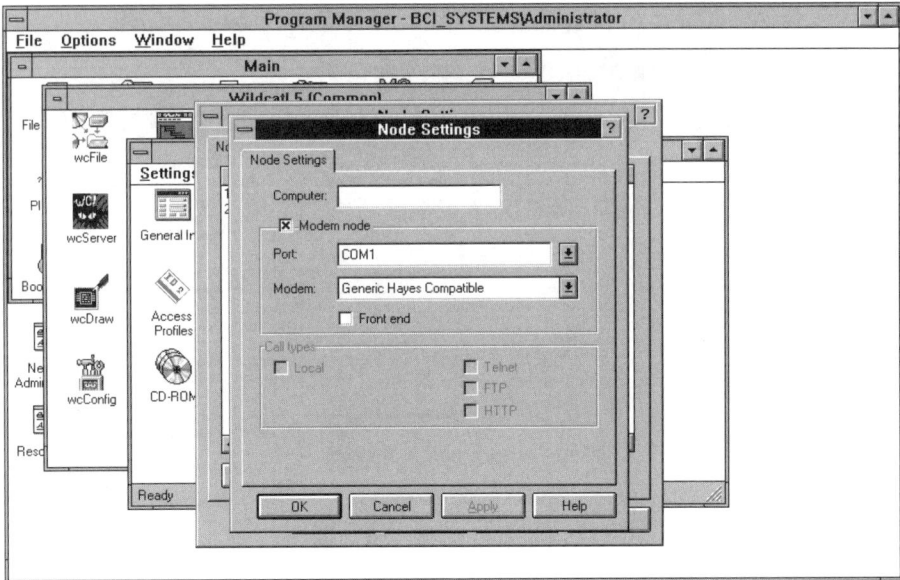

Figure 12.11   Node configurations.

wcMenu icon which opens the currently (and installed by default) established menu system, shown in Figure 12.12. The system is clear and concise, so you can easily alter the menus to suit your needs.

Other interesting features are the conference rooms Wildcat! installs. To see these rooms, double click on the wcConfig icon, then double click on the Conferencing icon. We'll discuss conferencing shortly.

Final Security Settings before Allowing Users

One thing we haven't yet considered is security. Before you allow users to log on, you have to set a few boundaries. *Access profiles* define how the user is allowed to use the BBS—what conference and file areas the user can see, and how the user is allowed to function on the BBS in general. The profile is for a group of users, not for one individual user. This approach eases administration just as it does in NT. Double click on the WcConfig icon and then double click on the Access Profiles icon. Wildcat! displays a screen that shows the currently installed profiles—New User, Registered User, and Sysop. For this example, double click on the Registered User profile, which is shown in Figure 12.13.

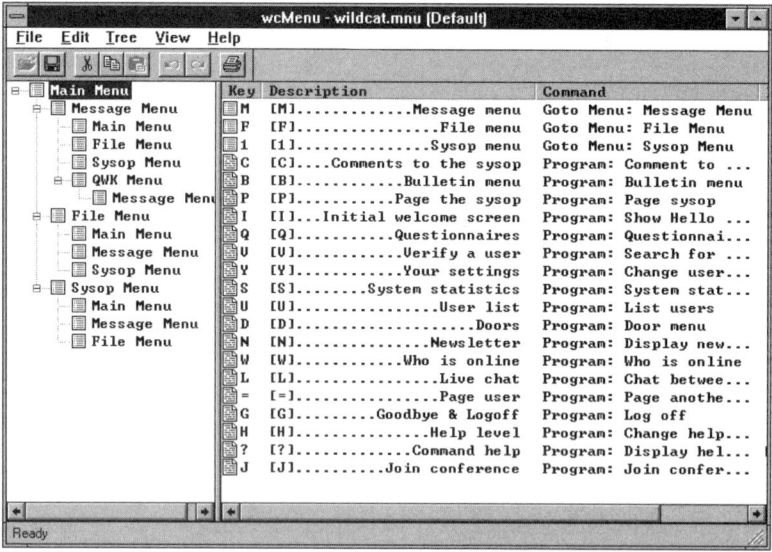

Figure 12.12   Customizing menus in Wildcat!.

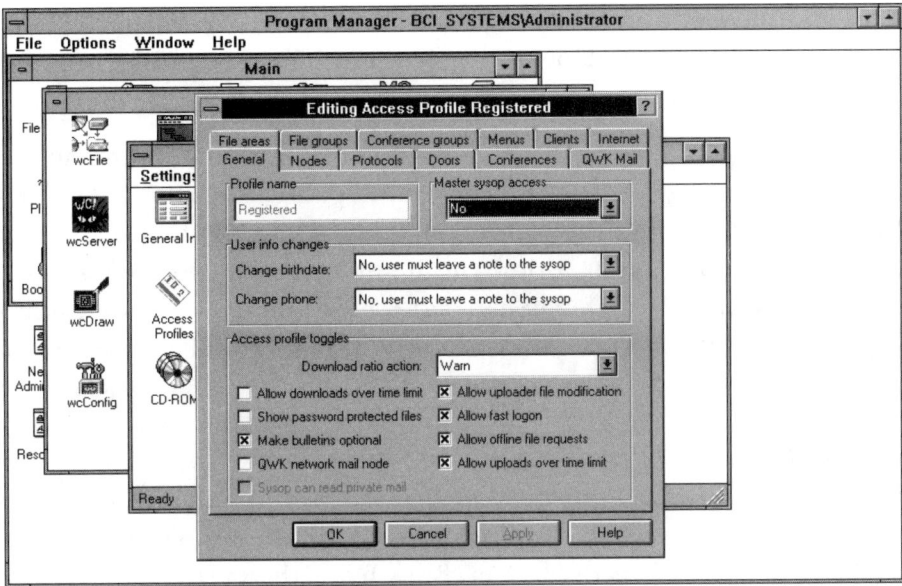

Figure 12.13   Reviewing Wildcat!'s access profiles.

Once you've modified the access profile, double click on the Security Profile icon. This profile allows you to set the security validation of the user by
requiring the birthday and phone number of the caller after a certain
number of logons, and to deny access if someone doesn't get it right. You
can also specify the volume of file transfers to limit the user to, or otherwise prevent someone from wasting time on the BBS. Make the desired
changes to the profile for your site's needs.

 If you allow someone unlimited file access to the BBS,
they could possibly upload files to the point that all avail-
able disk space is consumed! This has agonizingly det-
rimental effects on BBS operations.

There are a number of other configuration options that we would normally set for the BBS to operate fully, but I'm going to stop here because
our primary interest is how Wildcat! benefits us for Web server operations.
I'm going to cover three more functions before going into the Internet
Connectivity suite of tools, and these three directly affect how the BBS

serves up the Web. But, before you press on, try making a test call to the BBS. Dial the number, and log on as a new user. The new user logon screen is shown in Figure 12.14.

Answer all of the questions the BBS questionnaire asks, and remember to write down or remember your username and password—you'll need them when we install the Internet tools. Complete all of the screens that are presented, and take a look around at the menus. What you see is the default installed menus that Wildcat! did for you, and you can customize these as you see fit. After your tour, Wildcat! displays its default main menu, as shown in Figure 12.15.

Online Conferencing

If you've ever worked in any type of corporate setting, then you're surely familiar with the infamous "meetings." Normally, you simply round up the attendees and have your discussion. But what if the participants are scattered across the country? One alternative would be to fly the participants in, but that gets kind of expensive.

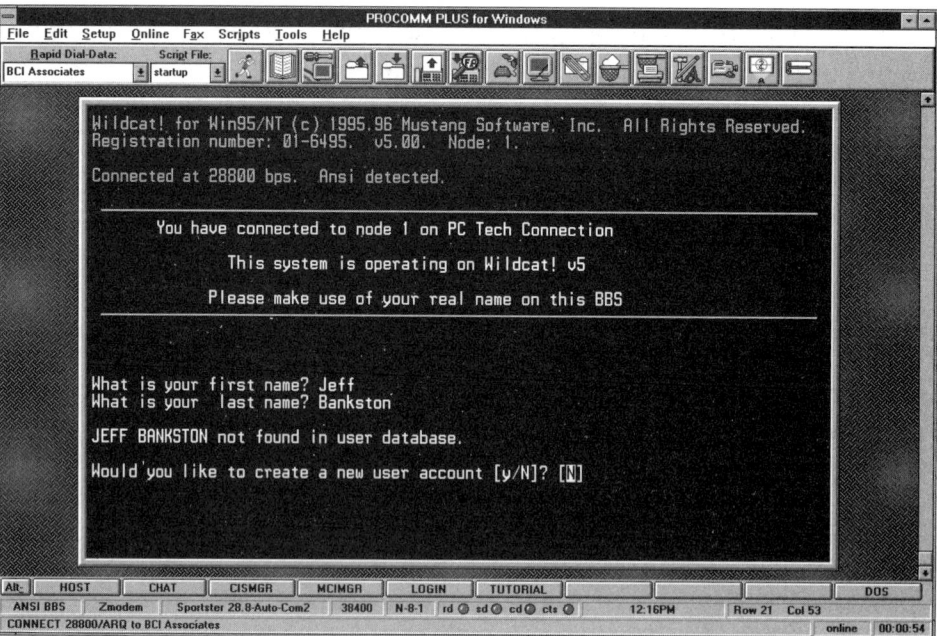

Figure 12.14 The new user logon procedure.

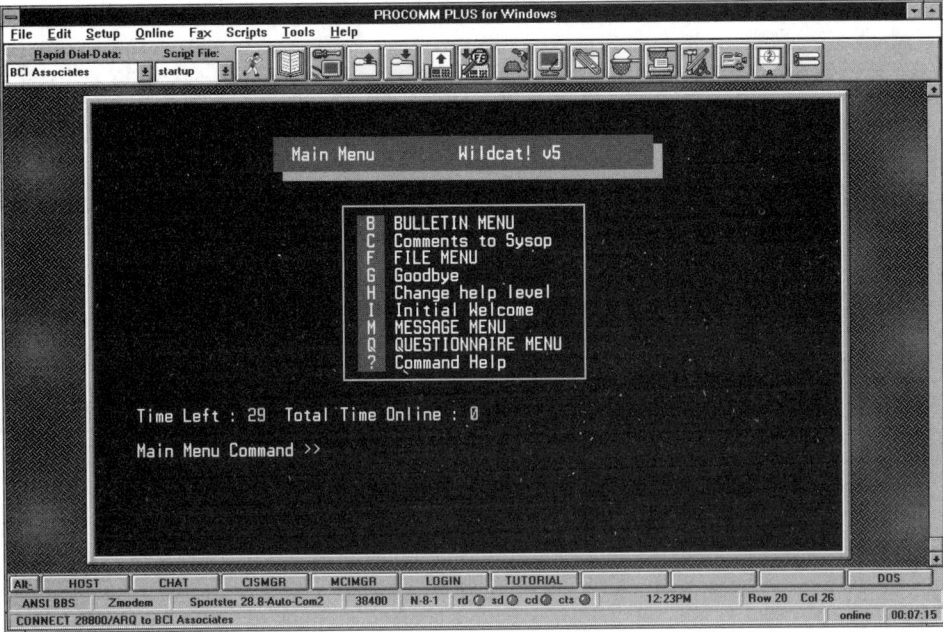

Figure 12.15 Wildcat!'s default main menu.

Another alternative is to set up video teleconferencing. This space age approach to business is big with companies that can afford it, but us small guys have to be resourceful. Enter Wildcat!. With a multiuser server (such as our Web server) and a 16-user license of Wildcat!, you can hold meetings that include folks from all over the country—sans the face-to-face contact of the other two alternatives. To set up Wildcat! for your conferences, double click on the wcConfig icon and then double click on the Conferencing icon. I've modified the rooms for my business, as indicated in Figure 12.16.

Before you can actually hold an online meeting successfully, you need to grant the necessary rights to read, write, and post messages into the conference room.

BBS Email

BBS mail is the same no matter where you go, so I'll just mention in passing that Wildcat! has superb mail functions. With Wildcat!'s full-screen editor, it's very easy to compose and send mail. Simply compose the mail and then press the Escape key to bring up a list of options for processing the mail.

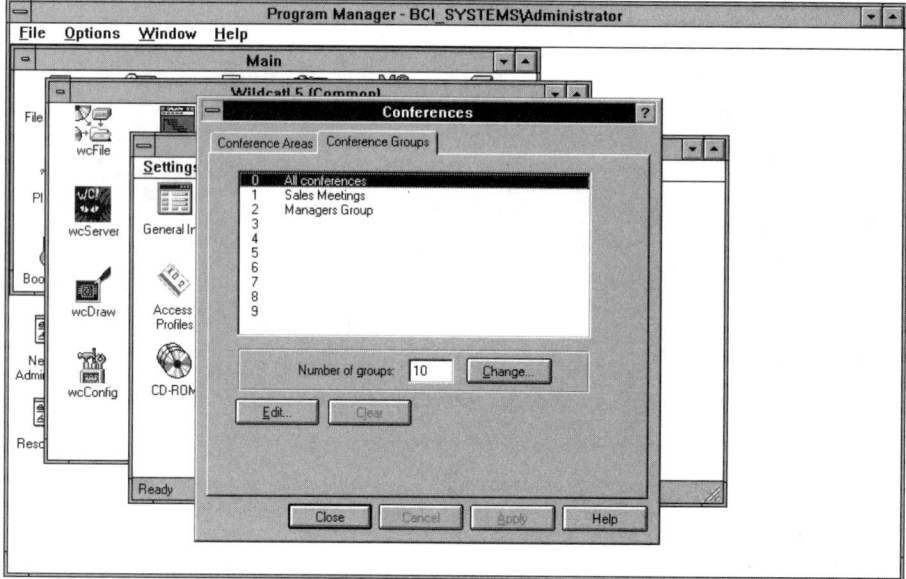

Figure 12.16   Hold online meetings in Wildcat!'s conferencing rooms.

Internet Gateway for NT Server

RAS forms a straightforward connection to NT and clears the way for Internet access for any user that has rights to log on. However, on your NT setup, you'll need a license for each logon user direct to NT by way of RAS because a RAS client is a direct client to NT resources.

On the other hand, Wildcat!'s connections are as an application running on NT, therefore your licensing is not restricted to NT but rather to Wildcat!. If you have a 50-user client pack for NT, and you're running 47 clients, then that all-encompassing conference coming up could be canceled abruptly. However, if you have a 16-user Wildcat! BBS, then your problems are solved. Those same users can now use the Web server to gateway out to the Internet. We'll explore this further after we install Mustang Software's Internet Connectivity Pack.

Installing the Internet Connectivity Pack couldn't be easier. It comes on a single 3½-inch high-density diskette, and installs in fewer than five minutes. Just insert the floppy and execute the Setup program, follow the prompt placing the software in the appropriate directory, and it's done. By default, the ICP is installed into the same directory as Wildcat!, and I suggest you leave it there so the Wildcat! menus can be updated and the whole program can be managed in the same location.

Wildcat! itself has three configuration settings for ICP—FTP access, HTTP Web access, and email access. The proxy servers can act somewhat as a security barrier to outside interference to your site. All you have to do to configure the Internet options is click on the wcConfig icon and then click on the Configuration icon. Open the nodes settings and check the boxes applicable to the type of Internet access that you want to grant to the calling user, as shown in Figure 12.17.

Once you've defined these settings, you'll be up and ready to access the Internet…almost. You'll next need to modify your menu selections to add the Internet choices and any custom code that you want the users to have access to. To make these modifications, you'll need the wcCode Plus Pack developers tools to go with the Internet pack.

While a full discussion is beyond the scope of this chapter, it took me only an afternoon of playtime with wcCode and the ICP to have a full working set of submenus for Wildcat! for the Internet. I was amazed at how easy it

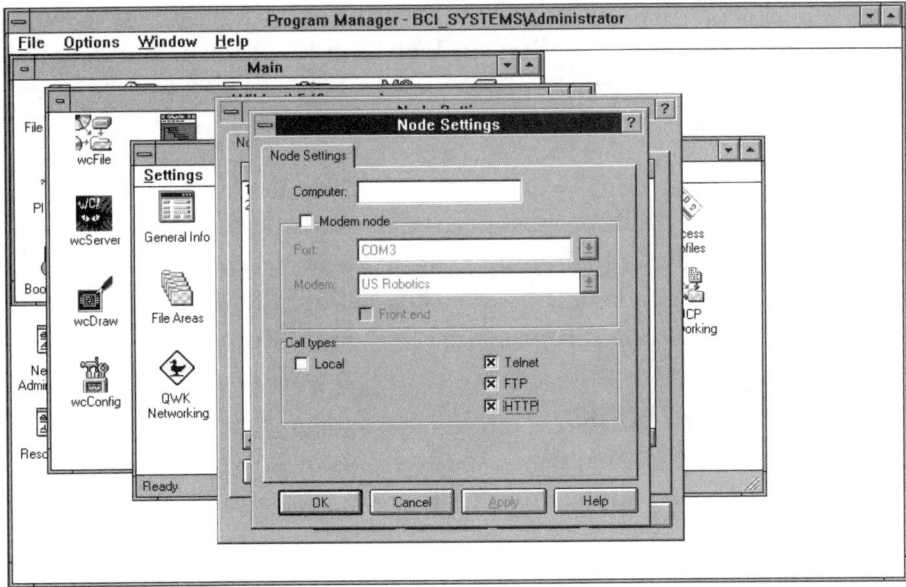

Figure 12.17 Internet configuration options for each node.

was to use the suite of tools for Wildcat! to build a usable set of accessibility functions for my customers. The manuals are clear and concise in their organization, and overall I had the entire BBS site plus custom code for the Internet operational in about six hours. As for the BBS itself, I had it operational in less than 30 minutes, but the total time here reflects installing the Equinox card as well. The Equinox/Wildcat! combination is remarkable all the way around.

NT Server Management Tools

In any Web server, it's always nice to know how the Web server is doing, and who is accessing it. The WebTrends system analyzer can perform these very essential operations. WebTrends uses the log files generated by the various Internet servers running on your machine, and produces clear reports in HTML and GIF file format. WebTrends is compatible with nearly every Web server on the market. You can reach e.g. Software, makers of WebTrends, at *http://www.Webtrends.com* or by phone at 503-294-7025.

Installing WebTrends

Installing WebTrends is quite simple. The program is stored on a single 3½-inch high-density diskette. When you execute the Setup program, it looks for any previous installations of WebTrends, and offers to install the software anywhere you want, as indicated in Figure 12.18. As a matter of habit, I installed my copy in a common directory beneath my other Web server software.

After you've installed the program, install the additional WebTrends software that handles the interpretation of the known Web sites in the world. This portion of WebTrends comes on two 3½-inch high-density diskettes which expand out to one monster file of nearly 5 MB.

Configuring WebTrends

WebTrends allows you to choose a path to a browser for the output files, and define or edit the templates used for the various reports. You can choose from corporate to business to quick summary and technical outputs, as shown in Figure 12.19. You'll find these templates a tremendous help when it comes to troubleshooting a flaky Web server. In the next section, I'll run one of these reports so you can see how helpful they really are.

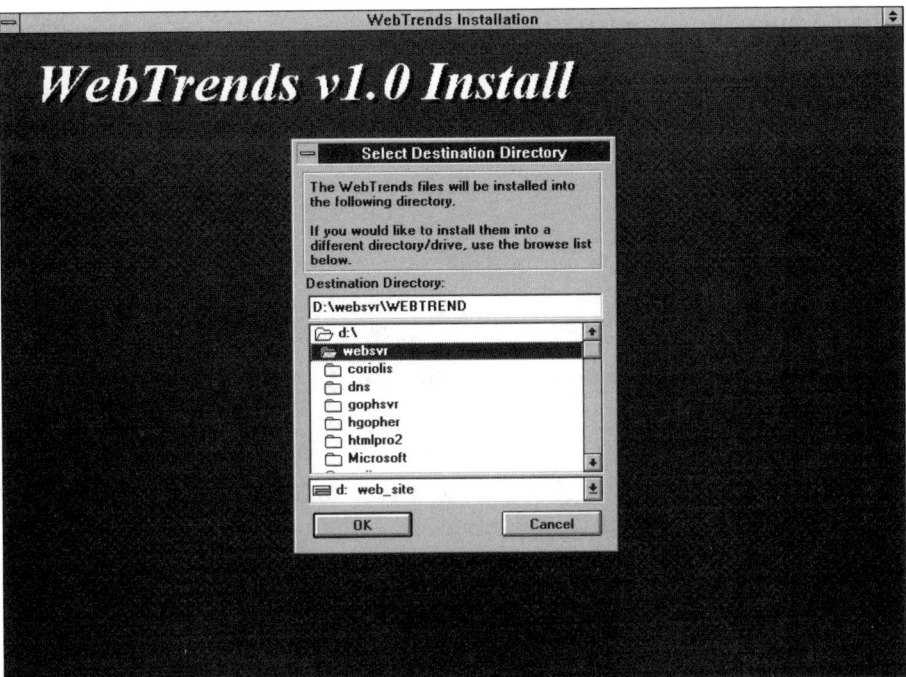

Figure 12.18   Installing WebTrends.

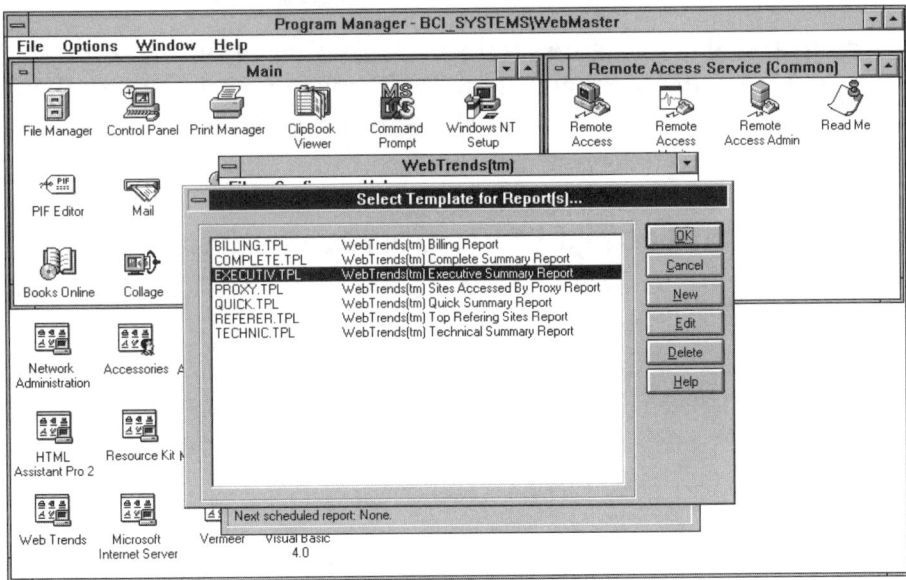

Figure 12.19   WebTrends' template configurations.

I added a template for my business' Web server to cover the accesses to the site by cataloging the log file produced and recorded to the Microsoft Windows NT Server log file. I let my logs go to the standard location beneath the winnt35\system32 directory, so I had to point WebTrends to that location.

Using WebTrends

After you've configured WebTrends, it's only a matter of starting the trend analysis against the log file. Be sure you've specified a Web browser for WebTrends to use to view the report by using the Configure button. Start WebTrends, and then click on the Report button; then select the log file to run the report against.

> *Note: The analysis process takes several minutes for each file process, and can easily take 10 minutes to process on a Pentium 100 if your site is very active. Be patient during the process.*

After the process completes, WebTrends automatically starts the chosen Web browser and presents you with a colorful report and analysis in HTML and GIF file format, as shown in Figure 12.20. The reports are saved, but are regenerated between each session in case the log file changes.

The report is chock full of useful data, as shown in Listing 12.1, showing you which HTML files were accessed, how many times, who accessed each file, and much, much more. This sure beats the heck out of looking over the log files and manually picking out the information you need.

Listing 12.1   NT Log File Source Used by WebTrends

```
204.49.131.51, TSD_Mgr, 4/4/96, 10:46:20, W3SVC, BCI_WEB, 204.49.131.51,
    1061, 344, 3773, 200, 0, GET, /Default.htm, -,
204.49.131.51, TSD_Mgr, 4/4/96, 10:46:21, W3SVC, BCI_WEB, 204.49.131.51,
    942, 278, 2667, 200, 0, GET, /samples/images/backgrnd.gif, -,
204.49.131.51, TSD_Mgr, 4/4/96, 10:46:26, W3SVC, BCI_WEB, 204.49.131.51,
    4907, 276, 4962, 200, 0, GET, /samples/images/h_logo.gif, -,
204.49.131.51, TSD_Mgr, 4/4/96, 10:46:28, W3SVC, BCI_WEB, 204.49.131.51,
    1472, 275, 1067, 200, 0, GET, /samples/images/SPACE.gif, -,
204.49.131.51, TSD_Mgr, 4/4/96, 10:46:28, W3SVC, BCI_WEB, 204.49.131.51,
    130, 276, 3051, 200, 0, GET, /samples/images/h_exec.gif, -,
204.49.131.51, TSD_Mgr, 4/4/96, 10:46:29, W3SVC, BCI_WEB, 204.49.131.51,
    1512, 276, 2635, 200, 0, GET, /samples/images/h_tour.gif, -,
```

```
204.49.131.51, TSD_Mgr, 4/4/96, 10:46:31, W3SVC, BCI_WEB, 204.49.131.51,
    1312, 276, 1047, 200, 0, GET, /samples/images/SPACE2.gif, -,
204.49.131.51, TSD_Mgr, 4/4/96, 10:46:31, W3SVC, BCI_WEB, 204.49.131.51,
    50, 276, 6284, 200, 0, GET, /samples/images/h_samp.gif, -,
204.49.131.51, TSD_Mgr, 4/4/96, 10:46:35, W3SVC, BCI_WEB, 204.49.131.51,
    4306, 278, 3371, 200, 0, GET, /samples/images/h_browse.gif, -,
204.49.131.51, TSD_Mgr, 4/4/96, 10:46:36, W3SVC, BCI_WEB, 204.49.131.51,
    1202, 277, 2982, 200, 0, GET, /samples/images/powered.gif, -,
204.49.131.59, TSD_Mgr, 4/4/96, 10:48:55, W3SVC, BCI_WEB, 204.49.131.51,
    1763, 183, 3749, 200, 0, GET, /Default.htm, -,
204.49.131.59, TSD_Mgr, 4/4/96, 10:48:57, W3SVC, BCI_WEB, 204.49.131.51,
    1873, 229, 2643, 200, 0, GET, /samples/images/backgrnd.gif, -,
204.49.131.59, TSD_Mgr, 4/4/96, 10:48:58, W3SVC, BCI_WEB, 204.49.131.51,
    2744, 226, 1043, 200, 0, GET, /samples/images/SPACE.gif, -,
204.49.131.59, TSD_Mgr, 4/4/96, 10:49:00, W3SVC, BCI_WEB, 204.49.131.51,
    4537, 227, 4938, 200, 0, GET, /samples/images/h_logo.gif, -,
204.49.131.59, TSD_Mgr, 4/4/96, 10:49:01, W3SVC, BCI_WEB, 204.49.131.51,
    5478, 227, 3027, 200, 0, GET, /samples/images/h_exec.gif, -,
204.49.131.59, TSD_Mgr, 4/4/96, 10:49:02, W3SVC, BCI_WEB, 204.49.131.51,
    2724, 227, 2611, 200, 0, GET, /samples/images/h_tour.gif, -,
204.49.131.59, TSD_Mgr, 4/4/96, 10:49:02, W3SVC, BCI_WEB, 204.49.131.51,
    1893, 227, 1023, 200, 0, GET, /samples/images/SPACE2.gif, -,
204.49.131.59, TSD_Mgr, 4/4/96, 10:49:06, W3SVC, BCI_WEB, 204.49.131.51,
    4005, 227, 6260, 200, 0, GET, /samples/images/h_samp.gif, -,
204.49.131.59, TSD_Mgr, 4/4/96, 10:49:06, W3SVC, BCI_WEB, 204.49.131.51,
    4106, 229, 3347, 200, 0, GET, /samples/images/h_browse.gif, -,
```

Now, which would you rather use for your Web server analysis?

General Web Server Administration

Another matter of interest to you in your daily Web server tasks is to ensure that the FTP server disk space doesn't fill up. For that matter, there are several new NT utilities coming to market that watch the disk for usage, allocate and manage space, and handle the hierarchical storage management tasks—moving the least recently used files off to temporary storage such as magneto-optical drives and journalled tape backup. Some servers also use backup mirrored servers to move old files off to conserve disk space.

System Backups

Another task that you'll be performing is a daily (if not more often) backup. Here's an exception to the rule of cheap and effective Web server operations.

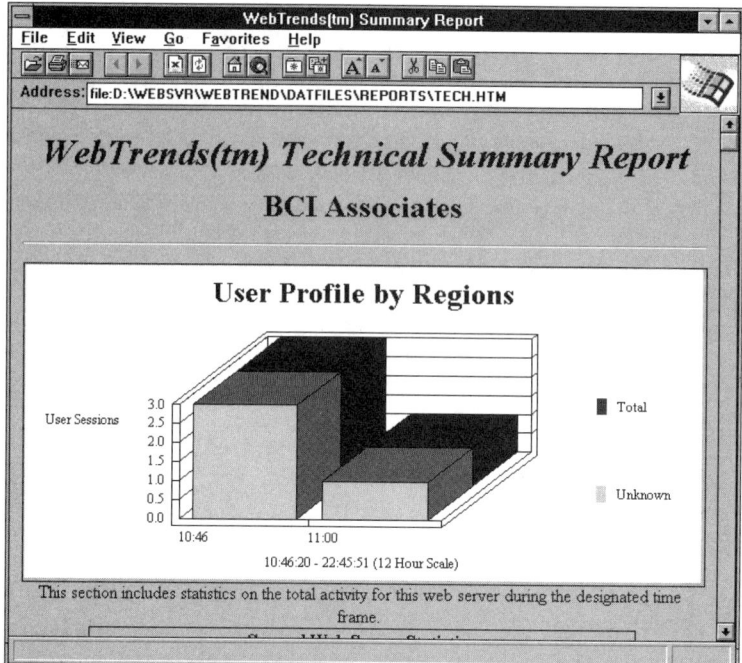

Figure 12.20　WebTrends' analysis report.

If this is your first Web server, then you're likely making the transition from an all-IDE disk-based disk storage system to one that's mixed IDE and SCSI or perhaps all SCSI. If this is the case, then your options for backups on Microsoft Windows NT Server systems have just dropped rather drastically.

You can no longer turn to the standard tape backup solutions for NT because the built-in backup for NT uses QIC drives. QIC drives are nearly impossible to use due to their limited capacity, and thus require a move to SCSI solutions. I've tested several tape backup solutions for my servers, and came up using Conner TapeStor 4000 drives as one method. As I'm writing this, I'm using the Arcada Backup Exec for NT Workstation v6.1, which is working fairly well. It has its quirks, but otherwise seems the best for our configuration.

Emergency Restoration

The last thing that any WebMaster wants to hear is the whining of a crashed disk drive, or the ringing for the umpteenth time of the phone with users asking why they can't get access to the files or Web pages. Even if you're confident it's only a security problem, the whining of the disk still sends shivers from your nose to your toes. A horrid thought, but one that may be faced eventually. Don't say it can't happen to you, because it can. In fact, I was faced with such a situation while writing this book, and it cost me a day to rebuild the server. I had been tinkering around with the software, and had only just reinstalled the server and had not created an emergency diskette. Nor had I saved off the partition configuration...nor done a backup since I had more software to install.

The worst possible situation came true for me, and parts of it might for you some day. One policy we adopted sometime ago was to create two separate backups of the Web server—one for NT and one for the data files of the Web server. Not the applications, just the data files, such as the HTML source, Visual Basic source, and the like. The applications have to be registered with NT when installed, but the data files can reside anywhere and thus can be restored from tape to anywhere. If the server crashes, you'll have to reinstall the applications anyhow, so what's the use in backing them up every time? Not much, really, for a Web server. But lose the source files, such as HTML and CGI pl files, and watch what happens to your job security. Those took hours upon hours to create, and even more to rebuild and test.

Microsoft Windows NT Server installs and remembers what hardware it's running on, and therefore needs to have that same hardware in the backup system.

Hot Spares Ready to Install

One last word of advice for you. If your site becomes critical, meaning that you can't afford to be down for more than several hours, you should have a completely installed and mirrored Web server. This is rather expensive as a backup mechanism, so if your company needs the emergency support, but can't afford it, you have an alternative: Use another server to install the software onto another hard drive, so at least the operating system is ready to accept the Web server. In fact, some even install all of the Web server software as well as applications.

If you take this approach for emergency services, be sure to observe software licensing.

Summary

In this chapter, we covered the hazards and fun you can have taking care of the Web server. Because you already knew how to manage Microsoft Windows NT Server, I opted to show you how to use alternative communications functions to access and manage the server, using Wildcat! BBS software. For each rock in the road, there's a way to smooth out the ride. WebTrends showed you how to find those rocks in the Web server road and let you remove them without cutting yourself to shreds. In the next chapter, I'll delve into Web server and NT security issues as they apply to your site.

Web and NT Server Security Models

Security is a very important part of any computing environment. The fun and exploratory nature of the Web brings with it new security issues, including virus attacks and intrusion. In this chapter I'll be focusing on the security concerns of your Web server in general. Specifically, we'll cover:

- The Department of Defense (DoD) security standards

- Standard NT Server security types and applications

- Implementing NT's C2 Security Level

- Firewall Security Models

- The Reverse DNS Lookup Model as a Security Measure

This order of approach should give you an introductory level overview of security measures from a layman's perspective. While each of these topics has a much deeper explanation, due to space limitations, I'll only be presenting the core technology of each.

Established DoD Security Levels

The Internet, by design, is a wide-open frontier given to the vices and virtues of the people inhabiting cyberspace.

As such, it has been raided and pillaged on numerous occasions. Any site supervisor worth his or her salt will tell you horror stories of what has—or almost has—happened with an intrusion or unauthorized usage of the systems. Whatever the cause, any network used for outside connectivity has, once upon a time, been subjected to this ill. And no one wants to be at an intruder's mercy.

DoD security is arranged into four progressively tighter security realms— D, C, B, and A. Also, with each increase in security comes a corresponding increase in cost to implement that level.

Level D

Level D is the least secure of any computing environment. In fact, there's no security at all. The whole system or network is wide open for anyone to see and use. Typically, this is a regular DOS-based or Windows-based computer. On the network, the users have open access to the server's applications, and even password security is not used. There is no way to discern who is using the computer at a given time..

Level C

Level C has two sublevels of coverage—C1 and C2. C1 is the next level up the security chain because the username and password pair of authentication is used for validation. The system administrator uses the NOS tools to assign file and directory access attributes for each user. The administrator may use group profiles for mass rights and permissions settings, remote system access, and printer rights. However, the system administrator has global access throughout the entire system, and there's no tracking mechanism to say what was changed or otherwise altered by the administrator. This level has another hole in it, since any user with the administrative password can access the system globally without differentiation from another administrator.

Level C2 addresses these issues, and C2 is what Microsoft Windows NT Server implements. C2 restricts users' access to only those areas of the network that they have rights to *and* also restricts permissions, allowing users to reach only the files explicitly open to them. In other words, a user might have the right to go to a certain directory and view the files, but this user might not have the permissions granted to use the files. If this user does have the permissions, and begins using these files, the user leaves an audit trail that NT Server puts into the log file as a record of access, as indicated in Listing 13.1.

Listing 13.1   NT Authentication Audit Trail

```
5/6/96  10:21:40 AM  Print  Information  None  10  sysmgrjb  BCI_PDC
     Document 15, Microsoft Word - PERMISS.DOC owned by sysmgrjb was
     printed on Domain Laser via port LPT1:. Size in bytes: 82114; pages
     printed: 2
5/6/96  8:52:44 AM  Print  Information  None  10  sysmgrjb  BCI_PDC
     Document 14, Microsoft Word - chap13.doc owned by sysmgrjb was printed
     on Domain Laser via port LPT1:. Size in bytes: 70742; pages printed: 2
5/5/96  8:34:59 PM  NETLOGON  Information  None  5711  N/A  BCI_PDC  The
     partial synchronization request from the server BCI_WEB completed
     successfully. 1 changes(s) has(have) been returned to the caller.
5/5/96  12:17:57 PM  Print  Information  None  10  sysmgrjb  BCI_PDC
     Document 8, Microsoft Word - chap14.doc owned by sysmgrjb was printed
     on Domain Laser via port LPT1:. Size in bytes: 347417; pages printed: 6
5/5/96  10:54:57 AM  Print  Information  None  10  sysmgrjb  BCI_PDC
     Document 7, Microsoft Word - chap14.doc owned by sysmgrjb was printed
     on Domain Laser via port LPT1:. Size in bytes: 179875; pages printed: 4
5/5/96  12:52:09 AM  NETLOGON  Information  None  5711  N/A  BCI_PDC  The
     partial synchronization request from the server BCI_WEB completed
     successfully. 1 changes(s) has(have) been returned to the caller.
5/4/96  9:48:47 PM  Print  Information  None  10  sysmgrjb  BCI_PDC
     Document 6, Microsoft Word - chap12.doc owned by sysmgrjb was printed
     on Domain Laser via port LPT1:. Size in bytes: 1210740; pages
     printed: 20
5/4/96  8:35:26 PM  Print  Information  None  10  WebMaster  BCI_PDC
     Document 5, Collage Complete owned by WebMaster was printed on Domain
     Laser via port LPT1:. Size in bytes: 251369; pages printed: 1
5/4/96  8:13:26 PM  NETLOGON  Information  None  5711  N/A  BCI_PDC  The
     partial synchronization request from the server BCI_WEB completed
     successfully. 1 changes(s) has(have) been returned to the caller.
5/4/96  8:00:02 PM  NETLOGON  Error  None  5722  N/A  BCI_PDC  The
     session setup from the computer HOME_SVR failed to authenticate. The
     name of the account referenced in the security database is
     HOME_SYSTEMS$. The following error occurred: Access is denied.
```

Take a look at the first few entries. First, the date and time are inserted along with the reason for the entry. Farther along is the username, sysmgrjb, followed by the domain controller that was recording the event, BCI_PDC.

The rest of the entry is self explanatory. This kind of information is valuable because you know exactly who did what while they were logged in. Even the system administrator gets logged into this system, which cannot be altered. There are, however, alterable events, called audit options, that affect all users. The system administrator is responsible for defining these options.

To define the auditing specifications, go to the Administrative program group, then open the User Manager for Domains program. Click on Policies|Audit to display the audit options shown in Figure 13.1.

NT SERVER TIP

If you try to track the entire world's events, then the size of the event file will match it! It's not unreasonable for a one week "System" log to reach 2 MB in size for a 10-user network. To control the size of log files, open the Administrative Tools group, star the Event Viewer, and then click on Log|Log Settings. Make the necessary changes to the sizes and control of the log files, as shown in Figure 13.2.

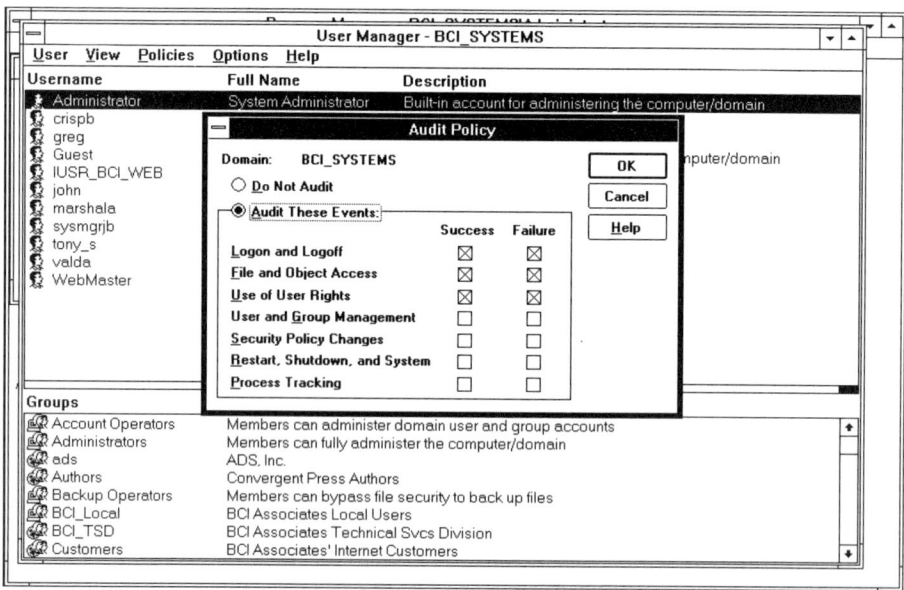

Figure 13.1   Setting the audit options.

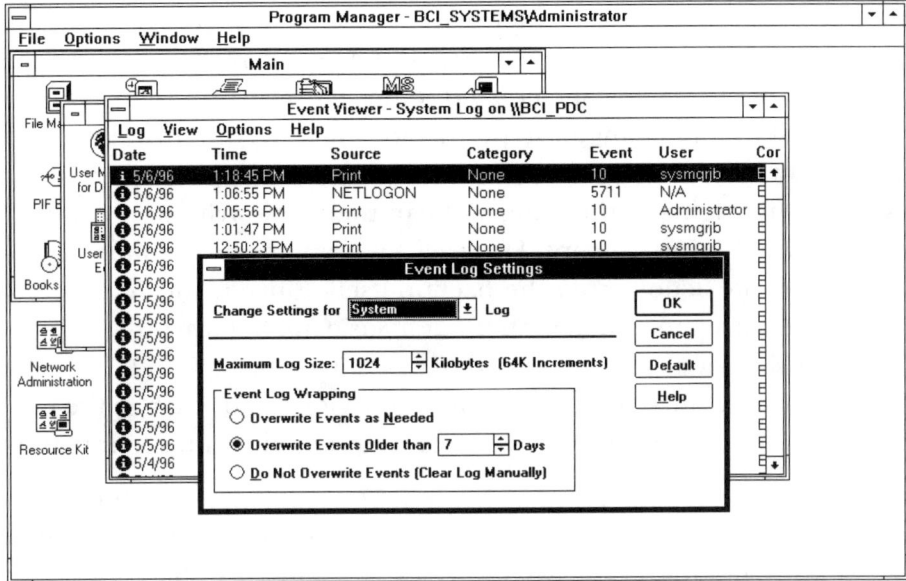

Figure 13.2 Log file size settings.

A little later in this chapter, I'll show you how to implement C2 level security on NT Server, but for now, we're going to continue on with our discussion of the DoD security model.

Level B

Level B security includes three sublevels to address increasing orders of security. Above C2, the next tightest level is B1, which says that an object—usually a file or directory but it can be a piece of equipment such as a tape drive—under mandatory control by the system will not allow the owner to change any of the permissions of the object. For instance, if one of the computer operators at your site is classified as the owner of a tape, and the tape drive has read and write permissions so backups can be done, then the operator can't change the permissions of the tape drive so that a different tape could be used to overwrite the operating system with different rights.

An Example of B1 Security

An example will be helpful. Let's say that Susie created a tape called Accounting (and is therefore classified as the "Owner" of that reel of tape), and Chuckie, as the system administrator, creates a reel of tape called "Master

OS." Access to tape drives is under strict control of the MIS group, usually. When Susie logs into the system to access the tape drive, she only has permissions to use tapes that she created under B1 security (the Accounting tape), but she can't change the permissions or the contents of the tape. She can add more backup data to the drive because the system knows she has ownership rights to the tape, and can therefore write to the tape for the purpose of doing backups. However, she can't erase the tape because that's a separate action from the backup itself. Since Chuckie's tape has privileged information on it, even though Susie might have physical access to the tape, she doesn't have rights to the contents of the tape and is therefore unable to restore the operating system. Such a job might change the rights and permissions of the entire system, thereby opening it up to intrusion!

Oh, in case you might be wondering where the good 'ol U.S. military security falls in this scheme of things, it's right here in B1 level. I could tell you how and why, but then I'd have to shoot you…and burn the book!

B2 Security

Level B2 says that every object in the domain must have a label. For instance, the disk drive that contains the operating system might be called "BOOT DISK" and the accounting department could be named "THE MONEY PIT." This approach further decreases the likelihood of mismanaged security rights because a user's rights and permissions would be indelibly tied to the object. Additionally, object-to-object security can now be formed by placing some objects in a hierarchical tree of control.

B3 Security—Adding Hardware

Level B3 is where you start getting into a more expensive secured environment. When secure systems are tightened up to the B3 level, you can be assured that most everyone has a security clearance and has been through an extensive background check. In the B3 level, specialized hardware is used to enforce security accesses to the system, as shown in Figure 13.3. One way this security level is employed is on clustered systems where disk drives are shared between servers. Using this approach, a circuit card programmed to allow access from specific domains is installed. For even tighter security, cards can be programmed at the user level, but this technique is definitely expensive!

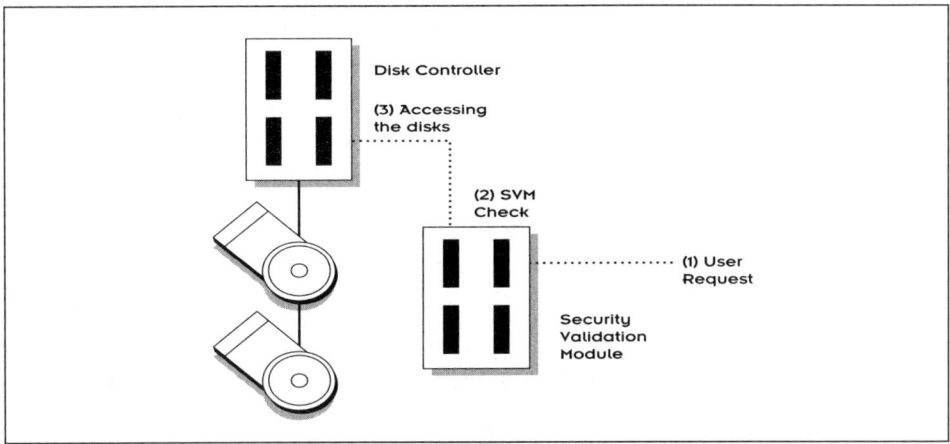

Figure 13.3   Hardware-controlled security access.

The procedure is usually classified or deeply confidential, but follows these general guidelines:

1. The user makes a disk request—like storing a file—which then goes to the security validation module (SVM).

2. The SVM card performs a lookup of the requestor's identification, and compares it to the list of authorized users.

3. A match allows the requested operation to be completed. An unauthorized request results in activation of a security alert or a log entry. (Personally, I think the best approach would be to install an ejection seat, which lifts off when unauthorized requests come in!)

Level A

This is the most stringent level of DoD security and is used by such government offices as the U.S. Postal Service for securing certified and registered mail. At this level, the SVM card discussed earlier is manufactured under tight control and the software that is used to program the card is written by programmers with high-level security clearances, and who earn a skijillion-dollar-a-year salary. The company that performs this work is usually a DoD contractor that has close security ties with our government. Several that come to mind are General Electric, Martin-Marietta, Loral Federal Systems, and Ford Aerospace.

Once manufactured and programmed, the SVM card is shipped from the vendor under tightly controlled routes of travel. The hardware that uses the card is closely monitored during transit, and the firmware circuits used to store the user database are closely guarded under lock and key.

Normal NT Security Issues

Now that you understand the government security features and functions associated with computers, its time to see how this applies to Microsoft Windows NT Server's security. If you already know the details of NT's security, you might want to skip this section and go directly to *Implementing C2-Style Security*.

User-Level Security

Any user connecting to NT has to pass some sort of security parameters within the server, whether it be login rights or file attributes. It's easy enough to define and control users by way of the User Manager for Groups function. I won't go into each right or permission for NT—you can refer to the Microsoft Windows NT Server Resource Kit for a deeper explanation—but we'll discuss the more important features.

Go to your server and start the User Manager. Select any one of the users on your system, and then click on User|Properties to see this person's attributes. All of these options cause some sort of restriction to be placed upon the user, whether it be the time and day that the user can log in, group permissions the user has, or which PCs the user can use to log into the network.

Notice the five checkboxes on the left side. The very bottom is not available now, but is automatically checked if the account gets locked. If that occurs, you'll have to uncheck this option to allow the user back into the network.

Group Security

Plan out your groups carefully, or you might wind up giving out full system admin access to guest users!

I usually don't start out a section with a warning, but this one is well worth it. Most administrators don't really think about the overall security issues and how they apply to users, or to collective groups of users, until they start adding users to the NT domain. I wholeheartedly recommend that you plan your network security on paper before you actually enforce it, to prevent security breeches farther down the road. Let's take a look at an example.

In my work with The Microsoft Network as a Category manager, I had rights to perform certain tasks closely related to the system administration of a server. Some of the other managers on the service had similar rights, but only for other areas specific to their job. As a result, their rights were a subset of mine. After changes had been made in the service, I noticed that these other managers now had rights into my functional area. There was no reason for this change. Investigating the problem uncovered a mistake in group rights setup, as shown in Figure 13.4. The zigzag lines show where the accidental rights were granted to a Forum manager. The private rights for the Category manager, indicated by the little boxes, were normally granted in an overlapping fashion, but were cut up by the improper group rights selection. Of course, this was a mistake; with some 700 users on the server, a mistake was bound to happen.

There's no telling how long this condition existed, but it was easy to spot when it occurred. The point is to be very careful and have your server's rights and user rights assignments clearly documented. Had the administrators planned security from the beginning, this problem would never have occurred.

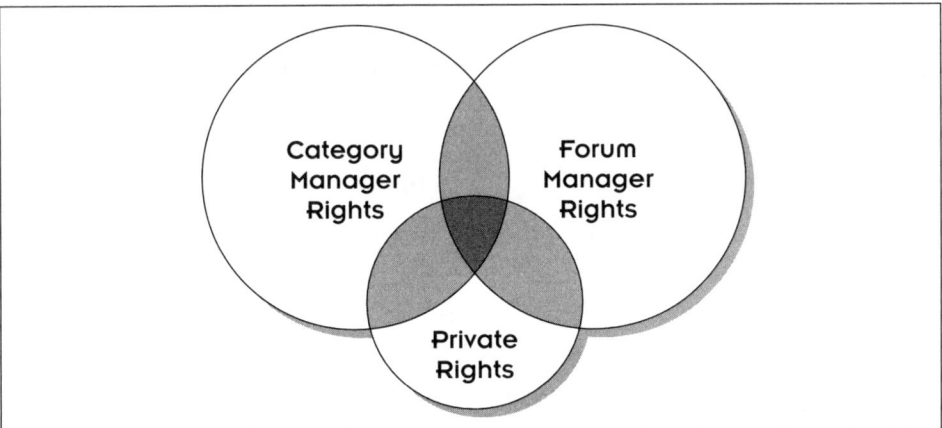

Figure 13.4   Various group rights overlapping.

NT Share Security

"Shares" is a method that NT uses (as do other operating systems) to make server resources available to the users in a controlled manner. A share can be a printer, or it can be an entire server's disk space, including the NT operating system data areas. The share tells NT which users are authorized to access the resource, and how they're allowed to access it—reading it, writing to it, or the ability to add or delete directories.

As long as a share is in force, any user connecting to the server will be able to see the share even if the user doesn't have the proper permissions set to access the data within that share. These shared resources have been known to open a server to intrusive users, because if a hacker can see it, he then knows the name of what he's trying to break into.

The key issue here is to grant access and the use of shared resources to only those users that use the data or applications. Figure 13.5 shows a share that forms an aggregation of the applications used for my Web server. In one fell swoop, I've limited the users to one controlled area of the server.

The drawback to a situation like this is that the security model is less flexible because so many applications are managed by the share. The up side is that all I have to do is change the permissions for the individual applications within the share to deny access to anyone I choose. The plus side is that when I map a drive letter to this server share, only one letter is used. My PC uses drive letters C through K for hard-drive partitions and optical drives, so I'm automatically using lots of drive letters. Because I'm the system administrator for four networks, I have drive letters mapped to three of these servers, resulting in the use of seven more drive letters! Figure 13.6 shows how I manage shared resources on multiple servers.

The more group shares that you create, the more demands you place on the server, and the more chance of a security problem cropping up as a result of the users getting mapped to multiple shares. When this happens, some user is likely to have a non-working application directory, or an administrator might goof, granting the wrong (or too many) permissions.

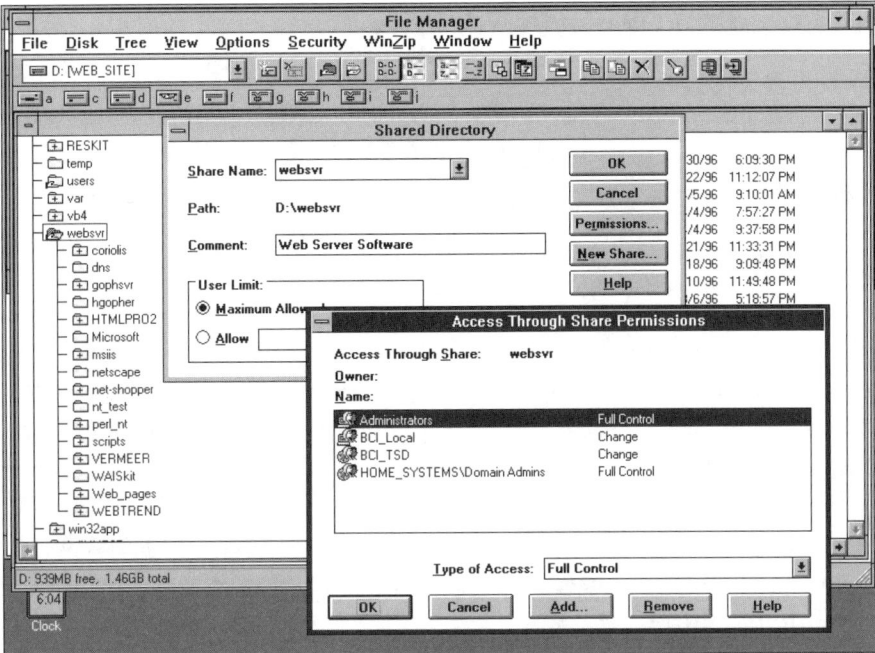

Figure 13.5   Limiting access with a shared location.

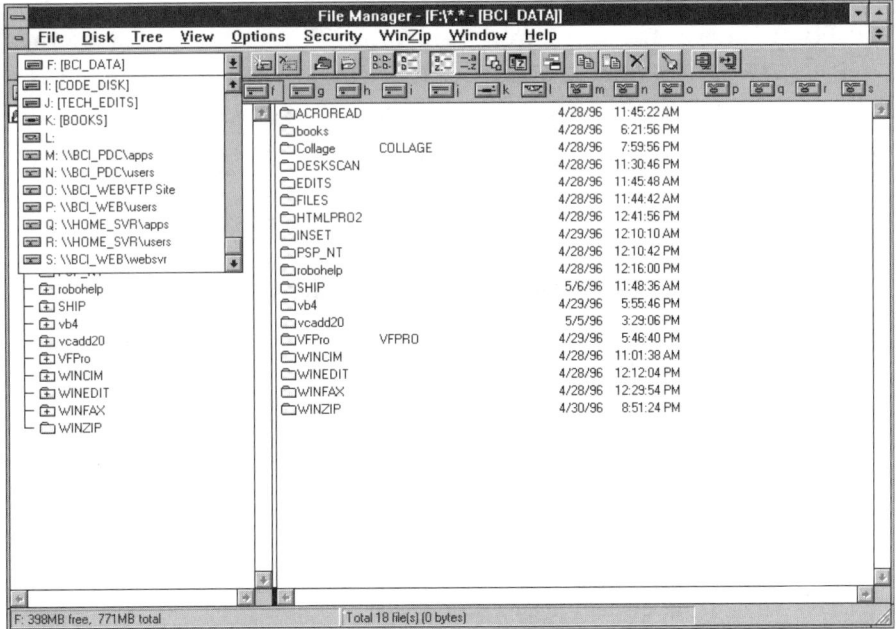

Figure 13.6   Multiple server shared resources.

Implementing C2-Style Security

Now that we've gone over basic NT security issues, let's focus on implementing the C2 security level. Just in case you didn't know, you can also implement this security level in an NT Workstation, providing the partitions are running NTFS.

What C2 Is

C2 is a comparable balance between resources that a user owns if their PC runs NT, and the requirements to secure an operating environment to the level that intruders can be effectively denied access. It is a methodology that is straightforward for the network administrator who understands security, networks, access controls, and systematical approaches to user controls. If you follow the C2 guidelines to the letter, then you'll most likely have a server secure enough for the most demanding and intrusive users or computer fiends. In order to implement C2, your server must meet the requirements shown in Figure 13.7.

> *Note: I won't be detailing each of these requirements. For a more detailed explanation, refer to the Microsoft Windows NT Server Resource Kit for v3.51.*

Notice that each of the functions shown in the figure has a lock icon displayed to the left of the function name. If the icon is in the unlocked position, then the NT function will not allow C2 to be implemented. If the icon is in the locked position, then the function meets C2 requirements.

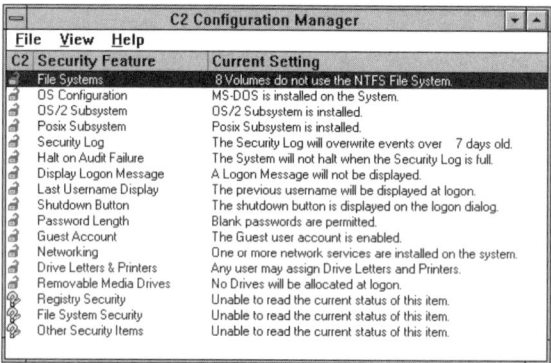

Figure 13.7 C2 security implementation details.

In this case, nothing about this NT Workstation meets the C2 security level. As a comparison, I implemented partial C2 level security, shown in Figure 13.8, on my domain server to show you the difference.

To fully secure a server to the C2 level, the server can't be running any software that opens a hole to intruders, such as a DOS partition where a user could access it by booting the server from a DOS floppy and seeing the partition.

And What C2 Isn't

Looking at all of the C2 requirements and understanding what they do might give you the idea that a fully C2-compliant server is the cat's meow for denying intrusion. C2 is meant to provide the most stable and secure server possible given the type of computers we use today, but it can't possibly anticipate every new development in the world of viruses and hackers. I'm not saying that Microsoft's implementation of C2 doesn't work—it truly deters all but the most adamant intruder from breaking into the server—but just be aware that it is not foolproof.

The Web is an open atmosphere and subject to break-ins due to its programmatical nature. CGI and programming tools like C++ are so powerful that in capable hands virtually any login security can be broken given enough time and computational power. You need to maintain your vigil with the users for passwords and physical access to the server. The moral to this story is: Don't count on C2 to keep your computing world safe.

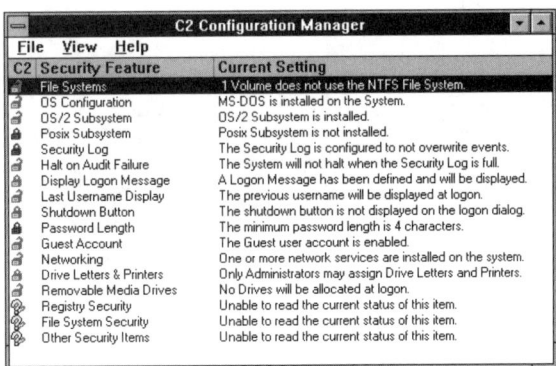

Figure 13.8 Partial C2 security employed.

Firewall Security

The last topic I'd like to share with you in the security department is the use of firewalls to help secure an entire network. A firewall can be thought of as a guard shack at an international border crossing. When you cross from one country to another, you have to present a passport to the guards. If you have the proper credentials, you're let through; otherwise, you're refused passage. Firewalls do the same, only with a TCP/IP address of the source and destination computers.

A Simple Firewall

Placing multiple network interface cards in the same computer, as shown in Figure 13.9, is one of the simplest firewalls you can build. This technique creates a method of internal routing, which is sometimes preferable to purchasing an expensive external router, to guide and direct network traffic between network segments. However, within NT you can use software to perform network routing between the networks.

This approach, sometimes referred to as a "poor man's router" reduces the load on a server by keeping network traffic for one segment to that segment only, and routing traffic to other segments only when it's required. The same technique can be employed to segment external Internet traffic from the internal business network, as shown in Figure 13.10.

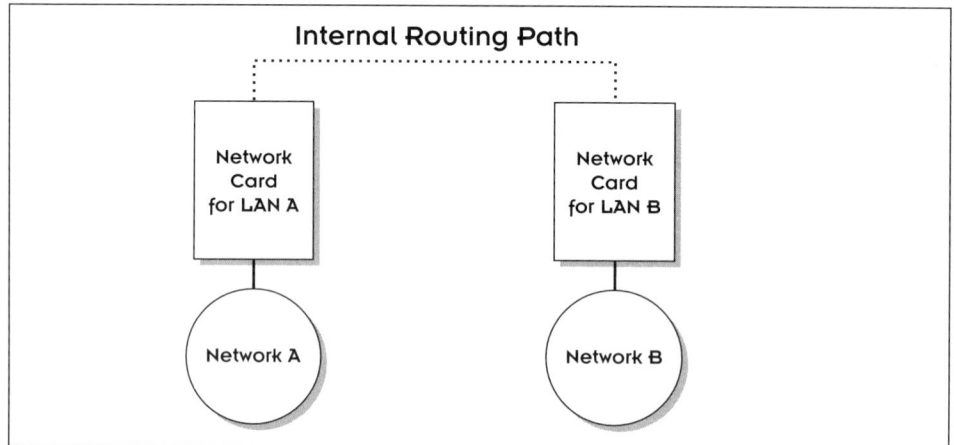

Figure 13.9   Using multiple network cards in a server.

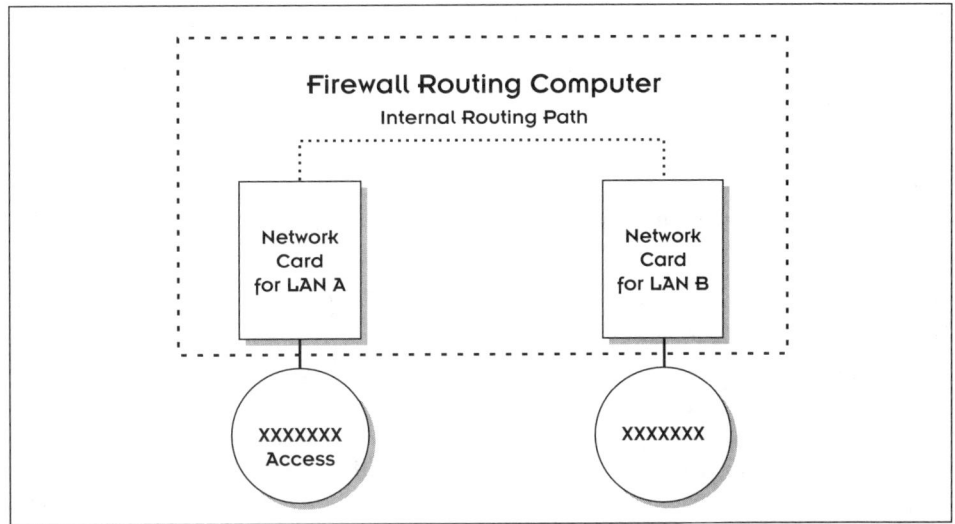

Figure 13.10   Separating external and internal networks.

Another technique is to set up a computer as a firewall and install hosting software to further secure the networks. At the time I wrote this chapter, I was unable to locate host software for firewall agents to perform this function solely and dedicated. All of the solutions I found—and there were plenty of them—were Unix-based.

Enhanced Firewalls

If you really need to secure your internal network and retain connectivity to the Internet, then you might consider implementing a *bastion host*. This double layer of protection is run in conjunction with a router, and screens or remaps the TCP/IP addresses to the *Media Access Control* (MAC) layer addresses of the network card of the workstation that resides on the internal network. The MAC layer is the second lowest layer in a network card's interface, next to the physical connection of the cabling. The basic theory is to use the model shown in Figure 13.10, and add a router between the firewall computer and the external connection. This router serves to filter the incoming traffic first, and then forward the traffic that passed the filter on to the firewall computer. This strategy forms a very secure two-way barrier to external intrusion.

Double Firewalls, Proxy Servers, and Sacrificial Hosts

If all of this is still not enough for you, and you absolutely must have a completely secure environment *and* tie your internal networks to the Internet, you still have an option. Such options, however, do not come cheaply. This system is used to store and forward incoming packets after having been filtered by the outside router and the outside firewall host. If the outside router says that the incoming data passes the filtering test, then the packets are sent to the outside firewall. Once this far, the packets can be interpreted by the outside host computer, commonly called a *sacrificial host*. If anything goes wrong, there's no great loss. Sure, the Web server comes down, but the internal networks are saved.

If nothing goes wrong, then the inside firewall serves as a proxy server to interpret and pass on only the packets that pass the filtering test to make the trip to the internal network. This method provides a double layer of protection by creating two avenues of opportunity for the administrator to stop intrusions. This setup is normally all that an organization could expect to create for the ultimate in C2 security. Beyond this, the B level of security demands the use of fiber optics and cryptological devices to scramble the packets using the Data Encryption Standard (DES) created by the U.S. government. DES encryption is commonly used in functions where the very best in protection is required, and is so good that it can't be legally exported outside of the U.S. In fact, several excellent utilities, such as PCTools for Windows, employ encryption algorithms that cause the application to be distributable only in the U.S.

Summary

In this chapter, we've taken a slight detour from normal Web functions to look at server security. I've introduced you to the different levels of security that you can use to implement a protective scheme for your Web server and internal networks. I wish I had time and space to go on; security is so important that I could write an entire book on the subject. Here's to a secure Web site and a productive future for it.

14

Avoiding Disaster— Troubleshooting Tips for Your Web Server

Any electronic or electrical device is subject to failing at any time, and without warning. And for all of us who work with computers, this statement couldn't be truer. (We have the empty Tylenol bottles to prove it!) Computers fail for many reasons, but few methods—especially effective ones—exist to prevent failures. Unfortunately, electrical failure is not the only problem you could encounter. Disaster lurks around every dark corner in the computer world. What exactly do I mean by disaster? Well, when speaking of computers, disaster generally falls into these categories:

- Power failures—expected and unexpected

- Lost air cooling

- Theft of equipment

- Vandalism or sabotage

- Virus attacks

You can hope that such things never happen to you (and I hope they don't too), but if and when you find yourself in a situation like the ones described here, you need to be prepared. This chapter is designed to show you how to respond to disasters. Some techniques show you how to prevent disaster before it happens, while others simply help you to recover as quickly and painlessly as possible after a disaster has occurred.

Preventable Power Outages

Details, details. When you plan a Web site, details should be your main concern. Forgetting tiny details can easily result in major disaster. Don't believe me? Well then I have a horror story for you, and I hope it scares the beejeebies out of you!

An experienced network administrator installed a new UPS unit on the network server that was to begin doing double duty as the company's Web server. A smart move to be sure. He followed all of the standard precautions during the installation. He installed the UPS software and even went to the Control Panel and made the proper settings via the UPS program. NT now knew that the UPS was there, and all looked fine. A week later, as he came into the computer room, the hairs on the back of his neck prickled. He smelled smoke. Frantically chasing down the source of the burning, he discovered that the UPS was fried and the server was shut down. He breathed a collective sigh of relief knowing that the UPS did its job. But wait...there's more (I told you this was a horror story). He soon discovered that not only did the UPS fry, so did various parts of his server!

As he began to decide if he should use a silver platter or a ceramic one to serve up his head to the CFO, he remembered that the UPS warranty covered any attached equipment up to $25,000 in replacement value. Whew! His blood pressure began to inch back down. This was a close call. So, he called the UPS vendor, reported the claim, and the vendor dispatched a local technician to investigate the problem (when money is involved, vendor's never just say I'm sorry!). Promising swift turnaround of the paperwork, the technician began his investigation, and the network administrator worked on getting the spare server operational.

(Now you can start humming the *Jaws* theme.) When the technician finished, he laid some pretty bad news on the administrator—the warranty is null and void! The UPS was connected into a power source that was not properly grounded, had a 15 volt difference of potential between the neutral leg and ground, and had an intermediate power extension running off of it that was not NEMA rated. Any one of these three problems was enough to void the warranty, and the UPS destruction was all but assured. These oversights also answered the nagging questions of erratic server problems that prompted the company to buy the UPS in the first place.

See what I meant by details? This real-life disaster shows that gremlins hide in every aspect of your computer installation. The power infrastructure of your site may run a typewriter and coffee pot just fine, but computers are very sensitive to power problems. *Have your grounding system checked and validated once a year.* If your equipment is in an office complex, ask the building manager to survey the power structure for problems. Of course, this is just one example. Other problems lay waiting to pounce on you. Did you remember to connect the serial cable between the UPS and the physical server? Did you install the proper software to control the shutdown of the server when the UPS senses a power loss? Of course you did. Because you know now that preventive medicine is your best bet to a long and healthy life for your Web server.

Temperature Induced Disasters

Another silent bombshell waiting for the opportune (or inopportune, as it were) moment to strike is searing temperature within the computer case and throughout the server. Every component generates heat at different levels of intensity, and it's all cumulative. The end result is a gradual degradation of performance in every component. To what degree (pardon the pun!) this temperature affects performance is somewhat of a mystery. However, the following sections provide you with methods of reducing this heat and show you where cooling can be best applied.

Direct Equipment Cooling

Direct cooling refers to the usage of heat sinks and cooling fans to reduce or eliminate heat. Most of you recognize that heat sink and cooling fan combinations exist for processors, but did you know this technique is also available for the I/O cards? All you have to do is mount two three-inch fans on a full length card to circulate the air. This approach breaks up the hot spots between the cards and gets the hot air rising to the top of the case faster.

The same is true for hard drives. Vendors are recognizing the need for additional cooling in situations—like those common to RAID drive installations—where many drives are installed one on top of the other creating one massive heat generator. One cooling solution is the use of 1½-inch fans that blow air onto the drive stack, as shown in Figure 14.1. Not meant to explicitly cool the drives, the fan merely circulates the air from the case and into the drive stack, resulting in a disruption of the built-up heat. In most server- size cases, there's ample room to mount these fans.

Indirect Cooling

Now that you've got the device cooling taken care of, what's the purpose of recirculating the same old hot air? In the majority of tower cases, the power supply is located in the top rear of the case with its own cooling fan. What a lot of folks don't realize is that the heat that rises to the top of the case is exhausted by being drawn into the power supply and blown out the back. The power supply is therefore being heated further by the internal heat generated by components. Not that the power supply runs cool on its own, but the additional heat isn't helping the power supply at all. In fact, the extra heat causes the power supply to run less efficiently.

So you can see, there needs to be a way to reduce the heat everywhere before something melts down Chernyoble-style. You can accomplish this type of heat reduction using several techniques, both inexpensive and otherwise. Full size tower cases built today routinely have a prebuilt place in the top of the case for a second fan to be added, drawing out the heat of the case, and not through the power supply.

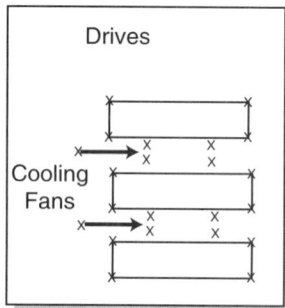

Figure 14.1 Direct cooling methods.

Yet another way is by the use of thermoelectric cooling plates that transfer heat from one surface to another. Although these plates are meant to be installed directly onto a device, they can also be installed onto the case in a location that causes cool air to be generated. Of course, you wouldn't want to install one of these directly onto a hard drive, but indirect case cooling works great.

Rack-Mounted Systems

Rack-mounted systems are the most expensive proposition, but they offer the greatest benefits. When your computer facilities grow to include several servers, then perhaps you'd be better served (pardon the pun!) by installing your computers into floor-mounted standup racks. These industry-standard devices are 19-inch-wide racks that allow you to mount the computer into a special chassis drawer that slides in and out on rails. All the computer components, including drives, are mounted inside this case. The case has vents and two cooling fans (in the rear of the case) that exhaust the air out the back while causing fresh air to be drawn into the front of the case.

When rack-mounted cases and cabinets like this are used, you can then use air conditioners to blow cool air through the facility's sub-floor computer room. What's a sub-floor, you ask? In a standard room setup where computers are sitting on the floor, the air they get is regular room-ambient air. A sub-floor computer room is one in which the computers sit on a false floor that is raised about one foot above the concrete floor by way of special floor mounts as shown in Figure 14.2. The rack-mounted equipment sits directly over an opening in the false floor, allowing the cool air to flow into the bottom of the cabinet, and circulating fans bring the cool air into the racked equipment. Pretty spiffy setup, eh?

In this type of setup, sensors arranged all around the equipment are set to monitor both air flow and temperature. If either gets out of whack, you could be notified automatically by beeper, or have the equipment shut down to prevent possible damage.

Don't have the money to build a raised floor? Don't fret, another solution exists! If you want to use rack-mounted servers, then you might want to explore floor-mounted miniature air conditioners. These little gems are

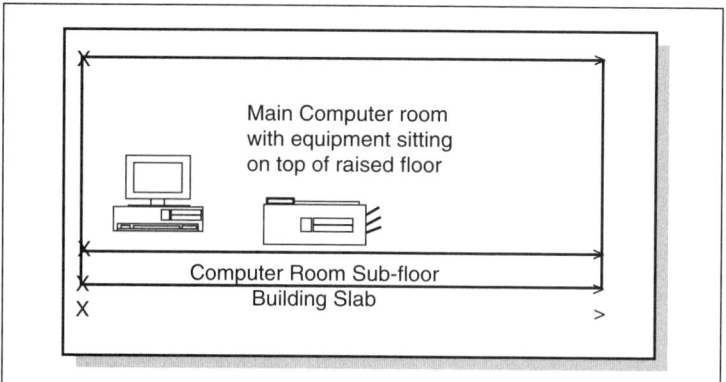

Figure 14.2 A sub-floor computer room provides additional cooling to computers.

rated in capacities ranging from 300 to 5000 BTUs, which is more than enough for a single rack. Operating on 120 VAC power, they produce enough cold air to satisfy a full rack of equipment.

The Sticky Finger Syndrome

Any computer operation is subject to the less pleasurable moments in computing life such as theft. These kinds of disasters leave you holding the bag with no possible way out, period. Pilferage in a computer room may or may not be a problem in your office, but rest assured it does happen in many locations. It could be nothing more than the loss of a floppy drive or a set of mounting rails for a hard drive, but some thieves pride themselves on their ability to pocket the big stuff. Unfortunately, many sites don't even think of the possible consequences of this event.

Lockable Hard Drives

If a hard drive is installed into a server, how can it be lockable? Open the case and there's the drive. True, but more high-end servers are incorporating the use of removable and hot swappable drives. Actually, using these drive types kills two birds with one stone. Not only can you prevent theft by locking the drive, but if one fails, you can simply remove it and replace it with a spare. The operating system then rebuilds the drive, if possible, assuming that this wasn't the main NOS drive itself. (If the main NOS drive fails, you're in deep trouble!) These units are all accessible from the front of the server and use a hexagonal key of sorts to lock or unlock the drive, or spin it down for removal.

Lockable Computers

When lockable drives aren't possible, or you have special needs that require securing the server, you can use lockable cabinets and server cases. Unfortunately, neither of these solutions is truly adequate because very few server vendors make a truly secure case. Sure, it has a keylock on the front of the case, but it's more like a steel latch hooking on a plastic case block. This isn't my idea of a lockable case. Make sure the one you buy has a steel lock slide onto a portion of the steel case itself. Additional software security should then be employed to prevent unauthorized access to the floppy drives and tape drive. In the unfortunate event that someone gains access to these devices, they have the ability to reboot the server with a floppy and gain access to the server software.

Lockable Computer Rooms

The last physical security issue involves locking the entire computer room. The office where I used to work contained over one million dollars in server and networking equipment to serve not only our local 200 plus users, but our wide-area users as well. The computer room was secured by magnetic card readers that controlled each door in the entire facility. The user swiped the card through the reader, much like you would at an ATM, and then punched in a password. A valid card and a valid password gets you into the facility. This is the ultimate in protection, but includes the ultimate in price tags, too.

Insuring Your Investment

Insuring your server is an obvious protection mechanism, but is an afterthought at best. If you have to seek reimbursement for covered equipment, then the damage has already been done. In the case of insurance, you should be aware of several things:

- Very few companies insure beyond several thousand dollars in personally used computers.

- Insurance underwriters for major data processing equipment have a variety of requirements that you have to fulfill before you can get the proper amount of coverage.

- Policy premiums are generally $10 per thousand in coverage. For the average network or Web server, you're looking at a premium of $250 a year for just one server.

- Insurability is sometimes judged by an independent survey from another computer firm. No matter how competent you and your people may be, an underwriter may require you to pay for a survey from an outside source.

In arranging the coverage for my equipment, I was required to have the computers and any networked devices centrally located in one facility that was bricked up on the outside, and all of the servers had to be running on UPS units certified by the underwriter as acceptable to them in protection. One such UPS is the American Power Conversion (APC) UPS, which comes with a $25,000 protection policy for any equipment plugged into it. For this policy to be in force, you must strictly adhere to the instructions that come with the APC unit.

Another safety measure I use is the Tripp Lite lightning suppressor for phone lines attached to equipment like my modems and ISDN router. Tripp Lite covers the replacement value of the devices attached to the suppressor if it's hit by a damaging electrical current. Tripp Lite requires that the suppressor be plugged into a wall outlet and not into a power strip or extension cord to ensure that the suppressor is properly grounded and attached to the correct polarity of the power lines. Suppression equipment, UPSs included, do part of their magic by being properly connected to NEMA-standard power sources.

Wall power must meet the standards of commercial power because your warranty will be void if the vendor finds that you are not adhering to the proper electrical standards.

Theft Versus Vandalism

While theft is an outright loss of property, it isn't the only way you can experience less than optimal operations of your site. Computer vandalism comes in several forms, ranging from someone cutting a cable between drives, to smashing fiber optics cables, to otherwise finding ways to disrupt normal operations. Both theft and vandalism cost your business money in the form of repairs, as well as loss of revenue if the damaged equipment keeps the business from functioning. As I mentioned earlier, it boils down to securing as much of the equipment as possible. Obviously, there's nothing you can do about the external cable plant operations between buildings or running along the telephone poles. We'll discuss how you can prevent theft and vandalism later in this section.

The Impact on Your Web Site

The overall impact of theft and vandalism is crystal clear—loss of productivity and money. And that's not to mention the contractual issues you may encounter if you can't provide the necessary support to your customers. Believe me, it takes time to regain credibility once you've compromised your integrity—even when it was not of your own doing.

On some occasions, the destruction itself masks the marauders entrance and exit so you'll never know what hit, or when. One of the best preventive measures for this situation is to have frequent and separate backups of your data files away from the operating system, and use password protection that only trusted employees (and only essential ones at that) know.

Preventative Measures

You can protect your business' internal investment with physical security implementations mentioned earlier, but be aware that "inside jobs" can and do happen. Luckily, you are not powerless in this case. One method you can use to combat inside vandalism is to enforce strict hiring practices. Unfortunately, a whiz of a programmer can easily create a back door into the system or a time bomb in the server. When you hire your programmers (or any employees for that matter), make sure you check their references. How trustworthy are they? Programmers are essential to many network operations and, therefore, have access to every single part of the network regardless of what server level security you implement! Even an employee with a good understanding of the operating system can wreak havoc if you don't take the steps to secure your investment. Don't assume the worst of your employees, but protect yourself.

Perhaps the best approach to sidestepping problems is to work with your people and make sure they understand your operations—what they can and can't do, and what will happen if they are found guilty of vandalism or theft. Normal security measures only go so far. Fostering a peaceful working relationship goes a lot further and is cheaper in the long run.

You can also perform a quarterly audit of equipment and software, which is a useful process for insurance purposes as well as to let employees know that the equipment is valued and accounted for at all times. Another option is to implement tight server-level security to prevent files from being copied or used after a certain time of the day, or limited to certain days of the week.

A Silent Marauder—Viruses

No matter how well you institute physical protection for the server, there's always the presence of a sly and devious creature called the computer virus. We've all been exposed to some form of virus attack in one form or another, but what was once a mysterious and seldom fatal attraction has rapidly become the scourge of computing. And what's worse is that over time, viruses have become more and more dangerous.

This section is intended to wake you up to the stark realization of what virus attacks can do and how to prevent them (or reduce the threat). And to finish this chapter in the same way I started, prepare yourself for another episode of "True Stories of Computer Disasters."

NT's Built-In Protection

Built-in protection is often a misnomer, but NT really does have a form of built-in protection, providing you implement the NTFS file system. NT's increased performance and operating characteristics come from the various parts of NT itself. One particular protective function of NT is called the Hardware Abstraction Layer, or the HAL, which performs the actual accessing of the physical hardware installed in the server. This serves to create a shield and a level of independence for applications and programmatical functions. As such, ordinary applications that used to run fine within Windows 3.x or Windows 95, and directly access the hardware, will not work under NT. The same is true for a virus because it's an application as well. Even TSR driver viruses can't install in NT once NT is operational because of this shield.

WARNING

Just because this shield is in place doesn't mean that you should forget about the possibility of a virus attack on a Microsoft Windows NT Server-based system.

Software Protection

What you should do, however, is check out one of the many fine anti-virus software kits available across the industry. Among the leaders is Symantec with its Anti-Virus for NT. Other vendors such as McAfee and Cheyenne Software also make NT-based solutions. As always, you should be diligent in maintaining a schedule of scanning and protection, or all is for naught. Also, you should invest in protection for any and every desktop PC that brings in data to the system. If you don't, you might unwittingly back up a virus during your daily administrative duties. You'll never know this has occurred until you restore the files (if that happens) and the virus activates. At that point, you may be totally defenseless.

An Example of a Virus Attack

Gather 'round the fire and prepare yourself while I relate another "True Story of Computer Disasters." In a company I used to work for some time ago, the MIS types didn't care much about virus protection, and those that did hadn't a clue about how to do it correctly. Unfortunately, a virus attacked the system and the damage was tremendous. Let's get to the details.

The entire computing community consisted of 14 networks spread across a campus-wide internetwork of some 13,000 users. A multiple FDDI ring was in place to connect all of the buildings and servers together. Several of the servers were of the Sun Workstation variety and five of them formed a cluster of operating software that worked together forming an apparently single unit. If you're not familiar with clustered systems, you can connect two or more computers together to pool their resources and build a considerably more efficient computing environment. In this setup, one server working at only 10 percent capacity can do some of the work of another server which is running at 95 percent capacity. This approach balances the workload and smoothes out the overall performance of the entire system. But there is a disadvantage.

In clustered systems, sometimes operating software on one server must be running for another physical server to work as well. When systems tie in tightly like this, disruption of one server frequently wreaks havoc on the others. This was the case when the virus hit the campus network. Although the actual circumstances surrounding the entry of the virus into the network was never pinned down, this is what we think happened. The virus was thought to have entered in a DOS-based machine and proliferated into one of the neighboring networks, and then migrated into another building where it infected several desktop PCs on its way to the network server for that building.

The virus was discovered when a user in the fourth network called the MIS group asking what MIS had done with his data files from a particular PC. Checking into the problem, MIS found out that the problem PC's hard disk was absolutely clean. Clean as in not even a partition existed! This was a key sign that something was definitely wrong, but the MIS person missed the wake-up call. The PC was repartitioned and the software was reloaded. The user then restored the data files from a recent backup, and away he went. Actually, he went off to lunch and returned to find his other PC wiped out as well. By this time, the network server for that building had been infected and wiped out as well.

At this point, the MIS group realized that a virus was loose and was destroying all PCs in its path, but they mistakenly thought that it was a DOS-only problem and that the Unix machines were not affected. Wrong! This was the second mistake the MIS group made, and it proved to be the worst mistake of all. With this network physically disconnected from the WAN, they cleaned up the infection, not thinking to disconnect the desktop PCs from the network while repairs were underway. They also failed to notify anyone else, but why should they? They're the MIS, right?

Well, they should have notified someone because by the time they "fixed" the original problem, the virus had replicated and polymorphized into another strain of virus and proceeded to infect the clustered machines, wiping them out, too. They weren't sure how this happened, and still aren't to this day. All they know is the business stayed offline for four days while the virus was eradicated.

 Take viruses very seriously or be prepared to pay the price. Educate yourself and your staff to the potential problems, and look for the warning signs that the MIS group in our story ignored.

Summary

If you slept through the entire book, I hope that you at least paid attention to this chapter because the information presented here is what will keep you in good mental health (not to mention gainfully employed!). The disasters we covered are all very real and occur in many different businesses. I'm confident that you now know what can go wrong, and will go wrong, in a Web server. I'm also confident that you now have the ammunition you need to protect your Web server from anything—including acts of God! Happy troubleshooting.

Appendices

PART

5

Common Terms and Acronyms

ARPA—A form of reverse DNS resolution allowing Web servers to check the alias used backwards against the calling server. This allows for a more secure server, but only if reverse resolution is enabled.

ARPANET (Advanced Research Projects Agency Network)—The first network infrastructure that was what we now call the Internet, sometimes referred to as the Web.

Bandwidth—The property of an electronic data circuit that specifies how much data can be safely carried on the circuit at one time. ISDN circuits have a maximum bandwidth of 144,000 bits per second, although most of the time only half of that is in actual use.

Bottleneck—The device that restricts any other device from performing at maximum performance. In a disk drive system, slower physical drives can be a bottleneck even though the disk controller is capable of faster performance.

C2 Security—The mid-level security that Microsoft Windows NT Server implements to form a secure computing environment. C2 was created by the U.S. Department of Defense.

DNS (Domain Naming Service)—The mechanism by which an alpha name (such as www.bci.com) is converted to the numerical IP address equivalent (206.139.150.35).

FrontPage—Microsoft Corporation's newly acquired HTML editor, originally owned by Vermeer Software. Allows the user to create fully described and integrated Web pages.

Filter—A function that checks an IP address, or an alias, and allows the data to pass on to the destination or to be rejected.

Firewall—A device, usually software, that prevents or allows users from the outside world to see your Web site. Normally, firewalls are created to prevent unauthorized users from entering your site, but they can be used to prevent intranet users from getting to the Internet.

Gopher—The Internet protocol that creates menus from disk drive directories and files. This was the early forerunner to what we now know as the Web.

Hop Count—The number of routers or processing devices that handle each data packet from the source to the destination.

HTML (HyperText Markup Language)—The basic programming tool of the Internet Web page.

HTTP (HyperText Transfer Protocol)—The language used to communicate between Web servers and the Web clients, or browsers.

ISDN (Integrated Services Digital Network)—A 144 Kbps link in which a pair of 64 KB channels is used to transfer digitized data between source and destination. A separate 16 KB signaling channel is also employed for setup and breakdown of the link. Standard modems are analog in nature while ISDN is much better at processing data and is less susceptible to line noises.

Internet Domain—The function that creates and defines the Web site. Each domain is a "territory" covered by the Internet provider with a block of 256 IP addresses and services customers of dialup modems. However, some domains are private sites that do not resell connectivity.

NT Server Domain—The NT Server principle of a collective computing environment. An NT Domain is usually an entire business having several different departments such as accounting, engineering, and logistics.

POP (Post Office Protocol)—One of the languages that email servers use to communicate and transmit email.

PPP (Point to Point Protocol)—One of two common protocols used to connect clients to Internet servers using modems. PPP uses a much improved error correction mechanism to ensure better data processing.

Proxy Server—Software, used sometimes in conjunction with a firewall, to build an impenetrable barrier to intruders. A proxy gives the user the illusion that they're accessing one Web site when in reality the proxy sends the user to another, based upon administrator-provided parameters.

Reverse DNS—Used to validate user access rights to a Web server. When you connect to a site, the site then checks with the server you use to make your Internet connection, and then validates who you are.

RAID (Redundant Array of Inexpensive Disks)—A system that uses two or more disk drives to form a logical disk drive, using a highly reliable scheme of data storage using various levels of protection referred to as RAID 1, RAID 2, and so on.

Router—The network device used to send data packets to the desired destination. The router helps prevent the data from going to the wrong location.

Storage Channel—A high throughput disk drive subsystem in which data is moved at rates of 100 MB or higher. This is the next generation of data storage for RAID systems, and uses fiber optics as the medium instead of cables.

SLIP (Serial Line Internet Protocol)—The first Internet access method used by analog modems to connect to the Internet.

SMTP (Simple Mail Transport Protocol)—The Internet mail standard used to send email to outbound servers. SMTP is capable of attaching files to the email messages using various formats such as BINHEX and UUEncoding.

Virtual Circuit—A communications path used by computers in which the path is not over the same physical server at any one point in time. This allows for a more flexible movement of data across links that could fail unexpectedly.

Web Server—The core operating software used to provide HTTP services from the server to the client.

B

An Extra Hand—
Information Resources

Computers are great tools when they work for us, but they can be a nightmare when things go wrong; and it usually goes wrong at the most inopportune moments. Many times, you'll be able to solve the problem yourself by using your wit, wisdom, or just plain blind luck. However, the one time in your computing life that absolutely nothing must go wrong, everything in the world will go wrong! The cat chews through the power cord, you spill Coke in the keyboard and the motherboard objects to it, and you remember that you forgot to plug in the UPS just about the time you see the first flash of a lightning bolt.

For whatever the reason, disasters will test your merit and inner strength. When that strength gets a bit frazzled (often around 3 AM!), you'll be reaching for a helping hand. Your list of resources will vary from site to site, so I've compiled a list of helpful resources that will aid you in troubleshooting a Web server problem, and how to apply the given advice to an actual Web server failure.

Microsoft Developer's Network

Wait, what's this programming reference; isn't this a Web server book? Sure it is, but there's plenty of programming involved with CGI code, Visual Basic, and the Internet protocols themselves. Microsoft Developer's Network, referred to as MSDN, is a collection of documentation, bug fixes, technical facts, and programming interface specifications for nearly all of the Microsoft stable of software. Not just for C++ or Visual Basic, it also contains information for Microsoft Office Developer's Kit, the Windows 32-bit Developer's platforms, and more. MSDN has three subscription levels: Level 1 contains libraries of files and documents, and costs $195 a year for quarterly updates. Level 2 is the same as Level 1, with additional documentation, SDKs, and developer's tools. Level 2 costs $495 a year to receive quarterly updates, with interim updates of special CDs such as beta products. Level 3 contains a complete set of all Microsoft software documentation plus Level 2 tools and drivers, including a 5-user license of BackOffice.

So how does this help you with your Web server? Let's say you're creating a very specialized front end to a SQL database using CGI and Visual Basic. The task requires you to send an email message back to the system administrator when a certain user accesses the database, and this user name check is performed every hour. In order to perform this check, you need to spawn another process on the Web server (actually on NT Server), but how do you do this in CGI?

These steps presume you already have MSDN installed, and for those of you who don't subscribe to MSDN, it will underscore its usefulness. Start MSDN while thinking of a keyword that will fit your topic. Just like any other search utility, you'll have to search a massive database with very distinct and accurate keywords if you don't want to have ten thousand topics selected as possible solutions. After you've started MSDN, you'll see a screen similar to Figure B.1.

The left side of the screen shows the major subjects supported on the CD. Many are non-supported, antiquated systems, but Microsoft is listing the information to assist in the transformation from older systems into modern-day technology.

Anyhow, back to the CGI issue. Click on the large pair of binoculars in the top center of the menu bar, and then click on the Query tab to type in the keyword that you're searching MSDN for. At this point you can also specify

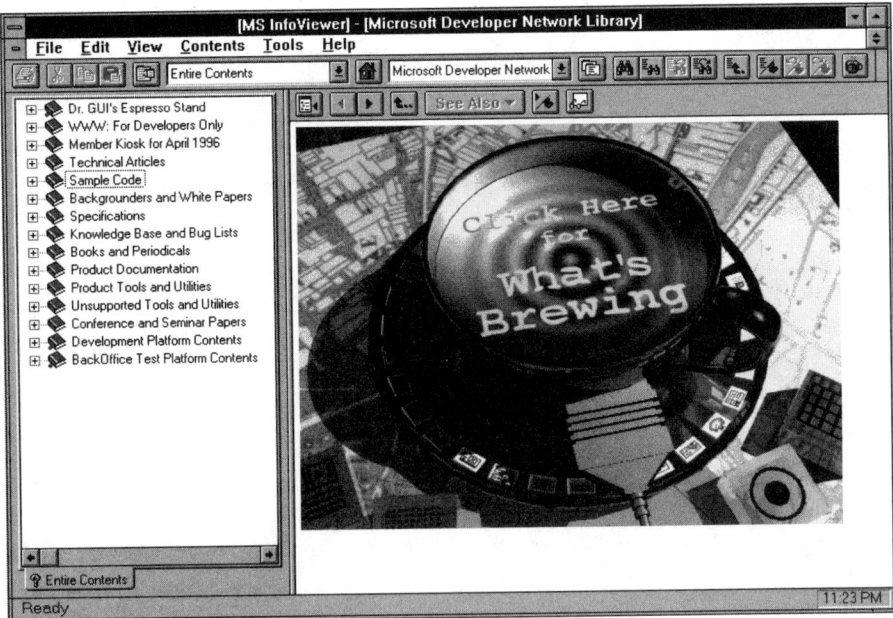

Figure B.1 The MSDN main screen.

a subset of information to search. In the search field, type in "CGI" and click on the Query button. Figure B.2 shows the results of the search.

This search uncovered several prospective answers to our CGI problem, but one stands out in particular—entry 9 on CGISPAWN—which turns out to be the one that will solve our problem. This is the essence of MSDN, and how it can solve some of your programming needs for NT-based Web servers.

Microsoft TechNet

TechNet is another Microsoft tool that helps solve problems. It comes in monthly updates at a cost of $195 a year. This set of two CDs differs from MSDN in that it only contains technical facts on Microsoft products, but also has other useful tips. TechNet looks like, and runs like, MSDN in every step of operation. If you know how to operate one, then you'll know how to operate the other. Figure B.3 shows TechNet's opening screen.

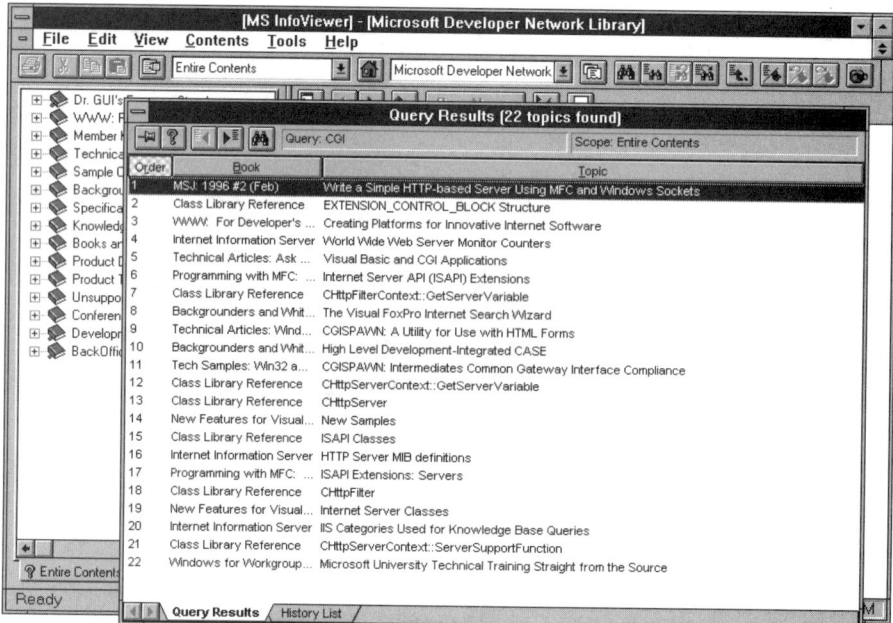

Figure B.2   The results of my CGI search on MSDN.

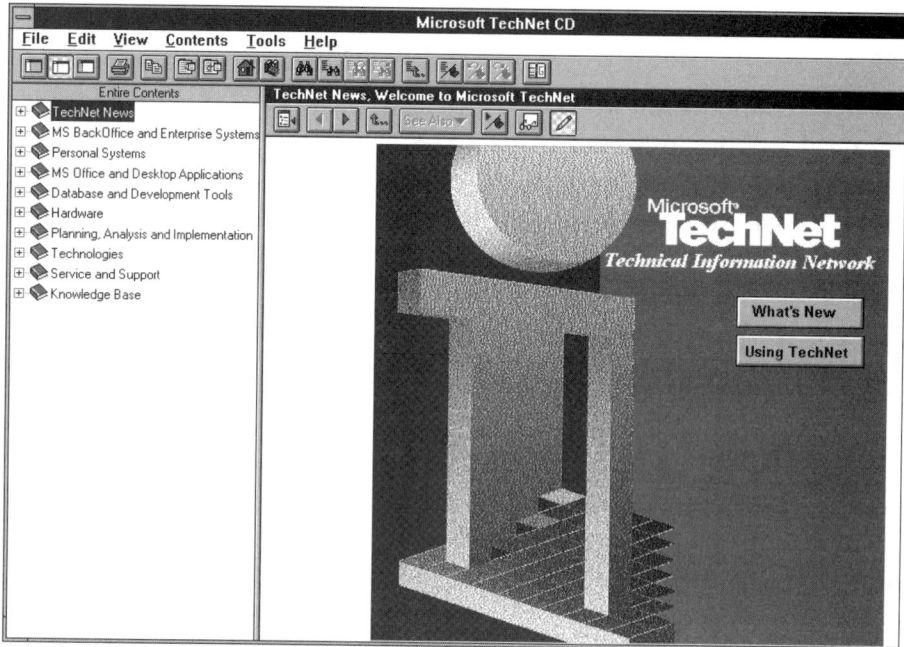

Figure B.3   Microsoft TechNet's main page.

CompuServe

Since the beginning of the computer revolution, online services have dominated the world of vendor support. These services can help you set up your Web server in a number of ways, including providing updated drivers, testing facilities for software, and places where users can gather to talk about their experiences. CompuServe is one such service that started years ago when the online services industry was in its infancy, yet it has held a firm footing and a longstanding customer base.

CompuServe Information Service (CIS) is made up of forums or electronic bulletin boards where users post questions and (hopefully) get answers to their problems. Vendors such as Intuit Software have a support forum on CompuServe where they provide updates and bug fixes to their users. All told, there's over a thousand such forums of support across CIS.

IBM Network

IBMNET is a subset of forums on CIS that support IBM products and services. IBMNET is broken down into forums such as IBMAPP (applications), IBMSYS (systems level support), and IBMHW (hardware support), to name just a few. Because it's named IBMNET, you might think that it's purely an IBM area, but that's not true. You can get some of the most complete answers to problems here, and from a very knowledgeable group of programmers. To get to the IBM Network, use the keyword GO CIS:IBMNET.

NT Resource Kit

The NT Resource Kit is a five volume set of manuals on managing NT Server and the networks under it. This includes a CD-ROM that is chock full of useful utilities and updated drivers for NT and tips on general maintenance of your NT Server. Two of my favorites are the domain planner we used in Chapter 2 to define the network and the NetWatcher utility which allows you to see who is connected to which NT resource on the server, regardless of the application. The NT Resource Kit is available from Microsoft and your local computer dealer for $395.

UseNet Groups

Don't overlook the UseNet newsgroups and circles that are available on the Internet. These are frequently either staffed or moderated by experienced users who at one time or another have been where you are now. One of the biggest advantages of UseNet newsgroups is that users are online 24 hours a day around the world, and you're bound to find someone that can help solve your problem.

List Servers

List servers are nothing more than large mailing lists of users that closely approximates forum participation in an online service like CIS. You get an email, answer it, and repost it on the list server. Someone else sees your message, answers it, and back it comes to you. One thing different here is that in a list server, everyone on the list gets the messages, not just the two carrying on the conversation. This can result in rather large message traffic across the Internet.

Summary

While this appendix is short, it is meant to let you know that there are numerous resources available to help you with your Web server problems, as well as other problems unrelated to the Web, such as physical server problems. There's no need to get hysterical in the middle of the night because of your NT server. There are plenty of people who have been where you are, and are willing to help you.

C

Installing NT Server

Throughout this book, I've presumed that you knew all about NT Server and how to use it. Microsoft Windows NT Server is by no means simple to use or administer, but it provides network administrators with a whole new outlook on computing life.

There are a few things you need to know about NT before and while installing it. For those of you who have installed and configured NT before, you might want to skip this appendix. For those of you who haven't installed NT yet, reading this appendix will help you understand what to expect of NT and point out a few pitfalls to watch for during the installation. This appendix is not intended to be comprehensive, but should help guide you through the rough spots.

Preparing the Hardware

You should know as much as possible about your server's hardware before a single byte of software is installed. That means knowing the exact name, type, model, and card settings of every device installed in the server. Once you get into the installation, NT will ask you to input several settings, and if you don't know what those settings are you'll have to abort the installation to check them. If you abort the installation, you'll have to completely reformat the disk used to hold NT during the installation. I've had to do this several times, and the only solid method I've found to recover from an aborted installation is to just start over. As you're building up the server, it's best to have a written record of the installed components. This assures that the next person who has to fix a problem on the server knows what's installed without having to open the case.

Make sure all of the hard drives have been formatted with DOS and that the C drive is bootable. If you decide later that you want to enable C2 security, then you can convert any partition to NTFS at that time.

Getting the Software Ready

When the hardware is ready, you'll need to format three 3½-inch blank floppies. The critical installation files from the NT Server CD-ROM will be copied onto them and the disks will then be used during the special boot process. This is a multilayered process that is performed by installing DOS and the necessary CD-ROM drivers on the server. At this point, all partitions are formatted and DOS is loaded on the C drive. Your CD-ROM should have all of its drivers loaded so the CD is visible to you on a DOS boot-up.

Insert the CD and boot the server to the DOS prompt. Make the CD the current drive, open the I386 directory on the CD, and run the winnt.exe program. Follow the instructions on how to copy the files to the floppies and the hard drive, and reboot when required. Rebooting will load the critical NT files onto the hard drive from the floppies that you created earlier. Follow the instructions to get NT running for the first time. This means that you'll have to choose a name for the physical server, and then decide if you want this machine to be a domain controller or a LAN server. See Chapter 2 for a complete explanation of these functions.

Once these choices have been made, the remaining installation options look very similar to those of Windows 3.x. Make the necessary selections for the applications and utilities, and then select the settings for the network card. *You must know the card's settings before you get to this point*, or the network will not run and the installation might have to abort, taking all of your hard work up to this point with it.

After these settings have been completed, you'll have to reboot for the server changes to take effect. After the server restarts, make the necessary user account changes to get your user base installed. Configure the shares, rights, and permissions that are needed for each of your users. At this point, and before any applications are installed, it's best to reboot the server once more and then log in as several different users with different rights to see if the security is correct. Double check the guest account to make sure that only guest privileges have been assigned to it. Make sure that the proper password security has been assigned and that auditing has been enabled.

Applications and NT Server

Once you've made it this far, you're well on your way to preparing the server for the task of Web serving. If your Web server requires programming tools like Visual Basic or Perl, now's the time to install and configure them. For the time being only install the tools that you'll definitely need. You'll want to make sure that the server is stable before installing and configuring the Web server tools, and having the users beat the server is an excellent way to do this.

However, if this is to be a Web server, and nothing else, you need to test it under fire! Install the Web software and set the security as needed for your site. Build the FTP directories and files for your customer base, and set security for both your FTP and Web services. If you set the FTP for anonymous logins, then you should allow anonymous entry for all locations on the site. You can still have private locations on any part of the server for test purposes, or to trade business secrets with your engineers.

Summary

While this seems a straightforward approach to installing NT, in fact it takes four hours or more on a good day without problems. This is only an overview of the installation procedure; it's intended to give you an idea of what to expect when you're installing Windows NT Server. The exact installation steps are covered in the *NT Installation Guide* that comes with each package of NT Server.

What's on the CD-ROM?

Keep in mind that much of the software on this disk is either shareware or freeware. Shareware means that the author or authors of the software are allowing you to try out the software with the expectation that if you like it, you will pay them for it or upgrade to a commercial version. Freeware means that you can use the software as much as you want with no charge, but there is usually a more advanced version available for a price. Check for a README or LICENSE file with each of the applications you use to see what restrictions the author has placed on the software and its distribution ad use.

Now, let's go through and take a look at some of the more useful applications on the CD. Don't be afraid to experiment a little and play with all the different types of software. Most of the software is described below, but for those that aren't, just check in the applications directory for more information.

Application: Purveyor
Where on CD: \WEBSVRS\PURVEYOR
Where On-Line: *http://www.process.com/prod/purveyor.htp*
Description: Purveyor is an advanced, easy to use family of World Wide Web Server software developed by Process Software Corporation, a leader in TCP/IP network solutions for over 10 years. Purveyor is design to allow organization to develop a world wide presence quickly and easily, yet provide a powerful array of features that cater to the most demanding sites. Introduced in April 1995, Purveyor was the first commercial Web server for Windows NT. The enhanced NT package, Purveyor 1.2, has just begun shipping. Purveyor is the ideal Web server for establishing a strong presence on the Internet for external applications, as well as communicating and publishing across the internal corporate LAN via the Intranet.

Application: WebSite
Where on CD: \WEBSVRS\WEBSITE
Where On-Line: *http://software.ora.com*
Description: The WebSite server lets you maintain a set of Web documents, control access, index desktop directories and use a CGI program to display data from applications such as Excel, Access, Visual Basic, and other programs. WebSite includes WebView, a powerful Web management tool which provides a tree-like display of all documents and links on your server, logging statistics, and searching and indexing features. The new Spyglass Mosaic 2.1 Web browser is included in WebSite, along with full online Help. New version 1.1 features include the HotDog Standard HTML editor which supports text formatting, link building, tables, and forms; WebView printing, so you can print a view of your Web contents; a new graphical interface for creating virtual servers; enhanced search capabilities; server side includes (SSI), to combine static and programmed documents on the fly; and a Visual Basic 4 framework with sample applications, which significantly improves the speed and efficiency of working with spreadsheets, databases and other programs.

Application: Clipart
Where on CD: \SAMPLES
Where On-Line: *http://www.lycos.com* (Search for "CLIPART ARCHIVES")
   http://sunsite.nus.sg/ftpmultimedia.html
   http://seidel.ncsa.uiuc.edu/ClipArt/funet.html
Description: This collection of clipart was gathered from many different places. You can find images here that can really spice up your Web pages. Check out the collections in \CLIPS\ART\COHEN and \CLIPS\ART\FUNET to see some really impressive line art pieces. Some of the more useful images are in the \BARS, \DOTS, and \SYMBOLS directories. These simple images don't take up much space, but they can really liven up a Web page and give it that custom look. There are also many images that can be used as separator bars and custom list bullets. Why stick to what Netscape has to offer you? Use custom images to give your page a unique style. But, be careful. Too many images can really slow things down!

In the \CLIPS\AUDIO directory, there are many sound effects and samples that you can use to give feedback to the people visiting your pages. Once again, though, you need to be careful that you don't use too many. Sound and video are also not supported on everyone's systems, so you may want to consider the people who will visit your site before you load up you pages with multimedia files.

Application: Adobe Acrobat Reader
Where on CD: \TOOLS\UTILS\ACROREAD
Where On-Line: *http://www.adobe.com/Software/Acrobat/*
Description: Adobe Acrobat lets you create electronic documents from a wide range of authoring tools for sharing across different computer platforms. Simply "print" files to the Adobe Portable Document Format (PDF). Now you can distribute your documents over the broadest selection of electronic media, including the World Wide Web, email, Lotus Notes, corporate networks, CD-ROMs, and print-on-demand systems. Adobe is pushing the PDF format as a replacement for HTML. Its advantages are unlimited options for layout, and what you design is what others see, which does not always happen with HTML. Good software to have on hand.

Application: Paint Shop Pro
Where on CD: \TOOLS\GRAPHICS\PSP3
Where On-Line: *http://www.winternet.com/~jasc/index.html*
Description: The complete Windows graphics program for image creation, viewing, and manipulation. Features include: painting, photo retouching, image enhancement and editing, color enhancement, image browser, batch conversion, and TWAIN scanner support. Also included are 20 standard image processing filters and 12 deformations. Supports Adobe style image processing plug-in filters. Over 30 file formats are supported, including JPEG, Kodak Photo-CD, PBM, and GIF. This is one graphics package you won't want to be without. It has many of the features of much more expensive graphics programs at a fraction of the cost. If you have never bought a shareware package in your life, this may be the first!

Application: LView Pro
Where on CD: \TOOLS\GRAPHICS\LVIEW
Where On-Line: *http://world.std.com/~mmedia/lviewp.htm*
Description: This application is one of the easiest image viewers and editors available. Some of its features include screen capture, transparent background, diagnostic information, quick print, image filtering, and many image enhancing attributes. Additionally, LView supports over a dozen different image formats. While not the fastest image viewer or the most complete image editor, LView remains one of the best all-around programs for viewing and manipulating images.

Application: QuickTime Player from Apple
Where on CD: \TOOLS\GRAPHICS\QUIKTIME
Where On-Line: *http://quicktime.apple.com*
Description: Although QuickTime has been a Macintosh standard for years, it is just beginning to catch on with Windows users. It offers a few features that Video for Windows does not have yet and some of the new technologies being developed for it are amazing. Check out the QuickTime Web page for the latest and greatest versions and watch out for the QuickTime VR players and editors that are beginning to appear. Note: There is a QuickTime VR player now available for Windows. Head up to the QuickTime Web site to download it, very cool!

Application: WS-FTP
Where on CD: \TOOLS\FTP\WS_FTP16
\TOOLS\FTP\WS_FTP32
Where On-Line: *http://cwsapps.texas.net/ftp.html*
Description: FTP remains one of the most widely used Internet applications, and WS-FTP makes this oft-used tool quick and painless. Configurability options include several alternative screen layouts, the ability to associate remote files with local programs, automatic logging, and quick screen-sizing. WS-FTP also comes preconfigured with an extensive array of FTP sites to check out. Multiple copies of the program can be launched to download multiple files at the same time. WS-FTP comes in two varieties: a 16-bit app and a 32-bit app. The only features missing are drag 'n' drop capabilities between local and remote file listings. WS-FTP is another of the must-have Internet applications.

Application: CuteFTP
Where on CD: \TOOLS\FTP\CUTEFTP
Where On-Line: *http://papa.indstate.edu:8888/CuteFTP/*
Description: CuteFTP is another stand-alone FTP program that expands on some of the features of WS_FTP. One of the best features of CuteFTP is its robust STOP command, similar in nature to the stop button found on many Web browsers. This command allows a user to stop any operation in progress while still maintaining the connection. Beyond the stop command, CuteFTP also integrates the file listing process with file descriptions obtained from the index files found at many anonymous FTP sites (extremely helpful for deciphering the cryptic file names found at many FTP sites). Caching of recently visited directories is another distinctive feature found in CuteFTP. In addition to fixing many bugs, the newer releases of CuteFTP have implemented WS-FTP's File Manageresque approach to listing both remote and local directories side-by-side, comprehensive login listings, selectable file viewers, selectable colors, the ability to recursively download directory trees, and the ability to easily send multiple files at once.

Application: HTMLed
Where on CD: \TOOLS\HTML\HTMLED
Where On-Line: *http://www.ist.ca*
Description: HTMLed incorporates many advanced features into a program that is extremely easy to use. Intelligent tag insertion, tag removal, automatic saving with or without HTML tags, word wrap, and configurable floating toolbars are just a few of HTMLed's advanced features. In addition, the task of creating background images and identifying colors for your Web pages is made easy. HTMLed also makes good use of right mouse button functionality.

Index